COUNSELING
WOMEN

To my mother
Ruth Hecker Collier
(1897–1975)
and to all the women of her generation, who lived lives of courage, compassion,
and distinction long before the present days of liberation,

I dedicate this work of love.

The Free Press
A Division of Macmillan Publishing Co., Inc.
866 Third Avenue, New York, N.Y. 10022

Collier Macmillan Canada, Inc.

Library of Congress Catalog Card Number: 82-70078

Printed in the United States of America

printing number
    2   3   4   5   6   7   8   9   10

Library of Congress Cataloging in Publication Data

Collier, Helen V.
    Counseling women.

    Bibliography: p.
    Includes index.
    1. Women—Counseling of.   2. Women—Mental health.
3. Psychotherapist and patient.   I. Title.   [DNLM:
1. Counseling—Methods.   2. Mental health.   3. Women—
Psychology.   WM 55 C699c]
RC451.4.W6C64   616.89′ 14′ 088042   82-70078
ISBN 0-02-905840-6   AACR2

COUNSELING WOMEN

A Guide for Therapists

Helen V. Collier

THE FREE PRESS
A Division of Macmillan Publishing Co., Inc.
NEW YORK

Collier Macmillan Publishers
LONDON

Contents

Contents

Contents

Acknowledgments

My deep appreciation goes to the following: my women clients—for sharing their lives with me over the years; my research assistants—Roslyn Klein, Cindy Carlson, Sid Reger, Mary Konovsky; my trainers in Gestalt therapy—Miriam and Erving Polster, Virginia Satir, and Jim Simkin; my editors—Kitty Moore, Senior Editor at Macmillan Free Press, and Gladys Topkis; my "former children"—Keith, Dan, and Heidi—for consistently asking how the book was going; my husband—G. J. Scrimgeour—for being my companion in writing books and living fully.

Bloomington, Ind.
1982

Introduction

This is a book for any mental health professional who has female clients. Its goal is to provide a straightforward approach to the special therapeutic needs of women for any professional, regardless of his or her original orientation. Professionals outside the field of mental health—doctors, lawyers, educators—will also find the approach adaptable to their needs.

The present needs of women show distinctive patterns which traditional therapies (and counseling) have failed to understand and which, in fact, outdate most of the training received by present professionals. This book attempts to show what the traditional disciplines of psychiatry, psychology, psychotherapy, social work, and counseling need to add or amend in order to make themselves responsive.

The book emphasizes techniques, but it also presents the theory of mental health on which those techniques are based. In addition, it contains statistical data showing the extent of change in women's situation in our society which has created the need for new approaches. In this respect, the book also serves as a reference to data and other ideas and theories in the field. The reader will also find sample exercises and approaches for use with individuals and groups of women, and a bibliography listing major sources from a variety of fields bearing on the needs of contemporary women.

Why a Book on the Therapy Needs of Women?

In the past, psychotherapeutic theory viewed the needs and the nature of women as merely complementary to those of men and, except in their neurotic manifestations, not as interesting. The values and life patterns of women, the processes by which they make their choices and decisions, those decisions themselves, the influences that determine their physical, psychological, social, political, and economic lives—all these were seen as subsidiary to those of men. The model human being, the proper object of a theorist's attention, was male; women were just an addendum. In theory we now know better, but practice changes slowly; the aim of this book is to help it change faster.

Until very recently, psychological theories disregarded the distinctive cultural realities of women's lives and minds: their life patterns, psychological processes, and personality development as females. Theorists remained especially unconscious of the sexist basis of our cultural expectations regarding women. They calmly accepted cultural definitions of behaviors, attitudes, and values appropriate for each sex at the expense of their development as complete human beings. As Juanita Williams (1977) points out, belief in the rightness of society's sex stereotyping pervades the work of Freud and his successors, and the habit went uncontested until the work of Karen Horney, Margaret Mead, and Clara Thompson in the 1930s. Psychological theory cooperated with the broader culture; it assigned women "feminine" characteristics which limited their behavioral options. Within the structure of the family, it assigned women only the approved roles of homemaker and mother—regardless of the realities of women's lives.

For women who have sought professional psychological help, the effect of theory has clearly been harmful. Restless females were encouraged to "adjust" to a reality which was either imaginary or damaging. Doctors routinely dispensed drugs to women to cure depressions which may have situational and discernible causes, or, as Phyllis Chesler (1972) has documented, declared their women patients neurotic or even insane when they expressed dissatisfaction with the traditional female role. Therapy, in this sense, was aptly called "cooling out" by Jean Lipman-Blumen (1975).

The message has been that normal women would not pursue roles which men were encouraged to fill, particularly those roles which lead to autonomy and power. Where men's roles were instrumental, active, external, and aimed at direct achievement, women's energies were channeled toward the expressive and the passive; they were told to be content with vicarious achievement gained through their menfolk and children. Because women's lives were seen as complementary and subordinate to those of men, women were regarded as less qualified than were men to deal with the whole spectrum of reality. They played an essential and admirable role but somehow were lesser human beings who should not expect as much from life and themselves.

Thus described, past personality theories sound ridiculous. Therapists currently in practice could not, one might think, have been taught mental health approaches which saw women as subordinate and complementary to men; but the generation of feminists, who began to subject past assumptions to rigorous scrutiny during the 1970s, have proved their case. (See for example, Rawlings and

Carter, 1977; Broverman, Broverman, Clarkson, Rosenkrantz, and Vogel, 1970; and Williams, 1977.) All the models for full human development concerned male behavior and, for the most part, still do (Holmes and Jorgenson, 1971; L'Armend and Pepitone, 1975; Johnson and Scarato, 1979). Textbooks routinely referred to both therapists and clients as "he" even though women have long been the majority of clients in counseling centers. The effect on therapists and other advisers of women was especially damaging because they were taught that autonomy was a legitimate and necessary goal for males but not for females (Broverman et al, 1970). Women, they learned, should actualize themselves through men, children, and others. Women who sought independence were deviant and probably by definition unhealthy—even those women who fled abominable situations in their homes. They were to be "helped" back onto the path to a proper dependence, back to the "relationships" where they would find their only real fulfillment. Others knew best. Others would make the major decisions in women's lives. Women would adjust.

The recent efforts to develop psychological theories and therapeutic practices which are sex-fair or feminist have the simple aim of counteracting the inequality with which therapists have been trained to view women. Their basic goal is neither combative nor doctrinaire. They see women simply as people, specifically as adult—not as somehow incomplete males. They emphasize the facts of contemporary life: that women, like men, have available to them all the roles of a fully developing self—worker, parent, politician, lover, spouse, child, president, whatever. Where they observe differences between the general states of women and men, they examine the reasons for and effects of those differences. They help clients to deal actively with the world and to make choices rather than to force themselves into a traditional mold. New research has generated new data; new cultural views of women have produced new theories of personality and life development. New approaches to counseling women are now essential.

Are the Helping Professions Still Sexist?

Despite their intellectual validity, sex-fair therapeutic theories are having difficulty in gaining the attention of practicing therapists. The lack of motivation to change extant within the helping professions seems to stem from their domination by males in terms of not just theories but also of power. In almost all counseling and mental health centers, most supervisors are male—except where institutions are established specifically by and for women. Some 67 percent of all psychologists and some 90 percent of all psychiatrists are male (*Women in Crisis*, 1980). Even though two-thirds of all patients seeking psychological help are women and one in three women (compared to one in seven men) sees a mental health professional at some time in her life, almost none of the professionals (female or male) have special training in the needs of women. In social services, not only are the agencies and clinics routinely headed by men, but the laws and regulations controlling clients are almost totally created by males even though a majority of the clientele is female (National Institute of Mental Health, 1979).

The training given to mental health professionals is still overwhelmingly dominated by males. A survey in 1974 showed that 85 percent of counselor educators were male (Haun, 1974); a survey in 1976 showed only two of 26 departments of counselor education to be headed by women, and of their 191 faculty members, 158 (83 percent) were male (Harway, Astin, Suhr, and Whiteley, 1976). In departments of psychology and psychiatry the imbalance is even worse, and in schools of social work only marginally better (45.6 percent of teaching faculty are women) as reported by the Council on Social Work Education in 1980. As recently as 1978, the APA's Division of Counseling Psychology produced thirteen principles for the counseling and therapy of women (APA *Monitor*, December 1978).

Though the worst sexism has disappeared from most college textbooks, they remain sex-biased. A recent analysis of the thirteen textbooks most often used in graduate psychology courses noted that gross sexism had been replaced by more dangerous features: sexism arising from omission rather than commission; failure to discuss sex differences; interpretation based solely on genetics; and unwarranted generalizations about people based on research dealing with males only (Birk, Barbanel, Brooks, Herman, Juhasz, Seltzer, and Tangri, 1974). Courses on the special psychological needs of women are extremely rare (Harway et al, 1976; Harway and Astin, 1977), and they are almost never required. Research into the differing needs of women was rare until very recently; there were fewer women researchers than men, and few of them were studying women's needs. "Women's research" brought contempt more often than it brought grants, tenure, or respect. Though there has been a vast improvement in this respect during the last decade, too much research has had to find its home in specialized and vulnerable "women's programs" rather than in the mainstream of academic disciplines (e.g., counseling or clinical psychology, social work, counselor education, sociology, anthropology, psychiatry, etc.).

Fortunately, the last decade has shown a strong attempt to correct this situation. Women have organized their own groups within the mental health professions: the Association of Women in Psychology; the National Women's Studies Association; Division 35 of the American Psychological Association; the Commission on the Status of Women in the American Personnel and Guidance Association; the National Committee on Women's Issues in the National Association of Social Workers; the American Educational Research Association's Research on Women in Education; the Women's Caucus of the American Society for Training and Development; and others. Federal funds have come through numerous if small agencies, and private foundations have helped. Traditional academic research and teaching may still be wary and inept regarding women's special needs, but they find it more difficult to ignore those needs altogether.

Thus the time seems right for a book devoted to the special needs and nature of women in relationship to the helping professions. There is a recent but firm consensus on several basics which make the subject essential in both training and practice:

1. The biological differences between women and men do not place women in a position of inferiority but do cause distinctive differences in development and life patterns.
2. Women have, for many reasons, a pattern of adult development that is distinctive. (See especially Lowenthal, Thurnher, Chiriboga, and Associates, 1976; and Troll, 1975.)
3. Today's women face practical realities different from those of men and from those of women in previous eras. Work, divorce, the gap between male and female earnings, patterns of the family—all are widely regarded as distinctive. Moreover, the culture is generally coming to accept uniquely female experiences (rape, mastectomy, etc.) as real and important.
4. We now recognize that women face special barriers to their full development, created by a society whose systems were built on the premise of sex inequality. These barriers may be external, but they have also been internalized by women who unconsciously hobble their own development. The socialization process that leads to sex-role stereotyping and the methods of counterbalancing the process are now recognized and even regarded as a proper object of attention by some therapists.
5. We have begun to understand the variations among groups of women which are caused by age, class, racial/ethnic background, or sexual preference; and we have acknowledged the multiple burdens of discrimination under which such groups of women labor.
6. As men begin to study themselves as males, the differences between females and males have become serious and legitimate objects of scrutiny which may help determine exactly what each sex has to offer the other in terms of full development as human beings.

These six realizations are the reason for a book such as this. The state of our knowledge has advanced to the point where I do not hesitate to say that mental health workers *must* understand the diverse needs of women as women and *must* build that understanding into their work if they are to provide their female (and their male) clients with the knowledge and skills that they need and professionalism demands.

What Is Uniquely Female?

This is a very difficult question to answer with any degree of accuracy. The physical differences between the sexes seem so obvious and the cultural differences between the roles assigned to women and men seem so "natural" that it is extraordinarily hard, even with real objectivity, to seek the facts and the truth.

A comprehensive analysis of research findings (Maccoby and Jacklin, 1974) summarizes those differences between the sexes which seem reputably documented. Females have greater verbal ability, first in early childhood and then again after age ten. Males excel in mathematical ability, especially after age twelve, and in visual/spatial ability, especially in adolescence and adulthood. Males are more aggressive—though the term "aggressive" and the causes of male aggressiveness are themselves being questioned in some depth. Sex differences in such matters as tactile sensitivity, fear, timidity, anxiety, activity, competitiveness, dominance, compliance, and nurturance are all still open questions since behavior is determined clearly by cultural expectations as well as by genetics. The sexes seem very similar in achievement motivation, as they do in task persistence. (The cause of the well-known failure of women to achieve to the same degree as that of men after high school is a matter of considerable controversy.)

Whereas some data suggest that the socialization processes experienced by males and females in early childhood are very different, what is remarkable is the degree of similarity between them. The only differences that emerge as particularly strong are those that deal with sex-typed behavior. Parents encourage their children to develop sex-typed interests by, for example, giving them sex-typed toys and rewarding sex-typed behaviors; they especially discourage male children from behaviors and activities regarded as inappropriate to their sex. Males seem to receive more punishment and also more praise and encouragement; males generally undergo a more rigorous socialization process than do females.

Thus, according to Maccoby and Jacklin, we can determine the following categories of sex difference, even though details are not yet settled: (1) biological and physiological factors; (2) behaviors shaped by parents and other socializing agents in accord with gender expectations; and (3) behaviors spontaneously learned by the child through imitation and modeling which are subsequently refined when adult.

Another scholar, Williams (1977), looking at the same evidence reaches very similar conclusions. Spatial ability, she concludes, may be the only cognitive ability which has a sex-linked genetic component, but even this is so affected by social and environmental factors that its genetic cause may be comparatively insignificant. The male tendency to show more aggressive behavior may have a physiological cause: a hormonally induced readiness to respond aggressively and other physical characteristics. But very young children are much more similar than dissimilar. Absolute differences between the sexes in behavior, cognitive ability, social and affective behavior, fearfulness, dependency, and anxiety have not been demonstrated during the first two years of life and therefore seem unlikely to have a genetic basis. Williams points out that most attempts to explore differences between the sexes ignore the much wider variations within each sex.

As a tool to measure differences between the sexes, genetics is less useful than study of the socialization process. Certain biological events peculiar to females (e.g., pregnancy and childbearing) obviously make women's lives different from those of men. A second clear difference lies in the roles usually played by women and men throughout their lives, some of which are unique to women, most of which have male parallels but different effects on each sex. The roles of parent, grandparent, single person, divorced person, offspring, worker, etc., though common to both sexes have very different economic, social, and emotional consequences on women and men. A third set of differences lies in the stages of adult life, as described by Lowenthal (1975) and Troll (1975). Each sex assumes activities, behaviors, values, priorities, and roles which drastically affect development and participation in the family, the working world, and society at large.

Finally and most important, the realities of the lives of contemporary women are very different from those of men (as well as from those of women in previous eras). The demographic data show recent dramatic changes among women in the family, at work, and in the larger world. Behaviors, attitudes, and values until recently seen as inappropriate for women—and still seen as inappropriate by some segments of society—are being adopted by increasing numbers of women as a result of economic necessity and cultural opportunity. Women's roles as earners, heads of household, and decision makers are clearly expanding; but they are receiving fewer rewards than do men and paying a higher price for the same or greater achievements. Because women today function more boldly in a society still not organized to help them, their task is much more difficult than that of men, who, in doing precisely the same things, are simultaneously fulfilling their own and society's expectations for their sex.

It is precisely in this last category that a mental health professional can be of major help, whether in practical or psychological areas. As women move into new roles, they have to cope with both the external manifestations and internal dynamics of the socialization process. In both respects, therapists have the opportunity to help their clients understand the different world into which they are moving and the new selves which they are developing.

Why Should Sex-fairness Concern Therapists?

The dynamics of the interaction between society and the individual woman should be singularly interesting to mental health workers. All societal institutions have the effect of encouraging individuals to internalize certain beliefs which produce attitudes, values, and behaviors which in turn lead to choices about family, education, and work (Smith, 1968). The life goals of women, the ways women relate to their peers, intimates, to authority, and to society in general are all determined by this process. So are the responsibilities they expect to assume or avoid. So is their sense of individual identity. So are their guilts and anxieties.

Therapists themselves are the products of the same process, and their judgments about clients reflect in some way, to a greater or lesser degree, their own socialization. Their professional responsibility to their female clients is to ensure that their work is not *only* a reflection of their own socialization, because that may well bring them to overlook the client's real needs. The area of therapy with women is one in which ignorant or unconscious judgments can do active harm to clients, and one in which therapists have a professional obligation to combat their own acculturation.

What should therapists do in the face of the barriers society places to women's full development? Should they attack them? Should they play "neutral," going along with them to a certain extent? Should they manipulate them? Should they knowingly or unknowingly cooperate with barriers which keep women from receiving their fair share of money, power, status, knowledge, or opportunity? These barriers may be less dominating than they were a decade ago, but they still manifest themselves in such areas as the limitation of job opportunities, the timing of a woman's career development, family systems which strongly discourage a woman's freedom, exclusion from the decision-making nucleus within an organization, the devaluation of a woman's accomplishments in favor of encouraging her as nurturer or office mother, or (perhaps most damaging of all) a woman's sense of powerlessness at the relatively poor pay and status which women's occupations are likely to produce. Which of these matters is or is not a matter of concern to a mental health professional? How much of it should therapists confront or ignore?

Of equal complexity are the internal barriers to their own development which the socialization process encourages women to erect. Most women unconsciously carry with them beliefs and expectations produced by the socialization process which they unconsciously use against themselves and other women (Bem, 1975). Studies show that women as well as men tend to devalue what women do or achieve (Broverman et al, 1970; Goldberg, 1968). They lower their aspirations to conform to society's expectations of women (Lipman-Blumen, 1972; Hennig and Jardin, 1977). They tend to accept other people, especially men, as wiser and more competent (Altemeyer and Jones, 1974; Unger, 1976). Moreover, unlike men, they tend to nurture others at the expense of their own needs. In general the consequence has been to undermine a woman's sense of freedom of choice by reducing her motivation to choose among the many alternatives that are in fact available to her. She does not see them as available, or she does not see them as suited to her.

It is not easy for a therapist to decide what to do in these circumstances. Some blame the victim (Ryan, 1971). Some let the woman make the choice without benefit of information or insight from a more knowledgeable person. Some overwhelm a woman with too much insight and information. Some encourage the woman to retain the barriers, while others want her to discard too much too soon. And some help the woman to observe and measure cautiously the self-imposed limits she has placed upon herself, to see what she has learned through the socialization process, to unlearn old ways and learn new ways which suit her needs and advantage.

Indeed, deciphering the complex of internal and external barriers is an exciting challenge for therapists. In the past, psychological theory has emphasized the intrapsychic origins of the problems brought to the therapeutic situation by the client (Zellman, 1976; Condry and Dyer, 1976), ignoring the societal structure which first taught through modeling and reinforcement what behavior, attitudes, and values were appropriate and functional and then reinforced that teaching by an elaborate and unconscious structure of economic, social, and political "realities" (Smith, 1968). This is why many feminists have accused mental health practitioners of being discriminatory agents of society, forcing the client into an adjustment that is essentially wrongheaded. But if it is outmoded to see a woman as purely a psychological entity apart from her background, so too is it unrealistic to expect all therapists to become revolutionaries in the cause of women's liberation or to think that that is what all clients need or want. What is needed is a skillful and professional compromise: the ability to understand an individual's whole situation and to use as much of that understanding as is appropriate for that individual. This is a challenge which any committed mental health professional will enjoy.

What Is "Sex-fair" Therapy?

No good mental health professional intends to be unfair to the sex of the client, but their unconscious acts are another matter. Occasionally, a therapist may escape the sex-biased values of our culture, but ordinary mortals are better advised to follow the advice given by Rawlings and Carter (1977), which is to examine and discuss values with the client rather than to attempt to breathe in a value-free vacuum. Sex-fairness itself is not value-free; it is simply flexible and equitable.

Sex-fairness is always difficult to achieve. Here, for instance, is an imaginative summary of contemporary personality goals which the author (Blocher, 1974) has synthesized from Rogers, Shaben, Health, Barron, Allport, and Maslow into a concept of the "effective personality." It is very attractive.

1. Consistency. The effective person is reasonably consistent in his behavior both within social roles through time and across social roles. . . .

2. Commitment. The effective person is able to commit himself to goals and purposes. He is able to take reasonable, calculated risks of psychological, economic, and physical kinds in order to move toward desired goals. . . .

3. Control. The effective person is able to control his emotional impulses and responses. He is able to accept the unalterable and inevitable without emotional responses that are inappropriate in nature or intensity. . . .

4. Competence. The effective person has available a wide range of coping behaviors. He is an effective problem-solver. . . . He is able to *master* environment within the limits of the possibilities available to him.

5. Creativity. The effective person is capable of thinking in original and divergent ways. He does not stifle ideas and impulses that are unconventional or novel. . . . [Pp. 97–100]

9

Beyond doubt these are worthy goals. And beyond doubt they are more difficult for women than for men to achieve—for the simple reason that all are characteristics which society actively discourages in women. Consistency: our culture asks women to be inconsistent across roles and through time, assertive as a worker, deferential as a homemaker; sex object when young, asexual when old; and so forth. Risk-taking: accident data show that males characteristically engage in riskier behavior than do females, and our culture rewards them vociferously whenever they forestall a woman from being exposed to risk, whether it be physical or financial (as for instance in serving in the front line or running a corporation). A risk-taking woman, on the other hand, is seen as exceptional, hard, and fanatic. In the matter of control, women are permitted to be more emotional in some narrow ways (crying, timidity) but less emotional in others (determination, ruthlessness, anger) to the point where both control and lack of control work to women's disadvantage. It may be, indeed, that they are societally encouraged to avoid *effective* control. In both competence and creativity, our culture generally sets women's limits narrower than men's. It does not encourage them to be unconventional, and it does not especially enjoy seeing them "master" their environment. In sum, Blocher's synthesis creates an essentially male ideal of personality effectiveness, one harder for women than for men to achieve. A female client striving for such goals will be fighting the other characteristics seen as appropriate for her sex, so the process of achievement will simply not be sex-fair.

Other theories of personality, fortunately, make sex-fairness somewhat easier.

Androgyny

One method of overcoming the harmful influence of sex-role socialization is to see every individual as a different mixture of characteristics which society chooses to describe as "female" and "male." Society sees its members as collectively possessing feminine, masculine, and neutral traits; many individuals within that society can choose, from any category, those traits which are best suited to any particular situation (Bem, 1974). Research indicates that such androgynous people are more creative and flexible and less anxious than extremely masculine or extremely feminine persons. (For greater detail, see Bem, 1977.) Thus the concept of androgyny is useful to therapists because it suggests a low-stress method of opening up other categories of behavior and feeling as options for the client without denying the validity of the female/male categories (Kaplan, 1979; Marecek, 1979). The choice of a particular behavior to fit a given situation carries a low level of threat to one's identity, allowing the personality to become "effective" without engaging in a contest against sex-role socialization.

Sex-Role Transcendence

The concept of sex-role transcendence (as developed by Hefner, Rebecca, and Oleshansky, 1975) goes a little deeper into the individual personality. Personal development is seen as having three main stages. In early childhood, sex roles are undifferentiated; the child has no clear conception of the behaviors which are encouraged or culturally restricted because of biological gender. Later comes the stage of sex-role polarization. The child feels the need to follow prescriptions for behaviors, thoughts, and feelings appropriate to its sex, and in this she or he is encouraged by cultural institutions. Some individuals finally reach a third stage wherein they transcend polarization to move freely from situation to situation with behaviors and feelings which are appropriate and adaptive, to make choices without rigid adherence to sex-role characteristics, and to behave and feel according to their personal needs as a whole individual rather than only as a woman or as a man.

Sex-role transcendence used to seem utopian, but since more individuals now operate freely in this manner, it has become a realistic goal for the therapist of women. Transcendence challenges the socialization process more strongly than does androgyny. In the latter the sex role is important: one consciously chooses between the various options. In transcendence, the sex role becomes unimportant; one is oneself rather than female or male—obviously closer to self-actualization. The developmental process of transcendence rather than the operational principle of choice between sex roles is the object of the therapist's attention (Garnets and Pleck, 1979).

As concepts for therapists, androgyny and sex-role transcendence are more useful than other theories of personality because they directly confront and use the effect of socialization on the individual. This serves four functions for therapists. First, it opens up any aspect of the client's life for consideration while still retaining a sense of coherence among all aspects. Second, it leads to individualized counseling by forcing attention on the particular developmental barriers which this particular female client has encountered. Third, it reassures the client that her situation is not an individual oddity but the result of cultural pressures to which we are all subject. Fourth, it allows the therapist to present options to the client in the form of choices which she may or may not make; there is no obligatory "model person."

Self-actualization

Both androgyny and sex-role transcendence are in line with the more familiar counseling goal of "self-actualization." Indeed Maslow, in 1942, was one of the first to report on the androgynous model of healthy women. (He found that women who were high in self-esteem were also tolerant of others, assertive, willing to take the initiative, decisive, self-reliant, independent, and ambitious.) Maslow focuses on the healthy, creative person rather than on the pathological or negative aspects of personality. He sees the environment as crucial in determining whether the individual grows from within in a healthy manner or whether inner needs and capacities are thwarted to produce a miserable or neurotic person. For this reason, counselors have found his concept of self-actualization a useful

11

model, and a glance at the characteristics of a self-actualized person shows them to be sex-fair. According to Maslow (1968), self-actualized persons

- have a realistic orientation
- show democratic values
- tend to be spontaneous, open, and relatively free of neurotic defenses
- exhibit an unstereotyped appreciation for people and things
- are problem-centered rather than self-centered
- resist conformity to the culture, often by creativity
- have a few deep relationships with certain important others
- require privacy and enjoy solitude
- do not exploit other people
- display philosophical rather than hostile humor.

All these characteristics apply to women as well as to men.

Thus we have at least three concepts of personality which are free of sexist overtones yet do not deny the force of sex-role socialization too easily. All three show the proper goal of sex-fair therapy, that is, a client who is sufficiently flexible, creative, and spontaneous to choose whatever behaviors are appropriate rather than those which are derived from the sex-role socialization process. By abandoning therapeutic goals which are advantageous primarily to one sex or the other, one makes it more likely that a client of either sex will function as a full adult rather than as an adult impeded by childlike sex-role behaviors learned and reinforced regardless of their real appropriateness.

Nonsexist and Feminist Therapy

Two other approaches to therapy aim specifically at being sex-fair: nonsexist therapy and feminist therapy. The major distinction between the two is that feminist therapy incorporates the political and philosophical values of the women's movement, thus actively combating sex-role stereotyping, while nonsexist counseling emphasizes the need for *all* human beings to be able to actualize themselves regardless of biological gender. Neither approach is linked with any particular set of therapeutic techniques though both stress an egalitarian relationship between client and therapist. Both assume that women and men by nature may be different from each other, but both see cultural influences as much more important than biological differences in the creation of differences and inequalities.

It is not useful to argue about which approach is better. The issue, rather, is which approach is more appropriate for the individual client. After analyzing the two approaches in some detail, Rawlings and Carter (1977) conclude that nonsexist approaches may be more suitable for a woman with traditional values to whom feminism is threatening, while feminist approaches may be more appropriate for a client who finds the cultural prescriptions for women restrictive and wishes to explore alternatives. In my own experience, both approaches may be used at different times with the same client; neither is relevant for all clients at all times. The basic issue determining the therapist's choice must be the belief that good therapy always begins where the client is and moves with her to whatever place she is able to move at that point in time.

The major difficulty which many counselors experience with feminist therapy is the strong value system which it requires the therapist to have. Many feminist theorists maintain, for instance, that no male can satisfactorily undertake feminist therapy (Chesler, 1972; Rice and Rice, 1973). While I certainly agree that many women need feminist therapy and that only feminist therapy will help them at particular periods in their lives, I also believe that many clients do not need *only* feminist therapy and that any therapist, male or female, can and should use enough of the ideas and information of feminism to make her or his therapy more useful to the client. One does not have to be a committed feminist to use the information and attitudes common to feminist therapy.

It is important to realize the similarities between feminist and nonsexist therapy. Nonsexist therapy assumes that the problems of a female client do not lie totally within her but are partly based in society; it sees a woman's development and behavior as determined more by being human than by being female, and it sees her goals as human rather than sex related. Feminist therapy generally agrees with this posture, and it shares many of the goals of nonsexist therapy: self-esteem, independence, power over one's life, achievement, individual growth free of traditional sex-role stereotypes. Both approaches emphasize the need to nurture one's self and to pay attention to one's own needs as well as to those of others (thus standing accused of encouraging "selfishness" and "narcissism" by those who know little about the operations of the personality), and both encourage the client to define one's self and one's goals only partially by reference to external or cultural values.

In addition, feminist therapy has something which nonsexist therapy needs: a clear specification of the source of a woman client's problems. Feminist counseling and therapy have been growing out of the larger political movement since the 1960s and they are bolstered by a great deal of new knowledge, fresh research, and steadfast revisions of and additions to existing theories and practices. When feminist therapists speak of women as experiencing problems and difficulties unique to their sex (and different from those of the past) and as requiring specific kinds of support to handle their difficulties in daily living and lifetime process, they know—very precisely and accurately—what they are talking about. It would be unconscionable for any therapist *not* to make use of this information and knowledge, and it is indeed exasperating to find therapists who willfully refuse that knowledge. A common goal of feminist therapy is to help clients become aware of the social and political context of their problems. Whether or not a therapist proceeds with that step, she or he has the responsibility to be informed and aware.

The goals of feminist therapy are not ultimately different from those of all therapy: the alleviation of personal distress and difficulties and the removal of

13

growth-inhibiting influences so that the individual may live more fully and effectively. The difference is the extent to which feminist therapists see social institutions and stereotypes as causing and worsening women's problems and the manner in which they encourage the client to examine these forces and combat their effects on her life.

Sex-fair therapy is the goal. To achieve it, one probably needs a healthy dose of feminism, certainly a desire to be nonsexist, and inevitably a great deal of skepticism about psychological theories which do not take into account the special situation of females in our society.

Which Theory of Therapy Best Fits the Realities of Women?

The common thread in all definitions of the nature of counseling is the interaction between two persons—one of them with expertise and training—aimed at creating an active and pragmatic state of change. As one of the major texts states, "Counseling is a process by which a person is assisted to behave in a more rewarding manner. Assistance is determined by the counselor; that which is more rewarding is determined by the person being assisted with the aid of the counselor" (Delaney and Eisenberg, 1972, pp. 2-3). In therapy, greater understanding is created in order to lead to changed actions: "Counseling is an interaction process which facilitates meaningful understanding of self and environment and results in the establishment and/or clarification of goals and values for future behavior" (Shertzer and Stone, 1968, p. 26). The role of the therapist is to be more objective and better informed than the client. As Lewis (1970, p. 10) puts it, the client changes "through interaction with an uninvolved person (the therapist) who provides information and reactions which stimulate" new behavior.

With adults, therapy is a highly cooperative act, two people working with each other. As Schlossberg, Troll, and Leibowitz (1978) state clearly, adults have "an identity, a history, a long-range perspective on time. During their lives, they have probably passed through various transitions and role changes, learned certain coping skills, experienced and observed much of life. Their greater experience, longer time perspective, and broader view of their history can be used as resources so that client and counselor together can build a foundation for dealing with particular problems and can develop strategies for handling future problems" (p. 57).

Adult therapy most often deals with problems caused as much by practical and "real-life" dilemmas as by psychological maladjustment. Schlossberg (1977) emphasizes its nature as an intervention process which facilitates change in an individual going through a transitional crisis. Farmer (1977) accentuates the importance of therapy for making decisions regarding various aspects of adult life: educational, vocational, and interpersonal issues. Other theorists emphasize habit problems which lead to crises (e.g., math anxiety, obesity, alcoholism) or interpersonal problems (such as difficulties in marriage, couples, families, parenting). All theorists see unresolved problems as a potential source of more serious disturbances in the emotional, social, and economic realms of the individual's life. They see therapy as an opportunity for the client to develop new insights, to change behavior, to have different expectations and attitudes, and to find fresh values. My own emphasis is on the practicality and realism of the therapist's goals. The dilemmas brought by the client demand solutions which must be pragmatic and often cannot be leisurely. The therapist must be knowledgeable not just about the individual client but also about the world within which she moves and in response to which she has to make her choices.

This is particularly true with female clients. Though as adults women have vast experience as women, the female experience of the world at large tends to be very limited. Women normally have not explored a large portion of the spectrum of adult roles and behaviors which is in fact available to them. At the same time, more women know that society now offers them this spectrum of options and are trying to explore them for the first time, even while they know little about them or their own suitability as explorers (Moulton, 1977). The art of therapy therefore lies both in working to utilize the experience and skills which a woman brings into therapy and, at the same time, assisting her to expand herself and the number of options which she is capable of choosing.

Therapy with women should therefore be seen as an intervention process in which the trained and objective therapist provides a woman with the means of becoming her own change agent, independent of the therapist in the future and capable of making her own confident choices about her situation in the world.

This is to be accomplished by three distinct actions on the part of the therapist. First, the therapist seeks to *counteract the negative consequences of socialization* in the woman client's life. This may be done by teaching her decision making skills and processes which she did not learn as a female, by broadening the options she sees in her adult roles and her behavior, attitudes, and values in any aspect of her life, and by replacing dysfunctional with functional models of thinking, feeling, and behaving. The goal of this first action by the mental health professional is a woman who recognizes and trusts her own expertise and power and knows how to use her accumulated experience and skill to deal with future choices. Second, the professional should *provide the client with whatever she is unlikely to get from her own environment*: nonsexist information, knowledge of resources, and the emotional support to enable her to take charge of her own growth. Third, the therapist must *work openly with any crisis or problem in any aspect of a woman's life*, seeing her as a whole person, helping her to see beyond the immediate problem, and encouraging her to clarify both the dynamics of the immediate problem and the variety of choices that lies in front of her. The goal of this third action by the mental health professional is a well-informed woman who does not feel passive and helpless in the face of crisis.

1

The Therapeutic Process

There are three critical elements in conducting therapy with women. The most crucial element of the therapeutic process is the existence of *two realities* which affect every client: the external world and the internal world. The crucial task of the therapist is to pay attention to the interaction between the two, at the very least helping the client to distinguish between them and to decide where she wants and needs to put her energy. The second critical factor involves the *values, attitudes, and behavior of the therapist.* Our culture demands that therapists make their own acculturation conscious to assure that the counseling process will remain purposeful and fair. The third crucial element is the *direction of the relationship* between therapist and client. All therapists function as agents of change with the end goal of having the client take charge of her or his own life. This process is more important with women clients than with men, both because of the variety of harmful consequences which a therapist's special agenda may create for a woman and because of the general tendency of our culture to have women give control of their lives to others.

In counseling and therapy, process and product are almost indistinguishable. The product appears constantly as part of the process, and the process cannot really take place unless the product steadily appears in the form of the client's growth. Nonetheless we can analyze the two in sequence as follows.

The Process

In the therapeutic situation, both therapist and client have "informal" and "formal" roles. In formal terms, the client presents her problems or difficulties and

16

herself to the therapist. The therapist uses professional and consciously developed skills to serve as the agent of intervention. This neat diagram is unfortunately complicated by the force of the informal event which underlies it, caused by the reality of both client and therapist as acculturated individuals who bring all their own values, attitudes, assumptions, expectations, behaviors, feelings, thoughts, physical presence, and *confusions* to the situation.

The task of both individuals in a therapeutic situation is to be very clear about themselves. The importance of that task may be why Fritz Perls' declaration has so quickly become a truism: "I am not in this world to live up to your expectations, and you are not in this world to live up to mine." This declaration is especially important in the area of counseling women.

The task is difficult if the therapist is female, more so if he is male. In general humanistic/existential terms, Arbuckle (1965) concludes that the ultimate goal in counseling is for any client to move toward her or his highest potential. The values of the client may differ from those held by the counselor, but the counselor must nonetheless accept and respect them. "The goal of the counselor regarding the item of sex," he writes, "should be to move toward being neither a feminist nor a masculinist but rather a humanist who can experience compassion and love for all people." Undoubtedly a pleasant ideal. But what of the reality of sex differences, regardless of their origin? The counselor must accept the reality, continues Arbuckle, "that at certain times a man will behave in a different way toward a woman because she is a woman and a woman will behave in a different way toward a man because he is a man. For the sake of the human species, let us hope that this difference continues to exist" (pp. 384–385). This is not a cheap *vive la différence* joke, but a genuine recognition that women and men are different, tend to relate differently to each other because of their sexes, and, regardless of whether they want to or not, bring different gender-based expectations into any communication. To achieve the humanist ideal, one cannot ignore the human reality. The implication for therapists is obvious; whether female or male, they have to study themselves as closely as they study their clients.

Rawlings and Carter (1977) point out not only that a therapist's personal and professional values influence the process of change in their clients but also that many of those values are induced by their professional training itself: "Professional values stem from the personality theory with which therapists identify, their models of psychotherapy, and their models of mental health. These professional values converge to determine technique and goals" (p. 6).

Therapists also need to pay close attention to the holistic concept of therapeutic interaction as discussed so carefully by Satir in *Peoplemaking* (1972). Regardless of our values and beliefs, we are also individuals. The way we look, the way we talk, the way we move, the way we feel, all affect how other people respond to us. The way other people behave influences how we respond to them; therefore we need to be very and sometimes overtly *aware*. This is particularly important in any interaction between client and therapist of different sexes, since outright sexual attraction (or repulsion) will play a role, sometimes minor, sometimes major. Two factors combine to affect the female client with a male therapist: the nature of any sexual response within either of them, and the tendency of most women to be submissive. Sexual seductiveness (by either sex) can easily become emotional or intellectual seductiveness if both partners are unaware of the dynamics of the communication.

Awareness of the probable areas of difference between client and therapist is the first and crucial step for counseling women fairly. These are as follows:

1. *Cultural values and biases.* These set the parameters for what is appropriate for females and appropriate for males. They therefore define what is healthy for women and men. To become aware of the effects of cultural values and biases on therapy, one has to ask repeatedly: what are the cultural values which, as a result of socialization, we both bring to this situation and which either blatantly or subtly restrict the choices, options, issues, and alternatives which we examine?

2. *Unique and common experiences.* Therapist and client will have some cultural experiences in common; others they will not share. What happens, for instance, if the therapist is male and his client is dealing with abortion or rape or mastectomy? Or what if a therapist of either sex believes that a lesbian woman should ultimately find her satisfaction in marriage, home, and family, or that menopausal women are erratic? What if a female therapist is too young to have experienced the more blatant sex-role stereotyping which affected a woman her mother's age? These questions must be brought into awareness, as must those experiences which we all share to some extent.

3. *Expectations from therapy.* This is an especially important area for clients who are receiving counseling for the first time. One learns to be a client or a therapist, and in either role experience affects outcome. One has to examine whether both the therapist's and the client's expectations are clear, appropriate, and realistic, and in making this determination the questions may be subtle. Is the woman, for instance, dealing with passivity yet expecting the therapist to act as one more authority figure on whom to lean? Or do the therapist's expectations for the ideal woman lead her or him to define and demand goals? Does either client or therapist expect to play out a sex role in this situation? Does one do so, but not the other?

4. *Expression.* When the client is confused or nervous and the therapist takes a posture of care and caution, there is potential failure of communications, both verbal and nonverbal. Cues are sent out unconsciously and may be misinterpreted. The issue here is to determine whether the verbal and nonverbal messages are congruent, and the aim is to make them not only congruent but clear.

These are not the only areas in which awareness is necessary, but attention to each of them, though it demands extreme alertness, will enable the therapist to make some basic judgments about the degree of sex-fairness in her or his professional relationships.

Process Goals

The second main method of measuring one's sex-fairness is to look at the outcome of the therapeutic process. What are the goals of counseling women? As with all therapy, goals do not all come at the end of the process. Sex-fair interaction is itself a major goal, and good outcomes for the client therefore require having a healthy process. Further, some of the goals of the process should enable the therapist to measure consciously the quality of her or his own therapeutic process.

For instance, the therapist can recognize whether or not he sees a client's behavior as being the result of her biology ("After all, she is a woman") or the result of learning and acculturation ("She has acquired only the spectrum of female behaviors, values, and attitudes so far"). A therapist can also recognize whether he is familiar with the mundane and usual realities of a woman's life (as contrasted with that of a man) and whether or not he sees the client as an individual or simply as part of a class or a pattern. With discipline, therapists can also determine whether their intervention, intended to provide new insights for the present stage of the client's life, is also attuned to her long-term development and actualization as an independent human being. There must be, in other words, some kind of harmony between long-term and short-term goals. All these might be described as characteristics of the process about which the therapist consciously and repeatedly *thinks*, the elements by which one evaluates one's own skill. They are, in other words, goals by which one measures the health of the process itself.

The most pertinent of these process goals is probably the ability to view the client as an individual. Actualization for a woman who is 28 years old is unlikely to be the same as that for a woman who is 52. Actualization for a black woman is not necessarily the same as that for a Latino, an Asian, or a Caucasian. A skilled worker is not necessarily going to find happiness by becoming a professional. When a client finally makes a choice which seems "wrong" to the therapist, whatever frustration the therapist feels is probably due to her own agenda, which the individual client has failed to meet, and is thus more the problem of the therapist than that of the client.

Again, this is usually more important when counseling women simply because they have been acculturated to make their choices according to others' expectations. The therapist may feel that the client should divorce her husband or go back to school or get a better job, but the client chooses not to. Who is right? Perhaps both. The therapist may have the "better" idea; but the key matter is that the client is making her own choice. At this point in time, her actualization may lie in the "wrong" alternative. She may well choose differently later. The important factor is that she recognize that the choice is hers, that she is in charge of her own life for good or ill, and that she can therefore change her choices later and at will. This sense of power over one's life has to be developed slowly throughout the entire counseling process.

Finally, the process goal most directly affecting the therapist herself or himself is avoidance of reflecting the inequality with which society in general regards women and men. Our culture is replete with cute expressions and gestures which all add up to the belief that men are to be dealt with seriously while women are "like that." None of the attitudes revealed by these expressions can be allowed to affect the counseling process, but their elimination is extremely difficult. The whole force of the socialization process directs both therapist and client to believe in inequality no matter what they say they believe, and only the therapist has the training to note and eliminate the subtle manifestations of that cultural force.

Product Goals

The product of the counseling process can tell us whether we have achieved intermediate goals. For example, one very desirable product is a woman who no longer needs the therapist. Some women clients simply transfer their dependence from an outside individual to the whole mental health and social service system, repeating in another form the old cultural message that "someone else knows better than I what is good for me." The aim of the therapist is a client who makes changes and choices without unnecessary dependencies on outside influences, including the therapist's plans for her.

A second product should be a client who can use either feminine or masculine behavior as is appropriate to her needs. It is conceivable that a client may choose to attach the same old adjectives to her descriptions of "feminine" and "masculine." (Women are nurturing, passive, home-loving, nonaggressive, sensitive, caring; men are self-reliant, competitive, active, achieving, intelligent, etc.) What is more important is whether she sees both "feminine" and "masculine" behaviors as available to her when appropriate. She should not, in other words, feel less feminine displaying "masculine" characteristics when they are required to function successfully.

A third goal is that the client should not feel that she has to display traditionally "feminine" behavior if it works to her disadvantage. She is not obliged to be a sex object, a housekeeper, a poor earner, or a submissive individual to be and feel that she is a woman. A client should see that in today's society practical concerns—not sex-role stereotyping—should determine how she behaves and feels. Whether within the family or in the world of work, traditionally feminine behavior may be psychologically and economically harmful. The therapist's goal should be to help the client choose or discard the traditional sex-role prescriptions for herself on the basis of a sensible judgment of her own situation.

Ultimately, these three goals define what one means by a therapist functioning as a change agent who helps a woman become her own change agent. The role of the therapist is partly educational, partly psychological, partly supportive. On the one hand, therapists work to change the external barriers which prevent women clients from developing fully. On the other hand, therapists equip women to deal with these barriers by overcoming the internal barriers which the socialization process has erected within them. A therapist may have to serve as a change agent who removes the external barriers directly. A therapist will certainly help the woman learn to remove barriers for herself and to function with some sense of autonomy, independence, and control over her own destiny.

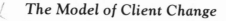

The Model of Client Change

To understand the specific therapeutic approaches recommended in later chapters, it is important at this point to look at the model for client change on which they are based. The model draws from humanistic and Gestalt concepts, especially those of Satir (1972, 1976) and Erving and Miriam Polster (1973), with additional emphasis on nonsexist and feminist ideas.

The model deliberately emphasizes both the internal and the external aspects of a woman's life. What goes on in our personal lives—body, mind, and psyche—has an intense and total relationship with the external world through

CHANGE MODEL FOR THE WHOLE WOMAN

Focus of Attention	Elements of Awareness	Change Objectives
A. *Internal*	*Body*	1. Expanded and positive self-esteem
What do I own as true for me? What part of reality do I accept responsibility for?	Breathing, voice tone, posture, armor, sensory perception, physical care	2. New skills and new behaviors
What barriers do I erect which create and/or compound the situation?	*Mind* Cognition, knowledge, learning, planning, restructuring, deciding	3. New communication styles, verbal and nonverbal 4. New rules and new expectations of self, others, and the world
	Psyche	
B. *External*	Feelings, wants, desires, dreams, needs, fears, frustrations, intuitive sensing	
What is outside me that I must respond to? What part of reality do I place the responsibility for outside myself? What barriers are erected outside which create and/or compound the situation?	*Actions* Choices, deeds, behaviors, creation, work, achievements	

which we move as we express our relationship to that world through our actions. The various elements of our personal lives are similarly linked with an intensity that specialized professional disciplines often ignore. Mind and body interact, emotion and actions are interdependent. To be aware of one and ignore the others is perilous. On the other hand, to concentrate on one in order to understand the whole is a simple and flexible technique. The objectives of change can be achieved in a variety of ways and measured by awareness of any or all four elements; all four objectives will interact in such a way that each will be visible in the other three.

Any therapist, for example, can use the simplest techniques of observation in order to perceive elements of the current psychological state of a client. It is a matter of being able to see and hear with *purpose*. When a client attends a session, I am constantly and consciously aware of such matters as these: is her posture unusually slumped or tight? Is her walk self-confident, or shy or defeated? Does she sit solidly, does she slump, or does she perch nervously? Does she restrict parts of her body, especially her hands and legs? How does she use her eyes, to express or conceal? To look at me or the floor or inside herself? I also pay attention to dress since it expresses the client's state of being and demonstrates the signals she is sending to other people. Is she, for example, unusually sloppy or stylish in her dress? Does she always wear dark colors? Is a new attitude toward dress, and therefore self-image, emerging? Does she fuss with or about her attire inappropriately? I also listen carefully, starting with observation of the pattern of breathing. Is her breathing very shallow? Does she hold in her breath for long periods? Can she laugh or cry freely? Is the pitch of her voice too "girlish" for her age? Is its tone appropriately variable or monotonous?

The point of this observation is to enable me to measure how the client is with herself and how she presents herself to the world and to me. Is she, for instance, afraid, confused, compliant, rigid, aggressive, defensive, withdrawn? Is she out of touch with or strongly repressing her own strength? Is she cut off from her own source of power stemming from the body and therefore from her true self? In these matters, the body is a metaphor for the psychological being; through this metaphor both I and the client can become aware of the mind and psyche.

When a client begins therapy, I always ask a series of questions about her, such as: what brought you here? What's happening in your life right now? What special plans, problems, decisions, new realizations engage you right now? What do you want from therapy, from me, from yourself? Though the answers are very often misleading or incomplete, all of them begin the process of *clarification* which the psyche requires. They start both me and the client thinking about her as an entity. They also reveal *lack of congruence* between various aspects of the client's life or with other elements of her behavior, particularly impaired ability to appraise the world and the self realistically because of, say, chronic unrecognized depression or anger.

Observation of actions both within and outside of therapy gives crucial insight into mind and psyche. A client says, for instance, that she "really wants" a relationship to work, but in action she criticizes or belittles her companion routinely or systematically refuses to join in shared activities, or, having brought her companion to a therapy session, she tries to control what she or he says. Another revealing pattern is that of a client who never gets around to doing what she says she wants to do. This action may be giving something up, such as drinking too much, dating too many men (or one particular man), or staying at home alone when depressed. It may be failing to fulfill a promise to oneself. A client, recently promoted to a management job, reported that she was very eager to learn how to manage people, but she failed even to read a series of books on management, bought at great expense. (Eventually she realized that she did not want a management job and resigned.) The therapist wisely looks for any sign of conflict between a client's actions and the other elements of her being. Wherever there is such conflict, there is room for growth, and that growth will be toward congruence between the elements outlined in the change model. The therapist should also look for the absence of any significant element in the mind or psyche or actions; lack is a signal of need.

There is no sense in which significant personal change can be anything but total. If change sometimes seems to involve less than the total person, that is simply because the individual or the therapist is concentrating temporarily on one avenue toward change. Paraphrasing Satir, we can say that change comes from four main directions:

- Self-esteem: how do I feel about myself?
- Communication: how do I communicate with others, verbally and nonverbally?
- Rules and shoulds: what are the rules or "shoulds" by which I determine my choices and actions?
- Behavioral risk: what new behavior am I willing to try, to test, to risk?

Change any one of these areas, and it will have an effect on the others. For example, suppose a change occurs in the client's rules or shoulds: "a woman should always place others before herself when making choices" becomes "a woman can put herself first when making choices." To be more than just words, this new rule must manifest itself in changes in self-esteem, communication, and behavior. Another example, this time in behavior: "I will set my own schedule for getting the day's office work completed." That behavioral risk requires changes in communication, is the abandonment of an internal rule, and will probably result in greater self-esteem. The four avenues lead to the same central point, as is apparent in Figure 1.1.

A major implication of this model for therapists is that one can start working for overall change with any small aspect of behavior, attitudes, or values. This makes the model very pragmatic. The attempt to make too large a change can cause a client to fail to make any constructive change at all. Women usually find the achievement of one small step easier, more rewarding, and certainly more effective than the giant leap for womankind that causes one to fall flat on one's face. And therapists who see where the client's "core" should change and grow frustrated because the client lets the "details" slow progress can, using the model, start with small, measurable changes in accessible matters so that the sense of change rapidly reinforces the client's efforts. Change is not a product but a process which is never completed. It results from the interplay between personality and behavior. The changes may be delicate and subtle but can also be very powerful.

The therapist cannot bring about all the changes that a woman needs to make or will make during any given period of her life. However, a therapist using this model can train a woman to understand the process of change and to use the skills and techniques which all change requires so that she has the power to make her own changes, so that she can truthfully say: "I am my own person. I can take control over my own life. I can use help from others, but I am my own best expert."

The other major conclusions of the model, which will be demonstrated in detail in subsequent chapters, can be summarized as follows:

1. Therapy is a process of intervention wherein a trained professional provides a woman with experience of the skills and techniques which she can use, for herself, to gain control over her own life in connection with both present and future problems.
2. The most crucial role for the therapist of women is to remove the external and internal manifestations of sex inequality by manifesting and encouraging feminist and sex-fair attitudes.
3. The therapist serves as a catalyst or nurturer for the woman's undiscovered

FIGURE 1.1. *Adapted from a theory developed by Virginia Satir, in* Making Contact *(1976).*

CHANGE MODEL

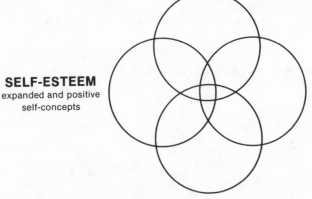

COMMUNICATION
new verbal and nonverbal styles

SELF-ESTEEM
expanded and positive
self-concepts

TAKING RISKS
new behaviors and skills

RULES
new and changing expectations
and "shoulds"

and unrealized potential. The goal is the client's actualization as an adult human, unburdened by whatever is dysfunctional in traditional sex-role expectations and behavior.

4. Change comes about through dealing with the total person as she manifests herself in body, mind, emotions, and actions. Separately and together, these elements are those upon which the therapist must teach the client to concentrate.

5. Therapists should concentrate on both the externals and the internals of a woman's situation because most problems and opportunities for growth lie in the interaction of the two.

6. Changes occur most easily in a supportive environment. Directiveness is best limited to drawing a woman's attention to matters of which she is not fully aware, to the dimensions that surround her present plight, rather than to a narrower solution of the problem first presented.

7. A supportive (as opposed to directive) environment means: (a) meeting a woman wherever she is, so that one may begin with her experience and her present reality in some detail; (b) helping her to recognize and discard values and behavior which she recognizes as restricting her development; and (c) providing her with new information, skills, alternative roles, new communication styles, behaviors, and expectations or rules for herself so that if and when she begins to question her present way of being, she will have the option of alternatives that are nonsexist, androgynous, or transcendent.

One final point should be made. The model discussed above is clearly assembled from a variety of disciplines which often like to emphasize their differences from each other. It is not my objective to throw everything into the same pot, to make guidance seem like psychotherapy, counseling like analysis, or career development like psychiatry. A psychologist is not trained to help a woman decide whether she should take a typing course or enroll for an M.B.A.; a guidance counselor cannot help a woman resolve childhood trauma; and a social worker is not trained to be a career counselor. However, it is clearly the intent of the model to show the common ground which all disciplines share, the base upon which each can build its own strengths. All the data and all our past experience show that each of these disciplines working in isolation and ignorance of each other has not done as well for women as we might wish. Too often, each ignores or is unaware of factors in a client's life which are officially the realm of some other discipline, and this has created a dichotomy between the practical and the psychological which is false and disastrous to many women. The suggestion contained within the model of client change presented in this chapter is not that each discipline acquire the skills of the others, intrude upon the others, or even necessarily cooperate in any formal manner; it is simply that each in its own way start from the same common ground—the client herself and her situation in society—so that each in its own way may end up with a worthwhile outcome: a woman in charge of her own life and development.

2

The Mentally Healthy Woman

Introduction

This chapter deals with mental *health* rather than mental *illness*. It is not about psychopathology, psychosis, or even severe neurosis in women. Many women seeking mental health services do not fall into these categories even when symptoms such as depression or anxiety are displayed. Their mental health and emotional stability have been threatened not by mental illness or disease but by their status and situation in society. The needs of these women are the subject of this chapter.

Our society tends to overdiagnose women as mentally ill. A culture which labels femininity irrational, immature, and childlike easily produces diagnosticians who see women's signs of psychological stress as induced by some internal weakness connected with the biological state of being female. Diagnosticians rarely look first to the external situation to see whether the client's behavior might have its source there. In the case of depression, for instance, most diagnosticians think first of making an adjustment in the woman rather than of the woman making an adjustment in her life—even though there is a plethora of research demonstrating the strong link between depression and attempts to fulfill sex-role stereotypes imposed by society. Many depressed women, in fact, are not showing signs of pathology at all. They need to understand their situation and the sources of their frustration, confusion, pain and self-doubt; they need to change the way they are living and the way they see themselves. Even the small proportion of women showing signs of pathology needs help in handling external matters about which diagnosticians rarely inquire.

Our society has tended to see a desire for therapeutic intervention as prima facie evidence of mental illness. People who need help to function as independent adults are seen as having something wrong with them, as less than completely adult. This attitude often joins with the social stereotype of womanhood to explain, incorrectly, why more women than men come to therapy. As less than fully adult, women are seen as more needy and weak and therefore more susceptible to mental illness. The opposite, I suspect, is true. Many women coming to therapy are already healthier than others who do not seek counseling. They want greater understanding of themselves and more personal growth. They want to deal directly with the issues and themes of adulthood and the limitations which sex-role socialization imposes on them. They are using a constructive method of dealing with their psychological disturbance and displaying a flexibility and courage that bode well for the continued growth they seek.

Mental health counseling with such women wastes energy on a search for diagnostic labels. The task of the therapist is, rather, to sort carefully through the complexity of themes presented and to identify the predominant issues for combined exploration and work. The therapist does not function like a doctor, who can diagnose and treat an illness without transmitting any of her or his knowledge to the patient. She or he is, rather, a collaborator of special expertise who will transfer knowledge and ability to the client as rapidly as possible. Viewed in this light, therapy is a process of exploration, collaborative work, and the weaving of separate themes into an integrated whole whose pattern is visible to the client as well as to the therapist. This is the approach to mental health counseling for women which this chapter discusses.

The Difference Between Women and "People"

Why discuss women's mental health rather than people's mental health? Is a healthy person not simply a healthy person, regardless of gender? Is illness not illness, whomever it afflicts?

The most basic problem affecting the mental health of women becomes visible when one looks at the characteristics which our society calls "masculine" or "feminine." In the process of designing her Sex Role Inventory, Bem (1974) surveyed a large number of college students to discover the adjectives most used to describe the typically feminine person and the typically masculine person. The resulting adjectives for "feminine" were, for example, gentle, yielding, sympathetic, understanding, childlike, and sensitive to the needs of others. Those for masculine were, for example, ambitious, athletic, self-reliant, independent, assertive, dominant, and competitive. Looking at these two lists of adjectives, one can easily see which qualities—masculine or feminine—our society most clearly values and rewards in "people" as a group. Those attributed to masculinity are those which society sees as belonging to a healthy adult, a person who survives, copes, functions well, and gets ahead. A man possessing those qualities can pride himself on being both a healthy adult and a real man. A woman, however, must choose: she may become either a real woman *or* a healthy adult (Broverman, Broverman, Clarkson, Rosenkrantz, and Vogel, 1970). A woman possessing all of the feminine and none of the masculine qualities will either not do very well in society or will survive only by being dependent and subordinate. In other words, society's values build role conflict out of the man's struggle to be mentally healthy and into the woman's similar struggle.

The mental health of men today is threatened often enough, but that of women is threatened more often according to the frequency with which they are called upon to act as independent adults in conflict with their sex-role conditioning—a frequency which is steadily increasing. Few people realize that the same event or situation may seem normal to males but highly stressful to females—simply because of the "feminine" and "masculine" qualities which they have been trained to develop differently. If a woman's stress is observed, she is likely to be blamed for experiencing it: "Well, if you want to live in a man's world, then do a man's job . . . " Or, "Women are not as tough as men." Or, "You can't expect a woman to be able to . . . " Even kindness can debase women by reflecting society's low expectations of them. A depressed woman may be allowed simply to remain in her home unnoticed when a man would be judged unwell for not going to work, and women are given antianxiety drugs more often than are men because, expecting women to lack the mechanisms to deal with life's realities, people more readily offer them crutches. When faced with conflict, women more often than men are allowed to give up rather than encouraged to endure or prevail. Thus, a woman is ultimately undermined in the adult's most necessary characteristic: the sense of power over life.

In pursuit of the need for help or advice, what are women likely to encounter in the mental health professions? The answer is not cheerful. Whether they go to psychoanalysts, psychiatrists, or psychologists, to sex therapists or career counselors, to personnel managers or shop stewards, or to professors, lawyers, or doctors, the probability is that their problems will not be faced in a sex-fair manner. As The National Advisory Council on Women's Educational Programs recently stated, "Counselors, [like] other mental health professionals, often hold negative or ambivalent attitudes toward women" (1977, p. 5).

Although research on bias and sex-role stereotyping in the mental health professions is still in the developmental stages, their existence is already well documented. Precise knowledge began with the large studies published by Broverman et al in 1970 and 1972, and it has been defined further by such studies as those of Sherman, Koufacos, and Kenworthy, 1978; Fabrikant, 1974; Brown and Hellinger, 1975; Aslin, 1977; and Stricker, 1977. In 1975 came the extensive report by the American Psychological Association, whose Task Force on Sex Bias and Sex-role Stereotyping in Psychotherapeutic Practice reviewed the research and surveyed 2,000 female members of APA in order to identify the concerns of females as both consumers and practitioners of psychotherapy. Four general areas emerged as widespread matters of concern:

28

- the fostering by counselors and therapists of traditional sex roles;
- bias in expectations and devaluations of women;
- sexist use of psychoanalytic concepts; and
- responding to women as sex objects, including seduction of female clients.

The problem is particularly serious among male professionals. Brown and Hellinger (1975) surveyed 274 psychiatrists, psychiatric residents, psychologists, social workers, and psychiatric nurses. They reported that female therapists consistently held a more contemporary view of women than did male therapists. Sherman, Koufacos, and Kenworthy (1978) not only confirmed the finding of bias as more likely among male than female therapists (social workers, psychologists, psychiatrists) but also found that 70 percent of the professionals saw a special need for training to work with women clients.

Thus, when Division 17 of the American Psychological Association in 1978 laid down some basic principles concerning counseling and therapy for women, they asked only the most preliminary of efforts from mental health professionals: "Competent counseling/therapy requires recognition and appreciation that contemporary society is not sex fair. Many institutions, test standards, and attitudes of mental health professionals limit the options of women clients. Counselors/therapists should sensitize women clients to these real-world limitations, confront them with both the external and their own internalized limitations and explore with them their reactions to these constraints." Women, said the APA, constitute a special subgroup and "Although competent counseling/ therapy processes are essentially the same for all counselor/therapist interactions, special subgroups require specialized skills, attitudes and knowledge" (*The Counseling Psychologist*, 1979, p. 21).

Women clients themselves may make things worse, for in the helper/helped relationship traditionally feminine characteristics encourage the helped to give power away rather than to take it. The role of patient is more compatible with the female than with the male sex-role prescription—weak, dependent, irrational, indecisive, childish, submissive, accepting, and needy (Rawlings and Carter, 1977). With the woman's physician or therapist already likely to share cultural assumptions about women's personalities and behavior, her femininity and her role as patient or client are likely to make a disastrous combination; if she displays the characteristics of an adult in command of herself, she is likely to evoke a negative reaction as both patient and woman.

To show the effects of the combination, one can look at the group of helpers women most often visit—physicians—and the most likely result of the visit—a pill. Women get 60 percent of the prescriptions for nonpsychoactive drugs and 67 percent of the prescriptions for psychoactive drugs. They are the major consumers of barbiturates, other sedative hypnotics, relaxants, minor tranquilizers, antidepressants, pep pills, diet pills, and noncontrolled and controlled narcotics, though not for heroin (Prather and Fidell, 1975). There may be good reasons for all of this which we do not yet understand, but most stated reasons are ludicrous.

For instance, Brodsky (1971) found that physicians feel secure in prescribing tranquilizers for housewives because they can always take naps and do not need to stay alert. The sexism that underlies the giving of prescriptions is evident in a study of drug advertisements in medical journals over a five year period. This showed that nonpsychoactive drugs ("real illness") tended strongly to be associated with males while psychoactive drugs ("mental illness") were associated with females. Further, the male patients depicted in association with psychoactive drugs had specific work-related symptoms, while the depicted females complained of diffuse anxiety, depression, and tension. All this occurred in addition to the familiar gratuitous insult that none of the advertisements contained a woman physician (though 7 percent of physicians are female) while all the nurses were female. There is in fact a widespread belief that physicians as a group do not take women seriously until a physical symptom is visible. When one study asked physicians to describe the kind of patient to whom they feel negative, the "typical complaining patient," of the 76 percent who spontaneously identified that patient's sex, 72 percent chose female and only 4 percent chose male (Cooperstock, 1971).

Illness apparently is not just illness regardless of whom it afflicts; a healthy person is not simply a healthy person; and women's mental health is indeed an issue distinct from people's mental health.

How Major Psychologists Have Viewed Women

For the most practical and professional of reasons, the questions which every therapist should ask herself or himself during the next decade are as follows: What is "mental health" for women? What kind of woman can be described as "mentally healthy?" What power over her emotional/psychological life does each woman need in order to develop as a fully effective adult?

Traditional psychotherapy has simply not asked these questions. The legacy of Freudian analysis was to see women as doomed by nature to be incomplete men suffering from envy for the penis. In his old age, Freud continued to see women as inferior and mysterious. "Despite my thirty years of research into the feminine soul," he wrote, "I have not yet been able to answer the great question that has never yet been answered: What does a woman want?" In his mind, that frustration was clearly women's fault rather than his own. The subsequent history of psychological theory upon which all practice was based, in which all practitioners were trained, shows a similar sexist coloring.

Freudian psychoanalytic theory included the ultimate derogation of women: biological determinism. Anatomy, say Freudians, is destiny; since the lack of penis makes women inferior and incomplete adults, then clearly one need not pay them much attention. A great deal of psychoanalytic theory overtly sees the female—whether neurotic or healthy—as characterized by narcissism, masochism, low self-esteem, dependency, and inhibited hostility resulting from the unsuccessful adult resolution of childhood's inevitable and harsh truths. To be fair, these characteristics often do mark the female who follows the culturally prescribed role of the feminine. The basic problem, however, was that psychoanalytic theory of personality used males as the model. When later Freudians sought redress in the way of adjustments to the basic theory, they helped neither the theory nor our understanding of women very much. Indeed, they served only to draw attention to the lack of adequate study of women by psychoanalysis.

An interesting example of this process is provided by the distinguished neo-Freudian Erik Erikson. In *The Inner and Outer Space* (1964) Erikson states that biological difference does not mean that women are necessarily inferior. If the psychology of men is determined by their possession of external genitalia, he says, that of women is determined by their "productive inner space," i.e., the womb. To what destiny does this anatomy lead Erikson? Men, of course, exploit and manipulate the external world. Women, by nature, are conserving and nurturant. Thus Erikson finds a theoretical justification for the traditional economic double standard, the conventional split between masculine and feminine, the adjectives assigned to the two sexes by Bem's college students, and the sexism found in mental health providers by Broverman.

The effects of the basic theoretical stance are subtle but eventually stunning. Take, for instance, Erikson's famous analysis of the psychosocial development of "humans" into the eight stages of "man," which he formulated on the basis of knowledge about males and then adjusted to accommodate females. The theory itself, and the detailed observations, *may* be quite accurate; as Williams (1977, p. 58) points out, "the value and accuracy of these observations are empirical matters which can be validated by research yet to be done." The basic problem lies elsewhere—in the identification of "human" development with "male" development, to which female development then becomes a series of exceptions and footnotes. "If women are an exception to the theory," writes Williams, "then it is not a theory of human development. What the theory does is to provide a background against which women appear as an anomaly. Either separate explanations must be made for her, or she is a silent presence who is lost somewhere among the assumptions underlying the theory." Similar criticisms can be levied against almost all psychoanalytic theorists. The problem is basic; as long as the body is seen as the essential determinant of personality and behavior, there will be a double standard to explain "human" behavior. And as long as the theorists are male (one suspects), females will always be seen as deviations from the norm and aberrations from the ideal.

Any personality theory built on the premise that psychology remorselessly proceeds from biology, without due reference to sociological context, is vulnerable to challenge as sexist because it affirms the correctness of a socialization process that encourages women to behave in "feminine" ways and regards women who depart from the "feminine" as being deviant. Critics point out that the effect of such theories is to accept that any problem must arise from within the

31

maladjustment of the individual, not the environment. The world outside may be maintained; whatever exists is right. In a society in which women are given an inferior status, critics thus see personality theory of this kind as another form of social control preventing women from attaining equality. (Defenders of other minority groups see existing psychological theory as having the same effect on all minorities.)

Personality theory has obvious political implications in that traditional mental health models require women to adjust to the traditional behaviors defined by her culture as desirable. It is therefore not surprising that the traditionalist approach should have dominated and should still dominate mental health services. Most therapists are white males; almost all have been trained during a time when, and in institutions where, nontraditional alternatives were absent. Most of them work inside a health care system and institutions supported by society at large and intended to disseminate existing cultural norms. Faced with a woman behaving in "unfeminine" ways *or* in feminine ways undesirable in society, the therapists seek to help the woman "adjust to reality," that reality defined as the expectations created by social norms for someone of her biology. She should develop as a woman rather than as a person, and the stereotype of a woman's behavior so clearly defined by society is the easiest path for her to follow. There cannot be, say the traditionalists, any real conflict between being a healthy woman as defined by society and being a healthy adult.

There is little malign about all this, and were our society as homogeneous and rigid as some others, there might be no real argument with the role of mental health practitioners in perpetuating tradition. But our society is neither homogeneous nor rigid, with the result that traditional models for mental health are out of date, out of touch, and in danger of being justly labeled oppressive. How can a tradition function unchanged when any minority group not only becomes aware of its nature and situation but offers viable alternative theories? If it then fails to change, it is doomed to see as unhealthy those who are healthy. It may rapidly become actively oppressive; it may indeed drive those better in tune with reality to the "madness" so persuasively described by Phyllis Chesler (1972), a result so far from the intention that it is poignant. There is thus an acute need for psychological definition of the mentally healthy woman which takes into account the cultural source of mental problems, the socialization process which has a profound effect on our attitudes and behavior.*

This has been the thrust of opposition to traditional psychology from the very beginning. As early as 1927 for instance, in a chapter on sex in *Understanding Human Nature*, Alfred Adler recognized the damage done to the psychic life of

---

*Evidence of the double standard existing in the theory and practice of psychology has accumulated rapidly since the original study by Broverman, Broverman, Clarkson, Rosenkrantz, and Vogel (1970). See, for example, Broverman, Vogel, Broverman, Clarkson, and Rosenkrantz, 1972; Chesler, 1972; Bosma, 1975; Maslin and Davis, 1975; Delk and Ryan, 1975; Aslin, 1977; and Sherman, Koufacos, and Kenworthy, 1978. Classic counseling textbooks (e.g., Krumboltz and Thoresen, 1969; Shertzer and Stone, 1968) have followed the famous theorists in referring to all clients and counselors as "he" and "him."

women by the assignment of inferiority to women as a sex in both theories and institutions. Though he was a psychoanalyst associated with Freud, Adler saw all individual psychology as determined by the conflict between individual and environment; he saw as normal the striving for superiority within individuals, whether male or female. Between 1923 and 1935 Karen Horney, the first of the great female theorists, began to publish her work on feminine psychology. Later she formulated a theory of psychology which linked human growth and its limitation to the quiet interplay between individual and environment; her major work, *Feminine Psychology* (1973), contains a clear delineation of the complexity she saw. A second female psychoanalyst trained in Freudian theory, Clara Thompson, rejected biological determinism in favor of sociocultural explanations of feminine psychology as early as 1942, in a paper entitled "Cultural Pressures in the Psychology of Women" (1964). By that time anthropology was making major contributions, especially through the work of Margaret Mead. Her attitude toward women was one of the major sources of interest even as early as *Coming of Age in Samoa* (1932), in the use of cross-cultural studies to demonstrate the malleability of human behavior. In later work (1974) Mead discounted entirely the penis-envy concept of the Freudians as being hopelessly culture-bound. Mead never rejected the possibility that some psychological sex differences are determined by biology, but she insisted that much more research was necessary before their existence could be assumed. This was the general thrust of the mavericks in the first half of the century: what had been taken for granted on the basis of speculations about biology could no longer be taken for granted, especially in the light of alternative explanations. (More detailed discussion of the work of these theorists appears in Williams, 1977.)

Current Theories of Personality

In the 1960s new theories of human psychology began to have a dramatic effect on theories of feminine psychology. First, the ancient term androgyny was given new force. According to concepts of androgyny, all individuals display a mixture of traditionally feminine and traditionally masculine characteristics which may be more or less suppressed or developed. Male and female traits thus form a spectrum of qualities, and on that spectrum the individual may find her or his place. If anyone is "abnormal," it is she or he who lies at the extreme of the spectrum—the wholly feminine or wholly masculine person. In an important issue of *Daedalus* in 1964, Alice Rossi was one of the first to point out the value of this concept for therapists working with contemporary women; it allows a much broader mix of behaviors appropriate to their needs and natures. During the 1970s, through the work of such people as Bem (1974), Spence, Helmreich, and Stapp (1974), and Berzins and Welling (1974), the androgynous approach won a valid and even popular place in contemporary theory, accompanied by the development of instruments for measuring and describing the degree of androgynous orientation within an individual. A special issue of the *Psychology of Women Quarterly* (Spring 1979) examined in depth the use of the androgyny model by practitioners and its value in further research. The concept has two major virtues; biology is one of the factors which it recognizes as creating and influencing the individual, but by no means is it the sole factor. Thus it allows both women and men the flexibility which both sexes need. Further, it is genuinely a model for the development of all humans. Neither sex is accepted as inferior to the other, so the theory does not further propagate any kind of double standard.

Where this concept may lead is the concern of current discussion by Kaplan (1979). Worried about the dualism of masculine/feminine inherent in early definitions of androgyny, Kaplan suggests as a goal a hybrid state further along the continuum in which the masculine/feminine dichotomies "come to coexist, to be tempered one by the other, to unite in the formation of truly integrated characteristics." Behavior would not be an either/or but a both/and. Anger, according to Kaplan, would be tempered by love, dependency by assertiveness, and so on, so that in any given situation one would not have to choose between the two qualities. The linkage of superficially opposite qualities would recognize the legitimacy of both at the same time. Joining assertiveness with dependency, for example, signifies acceptance of the legitimacy of dependency needs while offering an active way by which to fulfill them, destroying the equation of dependency with weakness or of assertiveness with strength.

Practicing therapists may recognize Kaplan's goal, one we achieve too rarely, that of an integrated but truly flexible adult. Perhaps to compensate for the infrequency with which therapists actually reach that goal with their clients, Kaplan draws attention away from the end point and towards the process by which a client strives for integration. The thrust is not that the therapist should measure the client's status as an abstraction—is she or is she not now and forever a whole person?—but in any particular area the striving should be toward integration. A woman can be angry in one situation, loving in another, hybrid in a third, and still be the same person. Quite rightly, Kaplan points out how much self-development this requires on the part of the therapist. "All this places vast demands on the therapist's self-awareness," she writes. "We must sensitize ourselves to our own reactions, the theoretical implications of which only emerge through the very process of identification. At issue is the constant exploration of one's self in relation to the model of androgyny on the one hand, and to the cultural constraints that impinge upon us on the other" (p. 229).

Another theoretical construct has emerged in the 1970s as an alternative to the polarities of sex roles. Termed "sex-role transcendence" in the formation of Hefner, Nordin, Meda, and Oleshansky (1975), the model describes three developmental stages. In early childhood sex roles are undifferentiated, the child having no clear conception of the behaviors encouraged or restricted by the culture because of biological gender. In the second stage, sex polarization occurs as the child follows cultural prescriptions for behavior and feelings appropriate to its sex. In the third stage, the individual learns to move freely with adaptive feelings and appropriate behavior and to make choices according to her or his needs as an individual rather than as only a female or male; this is sex-role transcendence. It is a new concept requiring further refinement and testing, but, like androgyny, it offers a way out of the traditional polarities. Both women and men can by its means define themselves as individuals, using the traditional masculine/feminine division as only one measure among many.

In all three theories just mentioned, the evident goal is self-actualization rather than social conformity. The individual self is seen as having rights and responsibilities beyond those given by societal sex-role prescriptions. Like the concept of self-actualization, therefore, these theories can account for the development of the antisocial as well as the social individual.

Nonsexist and Feminist Therapy

The best new approaches to therapy take into account the information recently acquired regarding sex difference, the psychology of women, the internalization of sex-role stereotypes, and the societal norms for healthy adult behavior as they affect women and men as individuals. To compensate for previous inherent sexism in psychological theory, new approaches tend to be avowedly nonsexist or feminist, and both terms are now heard frequently in reference to both psychology and psychiatry.

Neither nonsexist nor feminist therapy subscribes to a particular set of therapeutic techniques. Both can incorporate any technique except Freudian analysis. They assume that women and men may indeed be different from each other by nature, but they view as more important those differences imposed by culture. They regard culturally prescribed sex roles based on biological differences as unduly constrictive. They seek liberation for the individual, and they tend to seek equality between women and men. They oppose restrictions on behaviors and values based only on biological gender. Nonsexist approaches have a strongly humanistic bias, and they are often accused of political naivete. Feminist approaches have a sociological base and are often accused of being too political. Conflict between the two may grow bitter at times, though they have so much in common that the conflict is hardly inevitable. My own experience has been that neither is "better" than the other, simply more or less appropriate at a given time with a given client.

What both approaches share is a vital rejection of the inferiority of women as human beings. Good mental health counseling starts with where the woman is and keeps pace with her progress, without setting authoritarian rules about where she should be. This is the touchstone for measuring nonsexist and feminist therapy since it is the standard by which traditional psychological theory so egregiously failed and since both nonsexism and feminism believe that no source outside the woman knows better than she herself what is best for her. Both maintain that to gain equality and development she must learn to know, to respect, and to use her own self-understanding; and both theories direct their efforts to this end.

Nonsexist therapy works with both women and men although it is used more commonly with women at the moment. Its goal is that the client assume freedom, responsibility, and equality as an individual within the larger society. It sees the intrapsychic origins of an individual's problems as—on the whole—less influential than societal and sex-role expectations. The guilt and anxiety often associated with individuals who differ from society's prescriptions are relieved, in nonsexist therapy, not by relinquishing differences in favor of conformity but by acceptance of the individual's right to live variously in a variegated society.

The basic assumptions of nonsexist therapy (Rawlings and Carter, 1977) are as follows:

1. The therapist should be highly aware of his/her own values, especially as they relate to expectations for "males" and "females." Since the evidence shows that most therapists are subject to the same biases as are the rest of the culture, this is already a professional requirement which most are unable to meet without special training.
2. Differences from the norm in sex-role behavior are seen as normal and appropriate. Choices should be made on the basis of what will work best, not on what should or should not be.
3. The dominance of biology in determining sex differences is rejected, though it is usually seen as a factor.
4. Behaviorally, reversals in sex-role predispositions are not seen as pathological and the desired outcome for all clients is the ability to choose adaptively.
5. Females and males are viewed primarily as individuals. Females, for instance, are seen as capable of the same autonomy and assertiveness as males, and males of the same expressiveness and tenderness as females.
6. The therapist avoids using the power inherent in her or his position to reinforce or punish behavior which appears to be decidedly masculine or feminine.
7. Test instruments which contain sex bias are avoided.
8. Diagnosis does not depend on a client's "failure" to achieve behavior in accord with her or his culturally prescribed sex role.
9. Therapist and client work cooperatively to achieve the values and choices appropriate for this person in this situation regardless of her or his gender. Sex-role transcendence is the goal.

Unlike nonsexist therapy, feminist approaches explicitly incorporate the values and philosophies of feminism, as promulgated by the women's movement, into their therapeutic values and strategies. Feminist counseling and therapy in fact arose from the women's movement of the 1960s and 1970s and from the wave of exciting new research which accompanied that movement. Feminist counseling believes that females and males should seek and have equal opportunity for personal power, economic wellbeing, and political/institutional influence. It insists that interactions between individuals should be egalitarian, and in this respect the egalitarianism which the therapist displays is itself a political statement. (For details, see Rawlings and Carter, 1977.) Feminist therapists, even more strongly than nonsexist therapists, seem to endorse cultural as opposed to biological determinism and the environmental model of psychopathology. Sex-role transcendence is clearly the model for mental health. Feminist therapy is particularly useful because of its specialization in sex-role socialization, that of males as well as females, in cases where either sex is trapped in the cultural bog.

The basic assumptions of feminist therapy (Rawlings and Carter, 1977) are as follows:

1. The inferior status of women in our society and others is due to their having less economic and political power than do men.
2. Though the circumstances in which a woman exercises power will vary according to her economic and/or social class, social class does not affect her individual value to the same extent as does her gender.
3. The main source of a woman's problems is likely to be social and external, not personal or internal, but focus on the external as a source of problems does *not* relieve the individual of responsibility for her choices. On the contrary, the individual can change both herself and the external world.
4. Friendship, love, pairings, and marriage should be based on equality of personal power.
5. Other women are not the enemy; nor are men. Both are victims of sex-role socialization. Social change is an important goal for the individual, who should concentrate on choosing behaviors that are appropriate rather than sex-role stereotypical.
6. Economic and psychological autonomy are both important goals for women.

A view of the strategies which tend to be used by feminist counselors and therapists shows how thoroughly this approach defines the individual as a sociocultural rather than as a biological being and how much more activist it tends to be than is nonsexism. Normally, a feminist therapist will make her values regarding a woman's role in society explicit to the client; thus the client is immediately faced with choices which demand autonomy and evoke equality between therapist and client. These events will usually precede development of a contract for specific behavioral changes on the part of the client, whose responsibility is to provide measurable goals for therapy, to remove the therapist's power as magician, and to emphasize the "how to" rather than the "why."

The feminist therapist has many qualities typical of a good teacher. For instance, although the therapist confronts contradictory behavior, she or he does so without instructing which element of the behavior should be discarded. What a client says is taken at face value rather than subjected to subtle interpretation, but clients are taught how and when to use straight communication. Sex-role analysis is often used as one treatment technique since it provides emotional support, which simple encouragement to develop herself will not offer, during the process of an individual's analysis of the emotional and political barriers to her goals. Women are consistently seen as capable of more autonomy than they have traditionally displayed. The therapist assumes that the client is her own best expert on herself, simply adding to the tools which a client may use. For this reason, diagnostic labels such as those in conventional patient records are useless and unused, and if diagnostic testing is done, its results are available to the client—along with all other charts and records.

Four basic observations are often made about feminist therapy, sometimes as criticism, sometimes as praise. First, it requires strength and initiative on the part of the client. Critics say many clients do not have these qualities; supporters say that the technique develops them more rapidly than do other strategies. Second, many claim that feminist therapy is less effective in individual therapy than in group situations; others maintain that groups wherein women learn from and support each other, diluting further the therapist's power, are ideal for the individual woman's growth. Third, many therapists are uneasy about the technique since it requires activism on the part of the professional as well as that of the client; supporters say that without activism feminist therapy is only "Band-Aiding" and easily becomes part of the problems which already plague the client. Finally—and this is a criticism sometimes levied by feminists themselves—critics say that feminist therapy too greatly emphasizes the need for women to have the skills to be financially independent, pointing out that this is very difficult for many women, especially those in minority groups. Supporters maintain that not only is financial autonomy the only way an individual in our society can maintain a sense of personal power but that it is a legitimate and measurable goal to some degree for any client.

Radical Feminism

"We, as women, can and must free ourselves. We can effectively take care of our own and one another's heads and souls. We should seize the means of producing and preserving our own mental health. Women already have well-developed skills and intuition and insight; as oppressed people we are accustomed to adapting and compromising to the desires of others, to tuning in scrupulously to other people's feelings, and to taking care of their unspoken needs. When these skills are coupled with permission and training to be strong, to take care of business, to think rationally, and to talk straight, the result is a skillful and powerful people's psychiatry" (Wyckoff, 1977, p. 371).

These words of Hogie Wyckoff describing radical feminist psychiatry take us a long way from the inferior nature of women depicted in early psychoanalytic theory, and their debt to politics is quite visible. The aim of radical feminist psychiatry is the training of women to work at healing other women and at "co-opting power from the medical establishment." Traditional psychiatry is seen as having actively harmed women; in radical feminist psychiatry the term "psychiatrist" is interpreted by reference to its Greek roots as "soul-healer," reflecting the task which faces its proponents. It is not merely an alternative to traditional psychiatry but a counter-movement specifically intended to bring the practice of soul-healing back into the hands of the people—in this instance, women.

Each separate premise of radical feminist psychiatry is solidly based. In terms of psychological theory, it uses a problem-solving approach based on the theories of R. D. Laing, Fritz Perls, and Claude Steiner. In terms of factual base, it uses numerous research studies showing the prevalence of females as patients, of males as practitioners, and of sex-role socialization as a harmful force. In terms of politics, its source is minority radicalism, the belief that woman have been oppressed as a class (deliberately and fortuitously), and that traditional psychiatry functions as a force maintaining the status quo evident in sex-role socialization. In terms of orientation, it has a missionary force; the strength of its antagonisms to the establishment coupled with the militancy of its vocabulary discourage many people from paying it due attention.

Several concepts are central to radical feminist psychiatry. It asserts that oppression leads to considerable alienation of women. Deceived into believing that there is something wrong with them, that their experience is not valid or even real, women succumb to collusion with their oppressors rather than recognizing their exploitation. For example, society creates massive alienation in the women who are told that they are "bitchy" or menopausally depressed when in fact they are correctly sensing the end of the only values society sees in women—as producers, homemakers, and vases for youthful beauty. Awareness of oppression then becomes a major force, creating anger that focuses the energy needed for a fight to reclaim full humanity: "Once a woman is aware of her injury and becomes angry, she can move against the real culprit" (Wyckoff, 1977, p. 373). Anger should obviously lead to action; action requires contact or support from others. Contact includes all forms of positive human recognition—credit for hard work, compliments, hugs, caresses, being heard, being seen, being understood—very much as outlined by Satir (1976) as the four "contact points": being seen, heard, understood, and touched. Women's support groups bring contact to their individual members.

According to radical feminist psychiatry, the force leading to the inferior status of women is neither biology nor psychopathology but a combination of societal oppression with what Claude Steiner called *banal scripting*, the development of some parts of the personality and the suppression of others. This explains self-definition according to biological sex. Under the banal script, women are conditioned to see themselves as the male's complement. They are programmed to adapt, to take care of others (especially their men), to be nurturing, and to avoid being strong adults. They are trained to feel powerless, not to feel adult, and to look to men for rescue and protection. Women and men are scripted to go together like hot and cold or yin and yang; they must be put together to make one whole person, which is an absurdity. Thus radical feminist psychiatry becomes a counterforce by helping women: (1) to reduce their other-direction, their training to look to others, especially men, rather than to trust themselves; and (2) to turn to other women for support in using their intelligence, confirming their experience, affirming their power to make decisions on the basis of their own understanding, and taking responsibility for the decision to change. (For fuller descriptions, see Steiner and Wyckoff, 1974; Wyckoff in Steiner, 1974; and Wyckoff in Rawlings and Carter, 1977.)

Far from conclusion, the debate stimulated by radical feminist theories has scarcely begun. Despite the discomfort often caused by its vocabulary, it has been unusually influential to other schools of thought; and because it has a consistent explanation for each antagonism that it raises in others, it is hard to ignore. Traditionalists tend simply to dismiss it. Critics who prefer the middle-of-the-road dispute both its strategies (too radical for a minority) and its conceptual base (inattention to psychopathology, overemphasis on cultural causation). Proponents and sympathizers are favorably impressed by the amount of energy it releases within both individual clients and groups of women. While unlikely to replace traditional psychiatry, radical feminism does act as a cutting edge in the process of change which the field of psychiatry needs to undergo.

Summary

The field of psychological theory has seen an extraordinarily rapid development from original premises which presented women as inevitably inferior to a current state in which the psychology of women is seen as being different from and as important as that of men. This has been accompanied by a strong and desirable emphasis on the role of culture rather than biology in creating typical female psychological patterns and problems. Nonsexist therapy, feminist therapy, and radical feminist psychiatry all use valid conceptual and factual bases and are much more responsive to the needs of women today, in terms of both basic approach and specific strategies, than are Freudian psychoanalysis and traditional male-dominated psychiatry and psychology. The fields of counseling and therapy are necessarily responding to these changes, with productive results.

Mental Health and Social Roles

There is considerable evidence that the change in women's social roles during recent decades may have been accompanied by a decline in their mental health. Of course, mental health rates are extremely difficult to determine because of the absence of complete data and the changing definitions of mental illness; but we are reasonably certain, on the basis of community surveys, admissions to treatment centers, and private and public clinical surveys, that since World War II the industrial nations have seen a higher rate of mental illness among women than among men (Weissman and Klerman, 1977), whereas before the war the rate appears to have been higher among men (Klerman and Weissman, 1980). While more men than women commit suicide, more women than men attempt suicide, and this rate has increased during the last 30 years (Klerman and Weissman, 1980). Data on depression show a similar pattern (Goldman and Ravid, 1980).

Two major explanations can be given for such differences between male and female mental health: the biological and the cultural. The biological explanation has steadily lost adherents in recent years. Only four behavioral invariates related to sex are now clearly acknowledged: males impregnate; females menstruate, gestate, and lactate. All other criteria of sexual differences stem from these and are now generally considered to be optional according to time, place, culture, and environment. Important studies in human sexuality have had a major impact on our attitudes. Money and Ehrhardt (1972), for instance, studied individuals who, because of natural or human error, required sex reassignment and were reared with that reassignment from a very early age (e.g., male infants raised as girls after loss of the penis). By showing the overwhelming importance of sex assignment at birth and during rearing to the formation of gender identity and sex behavior, the study showed the relative independence of gender identity from biology, in turn emphasizing the importance of cultural influences. After studying research of the relationship between sex and behavior, one must come to the conclusion that major differences solely due to biology cannot be demonstrated (Weissman and Klerman, 1977; Makosky, 1980).

For example, though women as a group seem more vulnerable to depression than do men, the difference seems not to have a biological cause. While married women are more depressed than married men, the same difference does not appear among widowed and never-married persons, suggesting some factor other than biological gender as the cause; factors known to be related to depression—poverty, lack of education, race, age, nutrition, and others—have no basis in gender. Current thought about mental illness is therefore much more interested in studies which show that groups of women who feel powerful score comparatively low in depression—women with advanced education, high status jobs, high income, and women who do not marry (Radloff, 1975). While the problems which typically trigger depression may well be sex-typed (Beck and Greenberg in Radloff, 1975), all triggering events seem related to a sense of powerlessness over one's own life. If this is true, the explanation for the higher rates of depression among women may be that they are more likely than men to learn and to experience helplessness as part of their social role.

At present many behavioral scientists believe that the sociopsychological environment is the major cause of women's mental health problems (Horney, 1973; Mead, 1949; Gove and Tudor, 1973; Williams, 1977; Radloff, 1975; Weissman and Klerman, 1977; Guttentag, Salasin, and Belle, 1980). Recognition of environmental stress as the major source of internal stress is reflected in psychotherapy's current emphasis on the dynamics of sex-role socialization. As Weissman and Klerman (1977) cautiously state, "social role plays an important

41

role in the vulnerability of women to depression." The sense of powerlessness accompanying depression seems to increase when conflict exists between the individual and the traditional female sex role; since this sex role is learned rather than acquired before birth through genetics, the attention of mental health theorists is clearly shifting away from emphasis on identity as determined solely by biology.

Learning Social Roles

The process in which we learn our sex roles from the general culture occurs in a variety of ways. Through rewards and punishments, modeling, social learning, sex typing, and sex stereotyping, women learn to behave and feel in certain ways. Rewards and punishments given by parents and others in the environment quickly provide the reinforcement to establish behavior while a child is very young. Modeling, or imitating the behavior of significant others, becomes a factor with almost equal speed. Social learning of a cognitive/developmental nature, when a child recognizes its own sexual identity and learns society's prescriptions for that sex, also starts very young. Sex typing assigns different qualities, activities, and behaviors to females and males, and it starts with birth. Sex stereotyping, which prefers generalizations about categories of people to discrimination on the basis of infinite individual variations, rapidly takes over. So forceful are these factors in the acquisition of sex-role identification that they overwhelm predispositions created by biology. By the time a woman reaches adulthood, she has so thoroughly internalized the sex-role belief system she has learned that it seems provided by nature or the deity. She will function according to sex-role concepts which seem not only appropriate but inevitable, even if they harm her interests and her mental health.

The sex-role socialization of females puts them in a worse psychological situation than does that of males. In studies of sex typing and socialization, for instance, both Maccoby and Masters (1970) and Mischel (1970) conclude that females are socialized for dependence and males for achievement and autonomy. Hoffman (1972) similarly concludes in a review of the literature on socialization that girls are not encouraged to become independent. Through being protected more than are boys and exploring their environment less, they grow dependent on adults to solve their problems. Block (1973) reports that cross-cultural studies of sex-role socialization show boys pressured to behave as agents, doing and competing, while girls are encouraged to behave in communion with others, talking and being reflective; failure by females may be rewarded. In a study of high school students, Feather and Simon (1975) found what any plain bright girl suspects: that both successful males and unsuccessful females were rated more acceptable as people than either unsuccessful males or successful females. Males, in addition, were seen as personally responsible for their success and females as personally responsible for their failure. This last finding is confirmed by Frieze, Fisher, McHugh, and Valle (1975) in a review of causal theory and studies which showed females blaming themselves for failure and crediting luck for success, a pattern correlated with low self-esteem and lowered expectations for future ability to perform well. A careful study of 500 adults by Kaplan (in Fann, 1977) found that the higher rate of depression in females was associated with the effect of socialization experiences which inhibited women from adopting patterns which would permit them to deflect blame from themselves for any blameworthy situation.

The effect is visible in childhood. Dweck (1976) found that children react differently to failure according to whether they blame themselves or external factors. Girls, blaming themselves, tended not to improve even when the situation changed (as in promotion to a higher grade); whereas boys, tending to blame external factors, maintained their belief in their ability to succeed and showed renewed effort in a new situation. Girls seem already to have learned powerlessness, boys power. Fortunately, training can alter a child's perception of the reasons for failure and its reactions to failure (Dweck, 1976). Girls tend to improve if given feedback by peers rather than by adults, boys if given feedback by adults rather than by peers (Dweck and Bush, 1976). In sum, the sense of helplessness and power can be learned and unlearned.

The implications about the cause and cure of depression are obvious. For instance, Albin (1976) concludes that if learned helplessness is a strong factor in causing female depression, then learned mastery can immunize them against it. Albin recommends, indeed, that therapeutic intervention directed against learned helplessness may be the most effective preventive measure against depression. If people who see themselves as powerless over their external situations seem more depressed than others (Abramowitz, 1969), then those who learn a sense of power can at least mitigate that depression. Women can improve their mental health by learning new behaviors and new social roles.

Sex Roles as the Cause of Mental Problems

Depression is the most widespread symptom and/or cause of mental problems in our society, and a great deal of effort has recently gone into study of its causes to generate better statistical information than is available in most psychopathology. Depression is more common among women than men, but there are some highly significant variations in the data. Gove and Tudor (1973) for instance, reporting higher rates of mental illness among women than men, found that while among married persons women have the higher rate, among unmarried persons of all categories men outstrip women. Gove and Tudor, along with Bernard (1975) and Radloff (1975), suggest that marriage has a protective effect for males and a detrimental effect on females. Studying unipolar depression (i.e., depression without periods of euphoria), Radloff found that women scored higher on depression scales than men among both the married and the divorced/separated, but lower or no higher among the widowed and the never-married. Adjusting for many other possible causes of depression, Radloff found that among men the married are the least depressed and the widowed the most, whereas among women the never-married are the least depressed and the divorced/separated the most.

What is the explanation for these differences? Biology is tempting. The chemistry of women is more complex than that of men due to the major life events of menstruation and gestation, and marriage is likely to increase the complexity caused by these life events. There is evidence that genetic factors contribute to depressive illness; but after examining the evidence, Weissman and Klerman (1977) suggest that it is insufficient for conclusions about either the mode of transmission or the apparent sex differences. They also examine evidence about premenstrual tension, oral contraceptives, menopause, and the postpartum period, which are all associated with depression in common lore; and, while there is evidence for the existence (though not the hormonal cause) of postpartum depression, in the other three areas any chemical effects are minimal, depressions are by no means universal or even normal, and they have no distinct clinical pattern. We can safely conclude that biological chemistry does not explain the differences between men and women in rates of depression because of the lack of evidence relating mood changes and clinical states to altered endocrine balance or specific hormones. (It should, however, be noted that psychopharmacology is currently in a state of rapid growth. New experimentation may well produce new evidence during the coming decade.)

In the absence of an explanation due to chemical biology, what alternatives exist? Weissman and Klerman surveyed the literature on a series of other topics: the psychoanalytic explanation by means of intrapsychic conflicts; marriage; the psychological disadvantage of women's social status; the rising expectations of women, and stress caused by rapid cultural change; and the contribution of the mental health system itself in promoting dependency through reinforcement of stereotypes. None emerged as a convincing explanation. Weissman and Klerman concluded only that the different rates between the sexes are not the result of a reporting artifact, which has often been suspected, nor of women's health care behavior. The latter is significant. It could be that women respond to events with more depression, recognize depression more readily, or complain of depression more often than men. Again, however, none of these explanations is sufficient. Men and women do not appear to evaluate the impact of standard life events differently. Women do report more symptoms, especially affective depression; they do use the health care system more often than do men, seeking help of all kinds more often. This, however, is probably a consequence of male sex-role socialization; men tend not to seek medical attention, especially for minor illnesses, and the structure of the health care system tends to make it inaccessible to men. Men and women may have quite different responses to both anger and depression. While women predominate among patients, for example, men vastly outnumber them among criminal offenders, especially the violent; and men use and abuse alcohol at much greater rates than do women.

Other sociological explanations have been offered. Work outside the home is often indicted. Radloff (1975) found that women in professional or managerial jobs had very low depression scores, even lower than comparable husbands. This may mean that status in the work force is an important variable, or it may mean that undepressed women do better at work. On the whole, Radloff found that both working wives and home-bound wives were significantly more depressed than working husbands, which suggests that marriage, not work, is the important variable. As for the high depression scores among divorced/separated women, this seemed to be explained by the presence of children and the absence of money—indirect consequences of the absence of marriage. In sum, there is enough information in Radloff's data and in other studies to indicate that the work/marriage/home matrix merits much deeper investigation, but not enough to indicate that any particular status is enough in itself to be *the* cause for the magnitude of female depression.

We should, clearly, look at the more complex interactions between women and their environment. Here three theories of the source of depression for both males and females offer some insight. Both Ferster (1974) and Lewinsohn (1974) state simply that depression results from a lack of experiences which the individual finds pleasant in life. Their "cure" is positive reinforcement, a therapeutic technique in which the person earns pleasant events as a result of her or his own actions. Seligman (1975) indicts learned helplessness, in which a person applies the unrealistic generalization that "nothing I do matters" to situations where action could indeed make a difference, so that behavior becomes self-defeating. Beck (1974) uses a similar but more cognitive model in which the unrealistic pessimism of "I can't do *anything* to get what I want" dominates thought and deed. All three theories, I believe, are interesting because of their emphasis on the learning process: the importance of rewards, getting what you want, getting rewards through your own actions, and believing that your actions can get you what you want.

The concept that learned behavior generates depression confirms or explains data from other sources. Surveying studies on both child rearing and adulthood, for instance, Radloff concludes that "competent behavior" of the kind highly praised in our society brings fewer rewards and more punishments for females. Costrich, Feinstein, Kidder, Marecek, and Pascale (1975) found that aggressive females are much more likely than passive females (and than aggressive males) to be deemed "in need of therapy," a form of social penalty for deviating from the sex role. Wolman and Frank (1975) found that women in otherwise male peer groups became isolated. When their attempts to influence the group were ignored or rejected, they gave up and became depressed. More obviously, we treat successful women with social rejection or scorn, calling them castrating, while secretaries may be given flowers for being nurturing—along with lower pay. The same competence does not earn women as much pay or status as it does for men. There is plenty of varied evidence that experience as a whole teaches women to feel powerless and leads them towards depression, and this experience of failure stems from their role as women in society.

Most women coming to counselors and therapists, in my opinion, are likely to suffer from a depression caused at least in part by their learned sex role. The mental health issues of the typical woman client arise more often than not from the sociopsychological realities of her life as a woman in a culture which regards women as helpless, second-class, and incompetent, and which leaves them without the share of the culture's resources—money, status, control—which would combat their training in powerlessness. Thus the stress caused by friction between the individual and her sex-role assignment directly creates mental health problems of the types most often seen by therapists. Lack of self-esteem, conflict and ambivalence regarding choices, passivity in the face of challenge, helplessness, dependency, the given permission to be made a psychological, political, and economic victim—these are characteristics much more widespread among women and female clients than amongst men and male clients. Their sources may be obscured since women so often blame themselves for failure rather than blaming external structures, rules, or other people, but analysis of the situation will normally reveal the pervasive effects of socialization.

Depression is a likely danger for anyone—female or male—who feels too little control over her or his own life; but women are more vulnerable to powerlessness, both real and perceived. Many theorists have indicted the lack of power at both personal and political levels as a major factor in determining the mental health of women. (See especially Bernard, 1973: Chesler, 1972; and Gove and Tudor, 1973.) Women have more training in learned helplessness and experience more real helplessness in conditions where they do not in fact have control, whether that situation is a bad marriage, the poverty brought by divorce, the absence of proper education or training, or job discrimination. In response, many current programs for women seek to restore their sense of power in a given situation—rape centers, battered women shelters, homemaker retraining programs, and so forth. Further, society is currently changing its laws and rules and some of its institutions so that women may have greater access to power. My impression about divorce, for instance, is that many women are using society's new procedures and attitudes specifically to combat the feature which Radloff considers to be the most convincing evidence of social roles as a cause of depression—the inequality that causes marriage to have a protective effect on men and a detrimental effect on women.

Autonomy, self-determination, independence—in our society these are the signs of the mentally healthy person's relationship to the world; they can be encouraged by therapists. They will increase as we eliminate helplessness training in child rearing, education, marriage, the media, or in therapeutic situations. They will increase if women are given training in how to be aware of what they want, how to get it, and how to take credit for getting it. They will increase if the environment changes in the direction of rewarding rather than punishing female autonomy; they will increase if the environment stops protecting her and doing things for her, so that she may initiate her own actions and, as a human being should, learn their natural consequences.

3

Problems Women
Bring to Therapy

The solution to women's mental health problems can be found in the interaction
between the individual and her enviroment. Therapists need to pay close and
constant attention to both the woman *and* her environment, to work with internal perceptions and concepts without losing sight of external realities and potentials. While one often works for a time with just one or the other, over the course
of several sessions both should be given approximately equal attention. The
therapist's vision of the client becomes curiously binocular; what is "ground" and
what is "figure" may alter from session to session, though both remain present.
Diagnosis takes on a significantly different character as the fluctuating roles of the
individual and her environment emerge at different times as "causes." Solutions
are similarly unique, as first the individual and then her environment respond to
values, attitudes, and behavior generated within therapy.

This chapter examines women's typical mental health needs from that
binocular viewpoint. It discusses the factors that usually bring a woman to
therapy, thereby emphasizing her environment, past and present. Then it
discusses the problems which a woman usually brings to therapy, emphasizing
the internal effects of the female lifestyle. Put another way, this chapter looks first
at the external barriers, then at the internal barriers to women's mental well-
being. Of course, not all clients raise all these issues; this chapter is not a pattern
which the client must fit. However, it will serve as a checklist. If the therapist does
not know whether or not these issues are relevant, then she or he cannot know
whether the therapy is effective. For the most part this chapter avoids presenting
special therapeutic techniques, many varieties of which respond to the issues. If

the technique does not respond to these issues, however, then it is wrong for women.

What Brings Women to Mental Health Counseling

The typical woman coming to mental health counseling does not suffer from psychosis, severe neurosis, or psychopathology of the kinds which require extensive medical or clinical experience on the part of the therapist. Women seeking therapy often are anxious or depressed; their problems are typically multiple. They suffer from specific and generalized anxiety, they are experiencing pain, frustration, confusion, despair, loss, and a pervasive sense of powerlessness. Diagnosis by labeling is rarely their first need, and it is often dangerous. The widely used diagnosis of "hysterical reaction," for instance, is no more than a label by which the manifestation of stress enables a poor diagnostician to reflect her or his own view of women as generally irrational, immature, unhealthy, and childlike. The typical woman client is not lost in mental illness but, on the contrary, actively seeking health, grasping at what seem like thin threads leading to a life with greater meaning and satisfaction.

Women clients tend to experience some manifestation of the conflict between themselves and the roles given to them by socialization as women; this conflict may create such a high degree of stress that the symptoms may mimic those of severe illness. The task of the therapist is to make, and to help the client make, a series of realistic discriminations on which they may build toward better judgment. The process will be complex, probably dealing with the major themes of adult life but also revealing their roots in childhood; some form of neurosis or pathology may be intertwined. The therapist must separate major themes for individual attention, and the therapeutic process will normally be one of cooperative exploration, work, and change.

Outmoded Behaviors and Attitudes

Rapid change in society requires an individual to be flexible. Today's changes require women to give up many of the attitudes and much of the behavior which have been stereotypically feminine. The following lists of characteristics are taken from Sandra Bem's androgyny study (1974). Which set of characteristics would best enable today's women to survive and thrive among their new realities?

Feminine	Masculine
cheerful	aggressive
warm	ambitious
gentle	competitive
tender	dominant
gullible	forceful

Feminine	Masculine
loves children	individualistic
sensitive	self-reliant
shy	willing to take risks
does not use harsh language	
dependent	

Consider the list of qualities composed by Broverman et al (1970) from those valued in the traditional female and male stereotypes:

Female	Male
very aware of other's feelings	tough
gentle and submissive	aggressive
strong need for security	little need for security
unaggressive	direct
not self-confident	self-confident
not independent	independent

Clearly, a woman who wants to thrive today cannot afford to subscribe solely to the feminine stereotype. But giving it up exacts a price and cannot be done merely by willpower. The concept of androgyny makes good sense in this respect; it emphasizes the acquisition of new characteristics without demanding rejection of the old, seeing the traditionally feminine less as outmoded than as sometimes dangerously inappropriate. It emphasizes choice, and it is achieved by learning—themselves both adult characteristics.

Life Stress Events

Life offers some stressful events which may occur during any period of history: death of parents, leaving home for marriage, childbirth and child rearing, serious illness, and so on. These are expectable events and, as Neugarten (1976) points out, expected life events are less traumatic than the unexpected. In previous ages other expectations buffered stresses in a woman's life: marriage for a lifetime, two-parent child rearing, geographical stability, full-time and permanent housewifery, etc. But today's data show that women are now much less buffered by the predictable and that life may at any time present them with an unanticipated stress event. We will eventually adjust to the new realities—accept as usual, for instance, having at least one divorce—but at the moment and for the foreseeable future the transitional generations will experience greater stress in dealing with them. Problems typical of today's women—full-time work, divorce, stepping from affluence into poverty, aging alone—did not exist in the fantasies and training of most women alive today. Further, in the sense that today's stress events involve greater change, they may inherently be more stressful.

For example, the possibility of separation and divorce influences the whole of one's life. At any time this has meant acquiring the ability to live again as a separate person, no mean skill in itself; but if marital separation becomes predictable, then it affects all choices about work and career, lifestyle, romance and the first marriage, childbearing and child rearing, romance and the second marriage, and more. Another example, chronic illness or cancer. When medical knowledge was less and disease worse, major illness was a much more expectable event than it is today. Now, as increasing publicity surfaces regarding the multiplicity of cancer's causes and the possibility of cure, cancer and especially breast cancer have become persistent daily fears in the lives of many women, creating perhaps a higher anxiety than our ancestors experienced with a broader range of diseases because it offers a brute choice between mortality and mutilation. One must therefore carefully examine the stress event which brings a woman into therapy in order to measure its ramifications throughout her life with some fairness and—this requires emphasis—what it means to her as a female.

The following events are those which often precipitate the need for therapy; the first group consists of events in personal life.

Separation and divorce. The ending of any couple arrangement is probably the most frequent cause of women's entering therapy, for the very good reason that it attacks her both in the purely personal domain and in the wider social and economic world, changing everything about her way of being.

Loss of a child, either through death or disappearance, is less expectable today than in the past and therefore more stressful.

Aging seems to have become more stressful as our culture has increasingly emphasized youth and deprived older people of roles within an extended family. Particularly difficult is the condition of women divorced in their middle years after a long-term commitment. Aging has also become a threat not just to a woman's sexual marketability but also to her work, especially her ability to retrain herself and compete.

Widowhood may have become less stressful since it has become rarer at younger ages. It has long been a predictable event for women over 55 years of age.

Death. This retains its status with taxes as the only sure thing about life; but the current mass hypochondria apparent in our society, especially regarding cancer, shows that the prospect of one's own mortality remains a major force in our lives.

Mobility, whose stress falls principally on the woman in a marriage, is also a factor in the lives of never-married and divorced women who now face strange environments without companionship and perhaps with young children.

The second group of stress events revolves around work and money.

Job performance anxiety offers special problems for women who did not anticipate having full-time careers. It especially affects women who are expected to display leadership, those who are single parents, and those who combine work with a contemporary lifestyle (e.g., a woman starting to date again at age 38). As more women become solely responsible for their own economic well-being, they will experience greater stress in this area. Since many women occupy jobs which are the first to be eliminated when the economic situation turns sour, this stress has a firm base in reality.

Identity. The strain of integrating behavior on the job with that at home may cause major crises in identity and relationships. Many women are quite ambivalent about achievement and affiliation, feeling they have to choose one or the other. Many well-educated women work at jobs beneath their potential in order to avoid the conflict.

Overburdening. The superwoman myth, which now requires women to be both good workers and good homemakers, is a clear example of this syndrome. More frequently overburdening is caused by the low incomes typical of working women, especially when combined with loneliness of the kind that only expensive socializing can reduce.

Sex discrimination. Because most women are taught to discriminate against themselves, they are often unaware that their low status and high frustration on the job is due to the pervasiveness of sex discrimination; they therefore tend to blame themselves as if for personal failings. Discrimination is now less blatant but just as pervasive and, if a woman does recognize its presence, she may become frustrated and collapse into unproductive anger, potentially stifling her own efforts.

Retraining. Whether because of reentry into the job market at an older age or because of new ambitions, the need for a new career is a major factor in the lives of most working women.

Poverty or near-poverty characterizes the lives of most working women, especially in comparison with men. Added to this may be a sudden decline in standard of living brought on by the loss of a spouse.

A third group of stress events is in a sense more purely psychological, though induced by external changes.

Growth beyond childhood can be avoided by many traditional women who readily transfer deference and dependence from parents to spouse. When external change occurs to these women, unresolved personality problems emerge almost immediately. One of my clients had remained to middle age essentially the very shy girl she had been—by living a quiet domestic life with a dominant husband. Upon his death, when she was 38, her shyness prevented her from adjusting to the wholly new way of life required of her. She admitted quite frankly that she regarded her teenage children as better able to care for her than she for them. Had she not realized the need to restructure her personality as well as her life, depression would have led her to disaster.

Sexuality. The patterns, fears, and repressions of childhood can easily be carried into, or even through, a marriage. If a change occurs in a situation of this nature, trouble is likely. One client, raised in a fiercely conservative home and church environment, married her childhood sweetheart while young and had three children. He left her, at age 33, far from her original home—to which she

51

could now not return. Having faced all the responsibilities of singlehood bravely, she was literally horrified to find her adult sexuality stirring in ways that attacked her childhood morality—a problem she had never expected. This and the need to face the onset of adult sexuality in her children, raised in a totally different world, brought her to therapy.

Generalized anxiety. "There's another one of those women," said a male colleague. "All in a state about who-the-hell-knows what. I can't figure her out. You try." The client had, in fact, been through an improbable but real number of stress events in a short period. The colleague thought her irrational, immature, and illogical—qualities which she suspected and blamed in herself. My first step was simple: listen, help the client put her feelings into words, and reassure her that it was not irrational to respond anxiously to major stress. She emerged from the first session as a calmer adult again, which my colleague thought a miraculous transformation. What had misled him was the lack of a single presenting event, and in its absence he had used the label "hysteric." What had happened was that a woman, who had until then coped magnificently, had finally found things too much, given up acting adult, and retreated into a childhood pattern of helplessness. This reaction is frequently a result of female conditioning in childhood. This client created a metaphor which vividly depicted the source of much female anxiety: she saw herself as a huge ball of fire whirling through the sky, and she was pleased with the image of power. Then came the fear of breaking apart, exploding into millions of pieces and falling disintegrated to earth.

The case history of another client, Barbara, demonstrates the typical interaction between internal and external stresses affecting a woman. Barbara came to therapy scarcely able to talk, afflicted with uncontrollable weeping. "I don't *know* what is the matter with me," she said, over and over. We shifted to metaphor and she saw herself as a toasted marshmallow, burned on the outside, soft and squashy within, sitting on some rocks by a stream in the woods, watching the water rise and fearing that it would sweep her away. Barbara was 42 and accustomed to a marriage of twenty years ("lots of good times, some bad"). Her husband, Dan, now wanted a separation during which he would go to California "to find himself." Barbara had always managed finances for both of them and run the family, but Dan had been a steady provider. She had worked early in their marriage when they postponed having children; now they had children aged nine, eleven, and thirteen. Reasonable and cooperative as ever, Barbara and Dan worked out the separation: he would send money home each month, and they would sell the house and invest the proceeds in the completion of her university degree. It had seemed no insurmountable problem to Barbara—moving to an apartment, changing the children's school, returning to college, and becoming a single parent.

Then guilt set in; Dan wanted to leave her. "I must have done something wrong," she told herself. She felt anger, "burned" by him, then fear; she felt ugly and old at 42, "burned out," as she recognized the age bias operating against her at college. Helplessness followed; inside she was "soft and squashy," lacking the inner core that marriage and coupledom had lent her. She found herself waiting anxiously for Dan's letters and calls, avoiding going out, "sitting" by the stream watching life flow by, hoping it would not sweep her away. She had not given up the wife role at all. "Who am I," she asked, "if I am not a wife?" Dan had expressly set no limitations on her; she was free to date, to make friends, and to find other men. In actuality, the freedom terrified her—so she chose to continue living by rules she knew, those of the wife and mother.

The first task of therapy was to have Barbara listen to herself. She quickly realized some of the implications of her choice to remain feeling powerless, admitting that Dan had not "done it" to her. Having built her power base in the home and her self-esteem entirely on being a wife, she had made all her choices on the basis of being someone whom she was no longer. Even her role as mother was in question because she had always been wife/mother. Faced with being an independent individual for the first time in her adult life, she felt confused, timid, and incompetent—in a manner which she eventually recognized as typical of her early childhood.

For a long time Barbara wanted to continue making her decisions the result of someone else's choices. With Dan gone, she turned to the therapist; when that did not work, she turned to other members of a women's support group for decisions. If they gave her advice she did not want, she did not hear them (sometimes literally). After considerable private therapy, she began to show anger toward the people who had "put her" by the stream: Dan first, then the children, then her parents. As the anger was expressed in the women's group, it released energy. She made her first free choice—to spend money and time solely on herself by going away for the weekend to a resort with a female friend. Other choices followed, most of them surrounding the distinctions between her children's lives and her own; but each choice remained difficult, threatened to be overwhelmed by complexities and ramifications that paralyzed. She finished school and decided to look for a job, preferring the Midwest but feeling that she ought to be near her estranged husband in the West "for the sake of the children, even though they'd be better off in Ohio." A sudden regression followed and she asked Dan to make her decision. Fortunately, he refused to do so; and in the process of clarification of her own wishes, she became furious with him. Expressing that anger in a therapy session, she took off her wedding ring and threw it away, and this symbolic act seemed magical to her—she immediately felt relieved. "I'm not just someone's wife!" she said. Shortly thereafter she bgan dating, and she found a good job in Ohio. Three years later, she laughs at the idea of being a sitting marshmallow. She has a lover, a better job, and the new goal of an advanced degree in her field. Dan comes to see the children regularly and takes them with him for part of the year. They want to maintain separate lives but not divorce, for marriage (they believe) gives added financial and emotional security to the children; they will examine the situation again when the children leave. Now Barbara says, "Dan's a good friend. Not my best friend, but . . . I'm not the person I was when we were married. How could he know me that well now? I stayed young far too long."

Internal Events

As the seasons of life affected Barbara, so they affect all women. Everyone changes without specific reason, and the only problem is that they do not expect those changes. "I feel just like an adolescent! At 29! I'm too old to start exploring and rebelling! What happened?" "What's wrong with me? My job's good. Why do I hate it now?" "I feel lately like I've become a complete nobody. Mary is a mother. Christy is a secretary. Joe is a builder. But who the hell am I? Nobody!" "I just have this feeling *all* the time. I just want to run away and run and run and never come back to my life." "I always thought I'd love children, and I did at first. But now? I hate to say it, but they're monsters!" "Here I am married to John. Fourteen years. And I'm tired of fooling myself. It's women I love, and always have. I'm so tired of lying." "Is this all there is? This? For the rest of my *life?*"

These are the voices of everyday passion, the great drama of the humdrum; no major outside event is needed to precipitate them. Neugarten (1968, 1977a) suggests that some outside occurrence is usually associated with them, such as peer activities or expectations or frustration and boredom on the job. Others view women's rising expectations as the stimulus (Weissman and Klerman, 1977). Maslow (1954) believed that self-actualization was at work, the thrust of the person for health and significance in life. The theorists of life stages, like the poets, suggest that a transition from one adult stage to another is in process (Levinson, 1978). Freud would regard it as "the great question which has never yet been answered: what do women want?" When grandmother expressed these feelings, presumably others dismissed them with a raised eyebrow or the back of the hand —or locked her in the attic.

Such feelings are just as real and concrete as the husband's seven-year itch, the philosopher's desire to find himself, or the pilgrim's need to seek God. My own impression is that they represent the search for a separate identity and sense of self which Erikson (1968) placed in the adolescent years as the entrance to adulthood. Unlike most men, a woman is permitted—or even culturally encouraged—to postpone or possibly avoid forever the passage into adulthood by marrying, mothering, and nurturing others at home and on the job. As the sole objective of her life, this ultimately becomes an unbearable burden which she may attempt to throw off in a quest for health; one sees many women who have not. When the emotional dam fails to burst, the spirit so contained stagnates and a desolate dying takes place.

Unfortunately, research has not yet outlined for us the normal stages of a woman's developmental life as have the works of Levinson (1978), Erikson (1963), and Gould (1978) done for men. Though there are similarities, we strongly suspect that the male paradigm does not apply to women (Gilligan, 1978). Further, the "generational effect" outlined by Troll (1975) affects women so strongly that developmental stages will have to be drawn for different generations of women. Nevertheless, the feelings evolved are real, critical, and powerful, not just hysteria or purposeless malaise but the finest example of the kind of internal event which may bring a woman to therapy.

The classic example of internal events may be housewives' depression, a widespread phenomenon which leads to alcoholism on the one hand and dismissive laughter on the other. At 30, Anna came to therapy in that state. She had been raised in a traditional home in a conservative community where she remained through her college years and until marriage. Adopting fully the traditional characteristics of the feminine sex role, described everywhere as a nice girl, a good wife, a great cook, a fine hostess, she had never abandoned childilke attitudes. First father, then teachers, then husband knew best. At 21, still a virginal flirt, she had made an ideal wife for an older, goal-oriented man. She had set aside the education for which her parents had paid—the right college, a course of study which was easy rather than interesting. Now she kept a nice middle-class home in the right suburb, spent lots of time with friends, and entertained well because she was dedicated to Joe's career. She wanted for nothing and wanted nothing more: especially not children.

After nine years of this life, she came to therapy terrified because she had been depressed for months, had taken to crying for hours in the day, and had begun feeling that everybody except her was somebody—and she wanted the therapist to fix her up. In fact, she *was* almost nobody. In Gestalt terms, through introjection she had passively incorporated what the world had seemed to command, becoming what society and others told her to be to the point that she had no idea what she herself needed, thought deeply about, or experienced. "But I've always tried to be good!" she said indignantly.

Therapy began with relaxation exercises to quiet the turmoil which overwhelmed everything else. Then, slowly, we began to examine all the rules she had learned through the years. Her anger began to emerge in the form of the rebelliousness she had never shown at puberty and its target was predictably her husband, rather than her parents. She began by breaking an invariable rule: always to be home when Joe arrived. One night she came home a little drunk. She began an affair with a younger man who worked under her husband's supervision. For a long time the point of therapy was obscured by her need to create a smokescreen with these temporary issues, but eventually her rebellion led to discovery. Joe did not want his wife to work, but Anna took a job and found to her surprise that she loved the experience. When she decided to get an apartment of her own, Joe came to therapy with her and, both privately and in her presence, expressed his resentment and frustration with her. He was then, and still is, quite clear about what he wants: a traditional wife who will be home at the end of the day even if she goes to work. After some time in therapy, they agreed to a six month separation which ultimately led to divorce.

The pain and excitement of growing up was Anna's experience in therapy. She started at the chronological age of 30 emotionally going on 14—and ended at 31 going on 22. She has since spent two years finding out what she wants, feels, and thinks, loving the risks she feels free to take, setting new rules for herself, and engaging less in rebellion and more in exploration. She is now an experienced travel agent and she sometimes travels alone. With her own apartment, she functions as an adult practically and socially. She enjoys the freedom though she has kept two shelters: her parents still provide her with extra money; and every now and then she runs back home to Joe, who remains friendly but uninterested. He wants, he says, the other Anna, the way she was.

Working with Anna and Joe was painful in the sense that teaching and learning are painful. One watches growth in adults very much as one does in adolescents, regretting that external wisdom is no substitute for internal experience, and seeing the extremes of rigidity and rebellion as equally unnecessary. But they are necessary, of course, in the same sense that malaise, depression, and anxiety are sometimes necessary parts of the mysterious process of being an adult.

The Therapist's Response

To some extent all clients rely on the therapist to tell them what has brought them to therapy, and the task of the therapist is to be an observer and guide through confusion. Throughout therapy, therefore, the essential actions of the therapist are to watch, listen, and sense, to question and to wonder aloud, then to discuss and, if need be, to explain. I normally start with the client's own perception of what has brought her or him to therapy; is it a life stress event, an internal change, anxiety or depression arising from an unrecognized source or from some reality of job or role?

Both the perceptions of the client and self-reporting are, however, often unreliable. Revelations will come in layers as therapy continues, as the client learns to trust the therapeutic relationship, and as deeper issues unveil themselves. One client, for instance, a cheery and self-confident young woman, came to therapy originally because "Mother thinks I louse up my life without good reason, and I guess I agree with her, but I'm not *unhappy* about it." After three or four sessions, misery began to replace the cheeriness, and self-confidence gave way to the fears brought by self-doubt and self-blame; and the young woman was saying, "I came to therapy because I hate myself for always looking like I know what I'm doing. I don't." This later proved the realization at which true therapy began. Another client came to therapy reporting depression resulting from poor communication with her husband; not until the sixth session did she feel confident enough to say that she was a lesbian and that her "husband" had started hormone treatments to become a transsexual male.

In cases like these, clients need to learn both trust and self-knowledge; to assist this process, the therapist must teach the client her own skills as therapy proceeds. For this reason, I have a series of general questions which I initially ask myself, then later ask the client, and finally teach the client to ask herself or himself:

> What do I hear, see, and sense in the way of *patterns* regarding both behavior and attitudes, especially outmoded behaviors and attitudes?
> What is happening in the client's life which either induces or reveals *stress and conflict* within the self or in relation to others?

What about this person is *functional* or clearly *dysfunctional*, especially in regard to behaviors?

In terms of the person's relationship to the *outside world*, what do voice, posture, breathing, and movement reveal to both of us about the messages the client is sending?

What about the *inside world*? What is gnawing at her or his vitals—fear, frustration, anger, self-doubt, confusion, conflict, or hopelessness? What messages are being internalized to damage the client's self-esteem? Which emotions have real causes in the outside world and which do not?

Regarding long-term symptoms, what *unfinished business* remains from childhood and upbringing, in terms of either suppressed feelings (anger, pain, fear) or outmoded feelings?

As therapy continues, I also look for major themes which characterize the lives of many adults and which directly relate *feelings* to *actions*:

Is the person afraid to make free decisions?

Is she or he afraid to act, especially in making a genuine commitment to another person?

Is the desire for intimacy with another person (perhaps someone from the past or the unknown future) restricting the individual's power to create a life of her or his own?

Is there usually a rigidity of attitude, apparently due to restrictions of an unconscious or unacknowledged origin?

Is the client afraid of intimacy and self-revelation?

All of the above, of course, are present in all people; what brings most women to mental health counseling is an abnormality of *degree*. The response of the therapist is thus to help the client learn not only what has brought her to therapy but also that it is all right—that something can be done about it.

One final note of warning should be sounded: what brings some women to therapy is an appalling, real, life situation whose nature, for various reasons, they are unable to recognize and therefore do not report. This is often the case with abused wives or women who were abused as children, with alcoholics, with impoverished women, and with those driven "crazy" by living too long with a mentally ill person. While dealing primarily with the internal life of the client, the therapist should also carefully scrutinize her living environment for a degree of abnormality which the client is not capable of measuring.

What Women Bring to Counseling

Many women bring similar problems into therapy; this section will introduce some of these common problems.

Powerlessness

"In the case of both women and blacks, the fundamental problem has been that others have controlled the power to define one's existence. Thus, to whatever extent women and blacks act or think in a given way solely because of the expectation of the dominant group rather than from their own choice, they remain captive to the prevailing system of social control" (Chafe, 1977, p. 77).

Whites and males also submit to social control and feel powerless as part of the price of being a social being; but as a group women have been held in subordination by economic, political, social, and psychological means, with the result that the experience of powerlessness is a pervasive factor in the lives of most women. They are taught behavior which promotes and maintains powerlessness (Johnson, 1976); power, at best, comes vicariously through others when those others care to share. Psychologically, powerlessness shows in the aspirations of women and in the degree to which their self-images are impressed on them by others. There is a lack of validity to one's own experience; what a woman feels or wants is not automatically right or legitimate—or even extant. "He wants me to stay with him. He says we are all better off as a family," says a client. "He knows I'll be better off." Asked what *she* wants and feels, she looks surprised. "I don't know," she says. "I suppose he's right. I hadn't really thought about it."

Power is the ability to do, to act, or to effect. One may have power over oneself or over other people, but it is usually expressed in terms of relationships with others. We regard a sense of power over at least the basic elements of one's existence as the sign of a healthy and free person. Both illness and subordination take power away. A characteristic of what we call a minority group is its comparative lack of power, which is why women are classed as a minority group despite their larger numbers. Women's lack of power has at least four distinct layers: like everyone else, women lose power as the world at large takes it away or places limits upon it in the normal socialization process. In addition, they have less financial and political power than do men as a group. Third, the socialization process aims at teaching women not to seek or exercise power and to become or at least to seem subordinate, approaching men in particular only in the devious and seductive manner promulgated, for instance, by *The Total Woman* (Morgan, 1973). Many women feel very comfortable with this approach because socialization eventually persuades them to internalize fear and dislike of power—a word which is then likely to cause shudders of sinful delight or distaste in them, explicable only by a belief in magic. "Power is evil," whispers the inner voice, "and selfish, and you don't want it." Men are given exactly the opposite message. Without feeling personal power as a right, women have no basis to accept obvious power as legitimate (Raven, 1965). The subject is thus a matter of dispute among women, some of whom exercise extreme pressure against others who seek power as a right.

The power issue is proving quite productive in therapeutic terms; one of the most useful courses a therapist can follow is to have a client explore how much of a sense of powerlessness she carries with her. The power issue pervades so many areas of life—relations with men, children, parents, peers, friends, employers, and the social structure. Operating in any area with a sense of power is dramatically different from operating with a sense of powerlessness, and it is even more different from operating with a sense that power is selfish and wrong. In most practical matters, a sense of powerlessness prevents an individual from even considering a whole range of different feelings and behaviors—refusing to stay late at work without pay, having the children do the dishes, getting a husband to stop beating or start making love, making a consumer complaint, choosing a career or a mate, and so on.

It is often a difficult task to help a woman acknowledge that she is suffering from a loss or lack of power. Three general questions should be asked and eventually taught to the client:

1. Is she depressed without realizing that the cause of depression is her sense of powerlessness? I have seen this phenomenon often in women whose husbands were being unfaithful, those who had lost all control of their children while single parenting, those who lacked money, and those whose job situations were highly unpleasant. In such situations, many blame themselves for being depressed rather than blaming the situation for being destructive of their sense of power.
2. Is she aware of powerlessness but unable to grasp a position in which to start changing things? Powerlessness is a feeling which restricts individuals in all directions; they are sometimes unable to separate a general situation into its components which might offer a foothold for the "practice" of power.
3. Does she, in general, take such a powerless stance toward the world that she almost invites the world to take over, so that she is constantly losing control over more issues? The powerless stance is usually physically apparent in posture, voice, breathing, and immobility—the tendency to occupy a very small space and to appear, in common parlance, like a rabbit or a "push-over."

The task of the therapist is to look for sources of powerlessness, whether they are real or imagined, present or past. The therapist may also have to discuss and demonstrate powerlessness and power because confusion about them is so widespread. Finally, the therapist and the client cooperatively look for actions, small or large, which may give the client the experience of power—such as facing the same problem from a stance of powerlessness and one of power. Actions are crucial to a sense of power, and "homework" between sessions is very important. A housebound woman should be encouraged, for instance, to go to the library for one hour a day for a week to look at magazines. A new or overwhelmed single parent faced with a problem child should undertake to set a new limit on one element of the child's behavior and to stick to it regardless of consequences. An overly dependent wife should, for example, undertake to stay one night per month with a relative or friend.

One does not discard deeply learned helplessness easily. Therapists will normally find clients at different stages in the process. Those who feel most powerless are likely to be quite depressed. Normally following depression comes anger, which may lead to rebellion in major or minor matters. This usually evokes open coercion and increased pressure from elements of the environment and considerable discomfort within the woman, which will probably include guilt and a tendency to regress. It is the beginning of exploration, which converts the emotional upheaval into a learning process. The ultimate result is not a destructively aggressive and antagonistic woman but one who is constructive, forceful, and able to exercise her own power judiciously because she sees it as a skill, a necessity, and a right.

Limited Behavioral and Emotional Options

Socialization severely limits the number of options in feeling and behavior which both sexes exercise naturally. People veto their own behavior, emotions, and even their senses according to society's prescriptions, in order to think of themselves as either female or male. Studies in the area of androgynous characteristics suggest a productive way out of this often destructive process of self-limitation. Even in the Sex Role Inventory compiled by Bem (1974), in which the polarity between female and male is emphasized, neutral items emerged—traits acceptable in both sexes. These already offer certain options which lead away from the limits imposed by sex roles. In the thinking of Kaplan (1979), there is the concept of merging different characteristics from the masculine/feminine lists so that integration of two qualities rather than abandonment of one or the other offers another expansion of options. Still further, maturity brings a greater tendency to individuation, so that moving through the life span offers the individual the prospect of becoming more flexible, more diverse, more androgynous, and therefore less limited (White, 1979).

Expansion of options is a clear task for the therapist. Any client is certain to be restricting and repressing certain choices in feeling and behavior; any client is likely to feel uncomfortable, incompetent, or guilty about many available options. The basic skill of considering options, prerequisite to the ability to use them, is likely to be underdeveloped. Clients are likely to possess undervalued or even unrecognized skills, especially in the areas of affiliation and interaction. Inventory, a classification of present and absent skills, is therefore something which therapists and clients ought to make with the goal of using the unrecognized and developing the unfamiliar. Normally this means starting by developing that which is absent. The ultimate aim is not to choose either this or that but to balance and integrate traits and abilities as much as possible.

The more a woman has been socialized to accept the traditional female sex role, the more she will see certain behaviors and emotions as unavailable to her. Restriction of options will rarely appear openly, but the practice is so universal that certain syndromes can be pointed out. Whenever one of these appears, the therapist should be alert for both the nature and the source of the limits:

1. "Yes, but . . ." The therapist should ignore these words; the client means that she will act and feel only according to what follows them. It is important to point this out to the client, because we often trick ourselves by saying that we believe one thing while acting as though we believe something contradictory.

2. "It's just not *me*." Whenever a person claims not to be a certain kind of person, the therapist should be alert to the possibility of an unconscious and perhaps very forceful inhibition, possibly with a source in childhood rules. Again, clients may often trick themselves by presenting an intellectual open-mindedness which is not accompanied by permission to the self to be different.

3. The Good Girl. Usually stemming from childhood but often carried into and reinforced by work, marriage, and other relationships, this syndrome results in an individual limiting herself according to the opinion of others. She thinks and acts not to satisfy herself but to win approval.

4. The Voluntary Shut-in. This syndrome is usually signaled by a phrase such as, "No, I can't do that" or "No, I won't do that." Because the phrases may be spoken almost unconsciously, the therapist should draw the client's attention to them; and, as every parent knows, the meanings of "can't" and "won't" always offer room for interesting exploration. The syndrome is particularly frequent when a range or spectrum of alternatives is under consideration; often, the alternative most quickly rejected (e.g., divorce) becomes that eventually chosen.

5. The Dreamer. Some clients are full of intentions, plans, and fantasies. They often talk in terms of "What I really want . . ." and, "When X happens, I will do Y," and, "If other people would let me, I would . . ." The dreamers can be distinguished by their failure ever to take action consistent with their thoughts, so that their dreams become a substitute for deeds. In these circumstances it is crucial for therapist and client to agree on weekly homework which requires measurable, definable action, no matter how small.

Normally, a client's limitation of her behaviors and emotions will occur both within the therapeutic situation and in her entire life. Therapy then becomes an opportunity for practicing new behaviors and emotions; this is often what clients mean when they report feeling "safe" with the therapist. It should be emphasized that the feeling of safety should come not from comfort but from having taken risks and learned that one can survive, and that sense of security should translate itself as quickly as possible from the therapeutic situation to real life. Some clients cannot at first practice even within the therapeutic situation—even their dreams for themselves and their lives are restricted. It is important to teach these clients how to fantasize, and for this purpose imagination about the future is an important force: what do you or did you dream for yourself and your life? What would you like to be doing next week or next year at this time? What would your life be like if money (time, marriage, or children, etc.) were not an issue?

Anger

The sources of women's anger are numerous. The general devaluation by the culture of what a woman says and does is the background, making it easy to turn her from person into thing (sex object, mother figure, and so forth) so that she need not be taken seriously as an individual. Add to this the powerlessness that a woman is expected to display and the limited styles and manners which present her as feminine, and the stage is set. To feel valuable, she must perform in ways that will win the liking and approval of others, so she must be very careful about stepping out of her role even briefly. The childlike qualities of the feminine stereotype may not fit her very well; and when they are coupled with economic dependency on someone else and/or with physical strength and size less than that of a significant male, then extreme frustration is almost inevitable. The final touch is awareness of discrimination at home, at work, or in the larger society that is based entirely on her gender. In this light, the anger expressed by bra burning seems comprehensible.

But, surely women are less angry and aggressive than men? Bra burning is symbolic anger, scarcely directed at the oppressor, certainly not comparable to the riots in which young males all over the world engage. When the British suffragettes, to avoid force-feeding in jail, turned at last to violence in their despair, the houses they burned were already vacant, the bombed churches derelict, and the missiles nonlethal. And even when today's monstrous terrorist groups include women, are they not all simply followers of males, dominated and given orders as in the home? Certainly violence in our society is now and always has been primarily a male—indeed a young male—phenomenon to the extent that chemical biology is blamed for the sex difference, some undelineated hormonal effect. The overt expression of anger through aggression is unusual among females.

Hormonal effect perhaps; cultural influence certainly. Our society routinely teaches females not to express their anger—better, indeed, that they not even feel it. The target of a woman's normal anger is usually physically larger and stronger, so that rage leads only to ineffectuality or to physical harm to the woman herself. If not larger, the target may be much smaller, a child, so that guilt is almost inevitable. Either these targets of anger depend on her for love and protection or she depends on them for love, money, and a sense of worth. As the data show, it is simply much safer for a man to beat up a woman than for a woman to beat up anyone. Women therefore learn and are permitted to express their anger indirectly. Bitchiness, depression, sneakiness, manipulativeness, explicit sexual bargaining, and moodiness are all "acceptable" feminine characteristics whose source in anger is rarely acknowledged. But if a woman cleanly feels anger, let alone expresses it directly, then acculturation will tell her to blame herself.

Many women find the idea of anger unthinkable, no matter how much justification there might seem to be. Taught to hide or suppress anger or at most to release it indirectly, most women find their anger terrifying. It is easier to rationalize that the anger is not justified, is unimportant, won't do anything but harm, will not make a difference, and will stop all future nurturing. It is easier to ignore it, hold it inside, bury it, relieve it through scrubbing the floor, or condemn oneself.

Depression and enervation are the customary results of blocking feelings of anger, and so is an increase in the very qualities that led to the anger in the first place—especially feelings of powerlessness over self and others. It becomes impossible to deal directly with the anger-generating situation.

Because anger is the emotion which many women are likely to suppress as a result of their socialization, I look for it in every woman with whom I work. Clients may be angry with a person they love, with themselves, with a life situation in which they feel trapped, with a system through which they move (such as school, family, work, church), with past events still carried within, or with me. Because anger normally lies hidden in the body, I look for such signals as shoulders and arms held back from hitting or close to the body, tight jaws and mouth which keep words and sounds in, tight legs that want to run or kick, and a tone and pitch of voice that removes all strength from statements. I always choose an appropriate time to point out my physical observations to the client so that she may observe herself and connect these symptoms with her state of mind and feeling.

The therapist gives permission to the client to feel angry and to express anger. If it is near the surface, a simple invitation may be enough to stir exploration and release, e.g., "You must feel very angry about that." But words are often not enough; physical expression is necessary. I always have two encounter bats available for clients to strike at the floor, walls, chairs, and pillows. I have large pillows; I encourage some clients to give them names and then to pound on them. Most clients start slowly and then learn to hit and scream out their anger. With the most reluctant clients I join in, sometimes even starting off the process when I too feel angry at the cause of anger (e.g., a woman abused as a child, a rape victim, a case of sexual harassment, an intolerable home situation, work discrimination). I say: "I feel so angry when I hear you speak about this, let's hit and scream together!" In this way, I model the releasing of anger and its cleansing effect and I reassure the client that feeling rage will not consume and destroy either me or her.

Unblocking that energy is the task of therapy. The client must first identify feelings of anger in herself and then admit to them. External reasons for anger must be sorted in terms of validity, and the source of conflict must be examined. Release of irrational rage in safe circumstances may occur at any stage. The next step is for the client to recognize her right to feel anger and her power to deal both with it and with its cause; this new state of mind may accompany the first release when the client, as inexperienced as a child, discovers that rage need not destroy and that it does not have quite the degree of power she had expected. Once the energy of the whole person is available, learning can take place. The therapist's task is then to help the client learn to deal with anger directly through verbal and nonverbal communication styles, negotiation, confrontation, alliances and networks, compromise and resoluteness—all the difficult skills which mature people

63

try to exercise. The client also needs to learn safe times and places in which to vent her rage so she will not endanger herself physically or economically; it would be self-defeating to express anger in ways that might precipitate beatings or firings. This remark should not be interpreted as another way of discouraging women from feeling anger, as is apparent in the techniques recommended in some popular books; the task is not avoidance of anger, but its proper handling so that anger ultimately turns into a force for better survival.

An example of this process appears in the history of Joanie, a career woman in her early 30s with an 8-year-old marriage and a 2-year-old daughter conceived to hold that marriage together, who came to therapy considerably depressed and feeling a vague desire to run away. She was discontent with her job, where she had been passed over in both promotion and salary in favor of a younger and less qualified male; but this hardly explained her unhappiness. The marriage, she said, was normal though not very communicative, and she rejoiced that it had given her a daughter whom both she and her husband loved. He wanted another child; she found herself unable to explain why she was not equally eager. It was not until the third therapy session that she mentioned in passing that her husband often "hit" her while drinking on the weekend. "But he never hit the child!" she added hastily. Gradually her sense of humiliation emerged, but she was ashamed to complain. She supposed that she deserved his abuse, or at least she understood it because of work pressures and liquor. No, she certainly did not want to leave him. She had told neither family nor friends about the physical abuse, even when they questioned her about a bruise, because it was embarrassing and she felt guilty.

It took several sessions before Joanie admitted that she felt angry. When she realized that she was no longer ashamed to complain about his meanness she expressed resentment towards her husband. She knew it was not safe to express it to him directly. It was therefore important that she release her anger directly during therapy sessions over several weeks. We gave her husband's name to a large, dark brown pillow. At first she laid it on top of herself so that it smothered her; she could only peek out from under it. Later she cast it aside and spoke of it with contempt, then she began to poke at it and to address it directly. After another two sessions, she was able to kick and beat that pillow all around the room, screaming at it, treating this substitute for her husband exactly the way her real husband treated her. Her pleasure in this process frightened her, and she canceled her next session; but when she returned, she was calling herself Joan instead of Joanie. She reported having spent her weekend visiting family and friends with her daughter, and she was eager to resume the direct expression of anger not just at the pillow but about her husband. Very quickly this anger transmuted itself into rage at her dead father, an alcoholic who had beaten all his children while their passive mother had repeatedly stood by. In subsequent sessions Joan's submissiveness melted rapidly and she looked forward to "getting into" her anger at therapy. She had learned that she had a right not to be abused.

What of its sources in her husband and employers? She faced her employer to ask for a raise and promotion. He compromised and she quit, with the secret idea of finding a better job in another town. This led to a series of scenes with her husband which the therapist would not have recommended; but as a result of one of them, she packed up her daughter and belongings and moved out. "You're not going to make me into what my father made my mother!" was her proclamation. By moving to another state, finding a better job, and eventually filing for divorce, Joan has continued her personal growth with the support of women's groups and individual therapy. She has broken the pattern of victimization in relationships and she marvels in retrospect that she could ever have lived "that way." Both she and her therapists pinpoint the beginning of her change in personality to those weeks during which she slowly accepted anger as her right.

Inadequate Communication Skills

Two forces reduce our ability to communicate directly: (1) being unable to express ourselves fully and (2) not realizing that we have the right to do so. The latter force seems to impede women more often than does the former. The culture teaches women that they are mediators and conciliators, not direct parties to conflict; they are to be gentle, nurturing, softspoken, and unaggressive. But this suppression of the ability to confront frustration, disappointment, conflicts of interest, anger, and even minor irritation demands a high price. Most women need to learn how to improve the direct expression of their needs, wants, and feelings. This need is so widespread that it accounts for the instant popularity of what is called "assertiveness training," which gives women the tools for expressing themselves. The need of many women, however, is deeper; they need to learn that their emotions are valid, that they have a right to express them, and that other people have the obligation to respond. Tools will not work if a person cannot pick them up. Finally, like most people, women need to learn how to deal with conflict through negotiation and compromise—with the special understanding in their case that these techniques must not simply reinforce their habitual compliance.

After the end of her marriage, Edith at age 35 found that her major difficulty in being single again was in avoiding relating to people in the self-defeating manner to which she had been accustomed. With her children she was confident and direct, seeing herself as the authoritative and responsible adult. Not so were her relationships with other adults of either sex; she had developed a cyclical pattern: shyness, compliance, then withdrawal. Assertiveness training gave her new ideas and ambitions, but she felt rather uncomfortable about being assertive and made some discomforting mistakes. Her theme became, "I didn't mean *that*." She soon became aware that she did not know what she really felt and thought and that her emotions were, as she put it, "sloshing around inside." The techniques of value clarification helped her to realize her basic feelings and desires, and the reward of achieving direct expression in normal situations began to act as a positive reinforcement. Her next task was to deal with the greater amount of con-

65

flict—mild conflict—which her new assertiveness stimulated. She learned to negotiate so that the solution of a disagreement satisfied both parties. A negotiation that seemed very easy and normal was a great victory to her, such as when she learned to say to someone (male or female) not just "I don't want to see you this evening" but also "How about Thursday?" This therapeutic experience was a straightforward learning process, one through which perhaps the majority of women never move until older ages simply because their training as girls and as young women all moves in the opposite direction.

The first communication skill needed by many clients is direct expression to herself and to the therapist. My objective is to have the client hear herself, and I want her to be aware of my listening attentively and sharing what she says. My aim for her is clarity about her own existence and experience: thoughts directly expressed. Next most clients need training in simplicity and directness of communications; for this purpose I use a technique adapted from an excellent work, Miller, Nunnally, and Wackman, *Alive and Aware: Improving Communication in Relationships* (1975). In front of the client I place five cards headed Wants, Needs, Thoughts, Feelings, and Intuitions. She responds to each card with a single sentence beginning with "I" and expresses her perception right now and here at this moment in this place. Then she fantasies herself in another situation (past or future, elsewhere and with someone else) and responds to the cards similarly with her imagined perceptions. With those basics of clarity and simplicity learned, we can then move on to more complex communication skills—requesting, confronting, compromising, negotiating, and so on. In therapy sessions, we practice together dealing with typical situations or major events; in homework, the client tries her new skills with other people. Groups offer superb opportunities for clients to role play different styles of communication in various situations.

An important lesson from Gestalt theory which clients need to learn is that we often try to communicate too much and therefore communicate falsely (e.g., "I think we have a rotten marriage"). To counteract this tendency, clients need to learn that clarity, simplicity, and directness work best with the here and now and result in communication of a present reality—not an ultimate truth. Under these guidelines, the above statement might become, "This is hard for me to say, *and* I am thinking that you do not hear me when I say I want to talk about our lovemaking." Or, "I am very confused about what is going on between us and I want you to tell me if you have any plans and what they are." This form of statement emphasizes a truth about the person sending the communication instead of about the person receiving that communication.

Nonverbal as well as verbal communication skills are essential elements of the learning process for many clients. I train clients to be aware of such matters as breathing, tone of voice, posture, and position in a setting because researchers suspect that the impact of nonverbal communication is at least as great as that of verbal. Rather than talk about nonverbal communication, I have the client experience its varieties. For example, I have her say the same words in a little girl's voice and in a woman's voice, with breath held back or fully delivered, standing with all her weight on one foot or balanced between both, or while perched on the edge of a chair contrasted with being seated fully in the space which is hers.

Finally, I emphasize the behavioral nature of communication. Communication is an event. Although it expresses the mind and the psyche and it issues through the body, communication is ultimately a function which more or less precisely describes the boundaries between the self and the rest of the world. Communication skills are therefore not extrinsic decorations, not ornaments to be hung on the Christmas tree of the self, but are instead numberless deeds by which we define in measurable terms our selves and our world.

Failure to Nurture Self

The popular image of the traditionally feminine woman sees her as self-nurturing to the point of vanity and as cultivating prettiness and comfort to absurdity. In fact, most female self-nurturing is no more than skin-deep and is undertaken to meet the demands of image. Women are socialized to care for others more than or before themselves, and in the popular mind a wicked woman infallibly is one who is "selfish." The social task of women is to nurture others, to mother, parent, and tend, to create intimacy, to make things pleasant and beautiful, and to be aware of others' problems and their solutions. They are to be sensitive, affectionate, understanding, kind, helpful, cooperative, fair-minded, reliable and gentle—with others. When it is suggested that they display these same qualities to themselves, they laugh with shock; that would be selfish. As Miller (1976) describes the deeper issue, women are encouraged to concentrate on the feelings and reactions of others at the expense of experiencing their own. Miller suggests that a culture which demands that women center around others while men must center on themselves has caused suffering in different ways for both sexes. Further, the ability to nurture others is one area in which women clearly feel adult in comparison with men's childishness.

Before advocating the teaching of women to nurture themselves as well as others, I should emphasize a point which applies here and to all the other characteristics discussed in this chapter. One does not have to become less of a woman to become more adult. Phyllis Chesler puts the matter very well:

> Women whose psychological identities are forged out of concern for their own survival and self-definition, and who withdraw from or avoid any interactions which do not support this formidable endeavor, need not give up their capacity for warmth, emotionality, and nurturance. They do not have to forsake the wisdom of the heart and become men. They need only to transfer the primary force of their supportiveness to themselves and to each other—and never to the point of self-sacrifice. [*Women and Madness*, 1972, p. 301]

The point is easily made by a group experience. Each woman lists on the left side of a large piece of paper the ways in which she nurtures others. In the right-hand column go the ways in which she nurtures herself. The left-hand column

67

will be easier and longer, and the task is to take items from it and see how they can be converted into items on the right. All the sheets of paper then go up on the wall so that the group adds to the individual imagination. Invariably the common response will be: "I realize that I often do for others what I would love someone to do for me. Why not do it for myself?" Women are notoriously adept at finding meaningfulness in small things, while men are allowed not to be the same way. "Why wait for my husband to do it?" said one group member in wonder. "Why not buy flowers for myself?"

The ability to combine self-nurturance with nurturing others is a prospect which excites most women, but it is more than just an added pleasure. If a woman works and takes care of a home, is a single parent, takes care of grandchildren or aging parents, or is lonely because the children have left or she is living in a new community—or any of a dozen other circumstances which the data suggest are typical—then self-nurturance is a major avenue to mental health; its absence is almost a guarantee of unhappiness to some degree. To wait either for others to nurture one or to have others to nurture is a manifestation of powerlessness, especially in the crucial area of power over one's self.

Balancing Independence with Interdependence

Finding a healthy balance between autonomy and interdependence is a characteristically adult problem which is approached differently by females and males; both sexes need interdependence, but the ways they meet that need differ. Most men learn early in life to take care of themselves first (to "look out for Number One"), become accustomed in childhood to being cared for by women, and find the main avenue to interdependence through being adequate bread-winners. Acculturation encourages women, on the other hand, to satisfy others' needs before their own, to care for men even when they receive little care in return, and to emphasize interdependence even at the expense of being a successful breadwinner. Typically, therefore, men have trouble being interdependent in an adult manner, and women have difficulty being autonomous. Further, interdependence often leads women into dependency; starting as the supportive member of a relationship, a woman easily becomes subordinate. Starting as the one who is expected to please, she easily becomes submissive. The development of these characteristics then makes her less likely still to discover her autonomy. Simone de Beauvoir described the process succinctly in The Second Sex (1952). A woman, she wrote, "is taught that to please she must try to please." She must renounce her autonomy and act like a living doll, surrendering all liberty. Thus a vicious circle is formed, writes de Beauvoir: "The less she exercises her freedom to understand, to grasp and discover the world about her, the less resources will she find within herself, the less will she dare to affirm herself as subject [rather than object]" (p. 316).

The normal woman finds it difficult to establish her autonomy. The feminine sex-role stereotype encourages her to create her existence not by doing but by accompanying others who do. Her role is to listen, to tend, to care and understand —and to prohibit herself from expressing what she needs, wants, thinks, and feels at the expense of others. For this reason, women coming to therapy normally lack a sense of their own autonomy, are struggling to develop it, or have a conflict between their independence and their interdependence. Dependent women who establish a degree of autonomy typically experience very strong behaviors in search of interdependence. The fear of losing either one's own identity or one's relationships with others—in other words, the perception that the two are in conflict—is much more often a major problem for women than it is for men.

It may not be obvious to a male therapist, working with a female client, that her sense of autonomy is defective; he is unlikely to understand that society currently encourages her both to want and to avoid autonomy. If she expresses fear of being autonomous, he is likely to see that as a sign of immaturity. A woman working with a female client in a similar situation may err in a different way, depending upon her own discomfort with the issue. Her own unease with autonomy may cause her to avoid the subject; she may project her own lack of ease onto the client, or her own sense of the struggle in her recent life may otherwise distort her perceptions. Thus both female and male therapists may find it awkward to deal straightforwardly with an issue which is at the foundation of a client's sense of identity. Again, while an increased sense of autonomy is a major benefit from therapy, the therapist may feel uncomfortable about the consequences on a woman's life; the cost of autonomy seems to be much higher for a woman than for a man. The problems which follow the development of autonomy may be so complex that they seem disastrous. One major effect, for instance, may be separation from males. Many independent women live out their lives alone when their male peers choose less autonomous women (especially young women) as mates; these women will not surrender the pleasures of autonomy, which is the price many men demand for interdependence.

Finding the right point of balance between union and separation (Polster and Polster, 1973) is a continuing struggle in adult relationships. Both dependence and independence are necessary states, but the most desirable condition seems to be interdependence. As explained by Weingarten (1978), an interdependent relationship between a woman and another person shows the capacity to tolerate any of the following combinations:

Woman		Other
Dependent	/	Dependent
Independent	/	Independent
Independent	/	Dependent
Dependent	/	Independent

In other words, an interdependent relationship allows for the recognition of the need for dependence and independence both in oneself and in the other person.

Interdependence is a reconciliation of dependence and independence, but it is not a cure for them. For example, suppose that a client's relationship with the people important in her life (children, parents, lovers, friends) shows too much dependence. She may be giving away too much of her private self in order to have an intimate relationship, she may not dare to make behavioral changes in herself because her relationships might then crumble, or she may be expending far more energy than she should in fighting for freedom. Her next move, I believe, must be not to the ideal of interdependence but to the experience of independence. Thus I help an overly dependent client focus on her ability to act alone, her power to make decisions, her strengths, and the necessary responses to a critical situation in her present life. I will also investigate the sources in her life from which she learned her dependence (e.g., from parents, teachers, friends), then have her reenact those past events in fantasy from an independent viewpoint. She learned dependence; now she discovers that she can learn independence. This method must be applied even to the most practical manifestations of dependence. For instance, economics often bind a woman to dependency (money for graduate school from parents who want a dutiful daughter, a domineering husband with a salary three times as much as hers, "satisfying" a boss in order to keep a job) and even they must be dealt with therapeutically. At the very least she needs to discover how much of her dependence has an external source and how much comes from inside her as a result of socialization and habit; then she can practice independence where feasible.

After both dependence and independence have been experienced, the main need is to find interdependence; many women who leap from dependence to independence then find their relationships just as unsatisfying as before, but in different ways. They may especially fear that interdependence will lead them back into dependence. One client in her late 30s, Louise, had moved from a highly dependent marriage into highly independent single parenting, not only bringing up teenage children but also working as a semiprofessional while she earned a graduate degree. For six years she had avoided any serious relationship with a man and had grown increasingly lonely. "I've used my job, my children, school as an excuse to avoid really getting close to a man," she said. "I'm scared of one man I really care for. I don't know that I won't slip right back into dependence." Asked for a metaphor of dependence on a man, she said: "It is like sleeping in the featherbed at my grandparents' farm. I sink into the warmth and softness and I sleep so very safely, and in the morning it's such hard work to get up and so nice to stay there that I just lie and wait for someone to come and pull me out. And no one does." Asked what happened next in the fantasy, she reported growing restless, then angry that Grandma had put her in that bed, then angry at herself for being lulled by soft safeness. Finally pulling herself out of bed, she then went down to the kitchen and announced to Grandma, "I'll never sleep in that bed again!" Asked what her metaphor meant to her, she explained: "I love that safety and softness, and I'm tired of managing everything all by myself, and I'm scared that I'll sink into dependency with Tom, then get resentful, then start shouting at him that I'll never sleep in that bed again!" With this metaphor as basis, therapy could begin, weaving back and forth between present and past as Louise—through fantasy, body-work, reenactment of critical events, and so on—learned that dependence and independence were not her only choices.

The therapeutic relationship is itself an excellent laboratory for experiencing interdependence. Whenever I notice that a client is functioning either too dependently or too independently with me, I report that as an impression to her and we talk about it. In this way we are able to work together (that is, interdependently) on balancing the needs for both dependence and independence which therapy requires.

Lack of Trust in Self-direction

The subordination of women in our culture has a highly damaging effect on their ability to set their own direction—an effect even on their sense of the right to set their own direction. A man expects to be independent and to have the right to direct his own life; a woman expects to be interdependent or dependent and to have others direct her life. The feminine experience is not as legitimate as the masculine experience. Women sense that their needs, wants, feelings, beliefs, and experiences are not in some sense as valid as those of the dominant group in society; this causes a woman eventually to experience a lack of trust in herself. Here are some common examples of the effects of that lack: "I decided not to buy a car because my mother says it isn't right for me." "Dad says I should be grateful for what I have, so I suppose I shouldn't want life to be different." "He wants to move back home so I suppose I'll let him. He says it will be good for me, too." "He told me I made him so mad he had to hit me."

All these statements allow someone else to have authority over women and reveal women's lack of trust in their own feelings and desires. Women in therapy often have great difficulty answering simple questions about their sense of self-direction: what do you want in all this? How do you feel about that? What is happening to you? What do you need? Did you enjoy that? What excitement does that rouse in you? What do you want to be doing in a year? In five years? It is not so much that they have no answer but that they do not feel the right to ask the question. Given that right, a woman may find it exhilarating; she undergoes the experience of determining inwardly what she wants, and then she learns to express it outwardly. This is an essential therapeutic goal. As the woman claims her own experience of each moment in her life, she slowly learns to trust herself as her own best expert. To become her own change agent, she has to learn that she cannot abdicate the responsibility for defining herself to others, that she must cease devaluing her part in decision making, and that she must trust herself to set her own direction, regardless of outcome.

As in learning the balance between dependence and independence, the therapeutic relationship is itself a model for learning self-direction. Clients often want to give their power to the therapist, and the therapist must give it right back. I tend to say: "I don't know what is the right choice for you. I work constantly on

71

my own choices and self-direction, so I can share my experience with you and tell you where to get information, and I'll help you clamber through all this. But I can't make the choice for you, and I will support whatever decision you make for yourself. You know yourself better than I do."

Diffused Sense of Self

A sense of self means that one can define the boundaries between oneself and others or the world at large. Unwanted intrusion upon the self by others is therefore rare, and one does not intrude upon others' boundaries. Neither subordinateness nor superiority characterize a person with a good sense of self; equality and autonomy are the likely manifestations. Awareness of one's own needs and wants as separate and distinct from those of others is a prerequisite. Unfortunately, women as a group manifest a diffused and weak sense of self. They are characterized much more by what in Gestalt psychology is called "confluence"; that is, the tendency to yield to whatever comes along, investing little energy in choosing personally (Polster and Polster, 1973). This suggests that, in both personal and work lives, women tend to have greater difficulty choosing a path for themselves than do men; they tend to lack an innate sense of direction that will drive or lead them ahead.

Socialization encourages women not to develop a clear sense of self. The woman's role, they learn, is to invest her energy in responses to the situations of others. Thus, even if a woman is clear about her wants and needs, she may still regard them as invalid or trivial, and she will tend to dream rather than plan. In a study of the ways the two sexes create and manage their experiences ("ego-styles"), Guttman (1970) described major differences. Women tend to be "autocentric" in style, which means that they look at the order of events only to the extent that those events relate to themselves, whereas men tend to be "allocentric," which means that they see the order of events having a direction and logic of its own. For example, men tend to worry about the state of the economy, women about how they will pay the food bill. (Neither style is superior; each has its own merits and defects in terms of perceiving reality.) In psychological terms, autocentrism means that the boundary between the self and the other, or between the object and the emotion pertinent to that object, seems tenuous and permeable; in common parlance, women take things personally. They tend to see an outside stimulus, their appraisal of it, and their reaction to it as bonded parts of a continuous experience. Guttman believes that women thrive within this boundless world and that functioning within it is one of their strengths.

My own experience, however, suggests that the absence of a clear sense of boundaries is harmful in many circumstances and that many women coming to therapy have become worn down and exhausted from living in a world where everything has a personal dimension. A basic need of many clients is precisely to establish a clear sense of self and firm boundaries so that they can distinguish between what is self and what is someone else or something else. Gestalt psychology

72

is in this respect extremely useful when working with women, since the concept of boundaries is one of its basic tenets. Gestalt defines the self-boundary as the point at which each person makes contact with others and the world as separate entities. "The contact boundary," write Polster and Polster (1973), "is the point at which one experiences the me in relation to that which is not me, and through this contact both are more clearly defined." Translating this into Guttman's terms, the autocentric style encourages the individual not to define the differences between me and not me, so that the self can be easily intruded upon. In certain circumstances this leads to the acute perceptiveness about the outside world that men like to mock as women's intuition or to the apparent irrationality of, perhaps, looking at a politician on television and saying, "I don't listen to what he says, I like the way he looks, so I'll vote for him." In too many circumstances, however, it leads to simple and devastating confusion such as when a woman thinks a husband has the right to beat her when he is angry. One of my clients, defining herself as "the gal who can't say no," complained bitterly that, despite all of her prior resolution, when any man asked, she couldn't refuse—because she would then make him feel rejected.

There is also a perilous countermovement: personal boundaries too tightly drawn. Upon discovering the dangers of a diffused sense of self, many women move hastily in the opposite direction and take up a "retroflective" stance. This happens to many women who work their way out of the passive/dependent state but fear falling back into it. All their effort focuses on holding the self apart, all energy flows into maintaining and posting boundaries as the separateness of self is asserted, and all attention goes inward into guarding the intrapersonal rather than the interpersonal. All confluence vanishes, and the woman appears to be shy, withdrawn, cold, aloof, prickly, snappish, or too self-contained. Although not the most desirable of psychological states, departure from it, interestingly enough, has often been celebrated on film as the Plain Jane takes off her glasses and loosens her hair to emerge as the warm beauty she really is. Obviously, retroflection is not much healthier than either excessive autocentrism (personalization) or allocentrism (absence of affect). All extremes represent a fear that the self will be engulfed, overwhelmed, or swallowed up. Retroflection may, however, be a necessary step on the way to healthy balanced contact, a way of firmly separating the self from the world so that, when one returns to that world, there will be no risk of losing oneself again.

Therapists, perhaps especially female therapists, need to be alert for what I call "Swiss Cheese" clients—those whose boundaries contain holes large enough to tempt me to move in and take control if I choose. One of my clients had all the signs often apparent in a person with a diffused sense of self: a posture of waiting, shallow breathing, a sometimes faltering voice, head, shoulders, and eyes alert for clues in which direction to move, hesitancy in stating her feelings and thoughts, a surplus of emergencies—and a great affection for me. After many weeks of patient work, I found myself feeling impatient and angry—I wanted her either to stop being my client or to straighten herself out, and I was tempted to start telling her what to do. I was aware that flowing together with this client had caused us both to become lost in confluence. Having told her that I was experiencing these feelings, I then started new kinds of work on the specific contact boundaries outlined by Gestalt theory—talking, touching, hearing, understanding, acting, and seeing. We worked, for instance, on learning to breathe deeply and slowly so that all attention was focused on the self, rather than on the other. Starting from opposite walls, we met in the center of the room, looked at each other, touched, talked about what that was like, then moved apart and talked about what that was like. Eventually her unconscious fantasies for our confluence emerged: she wanted to be as important to me as I was to her. This perception enabled us to start work on her relationships with other people, and, very rapidly, the therapeutic experience became as satisfying as it had been frustrating. As therapists, our obligation is to work on our own boundaries, to keep our sense of ourselves as distinct from others, and to meet our women clients at their boundaries.

Much learning must take place before the sense of self can function appropriately, and experimentation seems essential. In a woman a clear sense of boundaries may manifest itself in such a simple circumstance as listening carefully to advice but then making her own deliberate choice regarding whether or not to follow it (i.e., avoiding either submissiveness or drifting). It is often manifest in her relations to children, to whom she can listen carefully, then choose whether to respond, when to respond, and how to respond. A woman with solid self-boundaries will negotiate, compromise, and confront with comfort because she has a sense of the validity of her feelings and wishes. In relationships and at work, a clear sense of self is invaluable. Since women's positions in these areas are usually subordinate, only a clear sense of self will prevent confusion and exploitation.

Confusion between Internal and External Causes

Many women coming to therapy have enormous difficulty discerning whether they or some other force are responsible for their problems, a characteristic of people whose sense of self has been broken down. This phenomenon is especially common among battered wives and the wives of alcoholic men, where the destruction is physical and economic as well as psychological and where one would expect them to identify clearly that the cause lay outside them. Not so; the almost universal tendency is for these women to blame themselves, not just for what is done to them, but as somehow (and the somehow is always vague) the ultimate source of the immediate cause for their suffering. This, of course, is the "blame the victim" syndrome with a vengeance, in which the victim internalizes society's message and blames herself. The victim caused the crime by being there, by being the bad kind of person to whom bad things happen, by somehow driving the criminal to a crime that would otherwise never have been committed. "I must have provoked him somehow," she says, and that is excuse enough for anything. To the therapist: "You don't understand. He's not really that way at all. It's my fault for not being what he wants and needs." The phenomenon is widespread among rape victims. When society blames a woman for somehow bringing about her own rape by enticement, teasing, or being provocative or for secretly wanting to be raped, it displays an especially clever viciousness, for many women are totally unable to comprehend the random violence that stimulates rape and therefore suspect that there could have been no cause external to them. "If only I had been smart enough to walk down another street," they say. "If only I had thought to come home earlier (or later)." Very few rape victims ever say, "He is solely responsible for his own violence, and would be even if I had provoked it deliberately."

Therapists face a danger when dealing with such confusion between external and internal causes because of the traditions within their own discipline; their almost inevitable tendency will be to blame an internal cause either directly or by implication. Traditionally, therapy sees problems as lying within the individual woman rather than in the cultural milieu. The therapist must make the client change because she is here—while the culture is outside the therapist's influence. Traditionally also, the success or failure of a relationship has been the woman's domain, responsibility, and blame; if a relationship sours, the woman's skills must be at fault. If a woman complains about her work environment—for instance, because of sexual harassment—do we believe or suspect her?

Thus the wise therapist examines the differing realities of both internal and external causes for whatever situation a client describes. On the one hand: what is she doing to oppress or limit herself? On the other: what external pressures function to keep her in a situation? Unless the therapist keeps the two clear in her or his own mind, there will be little prospect of training the client to do so; yet this is one of the most important goals in counseling women. It is probably most useful to concentrate on external causes first, even though this can be too doctrinaire; analysis of external causes will decrease guilt in the client as it leads to an understanding of internal reasons for sustaining the external situation. External causes reveal themselves in two major ways. Most revealing is the presence of a double standard based on sex either in a relationship, at work, or in a legal matter; i.e., is the woman's emotional, physical, social, or economic freedom crippled because some person or factor prevents her from functioning as a human with full and equal rights? Next are the messages which the woman receives from her environment. If she behaves in certain ways, will she rightly expect punishment, the absence of reward, rejection, or coercion which may create stress and hence anxiety? The answer to this question leads smoothly into internal causes: the woman's perception of what will or will not happen to her in different situations.

The eventual aim is to analyze and reconcile both internal and external causes, especially since they are linked inside each of us by the internalization of sex-role stereotypes. Typically, a woman's dilemma results from the interchange between her own inner dynamics and those of her environment. A major problem is that her self is likely to be the target of antagonism from both sources; someone else may oppress her, and she may oppress herself. The relationships between internal and external causes are infinitely variable, but an adult spends much of her or his life sorting out the two. Until a woman learns that both are equally real, and that she has the power to distinguish between them, she will not be able to function as an adult.

Old Rules and Expectations

An interesting experience in a group situation is to have the members write down all the old rules by which they operate, long after the need for those rules has passed. This may be amusing—and occasionally horrifying. We all carry about with us a grab bag of rules from childhood, the town where we lived, teachers, or simply the past; these old rules, which we never examine because they have become part of us, can cause great damage to us in the state of rapid change in which our culture demands we live. One man summed it up in a group; looking up with surprise, he said, "I've just realized. I always eat everything on my plate. Just like mother said. Even though my mother's been dead for ten years. Even though I pay for the food myself!" These rules which become as habitual to us in our emotional lives as rules would on a basketball court, and are every bit as detailed, are called "introjects" in Gestalt psychology—the "should" systems once given to us by our culture.

They fall into four main categories:

1. *Behaviors* which are acceptable in dealing with any situation productive of emotion, and those which are unacceptable. To see this in operation, one need only watch the players of any game for half an hour—and especially watch the differences between children and adult players or between women and men.
2. *Skills* for dealing with emotional situations in an appropriate manner and an inappropriate manner. A man who cries at a sentimental movie is seen as less than manly; a woman who does not cry at the same movie may be seen as less of a woman.
3. *Verbal communications* which are acceptable and those which are not. An interesting experience is to watch people's reactions to a man who habitually uses foul language and to a woman who does the same.
4. *Nonverbal communications* which are acceptable and those which are not. This is currently a matter of close study by the creators of television commercials because the nature of nonverbal communications from both women and men has been changing rapidly, and the success of a commercial depends less upon its verbal than upon its nonverbal message.

Many of the rules learned through sex-role socialization act as a sort of costume for the individual by which much about her or him is revealed to the world. When internalized, however, they are no longer ornaments but reality, and they associate closely with individual characteristics with varying degrees of comfort. "As a man," we might tell ourselves, "I can't afford to be seen as soft or to seem soft to myself." Or, "As a woman, I should always love my children." Or, "As a westerner, I should not be comfortable living in the East." These introjects often directly contradict our feelings; they may falsely dominate or confuse our behavior. They may result in our doing or not doing the most absurd or damaging things. The rules for dealing with emotional situations are specialized and detailed. A woman who negotiates expertly over the price of a refrigerator and a man whose job requires him to mediate between others for six hours each day may never be able to negotiate or compromise over their relationships as husband or wife; they learned the first skill, not the second. The verbal rules for women show some dangerous varieties of this specialization. A woman is expected to express love verbally but not anger—the first is being loving, the other bitchy. She should complain to butcher and friends if anything is wrong with the meat in the supermarket, but if there is anything wrong about her relationship with her lover, she should keep her mouth shut. The rules for women's nonverbal communications, especially the should-nots, have been widely publicized recently by several popular books. She should smile as much as possible, even if she is a weathergirl talking about tornadoes; she should be polite and clean and sweatless. She should not, especially when with a male, take up too much space. She should not seem pushy in any way, even in appearance, for only prostitutes look pushy; nor should she appear masculine in dress, walk, or habits lest she frighten away the men. She should assume little girl poses that will enable her to be called cute. She should not initiate eye contact and, once established, she should not maintain it too long (Chesler and Goodman, 1976; Frieze and Ramsey, 1976; Johnson, 1976).

We could never consciously learn all these rules, but we can consciously unlearn many of them and the unlearning can lead to an unraveling of many more. A particular example comes from voice training. Many women speak in a light, high, childish voice not because of physiology but because of acculturation. Learning to speak in a deeper voice, with better breathing and in a more direct tone, can change the entire personality because it suggests a whole new way of relating to the world. In group experiences, changes of posture are often very revealing. Having a woman demonstrate the body postures she uses when she is submissive and when she is assertive, then add her typical postures when dealing with spouse, lover, children, and boss, may suddenly illuminate her characteristic psychological stance to the world. One can cast off the old and don the new.

Some old rules must be completely abandoned. This is often true in enduring marriages, for instance, where roles and expectations which were quite satisfactory when the couples were young have since become outmoded and destructive as a result of age and altered circumstances; no matter how good they once were, these old rules must be abandoned now. Others must be restricted to appropriate situations. The key is flexibility coupled with choice, so that automatic obedience to a set of rules continues only where that is convenient. Therapists would be wise also to use the same principle, avoiding imposing their own "shoulds" and expectations on a client—even that one which says all women should be "liberated."

4

Role Transitions in Women's Lives

When we find ourselves expressing nostalgia for the 1960s and call the 1950s the good old days, then we know that the rate of cultural change is as rapid as Alvin Toffler's *Future Shock* predicted in 1970. Change is a fact of life with which any counselor or therapist of women must deal because, for many women, the state of cultural change has become acute.

Until the 1950s, women were still recognizably daughters of the nineteenth century. As the country became more urban, middle class, and technological, women's jobs became generally less strenuous and women grew more affluent, but the culture still saw females primarily as mothers, wives, and homemakers. The woman had responsibility for her family's well-being and was expected to find fulfillment through her husband, children, and home. If she was not home to welcome the breadwinner at the end of his working day, the marriage would go bad or the children would become delinquents. If she earned more than a man did, if she enjoyed the outside world too much, she would castrate the men in her life; in retaliation they would leave her to her own devices—a fate worse than death. The feminine mystique was a vital reality.

In some circles these beliefs are still powerful, but for most people times have changed and so have women's social roles. Society has different expectations for women of the future. In 1972 Alice Rossi foresaw that, in the future, marriage would no longer mean for a woman a "withdrawal from the life and work pattern she has established" but the "addition of a new dimension." Women and men would find marriage a "looking outward in the same direction." Women would be likely to marry not because marriage is mandatory but because they want mates,

78

and the bearing of children would be a matter of choice rather than automatism. Society would not judge a woman to have failed as a human being if she chose to go without mate, children, or nice home.

Alice Rossi's women of the future are already among us in great numbers. All women are now confronted with choices, whether they choose the old role or the new. Continual re-evaluation is a necessity since choices are no longer valid over a lifetime. Definition of one's role is a recurring obligation as women move in and out of various roles, selecting different options at different times and revising choices or having them altered for them. Contraception, abortion, divorce, and financial need demand decisions. Our culture now tells women that many roles are viable and even desirable, to the point that it may be in the process of creating a whole new social role for women.

A social role is a matter of both opportunity and expectation. As Havighurst and Neugarten (1967) define it, a social role is the "coherent pattern of behavior common to all persons who fill the same position or place in society and a pattern of behavior *expected* by the other members of society" (pp. 127–128). It involves both internal and external pressure. The behavior required by a role is incorporated in the self, so the social self largely consists of role behaviors which increase in complexity as one grows older. There is thus likely to be friction between the self and the social role at any time, but especially when both are in a state of flux.

The main areas of change are as follows: (1) in the world at large; (2) in the home and family; and (3) in interpersonal relationships. Everything or anything may become an issue—marriage, parenting, work, education, lifestyle, sexuality, living arrangements—any part of the whole range of life's major decisions and events. The future seems likely to endorse two major new rights for women: the right to make various arrangements in home life, and the right to develop as individuals. Because economic and cultural realities are changing, women will be both able and obliged to explore a greater variety of roles and lifestyles: remaining single, deferring marriage, postponing childbearing, remaining childless, marrying, divorcing, separating, heading households, getting more education, changing careers, running for office, holding positions of authority, and managing their own money throughout their lives.

Therapists will therefore have plenty of work in helping women deal with new economic, social, and psychological realities and assisting them to move through the personal transitions brought by the general cultural transition. There will be both external and internal barriers to women's development. Since society's structures and institutions change more slowly than society's expectations, women are still being defeated by, for example, the lack of child care facilities or flexitime work programs, poorly oriented and timed educational programs, or family structures which require a working woman to take complete responsibility for child care and housekeeping. In terms of internal barriers, women inflict wounds upon themselves through sex stereotyping: the inability to make long-term plans, uneasinesss with power, unwitting limitation of choices, or guilt about ambition or success (Collier, 1982). Therapists may legitimately work with both external and internal barriers.

The counseling process should not necessarily push a woman into change nor assume that all old myths are bad and all new myths good. A recent national survey (Bryant, 1977) reports that only half the women polled welcomed the current change in women's roles; the other half either resisted change or were spectators only. Thus no therapist can safely assume that a woman wants to change her social role or even needs. to. The art is to look for the dysfunctional. The obligation of the therapist is to know all the existing options and to offer them for exploration when appropriate; that is, a therapist must be aware when a woman is clearly being restricted by herself or others from using all the capabilities she might possess and need and when such restriction is harmful to her psychological, social, and economic survival or well-being. If therapists possess any of that magic which some clients attribute to them, the magic lies in knowledge of alternatives and when to offer them for consideration.

Alternatives and choices must be the central feature of therapy in a time of great social change. Twenty-five years ago, women behaving in ways that did not perfectly fit the traditional social role tended to feel that something was wrong with them because of the clarity of cultural messages regarding the right way of life for a woman. The tendency of therapy then was to help women fit into the proper social role, in essence if not intent agreeing that there was something wrong with them. That situation is no longer sensible in a culture that now encourages diversity. Therapists must now assume that what is right for one woman is not necessarily right for another, without there being anything "wrong" with either woman. The process of being an adult woman is one of change, choice, and discovery; many lifestyles are viable. The traditional is only one of many options, and the data show that it cannot be seen as more stable, suitable, or healthy than the others.

Change in Marital Arrangements

Until the last decade, the traditional nuclear family was the model for every individual's living arrangements; but it is now only one model among many, with the result that the choice of our living arrangements over a lifetime or for a time has become a major factor in our lives. People also change their concepts of home and family more often, so that a choice is rarely a lifetime choice. Indeed, one can no longer safely expect to make a final choice—our living arrangements have all become temporary.

In this state of affairs, therapists need to pay less attention to the single model of the nuclear family and more attention to the basic functions which a home fulfills: the creation of a secure and satisfying living environment and the opportunity for healthy parenting. Therapists also need to be at ease with the basic trends concerning marriage and the home which are affecting their clients' lives:

1. The inevitable association between marriage and childrearing which dominated previous generations has weakened because of new methods of preventing reproduction.
2. Marriage is no longer the basic reality upon which the creation of a home depends. More people than in any previous period of our history are choosing not to marry, to marry only for a certain period, or to marry a series of partners.
3. The social pressure to be married has declined at the same time that younger women, able to earn well, have become less dependent on marriage to keep them out of poverty.
4. In future the probability is that people will move in and out of the married state at different stages of life.
5. The norms within marriage are changing as dual-worker marriages increase, older women marry younger men, and sexual preference creates varieties among couples.
6. Marriage is not a permanent state which a woman can use as her goal in life. Most women are likely to spend most of their lives without a partner or with various partners.

Traditional Marriage

The data indicate that traditional marriage remains the norm by which other kinds of living arrangements are measured. About 85 percent of women live in a traditional marriage for at least some time (Bryant, 1977), and only about 10 percent of women and 14 percent of men never marry (Troll, 1975). The average age at marriage is 21 for women and 23 for men (Troll, 1975). In 1975, 56 percent of all adult women were married, living with their husbands, and not working (Women's Bureau, Mature Women Workers, 1976).

Insofar as these marriages remain traditional internally, they sharply differentiate the roles of women and men—the husband as breadwinner, the wife as homemaker. Being a wife means being housekeeper, mother, companion, lover, partner, manager of home affairs, nurse, ornament, sex object, and engine of the institution. A husband's obligations to the world outside the home are recognized as at least equal in weight to his family responsibilities; however, a woman's obligations are expected not to undermine but to reinforce her role in the home. A woman's life outside the home is her spare time; a man's life inside the home is his spare time.

Change, however, is overtaking these traditional expectations. More women are postponing marriage; in the age group 20 to 24, the proportion of women who had never married rose from 28 percent in 1960 to 43 percent in 1976 (NIE Fact Sheet, 1977). In other words, young women are no longer all proceeding directly from their parents' homes into their own without experience of the outside world. Younger women are also finding traditional marriage less acceptable. An International Women's Year survey (Bryant, 1977) showed that only 22 percent of all women wished to be mainly a homemaker, that a majority of those under 45 disagreed with the traditional role prescriptions (husband as worker, wife as homemaker), and that a majority did not believe that a woman's earning more than her husband created problems within a marriage.

Younger women tend to see traditional marriage as playing a vital but perhaps temporary part in their lives. According to the IWY survey, 49 percent of women choose to stay home while their children are young, but later they want to combine homemaking with work outside the home. Since this requires major changes in living arrangements during a lifetime, it may create significant problems for women in a society not yet oriented to their needs.

Thus, while traditional marriage is imperiled, it must be respected as a worthwhile choice for any woman because it is one she is likely to make for a period of her life. If acculturation has made a woman see it as the only possible choice or as a permanent state, the data suggest that she may be taking a risk; but the current tendency to deride traditional marriage may undermine the faith of many women in their ability to choose. As one 58-year-old woman said passionately in a women's group, "I'm *angry* at you younger women. I'm angry at anyone who sneers at traditional marriage. I refuse to be called 'just a housewife!' You devalue what I choose to do and was brought up to do, and you're wrong to think I feel unfulfilled. I live a good life, and I made the right choice for me, and I want to be *respected* for that choice!"

Dual-Worker Marriage

Marriages in which both partners work are now common and seem about to become a majority of marriages. In 1979, 49.4 percent of married women living with their husbands also worked (Bureau of Labor Statistics, 1980). The subject has already given rise to a major book (Bird, 1979) and to a tax-reform movement aimed at eliminating inequities for dual-worker families.

The assignment of responsibilities for the functioning of a dual-worker marriage varies between different couples. In one set of arrangements, both partners maintain both family and work lives but each holds primary responsibility for one of the two areas—what Bailyn (1978) terms a differential distribution based on specialization of function. In a second set of arrangements, both partners give equal commitment to both work and family, basing their responsibility not on function but on equal sharing. Any given couple may be evaluated as present anywhere on a spectrum between traditionalism and equality, and many dual-worker families change arrangements according to the requirements of either work or family at different times, affecting different partners.

More important than individualized arrangements within dual-worker marriages are the ways in which dual-worker marriages tend to differ from traditional marriages. Even when both partners are traditionally minded, even when the husband takes no greater part in home life than in a traditional marriage, differences are evident. In traditional marriage the husband alone sustains the links to the work world; in the dual-worker marriage, both partners sustain independent links while mutually maintaining relationships to family, nonoccupational institutions, and networks (Rapoport and Rapoport, 1978).

The stresses and satisfactions in dual-worker marriages are different from those in traditional marriages. A main source of stress is the effort required to maintain a balance between both partners in the matter of work and family responsibilities, which causes practical problems and psychological difficulties—sometimes for only one partner, more often for both (Darley, 1976; Pleck, 1979). But it does not seem true that dual-worker marriages are more stressful or problem-ridden than are traditional marriages (Hopkins, 1977). The greatest reward for a dual-worker family is the increase in income despite higher expenditures for such domestic functions as laundry, housecleaning, prepared foods, and day care; but money is not the only source of the high level of satisfaction found by surveys among married working women. For instance, one survey found that married working women are usually more satisfied with their jobs than are unmarried women, possible evidence that the combination of work and family life benefits both (College Placement Council, Inc., 1978). The Commission on the Observance of International Women's Year noted a trend for young, educated women to expect a life which combines marriage and work and suggested that this may be the dominant expectation of the future (Bryant, 1977). Women see fulfillment from work as an added satisfaction depending on two factors: the degree to which the work is itself satisfying, and the equality of sharing between partners in the management of home life (Heckman, 1977; Johnson and Johnson, 1977).

The danger may be that women accept work as well as home life as their responsibility without expecting any change in their ways of working or being in the home. If our society remains sexist, if it retains the male-designed structure of our work world and still sees a woman as having primary or sole responsibility for the home, then both women and men will simply expect more of the woman. She will be obliged to be worker and breadwinner as well as wife, mother, homemaker, and sexual partner—a situation in which some women already find themselves. In other words, if the male in a dual-worker marriage does not fulfill a variety of roles, and if the expectations of employers do not change, inequality between the sexes will have been perpetuated, and perhaps worsened.

The issue here is power. Will power be distributed equally between the two partners? Will women have the same right as men to choose a work structure suited to their needs? Or will women simply add another task to the variety of services they already provide? Simply to work is not enough; it is to the fruits of labor that we must look. Many theorists claim that the American family has evolved from its previous paternalism to a more egalitarian form. Others remain skeptical (Gillespie, 1976). Still others claim that we are only embarking upon the way to egalitarianism (Bird, 1979). For the most part the balance of power is still located where it always has been, with the male. Defining power as the prerogative of one who makes the decisions which dramatically affect the family, Gillespie suggests that such power is to a great extent a function of income and that, as long as women are the lesser earners, egalitarian philosophies will have little impact. Whoever makes the money, he points out, makes the decisions on which job to take, where to live, how the budget will be allocated, and all other basic matters; and since the income of males averages nearly twice that of females, men remain the ultimate arbiters. One should add, however, that unless a working wife is highly submissive, her independent income gives her more power than she would have in a traditional marriage (Scanzoni, 1972).

It is as yet unclear whether truly egalitarian relationships will be a product of dual-worker marriages (Scanzoni, 1972). Old stereotypes affect current marriages deeply, whether they are manifest in external forms such as salary differentials or in internal forms such as self-expectations or definitions of identity. The current generation of young dual-worker marriages is in an experimental state, outcome unknown; but as Bird points out, the next generation of children, raised in dual-worker marriages and soon reaching maturity, will disclose whether the traditional sex roles regarding home and work are coming to seem obsolete, even quaint. They may well accept androgyny and sex-role transcendence as the natural way of living in marriage.

Even dual-worker marriage can be a tender trap for women. As Troll (1975) points out, women are under greater social pressure to marry than are men because marriage still confers improved social status even though fears of being "an old maid" are not as pervasive as they were a generation ago. Marriage offers improved economic status and the satisfaction of vicarious achievement to the sex that society undervalues both economically and psychologically. Further, our society sees women as "marriageable" for a shorter age range than are men, even though women have the longer life span—with the result that there is always an oversupply of women potentially seeking partners. In 1980, the United States contained approximately six million more females than males; this means, to put it bluntly, that in the marriage market men are and will be the more valued commodity. Psychologically, therefore, there may be a strong tendency to perpetuate present lifestyles and marriage patterns which allow men to dominate. In particular, for all but a few women, their marital status is seen as more descriptive of them than their work. It is still true that a man marries a wife—while a woman marries a doctor, a pipefitter, an airline pilot, or a factory worker. It is still true that a man chooses his own lifestyle while a woman chooses hers by choosing a man. Until this imbalance changes, true equality will not exist.

Pessimism is not, however, obligatory. Bird (1979) is optimistic; among her case studies of dual-worker families, she finds an increasing variety that is very healthy. She explores the substantial effects dual-worker marriages are likely to have on politics, consumer marketing, population growth, changing social roles, marriage and parenting, adult life styles, the stages of adult development, and ways of working. She suggests, for instance, that the work ethic may decline: "a cafeteria offering different kinds of rewards will be needed to get work out of college-educated white-collar workers with two paychecks coming into their home" (p. 314). She sees the coming of new styles of family and child rearing and a major alteration in satisfactions. Equality of earning power will tend to increase psychological equality, to the benefit of men as well as women. "There won't be many more people than there were in 1979, but they will be better and happier people. More of them will be adults. More of the adults will be earners. And more of the earners will be working at jobs and schedules of their own choosing" (p. 322). This states exactly the long-term goal of those working for women's human rights—and the short-term goal of every therapist.

Serial Monogamy

Marriage till-death-do-us-part may never have been quite as universal as we have pretended, and it was certainly easier when life expectancy was shorter. More couples today are considering alternatives and meeting with much less social disapproval for deviance. Serial monogamy—marriage to one person at a time, but to several during the life span—has already become a widespread American phenomenon (Troll, 1975; U.S. Bureau of Census, Series P-20 # 312, 1975; Toffler, 1979).

Serial monogamy is a living arrangement, legally endorsed by the state, which two people may prefer for a limited period of life and terminate when it proves irrelevant or unsatisfying to either or both. It reveals the contractual rather than the spiritual side of the marriage relationship. Each marriage (and each period of nonmarriage) may be lengthy or brief; and while serial monogamists still find the concept of marriage as an abstract entity important, they seem to traditional monogamists to treat the state less seriously than they should. Some serial monogamists see it simply as part of the accelerated change required by life in the twentieth century, made easier by the fact that sexual intercourse no longer need result in conception; others—with a romanticism whose persistence is remarkable—look upon each new marriage as the last. Many young people view it as a planned temporary arrangement involving only two consenting adults, an attitude drastically different from the family affair of previous generations. Thus it is unwise to assume that serial monogamists are moral or immoral, foolish or smart, dumb or calculating; their behavior is simply different from the traditional.

A substantial number of young people think this problem through and actively plan to be serial monogamists. A client in her mid-twenties startled me some years ago by expressing the following intention in a life-planning session: "I plan to marry and have children within the next five years. That marriage will probably end, oh, sometime within the next fifteen years, after the kids begin to go their own ways anyway, and we want to do other things. I'll still take care of the children, of course, but I want to be working on my career seriously by then. I'll marry again in my 40s—someone who's also divorced, also with children. If that marriage ends later too—and who can tell? Men seem to prefer younger women!—then I might stay single. Why not, if I can support myself? But I'd certainly plan to marry again for company, if I met someone who wanted to grow old with me." This concept then seemed revolutionary, but working with others who have the same general approach has made me recognize its realism. Young people are well aware of the growing divorce rate, the change in childbearing patterns, the potentially liberated financial status of women, and the difference in life expectancy between women and men. They see life as inherently less stable than does my generation, and they seem realistic because they allow for flexibility. Of course their expectations may not be met, but their flexibility is a good quality for therapists to imitate nonetheless. In terms of marriage today, one cannot only look at outer form; one must look at function.

Other Forms of Marriage

During the 1960s other forms of marriage received publicity, and during the 1970s they became more common. Open marriage (O'Neill and O'Neill, 1972) is the most famous example of a variant form, but we have no real idea how many couples engage in it for longer or shorter periods—simply because discretion is one of its major elements. Therapists tend to see its unsuccessful aspects, as in adultery, often working to the disadvantage of women; but adherents point out that therapists see only its failures, not its successes. Open marriage is probably not as widespread as popular magazines suggest, although—now as in times past—many couples reject sexual possessiveness as an essential part of marriage. The popularity of "swinging," the open agreement to exchange partners for limited sexual encounters, is not as great as one is led to believe, either. The 1974 Hunt survey (reported in Troll, 1975) found that only 1 percent of couples had engaged in swinging, most of them during their 20s or 30s. On the other hand, studies by Kinsey (1953), Hite (1976), and others show that extramarital sex is at least as common as ever; and because of unstated agreements between the married partners not to pry, it may represent an alternative form of marriage. Although most therapists report that sexual infidelity is still a major issue brought to counseling by clients, and although women are somewhat more likely to engage in extramarital sex nowadays than in past generations, neither factor *necessarily* means a poor marriage. Again, the guide must be the internal reality of the marital relationship rather than only its external form.

Ménage à trois—usually meaning two women living with one man—is still an uncommon practice; so is group marriage (Constantine and Constantine, 1974). Nonetheless, both are genuine forms of marriage which represent an attempt (usually by the younger generation) to create a different kind of emotionally satisfying home. Communes have a similar goal, and they continue to thrive, usually with a lower profile than they had a decade ago. One cannot predict the patterns of sexual and marital relationships within a commune, each of which develops its own style; some condemn sexuality altogether, while others encourage polymorphous perversity. Some encourage regular and permanent marriage within the group, others forbid it; others demand arranged marriages not based on romantic love, and most foster the caring of children. As economic conditions worsen, urban communes which are neither sexual nor marital in intent are growing more common, offering homes rather like those of the boarding-houses that used to be widespread in our society. In fact, the basis of most group living arrangements is a sharing of some combination of economic, social, and political life; and while sexual partnerings are complicated, they are not the reason for communal living to the same degree that they are the reason for, say, certain ski resorts or cruise ships.

In 1973 Bernard pointed out that most communes of the 1960s did not manifest sexual equality. Males were leaders, females the subordinates. Feminists often, therefore, opposed the commune movement. However, four features of communes in the 1970s may change this situation; some communes are now organized on the basis of a product or business (e.g., solar energy, herbal teas, natural foods, or chemical testing) which offers women skills and responsibilities they might not normally acquire in more routine work. Other communes are evolving into communities with a strong humanist orientation ardently intended to overcome all forms of cultural stereotyping. All-female collectives have appeared. And finally, as a worsening economic situation makes it harder for lower-paid women to survive, work, and tend for children, cooperatives of various kinds are springing up everywhere. In sum, communal living with or without marriage is a definite alternative for creating a healthy home that provides for child rearing and creates an emotionally satisfying atmosphere for women. Some therapists believe that more clients should study it as an option for reasons both financial and psychological.

Change in Marital Status

Divorced and Separated Women

Most demographic data fail to distinguish between divorced and separated women. The International Women's Year survey (Bryant, 1977) showed that in 1975 2 percent of the female population were separated and 5 percent divorced. The number of divorced women has risen to 6.3 percent, as reported by Department of Labor statistics in 1980, with no information on separated women (Bureau of Labor Statistics, 1980).

Separation may be a temporary or a permanent state; it may be the prelude to a divorce or to reconciliation, or a form of marriage in itself. Both partners may have agreed upon it, or either the wife or husband may have initiated it. Large numbers of husbands simply disappear each year, leaving wives in limbo. The separated wife may or (more often) may not receive some income from her husband; she may enjoy the state or be miserable. In other words, counselors of separated women may face a variety of feelings and realities revolving around the client's sense of herself and her relationship to home; every individual situation requires subtle and cautious investigation. Where separation from children is involved, the state of the client is that much more complex.

Divorce has a greater clarity. The legal situation is more definite, and a divorced woman has greater potential for assuming the responsibility for her own destiny. Divorce is now also a familiar status, not the stigma it was during previous generations. Between the mid-1960s and the mid-1970s the divorce rate doubled, making divorce one of the decade's most dramatic social and economic changes. If this trend continues, the first marriage of one out of every three persons between the ages of 25 and 35 presently married will end in divorce, and four out of ten second marriages will have a similar result (U.S. Department of Health, Education, and Welfare, 1979a). In 1977 there were 1.1 million divorces, and the divorce rate was about half the marriage rate (U.S. News and World Report, 1978). One social scientist predicts that in the future each adult will have an average of 3.5 marriages over a lifetime (Skalka, 1978). Such data mean that regardless of moral judgments divorce, just like marriage, has become a factor in every adult's life. Though long-term marriage will continue, serial monogamy will become an accepted feature of the social picture.

There has been surprisingly little emphasis in professional education on dealing with reactions to divorce and depressingly little discussion devoted to its various effects on finances and lifestyle. Since it always involves a reorganization of the home base, it is always traumatic; but the degree of trauma varies considerably. Seemingly, older couples tend to find a less than happy marriage still capable of a financial and psychological flexibility that makes formal divorce the least desirable alternative and therefore very serious, whereas younger couples seem more likely to abandon unhappy marriages more rapidly. Examples of two couples who happened to come to therapy during the same period show the different expectations which couples may have regarding their living arrangements. Both couples were unhappy with the emotional satisfactions brought by their marriages. The younger couple decided on a divorce, even though they would thereby worsen their financial situation. The older couple, realizing that divorce would cause them both to lose a way of life which they loved, decided to stay married but to change the form of their marriage. In both cases, the couples wanted more emotional rewards outside marriage; the younger couple found that desire incompatible with marriage, while the older couple rearranged their marriage contract to cope with it.

The recent easing of the divorce laws brought a deluge of divorces among older couples: the number of divorces among persons 45 or older doubled from 164,000 in 1964 to 315,000 in 1974 (U.S. News and World Report, 1977). Easier laws were not the only cause. Society is less critical of divorce than it was, and both women and men feel more comfortable with the idea of pursuing new interests separate from each other. Where children have been the bond keeping a marriage together, they have now left, allowing a divorce which might have been contemplated for years to become a practical choice.

However, divorce is not the only option in an unsatisfying marriage; renegotiation of the basic dynamics of the marriage is becoming increasingly popular. Many older couples find that divorce and remarriage are not worth the time, energy, and money they require; and they are unwilling to demolish the economic base which they have spent many years building. When such couples come to therapy, their task is to re-examine their expectations of both marriage and other living arrangements. Middle age contains at least the beginnings of wisdom and some of the habit of patience, with the result that many middle-aged couples show great practicality about overthrowing outdated expectations and changing their lifestyles within marriage.

Divorce usually affects women adversely in some way. Financially, the woman is likely to suffer more than will the man and to be worse off than she was before marriage. Fewer than half of divorced women receive any alimony or child support (IWY, 1976), and those who receive support get a median annual amount that is inadequate (in 1975, for instance, $1300). If assets acquired during marriage are not equally divided, the woman probably will be in a much worse position because of lower earning power. In 1977, the median income for a female-headed family was $7,765 compared to $17,720 for a husband/wife family (National Commission on Working Women, 1979). Many female-headed families survive only because of governmental programs, and many women heading families face poverty for the first time. Their practical and psychological problems result more from that poverty than from divorce itself (U.S. Commission on Civil Rights, 1978).

Nonetheless, divorce does not necessarily make women unhappier. Studies show that women living in traditional marriages have a higher rate of depression than do divorced women, whereas divorced men are more susceptible to depression than married men (Radloff, 1975; Bernard, 1975). Younger women are more likely than older women to remarry and to have a job or career, and middle-aged women are more vulnerable to depression, but younger women's lives are more likely to be complicated by young children. The data show that displaced homemakers who are middle-aged do adapt to working lives; among women aged 45 to 54, 69 percent of those formerly married (and 76 percent of those unmarried) are in the work force (U.S. Women's Bureau, 1976b).

A divorced woman will probably be alone for longer periods than during any other stage of her life. Most divorced persons remarry, but men do so at a greater rate than do women. Under age 30, women are more likely than men to remarry; but after 30 the probability shifts to men and increases steadily with age. Mature women are much less likely to remarry than are either mature men or younger women (U.S. Bureau of the Census, 1975b), especially if they are black (Troll, 1975). According to the Women's Bureau (*Mature Women Workers*, 1976b), in 1974 31 percent of all women aged 55 and over were *not* living in families, and among these 93 percent of the Caucasians and 87 percent of the minority races were living completely alone. (These figures include widowed and never-married women.)

Widowed Women

The International Women's Year survey (Bryant, 1977) reported that 18 percent of all women had been widowed at some time and that 12 percent of all adult women are currently widows. The older the woman, the more likely she is to be a widow: by age 65, women outnumber men of the same age by 144 to 100; after age 75 the ratio is 171 women to 100 men; after 85 it is 200 women to 100 men (Sommers, 1974, 1976). But because younger men die at a much greater rate than do younger women as results of war, accidents, and heart disease, widowhood is not just a phenomenon of old age. Half of all widows are age 60 or younger, and there are an estimated 90,000 widows under the age of 45 (Troll, 1975).

Expectation may be the factor that often makes widowhood a harsher experience than divorce. Here are the words of two widows, the first aged 29, the second 74. Mary's husband was killed in an automobile accident at the age of 30. (Some 50,000 people die on the roads each year.) She was left at the age of 27 with a home and two young children. "We still miss him and he's been gone for two years—especially on birthdays or holidays or vacation times. Special days. When we used to share. I still feel his presence in the house. I miss him beside me in bed at night. I feel like he *should* be there. Oh, of course I've started dating again and gone back to work. It took *forever* to sort out the finances, the insurance mess, but life's back in order again. I suppose. I really miss him. It's our dreams that hurt most now. We had all these dreams for us, for the kids. Now they won't happen." Elspeth was widowed at 72. "Harold died two years ago," she said, "and it grieved me terribly, and I missed him. And at the same time I felt lucky, because he was 73 and he'd lived longer than we knew he was expected to. We'd shared so much together, and he's still very much with me in all those memories. We'd talk about it sometimes. We both knew I would probably outlive him and be alone for at least a few years after he died."

"We both knew I would probably outlive him." Elspeth's words reveal the process that Neugarten (1977) terms the "rehearsal for widowhood" that makes it less traumatic for older than for younger women. A women's life expectancy is 76, that of a man 69, and women tend to marry men older than themselves so that they half expect widowhood at some time. According to Neugarten, older women therefore have a sense of being on time when widowhood occurs, and they therefore experience less trauma. While they most certainly grieve, it is thought that they handle the process differently from younger women (Bequaert, 1976; Lopata, 1973).

Some 59 percent of all women over 65 are widows, and on the average a woman can expect to live 11 years as a widow. Many women spend their last years not just alone but impoverished. In 1974 the median income for elderly couples was $7,200; that for widows and other elderly women not living with spouses was $2,700. In 1975, 62 percent of older widows were living alone, and most of the remainder were in old people's homes. There were five times as many widows as widowers, and 79 percent of older men were still married (Bryant, 1977). The typical older widow, therefore, faces both the results of social discrimination against sex in the form of poverty and also discrimination against age. Isolation is accompanied by legions of practical problems: poverty, lack of transportation, poor health services, inadequate recreation, poor housing, physical vulnerability, and ignorance of practical matters.

Never-married Women

A generation ago it was almost inconceivable that a woman could *choose* to remain unmarried, but today increasing numbers are doing so. According to the Census Bureau, in 1978 there were nearly three million women who had never married, and the number is expected to rise because the United States already has a surplus of six million women over men. Bequaert (1976) believes this figure to be an underestimate because "it is safe to assume some women conceal their never-married status if it is a barrier to social acceptance, as it often is" (p. 10).

It is still more socially acceptable to be married than to be never-married. Society still sees sexuality as best contained within the bounds of marriage, especially for females, and marriage is still the preferred avenue to child rearing. Sexism sees a woman who retains her independence, plans her own life, manages her work, and supports herself in the world as less than fully feminine. Sex stereotyping sees marriage as a form of protection for a woman but not for a man, and marriage remains the most acceptable form of alliance against solitude and the world's dangers. Thus the never-married woman may still have to fight society's tendency, and her own, to see her as a failure even though she is unlikely to hear from a therapist—as she would have a generation ago—that her singlehood is the principal *cause* of whatever psychological difficulties she might have.

Nonetheless, Bernard (1973) suggests that more women are postponing marriage or never marrying simply because the alternatives have more attraction and less social stigma than before. Legal changes, such as in taking out loans or establishing a credit rating, are making it easier to stay unmarried. Now unmarried women can buy their own homes and establish whatever living arrangement they wish within them. The image of the "old maid" searching for burglars under the bed is being replaced by that of an independent and confident woman who is both worker and head of household. Many unmarried woman state that they have a stronger sense of individuality and independence than they could maintain in any kind of marriage, and instead of following the pattern of the home demanded by society, they prefer to establish their own homes with or without others (including children). In sum, there is no longer any implied connection between singlehood and lack of fulfillment.

Generalizations about the comparative satisfactions of marriage and nonmarriage are not helpful. One recent study reported that, in general, married persons are happier than singles and that women report less stress and men more stress after marriage. But it also found that women get along better without men than men without women, and that couples without children are happier than couples with children, suggesting that factors other than marriage itself determine the degree of satisfaction (Campbell, 1975). Other recent studies using different indices come to various conclusions (e.g., Bernard, 1975; Radloff, 1975).

The therapist may find the issue likely to be self-sufficiency and sense of identity—whether or not the woman is married. Marriage remains a woman's most likely choice; only the unusual woman chooses not to marry. But both types of women are likely to face the same basic issues in different guises: autonomy and choice.

Living Together

Increasing numbers of women live with other people without wedlock. The number of unmarried adults of opposite sexes living together increased from 654,000 in 1970 to 1,321,000 in 1976 (*U.S. News and World Report*, 1978) and is thought to have doubled since. The number of same-sex couples living together has also increased, particularly as a result of the rising cost of living space. (Some of these are lesbian relationships, which will be discussed later.) The living-together trend is one of the major social phenomena of our time.

Economics provide a major incentive for living together: tax laws which are more favorable when both are earning good incomes; social security benefits that are higher for two singles than for a married couple; the inflated cost of housing; the need for members of an impoverished subgroup (e.g., students) to pool resources. Sexuality is a second motive, especially when living together takes the form of trial marriage, cohabitation, a temporary sexual affair, or a transient relationship; but sexual relationships between those who live together are by no means inevitable. The more powerful motive seems to be the desire for intimacy. Living together provides companionship, love, support, stability, and pleasure without what some people judge to be the undesirable features of traditional marriage, and the assertion that such relationships are immoral has much less impact than before.

Many couples live together because traditional marriage does not meet their needs. Some are testing their compatibility, especially after they have been through a divorce. Others believe that early marriage is unwise, desire sex without promiscuity or sneakiness, or are postponing legal ties until both have taken their basic steps in education and career. Others have stronger motives, choosing not to marry in order to preserve legal, social, and psychological freedoms and responsibilities which they perceive as inhibited by marriage. Living together may be less limiting to individuals because it emphasizes interdependence rather than dependence, so many couples seeking to avoid the sex-role stereotyping encouraged by traditional marriage will prefer this option as a means of fostering equality between the sexes and growth of both individuals.

The four varieties of marital status summarized all have a valid place in contemporary society. To the therapist, the status chosen by any given individual has no right or wrong except in relationship to its suitability to that individual. Many women will move through all these different ways of living during the course of their lives; and for the therapist as for them, the keynote must be the ability to preserve a sense of self regardless of marital status.

Change in Parenting

Parenthood in the 1980s offers a spectrum of options almost as multicolored as that of marriage. Because of the steep decline in the birthrate during the last decade or so, the economic needs, personal activities, and psychological orientation of the generation which created the highest recent birthrate (1955, when the rate was 25.0 births per 1,000 population) differ markedly from those of the generation which created the lowest (1976, when the rate was 14.8 births per 2,000 population). Fertility rates dropped with extraordinary speed. In 1970, each 1,000 women could be expected to bear 2,480 children during their lifetime; by 1976, the number had decreased to 1,760. The same six years brought a decrease of 5.5 million in the number of children under fourteen. In 1960, 76 percent of married or previously married women in their early 20s had children; in 1976, only 58 percent had children (U.S. Department of Health, Education, and Welfare, 1979a). The effects on society and on the lives of adults are striking.

Both the causes and the consequences of the declining birthrate are related to changes in the status of women. Such changes as the widespread use of simpler methods of contraception, increased availability of abortion, postponement of marriage, easier divorce, and greater opportunity for rewarding education and careers for young women have combined to make the parenting role less *inevitable* for women (Lipman-Blumen, 1976a). In turn, the decreasing amount of parenting frees women to use their time and money differently and confronts them with options never before available. When women had little control over the choice to bear and rear children, many other options were irrelevant; now the deferring of pregnancy, the avoidance of pregnancy, and the choice to remain childless have become normal problems which face most women.

The larger consequence has been that women have regained power over their bodies, and that power has given them the opportunity to gain power over other whole areas of their lives; it has been a major force in the drive for equality. In the past, men in their 20s spent their energy on the education and work that would win a place in the larger world for them, while women of the same age used their time to bear and rear children. Now women can take their place in the world at the same time as men, and this affects the whole pattern of their lives: education, early work experience, choice of career, the period for which work is interrupted by child rearing, the age at which child rearing ends, economic status, marriage and divorce, and so on. (Women do not necessarily choose permanently between work and child rearing; the recent small rise in the birthrate is thought to be due to women who waited until their early 30s to have children.)

As Hammer (1976) points out, no woman can now avoid what has become the first major issue of motherhood: whether or not to bear a child. Most women still decide to become parents, but the issues of when and how to do so have become, for the first time in history, a matter of great importance for most of them (Sexton, 1979). As one client in her mid-20s said, asking for advice regarding whether or not to become pregnant, "The only older women *without* children are either old maids or unable to get pregnant, and they all seem to think there is something wrong with them. And the women who had kids think everyone should. How can they help me? Nobody had to *choose* like I do!"

Not Parenting

As recently as the last decade, women without children were seen as unfortunate; today the absence of children is no longer seen as undeniable failure or misfortune. In other words, not parenting has become a valid choice for women. The cost of child raising has become a major factor in encouraging women not to parent. In 1980 it cost $50,000 or more for the *necessary* expenditures of raising a child to age eighteen (Fadem, 1980). In addition, the loss of the mother's earnings during the child rearing years and the frequency of divorce, which often results in the mother providing full financial support for the children, have become major influences.

At the same time, the desire to have children is still strong in most women, and this has led to the widespread popularity of *planned parenting*. An important departure from the automatic or fortuitous quality of parenthood in previous generations, planned parenting is an attempt to parent at some stages of life and not at others. An International Women's Year survey (Bryant, 1977) showed that the tendency to plan pregnancies varies according to age, race, and education. Younger women tend to plan their pregnancies more often than do older women; more highly educated women plan more than do less educated women; white and Spanish-American women plan more than do other ethnic groups. About 40 percent of all white women engage in planning. The effect is that women in those groups which plan their parenthood spend fewer years on the process of child raising; this in turn has major effects on their careers and economic status. Thus the significance of women's freedom not to parent is the increased degree of control which they gain over their lives.

Two-parenting

Some 55 percent of children born now will grow up in the traditional two-parent family with both their biological parents (*Spokeswoman*, March 1978). But even the dynamics of the two-parent family are changing because of the increase in dual-worker families. Parents can now expect to change their roles within the family, at least over a period of years, and the number of working mothers alters children's perceptions of the female sex role.

Single Parenting

The remaining 45 percent of children will spend some of their childhood with only one biological parent in the home. The Bureau of the Census recently predicted that, of children born in 1977, 10 percent will be at least one year old before their mothers marry; another 5 percent will live for some time with a separated parent; 3 percent will live with one parent after the death of the other parent; and 27 percent will live with only one parent following a divorce (Glick, 1979). Others will live with women who have never married—as either illegitimate, adopted, or foster children.

Most discussions of single-parenting focus on its effects on the children, but the consequences for the female single parent are just as important (Hungerford and Paolucci, 1977). As both nurturer and provider, she is both the center of the home and its link to the wider world. Four main areas of responsibility now belong to her solely or principally: within the home; at work; in social institutions such as school and church; and in the personal network of friends, relatives, and particularly of the children's father (Rapoport and Rapoport, 1978). The consequent effort may be less than that needed to maintain a bad marriage, but no single parent can avoid major difficulties in balancing all these responsibilities. It is important to be aware that this fact is true regardless of the sex of the parent, as clearly depicted in the movie *Kramer vs. Kramer*. The multiple responsibilities a single parent must assume are consistent with the role. The emergence of growing numbers of single parenting men is bringing a new dimension to fatherhood and is a viable alternative in separation and divorce.

Step-parenting

Increasing numbers of women and men are now called upon to function as step-parents. The situation toward which society is moving has been called (Toffler, 1980) the "aggregate family," in which a number of adults have different parental responsibilities toward children who may or may not have a biological kinship. The result is a great complexity of roles; any parent may be called upon to act in two or more of these roles at the same time. Because children are most often placed in the custody of the woman after a divorce, and because men frequently choose not to be awarded custody at least until they remarry, step-parenting falls more heavily on women than on men.

Concepts of Parenting

The period following World War II is marked by a departure from the historical norm that amounted to an excessive preoccupation with children. As the number of children declines, as the population ages, and as women work more outside the home, the concept of parenting is changing.

It was, for instance, once accepted that a working mother's absence fostered juvenile delinquency. However, studies using psychological measures of the personality and adjustment of children show no correlation at all with maternal employment (Burchinal, 1963). Working mothers, it is now thought, may well create healthier children (Hanson, 1977; Gold and Andreas, 1976). One study showed that middle-class mothers who were working (either part time or full time) and working-class mothers employed part time were both associated with a higher degree of family interaction and with child rearing practices more likely to create autonomy and self-reliance (Douvan, 1963).

Another myth damaging to the mental health of mothers seems also to be declining in acceptance. The culture previously fostered the idea that perfect children were produced by perfect mothers and that a child's failure was a mother's failure (Wilborn, 1976). This concept was implicit in the child rearing handbooks of the 1950s; it placed an unjust strain on women, encouraging them to live vicariously and to lose sight of themselves as anything but mothers. No myth could be more damaging to the short-term economic status and the long-term self-image of women. Today, mothers tend less to submerge themselves in the lives of their children (Lipman-Blumen, 1976a). Interactions between mothers and children seem to occur more often in a framework of reasonable autonomy for both rather than on the polarity of dependence/independence.

Mothers have begun to realize that child rearing is only one of the processes of adult development and that attention to one's own development does not necessarily mean rejection of the children. Thus the major issue in parenting today is no longer the primacy of children's rights but the proper balance between the growth of the child and the development of the mother, with the assumption that the two, no matter how intertwined, need not impede each other. (For further discussion, see Satir, 1972; Dinkmeyer and McKay, 1973; Minuchin, 1974; and Hammer, 1976.)

Change in Relationships

The political and social changes induced by women's increasing equality during the last few years have brought important influences to bear upon women's relationships with men and with each other. The early stages of the women's movement almost immediately encouraged women to feel differently about men and, equally important, to express their feelings old or new much more openly. The ensuing cultural shock waves have made it difficult to keep one's balance; liberation seemed to bring up everything disconcerting that women had ever suppressed—anger, deceitfulness, resentment, and contempt—all wrapped in a sense of injustice. But this early anxiety seems to be declining as the shock passes. Women activists even acknowledge some men as allies; and while most men still play out their old sex role, many have come strongly to favor the cause of female equality—and some to admit that it is the best route to men's liberation. The depth and shape of the changes in relationships between the sexes will not be truly apparent for decades, but the signs of what seems to be one of the most potent cultural changes of our century are already visible.

The most widespread sign is in the area of sex-role differentiation. Both sexes—women markedly more than men—are trying out behaviors previously prescribed only for the opposite sex; it is now barely acceptable to suggest that a person does something or should do something simply as a result of sexual differentiation (Pleck, 1976, 1979; Farrell, 1974). The change is not yet as widespread as its publicity might suggest; studies carried out in connection with International Women's Year discovered that some social groups resist it much more strongly than others, especially the lower socioeconomic classes, the less educated, and older people (Bryant, 1977). Women themselves remain divided. As the National Commission on the Observance of International Women's Year put it, "The present times are critical and controversial for women. Half of them are now welcoming the efforts to change and strengthen women's status, while the other half of the female population is split between those who are change-resistant and those who are spectators to the controversy" (ibid, p. 46).

Nonetheless, evidence of basic change in cultural attitudes is readily available. In 1976 a survey funded by the Department of Health, Education, and Welfare reported significant changes in attitudes towards sex roles. All groups of women surveyed, for instance, showed increasing similarity in attitudes about whether a woman should stay at home or work, the crucial issue in women's search for equality. Women presently working are more egalitarian in this matter than women not presently working or women who have never worked, but since the number of working women continues to increase, so presumably will favorable attitudes towards the issue. The survey also shows men as affecting women's attitudes towards equality. The more educated the husband, the more likely was his wife to have egalitarian attitudes; this suggests that egalitarian women choose and are chosen by better-educated men or that husbands influence their wives' sex-role attitudes favorably, or both (U.S. National Institute of Mental Health, 1976). The survey's overall conclusion was that women are clearly developing a more egalitarian definition of the rights and responsibilities of females and males.

From the nonsexist viewpoint, the following attitudinal changes noted by various commentators seem the most significant:

1. The amount of behavior based solely on simplistic sex-role differentiation is decreasing. People are developing at least the "capacity to tolerate" (in the phrase of Weingarten, 1978) a variety of mixtures of dependence and independence in both females and males. It is no longer inevitable for individuals to frustrate their practical and psychological needs through rigid adherence to sex-role stereotypes.
2. Androgyny and sex-role transcendence, whether of personality or behavior, are becoming increasingly popular with both sexes but especially among women, who have more to gain in practical terms from refusing confinement to their sex-role stereotypes (Skovkolt, 1978).
3. Especially among the young, the newly emerging relationship between the sexes is a clear attempt at equality. As the authors of *Alive and Aware* express it, "role-making rather than role-taking is becoming the norm" (Miller, Nunnally, and Wackman, 1975).

4. As females have become a majority of the population, and as more of them do not marry and bear children, women are ceasing to be seen as only subsidiary to men. The female is increasingly seen as an independent entity, no longer fully dependent upon the male for either survival or fulfillment. Correspondingly, the range of possible relationships between women and men increases.

5. Marriage is more often perceived as a relationship in which responsibilities are shared rather than divided. Such burdens as earning or child care can be shifted from female shoulder to male shoulder and vice versa rather than confined to each partner as gender-prescribed duties and pleasures.

6. Women are developing a greater sense of control over their own lives and better ability to handle them. Their self-confidence and their sense of their personal rights are improving, resulting in more women who want and need men for better reasons than just to survive.

7. Equal opportunity to work and equal rewards from work are not yet a reality for women, but the possibility of attaining them is better than ever before. This movement toward equality may at times increase antagonism between the sexes; but in the basic matter of respect for ability to deal with the world of work, women are gaining steadily.

8. The next expression of women's search for equality appears to be greater assertion of their right to power within social structures, institutions, and professions which have traditionally been male-dominated. If women succeed in gaining power in proportion to their number, the structures and institutions will themselves change. Long a goal of the women's movement, this situation will present our culture with problems it has never before faced.

9. The basic shift in relationships stems from a fresh recognition of autonomy and interdependence. Our society has traditionally discouraged autonomy in both sexes and encouraged dependence in females; now it seems to be encouraging as mentally healthy the concept of linkage between autonomous individuals rather than "togetherness" or "subordination." The idea of partnership is widespread. As Weingarten (1978) states, "When interdependence works, there is sufficient flexibility to accommodate shifting stances frequently. Each person knows there is leeway and feels free to use it."

10. Finally, women seem to be finding it less necessary to define their relationships with the world only or primarily in terms of their relationships with men. They see themselves as people and as individuals, with all the needs and potentials of any—not just a female—individual.

One of the best signs that women are developing a sense of their own worth as individuals and as a sex is the changing relationship of women to women. The image of other women as "the girls," with its explicit derogation of adulthood, is so antique that it is embarrassing. Women today consider each other more seriously as individuals who are capable of existing anywhere on the spectrum of life's choices. Instead of merely sharing the trivia of being second-class citizens, instead of putting each other down or of seeing each other mainly as rivals for men, many women today see other women as the greatest means of support in their own struggles. The concepts of friendship, comradeship, and companionship have historically applied almost exclusively to males; now they characterize many female-to-female relationships. This is a major cultural change whose implications for the future are not yet predictable, but it may ultimately prove the basis for maintaining changes in all the other areas mentioned in this chapter.

Change in Work

Work is the most important area of current change in women's lives, and therefore the whole of Chapter 6 is devoted to it; but a brief summary of major changes in the area is necessary at this time.

Almost all women have always worked, and the patterns of their work have usually differed from those of men. Women have always worked within the home, where the family traditionally displayed clear sex-typed behavior and strong cooperation. The man brought home the pig and the woman made it into bacon, both working equally hard, each essential to the other's comfort and survival. Many women have also historically worked outside the home. When agriculture demanded the greater share of our labor force, much of the labor came from women, usually working the family's land but sometimes working as hired labor or slaves. When some families grew rich enough to afford domestic workers, they hired more females than males as servants. When factories came into existence, they hired echelons of women for what was euphemistically called "light" labor; and when offices expanded with the increase in commerce, women replaced men in clerical jobs. The invention of laborsaving devices for the home has since reduced the amount of physical work required as a homemaker, and agricultural mechanization has dramatically reduced the amount of human labor needed in the fields. Therefore, the greatest single change in women's working lives during this century has been the increase in the number of those doing paid labor for employers. Especially since 1960, the increase in women working for wages has been rapid; in 1960, 37.8 percent worked, in 1970 43.4 percent, and in 1979, 51.1 percent (U.S. Bureau of the Census, 1980).

The typical female patterns of work follow.

Worker and Homemaker

In 1978, the Census Bureau reported that almost half of all married women and 74 percent of divorced women worked outside the home. In sum, 50.7 percent of adult females (or 43 million) work and keep homes, indicating that it is now normal for a woman to balance both roles.

Full-time versus Part-time Work

Women working full time currently make up 28 percent of the work force and those working part time are estimated to be 18 percent of the work force (Bureau of Labor Statistics, 1980a). In addition most unpaid volunteer community and political jobs are done by women, most of whom are wives and mothers. Shifting between full-time and part-time work is thought to be more common among women than among men, partly because of child rearing and partly because of the low-paid jobs in which women cluster. Where men take the permanence of full-time work as a measure of both their social status and even their value, women must find other criteria.

Continuous versus Intermittent Work

The male pattern is to stay in the work force continuously until retirement; interruptions caused by unemployment or illness usually seem extraordinary and threatening to men. The female pattern is almost the opposite. Being occupied full time in the workforce is more unusual than not working; the normal female work pattern is intermittency. Some women work as continuously as do equivalent males, but most find interruptions in their work lives unavoidable for various reasons in addition to unemployment and illness. The average work life of a male is 45 years and that of a female 25 years, though the present generation of workers will reduce the gap considerably. Women adapt work patterns to fit family needs, making more frequent practical and emotional adjustments in this area than do males. Men average 4.5 years in one job while women average about 2 years.

Though the family sees the ability to work as an important contribution, it values the work life of an intermittent worker less than that of the continuous worker; the woman who works intermittently is essentially subordinate both on the job and within the family. For example, the female rather than the male will stay home for those periods required by child rearing; and when she returns to work she will find it easier to find another job both because hers is probably a low-paid occupation and because of the high turnover among similarly situated females. Intermittent or even potentially intermittent workers seem less valuable than continuous workers both to the employer and to the family. Employers, for instance, are suspicious that a young woman may abandon a high-level job because of pregnancy and therefore they prefer a male. Or when both spouses are executives or professionals, the wife will normally surrender her position to the husband's need for mobility, while the reverse is still rare (though there are strong signs of change in this area). Until very recently the law allowed the most common cause of intermittency (pregnancy) to permit employers and institutions to *force* a woman into giving up a particular education, job, or even career.

Intermittency carries a series of consequences. It is more difficult to display the steady upward rise characteristic of the "successful" worker. A woman cannot earn as much as does a man during a lifetime, even under conditions of equal pay. An intermittent worker cannot invest as much of herself in the future of a job or advancement within a career, and intermittency breaks the string of contacts and the flow of current information upon which job success depends. Thus intermittent workers gain less self-esteem from the area of work, even if their earnings are crucial to the family and their work enjoyable.

Heads of Families

According to the Bureau of the Census, in 1978 15 percent of our families were headed by women. Unemployed heads of families must rely on support from private or government sources. Thus many female heads of families face a difficult dilemma—either they must go to work and suffer the anxiety and stigma of not providing full-time child care, or they must stay home and suffer the anxiety and guilt of living on welfare. A woman who is homemaker, worker, and head of family occupies the most arduous living situation our society offers.

Heads of Household

The choice not to marry, divorce, and widowhood have made the woman who heads her own independent household a normal figure in our society. Preliminary data indicate that among women who begin heading their households while young, the pattern of work life is quite similar to that of most men.

Social change requires any woman to anticipate moving into any or all of these five categories at some time in her life. No woman can count on permanent membership in any one category, nor can she safely predict the length of time she will spend in it, nor can she fully control the time of her life at which she will enter or leave each category. Thus her work life is subject to much less control than is that of a man. The intermittent female worker appears normal to society; the intermittent male worker deviant. In both cases, departure from the status stereotyped as appropriate to one's sex brings problems—both society and the individual are more "comfortable" with a man who is a continuous worker and a woman who is an intermittent worker. This is the inner meaning of the statement that society does not regard women's work as highly or take it as seriously as that of men; this in turn means that neither society nor the individual woman regards her work life as worthwhile to the same extent as that of a man. The ramifications in terms of responsibility, training, promotion, pay, respect, and self-respect are evident. In sum, it is clear that the practical and the psychological realities of women's lives are intertwined and that a female has less inherent power over either set of realities than does a male.

An opposing tendency—to devalue women who do not work, or do not work for pay—has recently developed. Many women who chose to be homemakers exclusively justly complain that some people look down on them for not working, a cruel trick which uses the recent rise in social esteem of one group of women (the paid workers) to depreciate the value of other groups (homemakers and volunteers). There is a tendency for some elements of society to see paid work as not just the right but the duty of women; many men now take it for granted that their womenfolk will earn a full-time living and give full-time care to the home and family. Following a divorce, ex-husbands and many courts see a woman's ability to work as both her duty and their own justification for ceasing to give her financial support, even if the husband earns much more now and relied in the past on her earnings and/or domestic work to create his current status. Such men behave very much as though they had leased a car rather than made a marriage.

The major social change of our times in this area is that women have to take their work lives more seriously than before. A therapist cannot assume that working or not working is better at any given time for any particular client, though one needs to remember that full-time, long-term work brings the economic power that is a major source of much human status and safety. Other factors in the typical woman's life, however, require that both she and the therapist be flexible *and* engage in long-term planning. The data are undeniable; a woman can reasonably expect to be responsible for her own economic well-being for most of her life. At any time her earning ability may make the crucial difference to her family's well-being, especially to that of her children, as well as to her own. Every woman should therefore develop and maintain the ability to survive economically. The romantic viewpoint that encourages a woman of any age to see herself as needing to work only until she finds a man to take care of her is not just infuriating, but pernicious to the point of seeming deliberately intended to keep women powerless and inferior in status. Too many women still see the ability to earn a decent income as a bonus rather than a necessity. Too many fail to see that this alone is enough to force them into dependence upon men or the government. The need for women to be able to work, and to work preferably in well-paid jobs, is thus the single most important obligation which they should feel, the basic fact of female existence today and the brute reality that underlies the antiquated myths of femininity still promulgated by the socialization process.

Change in Education

Training and education are the keys to advancement in work, and the distinctive feature of this area is that too little rather than too much change is taking place. Women proceed far less often than do men to the advanced or specialized training that better jobs demand. The continuing differential between females and males in respect to education is evident in the data. Education reaches more people for longer periods than ever in the past; of all persons presently age 25 or more, the average length of education is 12.4 years and two-thirds have reached the high school level. Females are more likely than males to complete high school, but they are much less likely than males to pursue education beyond high school. Their proportion at each succeeding level of education declines rapidly: 43.3 percent of females and 35.0 percent of males stop after four years of high school; but 19.6 percent of females compared with 22.7 percent of males have completed three years of college, and 20.0 percent of females and 27.5 percent of males have completed four or more years of college (U.S. Bureau of the Census, 1980a).

Two distinct factors prevent females from receiving the amount and kind of education they need, both of them clear signs of society's discrimination against females. First, there are many external barriers to their advancement. Despite Affirmative Action programs strong enough to raise ire among opponents, institutions of education still have policies, practices, and attitudes which either operate against women or fail to encourage them. For example, policies on transfer credits, lack of deferred payment plans, lack of child care facilities, and the absence of role models among faculty and administration all affect women more adversely than they do men (Westervelt, 1975). Our educational system still perceives people as students, not as adults with complex responsibilities. These factors cooperate with external events in a woman's life to hobble her educational progress: early marriage, pregnancy, family tasks, loss of "attractiveness," etc. Such external barriers to advancement quickly create internal barriers—beliefs internalized by the female which guarantee the comparative unimportance of further education in their general view of life. The lack of rewards for women in the world of work, the lack of community support for female success, and the perceived inappropriateness of certain subjects and programs for women all create internal beliefs which either make educational effort seem not worth her while or give her a sense of conflict between being feminine and being an educational success.

In an effort to overcome these very serious long-term barriers, federal and state anti-discrimination programs have begun to envision the teachers and counselors within the schools as the major prospective agents of cultural change, and there are some optimistic signs. The number of women returning to school to earn high school certification or a General Equivalency Degree (GED), for instance, is thought to have increased greatly during the 1970s though the precise increase is unknown because the GED Testing Service does not report data by sex.

But the barriers are so strong that success for the present is at best dubious. There is the familiar example of the federal Comprehensive Employment and Training Act of 1973 (CETA) which funded states and communities to offer minority groups, including women, the training in the classroom and on the job that would improve their earning ability. In general, CETA programs have laudable goals: to provide low-income women with skills for finding and retaining jobs, to offer career counseling, to support entry into GED courses and post-secondary programs, and to give on-the-job training with pay. Like most such large federal programs, however, CETA is under attack, its ability to achieve those goals in dispute, and its funds a prime target for budget cutting. Charges have been made asserting that communities have used the funds to hire more women in low-paid, low-status jobs and that their advancement is not even discussed, since the communities tend to regard the money as provided for them rather than for the women. Another example arises from vocational education. The number of women enrolling in two-year programs of vocational education (secondary and post-secondary) increased by 200 percent in the decade prior to 1975, but evidence presented in that year to the Citizen's Advisory Council on Women showed the increase to have been mostly in areas leading to the traditional low-paid, low-status jobs. While females made up 55 percent of total enrollments, they were 92 percent of the enrollment in home economics classes, 76 percent in office job skills, and 85 percent in classes related to health occupations (U.S. Citizen's Advisory Council on the Status of Women, 1976).

Another example is taken from the apprenticeship programs run by the trade unions. Although females began active participation in the trade union movement as early as 1824, industry has always given them unskilled jobs and given men the skilled jobs. Apprenticeship programs leading to the acquisition of skills could legally prohibit females until very recently, with the result that in 1978 only 2 percent of all registered apprentices were female (National Commission on Working Women, 1979). In 1973, only 17 percent of all union members and only 7 percent of the governing boards of all unions, professional associations, and state employee associations were female (U.S. National Commission on the Observance of International Women's Year, 1976). Thus the major force in ameliorating the working conditions of males was simply never an influence on the work of women. The trade union movement chose to become a notoriously male bastion, its leadership almost without exception male, functioning to discriminate against women's employment by preventing their membership in some unions and attending to their needs only where they wanted to unionize an industry in which almost all the existing workers were female. Of course, women continued to work in nonunion jobs in which they provided a vast pool of low-paid labor. Some trade unionists realize that their movement's perception of women workers as threats rather than as colleagues may have been its single most important historical error, and there are signs that some remedy may now be sought; but regardless of future intention, the present effect has been to exclude women from the higher pay and greater benefits of union membership (Wertheimer, 1980). Unions report, in response, that women have been more reluctant than men to unionize, with the effect that nonunionized industries now tend to be those based on female labor. If so—if the women themselves are partially at fault—this situation is a particularly strong example of women's internalization of impediments to their own equality with men.

A major example of the difficulty of overcoming past patterns of educational and training discrimination currently arises from the country's military forces. As recently as October 8, 1975, the President of the United States signed legislation permitting women, for the first time, to apply for appointment to classes at the Army, Navy, and Air Force Academies. The U.S. Coast Guard and the Merchant Marine Academies opened their classes to women just as recently, with admission determined by competitive examination. (The Merchant Marine Academy was the first to graduate a female.) The resultant confusion has been one of the highest stress situations ever faced by our nation's educational establishment. Though the military's efforts to provide equality have been ardent and seem likely to be successful, they have required maximum energy from everyone concerned. They therefore provide our best example of precisely how difficult it is for the male educational establishment to translate a simple and undeniable demand for equal educational opportunity into a living reality.

Change in Politics

The country has made major progress during recent years in creating legislation to improve both equality and equality of opportunity for women, but it is noteworthy that almost all such legislation arouses controversy. Women's issues —the Equal Rights Amendment, abortion, funding for day-care centers, registration for the draft, CETA, even the Food Stamp program—have consistently been in the forefront of political debate, a fact noteworthy because it shows the amount of energy expended in the country not just in advocation of women's rights but also against them. One tends to assume that legislation has taken or will take care of women's problems, but the violence of the debate suggests that this is simply not true. Legislation is as much a matter of administration as of statute; a law enacted is not a law implemented, and it can swiftly become a law gutted. Especially if the country's economic situation worsens, present tendencies will continue to reduce women's rights and the funding for their needs and to pit them against other deserving groups (as in Affirmative Action or veterans' preference). To protect their rights, women will have to acquire permanent political skill and influence.

So far, men have enacted all the legislation affecting women's lives. Even today women hold less than 10 percent of all elective offices in the United States (*The Spokeswoman*, 1980). To the House of Representatives in 1976, a good election year for women's rights, there were elected eighteen women; in 1978, sixteen women were elected to the House and of the thirteen women who ran for the Senate, two won. In 1978 women won 10.2 percent of the total seats in state legislatures—the first time in history that their proportion reached double digits— and in 1978 there were two female Governors, four female Lieutenant Governors, ten Secretaries of State, and six State Treasurers (*The Spokeswoman*, Dec. 15, 1978). More women ran for office in 1978 than ever before, but *The Spokeswoman* commented: "A woman is much more likely to be nominated for a campaign against a sure-win incumbent than allowed a shot at a winnable race. Where there is an open seat with a chance of victory, the opportunity generally goes to the white male." Women have much greater difficulty raising campaign funds than do men. Clearly, therefore, most of the country's voters—male or female—do not yet trust women as much as men to make the decisions that drastically affect women's lives.

Those who determine the manner in which laws will be implemented are also overwhelmingly male. Women are a tiny minority among Justices of the State High Courts and of the Federal Courts and a scarcely visible proportion of the judiciary as a whole. The first female Chief Justice of a State High Court was appointed in 1975, and there had never been a woman on the United States Supreme Court until Sandra O'Connor's appointment in 1981. In our history we have seen only six women in the Cabinet, most of them quite recently, and there has never been a female Attorney General. In the executive branch of the federal government, where regulations as important as statutes come into being, women hold 43 percent of the white-collar jobs but only 3.4 percent of the highest-paid jobs where final decisions are made (U.S. Office of Personnel Management, 1978). The first female United States Attorney was appointed during the 1970s, and of all federal judges ruling on administrative law, only about 5 percent are female.

The issue of political and legal power, of course, is not clearly sexist. Many men in powerful positions pay very close and fair attention to the effects of their decisions on the lives of women as women, and many women in high office are not interested. The political issue is more one of being heard and of getting the right things done by our elected and appointed officials of whatever sex, and in this respect political powerlessness is analogous to women's habitual personal powerlessness. Here, as professionals, counselors and therapists can be surprisingly influential. Both legislatures and courts depend on information for their decisions; they need both anecdotal information and impartial opinion as well as documentation by statistics. They rely on the professions to make known the needs and concerns of their constituencies in a useful manner. They rely on them for information, regarding them as avenues for their own education. The legislative process, in fact, is not just a matter of lobbying and pressure groups but one of acquiring the best possible information over time. At the national level, several organizations provide information about the political interests of women to legislators and information about the political activities of legislatures to women.* This information may well not reach legislators or appointees at the state and local levels. A thoroughly professional role for the therapist and counselor, therefore, is to see that it does reach the right people and to evaluate it from a local perspective. This is an assertion of power not as a matter of strident militancy but as a matter of professional and civic responsibility, routine and natural in the operation of a democracy.

---

*The most useful organizations providing information about the political affairs of women are: The National Women's Education Fund, 1532 16th Street, N.W., Washington, D.C. 20036; The National Women's Political Caucus, Inc., 1411 K Street, N.W., Washington, D.C. 20005; The National Organization of Women, 425 13th Street, N.W., Suite 1048, Washington, D.C. 20004; and The Women's Equity Action League, 805 15th Street, N.W., Washington, D.C. 20005.

5

How To Help the Client
in Transition

The theme of preceding chapters has been that cultural change is now a basic issue in most therapeutic situations with female clients, regardless of the specific matter brought to therapy. Because our definition of what it means to be a woman is changing, and because this change places most women under pressures unique to their sex, standard mental health theories and techniques are out of date; therapists need to respond delicately to personal problems that are more than individual. In this chapter we examine some specific examples of how a therapist can bring the broader cultural dimension into the consciousness of clients.

Figure and Ground

The role of therapy in a world full of change is best understood by means of the Gestalt concept of "figure" and "ground." A client entering therapy normally presents a specific problem or symptom; that is, when she examines her situation, this particular problem or symptom emerges as the "figure" from the background of her life and experiences as a woman. In therapy, that particular figure will change and, in time, other figures will emerge from the background because, in the words of Erving and Miriam Polster, "the power of the ground is in its fertility" (1973, p. 30). The Polsters suggest that the "ground" of an individual's life contains three elements: prior living, unfinished business, and the flow of present experience. A therapist will find that the ground constantly produces new figures from any combination of those elements, even while she or he works with one emerging figure. In other words, the whole client is potentially accessible through any figure.

For this reason, traditional distinctions among the different branches or specializations of counseling and therapy are misleading, however practical. A woman coming to career counseling, for example, is presenting her work problems as figure but cannot solve them without making changes in all other areas of her being. A woman undergoing psychiatric treatment for depression will also, as she changes, alter the way she works, her relationship with her family, and her attitude toward her body; and if the treatment neglects an area such as career counseling, it may leave her perilously stranded. Ideally, every counselor or therapist should be able to deal with all these issues as each becomes figure for the client. In fact, they will respond very differently according to their own training, background, and preferences.

Take, for example, the range of problems faced by a newly divorced woman with children. Most of her problems will be those of poverty rather than of divorce: housing, schooling, budgeting, nutrition, medical care, work, the cost of entertainment and social life, the loss of luxuries which save time and energy, and the lack of money to purchase pleasure and rest. Insofar as these problems can be remedied by advice or by information, counseling and therapy can obviously help; they can also assist changes in attitude. Many women find single parenting a heavy burden, especially if they lack help from an extended family; but others find it not necessarily worse than dual parenting because less time and energy goes into arguments and decisions and because children prove capable of a greater maturity than expected. Professionals can help clients change from negative to positive attitudes by showing the client how to abandon elements of traditional dual-parent child rearing that are undesirable in a single-parent situation. To do this, they need to help in the much neglected area of self-nurture. The tendency of all single parents is to forget that caring for oneself is not just an individual right but an obligation to the family's mental health. Women in particular tend to equate "self-care" with "selfishness" and to give the children priority over themselves consistently. In turn, self-care will display itself in changed attitudes toward the practical problems induced by poverty. In that sequence, where does counseling end and therapy begin? Or vice versa?

The same shifting spectrum faces a woman unaccustomed to the world of work who has now become the head of a household. On one level, she will confront great practical difficulties—finding work, getting used to a new routine, retraining, and so forth. Her major problems will be time, money, and energy (U.S. Women's Bureau, 1975 and 1977d). On another level, however, she will soon face the problems characteristic of a mother accustomed to work: child care, time management, and loneliness. These could rapidly combine to overwhelm her with a sense of powerlessness. The fantasy common among married people, that divorced people face a joyful world full of social and sexual freedom, is just that—a fantasy. The main problem facing all divorced people is the formation of meaningful relationships (Bequaert, 1976), and this is worsened if their time and money is consumed by work and single parenting. Relationships formed while married tend to disintegrate, and marriage has usually hobbled a woman's ability to establish relationships on her own; the result is shyness, isolation, and loneliness. Some divorced women therefore fling themselves too hastily into intimate relationships and meet with disaster, often finding a new partner who surprises them by turning out to be very much like the old. Again, it is almost impossible to define by traditional terms the kind of mental health assistance which a woman in this situation needs.

Exploring Identity

At all levels the woman's need will be to explore and experiment. Divorced mothers need to see themselves in a new role, with new choices; and especially if they have another intimate partner immediately available, they need to examine thoroughly the factors in themselves that led or contributed to the divorce. This is particularly true of older women who have lived the role of traditional wife for many years. Thus all professionals need to foster exploration by the client. Exactly what form this will take varies according to therapist and client. Guided fantasy can be a powerful tool. Under the therapist's direction, the client may imagine that she has climbed with great effort to a hilltop. She is tired and needs to do something to refresh herself. What does she do? Now she looks out at the view that stretches beneath her; what does she see? What fears does she experience? What excitement does she feel? What new self emerges to match the new vista? What does she want to do first? And the real world can be as helpful as fantasy.

A divorced woman may need to join a social organization for singles, to move away from a community where singles are rare, to change her attitude to her extended family, to learn to distinguish between men who like her and men who use her, to take the initiative with a man who appeals to her, or to find support among women rather than men so that she does not equate the social with the sexual. What, in all this, will be the role of the mental health professional? Perhaps that role will be to encourage certain qualities no matter what the specific problem may be—to emphasize patience and allay excessive eagerness, to discourage passivity, to foster a sense of autonomy, to counter the feeling that a woman needs a man in order to be or feel like a complete person.

The newly divorced person has to establish a fresh sense of identity, and because a large part of our identity comes less from what we "are" than from what we do, the process requires equal attention to the practical and the psychological. A woman accustomed to deriving status and self-esteem from being a wife and helpmate, to gaining satisfaction from being the nurturer, homemaker, and power behind the throne, to merging her identity with that of her spouse, will have to establish her new autonomy by doing as well as feeling; incompetence in either area may bring on a severe identity crisis. Displaced, she may see herself as belonging nowhere and eventually as being nobody. Any restoration of her identity will involve her functioning as head of her own household; and the task of any mental health professional is to help her develop a sense that, though the home has changed, it has not vanished, and that her identity is not annihilated but new. Both client and therapist will therefore necessarily work with the whole range of behavior as well as attitudes.

Problems of identity often manifest themselves in seemingly trivial matters. One client, for instance, was obsessed with whether or not she should require her husband, as part of the divorce settlement, to buy her a lifetime membership in the club to which they had belonged as a couple. It may sound absurd—but it was her method of acknowledging the critical difficulties in re-establishing a social role which divorce dissolved. Another client was distressed for weeks regarding what she should do about the bowling team, sponsored by the church, to which she and her ex-husband belonged. Another repeatedly scheduled and postponed a vacation on the grounds that her grown children might disapprove. These are practical manifestations of the deep psychological difficulty of suddenly having to choose an individual life-style rather than merely accept and react to a given life-style. None of these clients could establish a new sense of identity without deciding these practical problems, but the problems could not be decided without a freshened sense of individual identity.

Life-style develops slowly over the years and is constructed largely out of habit. In a time of strong social change, habit works against instead of for the individual. The spectrum of choices brought by change can be overwhelming: live alone or with others? Stay here or move? Be "nice" or "naughty"? Divorce, widowhood, or the option of remaining single make women face problems of intimacy which marriage enabled them to *avoid*: monogamy, celibacy, promiscuity, bisexuality, or asexuality? Many encounter deep spiritual problems, such as when "Do I still go to this church?" turns into "Do I still believe in God?" All encounter the need to redefine home, a problem especially serious for women because the sense of home and the sense of self are apparently more closely intertwined in women than in most men (Lowenthal, Thurnher, Chiriboga, et al, 1976).

Thus any mental health professional will find a divorced or displaced woman dealing with all the following basic questions:

1. Life planning. How will I cope with the overall pattern of occupational, financial, and social matters in my life, first right now, then in the years to come?
2. Social relationships. How and how far do I move into the world, by myself and with others, in my daily life and in the broader picture?
3. Sexual needs. What really is my sexual being, and how do I find the kind and amount of sexual contact and of intimacy which best suit my new self?
4. Solitariness. How do I preserve the solitude I need, accept the loneliness I feel, use my independence to my advantage, and know when to abandon them all?

No client, of course, will state the issues of her life in these terms. For the client, the figure will more likely be presented in such terms as the following:

TRISH: I feel like an adolescent again, waiting for the phone to ring, worrying about what to say at a party, wondering who I can ask to go with me to the movie, feeling uncomfortable walking into church alone. I'm 39 years old; what's happening to me?

SHARON: I don't want to go to bed with anyone right now, and yet I long to feel a body next to mine again.

ALICE: There are lay-offs coming at work. I took this damn job because there were two of us supporting the family, and I'm stuck with it because now I'm the sole support for the two kids and myself. If I lose it, what do I do? But if I don't get laid off, I don't want to stay there—doing that for the next ten years!

MEG: I'm so lonely and down. I came home from work, made myself dinner, and sat in front of the TV and cried all evening. I've done that several times since I saw you last week, and the weekend was worse. What are you doing to me?

Solitariness is a most important issue. A woman will probably spend more time alone after divorce than at any other stage of her life. Most divorced persons remarry, but men do so at a greater rate than do women. Under age 30, women have a greater probability of remarriage than men, but after 30 the probability shifts to men and increases steadily with age. In addition, about 18 percent of all women are likely to be widowed at some time. Such a shift of identity as that caused by the move from marriage to singlehood can be resolved only with a strong sense of selfhood. Although the tendency in the mental health professions is to see the ability to make a commitment to merge one's identity with another person as being one of the crucial determinants of mental health, in fact, in a time of change, it is the ability to function as an individual that counts most. Here are the words of a divorced woman aged 36 who refused the opportunity to marry a second time: "I don't want to be married again. Sure, I'm lonely sometimes. So what? Married people get lonely too, and I'm not sure it isn't worse then. I can think of so many ways now to live my own life, and I want to experience what they are like. Right now, my kids and I rent a big house sharing with another divorced woman and her kids. It gives us all a good, big family *and* it gives me more time and freedom to explore in a way I never could when I was married. More time, more sharing of chores. I don't feel tied down. I plan to live this way as long as it's good for myself and my daughter and my son. When they leave home, I'll try something else. I've been having an affair for a year now, with a married man. I don't much like his being married, but it works fine so far because I haven't the least desire to marry him or even live with him. I date other men when I want to. I *like* not having a commitment to any man, just to my kids and myself. Happy? You'd better believe it! You know—there's more joy to me, in my life, in my kids, than there ever was before." These are the words of a woman who is clearly able to marry or

111

to live alone as circumstances—and the age of social change—require, a woman with a strong sense of her own selfhood.

Loss of Role

Loss of role is a feature of adult women's lives today, and one model (developed by Bohannan, 1972) for the loss of the marital role has been adapted (Aslin, 1976) to show the six elements which make up loss of role:

1. Emotional. For divorce, responsibility for the deterioration of the marriage; for widowhood, anger at and rejection by the spouse; in both states, grief and guilt.
2. Legal. For divorce, the settlement; for widowhood, insurance and inheritance arrangements.
3. Economic. Money and property division in divorce; fiscal planning in widowhood; reduced income and the need to support oneself in both.
4. Parental. In divorce, custody and visitation; in widowhood, single parenting.
5. Community. In both divorce and widowhood, new social roles, community relationships, and friendship patterns, the loss of the familiar being the major issue.
6. Psychological. The development of autonomy.

As a woman abandons one identity and establishes another, she feels loss and confusion in all these areas. Therefore, when I begin therapy with a female client, I carefully listen and hear, I see, I work to understand, I search with her for the changes in her life, and I watch for the reverberations and ramifications of any change in all areas of her life: economic and work life, family and intimacy life, physical life, and personal or psychological life. Is she clear as to what is "figure" for her? How does that figure fit into the "ground," the totality of her being? After a divorce, for instance, the figure may be the client's feelings of failure at not having worked out a successful relationship, but in the ground are her concerns about single parenting, new relationships, money, legal problems, and work, as well as her past learning and unfinished business from her childhood and early life. Or in widowhood, the figure may be anxiety and fear, but the ground includes her family and support system, her friends and potential partners, her children and their futures, her job and role in the community—all of which require her to rebuild. And in addition there are her models for behavior, learned in the past, which may assist, restrict, or restrain her growth.

At the beginning of a therapy group for women in transition, when each woman was to introduce herself and state what she wanted for herself, Vera broke into tears as she said, "My name is Vera, and I want to feel better." Asked by another woman what had happened, she replied: "I've been divorced one month today. Tom walked in one night six months ago and announced that he was leaving and wanted a divorce. I was so shocked, I agreed. Our marriage wasn't so hot, but it wasn't that bad. We argued, we had problems, but that's what I thought marriage was like after eight years. I found out after he left that he'd been having an affair with a secretary where he works for a long time. I was a fool!" I asked what precisely she meant by wanting to feel better. "Not to feel so confused," she said. "Not to feel so sad all the time." I asked: "Can you be clearer about what you feel confused and sad about?" She replied: "What I did wrong—why Tom left—what's wrong with me—and I hate him so much for what he did!"

A complex of strong emotions like this is typical of the loss of role: rejection, anger, grief, intense self-doubt, guilt, and more. They offer powerful avenues into self-understanding, and so, in the group, we began Vera's work with them. Eventually these immediate emotions became less important to her than other issues: frustration over the nature of her contacts with Tom about visitation with the boys; confusion about being a single parent; difficulty with the economics of a reduced income and becoming a full-time worker; problems in many other areas such as going to family gatherings alone, deciding what to do about former friends, dating again, and feeling comfortable with "them," as she called men for a time. What slowly emerged was the feeling of being Vera as she had never before been—but it took her a full year and much hard work within the group and in individual therapy before she could fully give up her previous roles and genuinely become a single woman.

When working with women who have lost roles, it is important to keep the six elements of loss in view. I often run through all six, talk about each, and ask how the client feels she is doing with each; what is figure now will later become background, and vice versa. Vera's original anger and sense of failure receded as other figures emerged, but one could not predict at any given time which element of the loss of role would be prominent.

The Power to Choose

The only avenue away from the sense of loss and confusion is development of the power to choose. *Reacting* to change leaves a woman powerless; *choosing* breeds in her a feeling of power. Thus, once the survey of changes in a woman's life is relatively complete, a therapist immediately looks for any area in which the client is able to make an autonomous choice, no matter how small. Choosing and acting always means development of a sense of power; we may not get everything we want, but we usually get something. Our choices change the flow of a situation. Negotiation, bargaining, and compromising give a level of control and power over the outcome that is essential to the development of self. When we act instead of reacting, when we choose instead of responding, we become an important ingredient in every event of our lives. The person who feels powerless in the face of change has to find points where she or he has the power to choose.

Every choice-point, whether minor or major, has the potential for giving a woman a sense of power. The therapist's task is to help the client see that these choice-points exist in every situation—whether or not to stay in a deteriorating relationship, try for another job, welcome or relinquish a child, move to another community, make a demand or request in a relationship, set boundaries on a child's or spouse's behavior, or pursue different behavior in a work setting. If the client experiences difficulty with choice, the therapist's task is to help her see that every choice-point challenges old behavior, values, expectations, rules, and self-concepts. The therapist's role is to show clients that passivity and activity are not mutually exclusive, that change need not make them powerless because they are an active ingredient in whatever change is occuring, and that they can influence the state of change. This can only be accomplished by examining the totality of a woman's being, both figure and ground, in order to identify those points at which she can make choices right now.

The therapist therefore comes to focus on the choice-points available in the course of a major change. My own tendency is to watch for all the choice-points which are occurring with changes and to help the client identify those points and examine, by means of options, all the choices in terms of the total self. Once the client identifies a comfortable choice-point, we then move through a decision-making process which both deals with the present concern and teaches how to deal with future choices.

 ## Making Intelligent Changes

The process of intelligent change consists of a sequence of fairly clear steps. (The following presentation of those steps is adapted from the Guided Inquiry Procedure developed by Farmer, 1977.)

1. Examine the overall situation, considering all possible options, no matter how unlikely at first glance.
2. Consider each option in turn, examining its advantages and disadvantages with the aim of making it seem a reality rather than an idea.
3. Choose a single preferred alternative.
4. Begin adapting this alternative in terms of actions and behavior, even if the first changes are minor.
5. Begin discarding old behaviors and attitudes which the chosen option makes dysfunctional.
6. Identify, practice, and learn new behavior suited to the new option.
7. Identify, learn, and practice new communication styles, both verbal and nonverbal.
8. Replace old rules with new rules that support rather than undermine the new option.

9. Evaluate to decide whether the new option is comfortable and functional, then revise, modify, or discard it and return to Step Three to make another choice.

Some clients move through the nine-step process without much delay at any step, but too often the pressures of money, time, or other factors make this impossible. For example, one middle-aged client came to therapy with a specific problem: whether or not to raise a 2-year-old grandson. She and her husband both worked, and they enjoyed the freedom from child rearing which had dominated the early years of their marriage. Of their five children aged 14 to 23, only the two youngest were still at home; but the eldest son, divorced with custody of his 2-year-old son, asked his mother to take over the raising of the boy. The client came to therapy filled with guilt because she did not want to take on the task. She judged herself selfish for wanting to have the freedom for vacations and luxuries rather than automatically wanting to care for her grandchild. She had to make a decision within a month. She also wanted to bring her husband to therapy so that they could eventually make a joint decision; but knowing that child care would be mostly her responsibility, she wanted to feel good about undertaking what her son wanted—and what her own background told her was the right thing. She had, one notes, already made her choice. She did not feel good about it, but the alternatives seemed worse.

A first attempt to study options did not work. Refusing to take in her grandson was an impossibility to her, and such alternatives as paying for child care by someone else seemed more complicated than she could handle. We therefore set out to analyze what her choice meant by fantasizing what her life would be like a month after the child arrived, in terms of both a typical workday and a typical weekend. Then we imagined what her life would be like at the end of six months, at the end of a year, and after five years. We studied this period in terms of money, work obligations, family time, social life outside the family, and especially in terms of her feelings about herself—her expectations, her sense of herself as worker, mother, grandmother, and spouse. By this time she was feeling more comfortable with her choice, seeing that she had alternatives from the kind of intensive child rearing that bringing up her own children had meant. Her husband and two remaining children came in for a lengthy session concerning their feelings and desires as a group, and shortly thereafter they made a compromise decision: to take care of the grandson for six months.

From the therapeutic viewpoint, the most significant feature of this choice was that the client had begun to see that much of her behavior was dictated by conceptions stemming from her earlier upbringing and experience that were now outdated by changing age and interests. She could not be the "mother" she thought she ought to be, and she accepted her feelings as legitimate rather than illicit. Hence the uneasy compromise on six months, and the decision to continue in therapy as an individual during those six months. Most of the time was now spent on behaviors, attitudes, and values that seemed entirely practical rather than "psychological"—rearranging the family's lives and schedules, reorienting work to satisfy the needs of child care, redesigning the social life of the family and her private life with her spouse, creating a new family budget, and so on. But in working on these details, she was in fact defining both what it meant to be a mother and grandmother, and what it meant to be her. By now she was fully aware that she and the mother/grandmother role were not coextensive, and that realization made her question the entire process which had made portions of her function on automatic pilot—the roles which she had grown up to fill.

A turbulent period of self-examination followed, characterized by a growing sense of her own rights and potentials. Before the six months were up, the decision whether or not to care for her grandchild had become a comparatively minor matter, one issue among many in her life-style. In fact, at the end of six months, it proved surprisingly easy for her to reverse her decision. She quickly found another whole option for providing her grandson with home, love, and care, as part of the process of going back to step one in the decision-making process, which was now radiating through her whole life. By the end of the year, all areas of her life were beginning to show substantial change. Particularly, she had changed her work and refreshed her relationship with her husband. She now felt grateful rather than resentful that her son had given her the "burden" of caring for a grandchild; that choice-point, forced upon her, had simply started a process which she had unwittingly postponed, a process which culminated in her feeling new energy and power over her whole existence.

Sometimes a client will spend a great deal of time at a single step of the process. Steps one and two were difficult for Beth, a divorced woman who found the task of studying all options very painful. She came to therapy with what seemed a strictly geographical problem which she could not resolve. After her divorce, she had continued to live where she had been married, in the city which her husband's career had first selected, even though her husband and their two adolescent sons had moved away. She had just sold her small business with the aim of moving to another town when her husband asked her to take over the two boys for their high school years which, both she and her husband thought, would be better spent in the town of their childhood. In therapy, she began to explore the ramifications of this choice, which was both imposed and self-imposed. This process had scarcely begun when her situation took a turn for what seemed the worse; her widowed father, living in a town 300 miles away, had a stroke—which meant that he needed home care. Beth, the oldest of eight children, immediately felt that she should be the one to provide that care by moving back to her childhood home, but this would mean that neither she nor her sons nor her husband would get what they wanted geographically. The situation seemed intolerably confusing to her; every way she turned, a new obligation and dissatisfaction seemed to face her.

In fact, this new situation proved therapeutically productive. Beth was faced with a violent conflict of "shoulds." As the oldest child, she had grown used to being the responsible member of a family—cleaning, cooking, taking care of younger siblings while both parents worked, and so on. She "should" be responsible because this was her role as daughter, but as a mother, she "should" also do what was right for her children, and, as an individual, she "should" be doing what was best for herself. She knew that both imposed situations were temporary; her father would not live many more years, and within five years her children would both finish high school and leave home. She felt the need to be "selfish," but she could not choose the option that would make her feel satisfied.

Under such pressures, therapy had to move on to the systematic study of each option in turn, and the only way to make sense of the various intolerable choices was to see that she herself was in control—one way or the other—of all the options. She began to realize that her concept of herself, rather than the wishes of others, was creating her list of "shoulds," and that the feeling of intense pressure stemmed from outmoded expectations and old ways of being in both her families. The real reason she was stalled at step one was because she had not, ever, envisaged step five—the discarding of dysfunctional and outmoded behaviors and options. That realization brought her back to the decision-making process with a whole new perspective; and as she worked at her own psychological development, the difficulty with her geographic choice seemed magically to melt away. With the help of a women's support group she was able to make her choices regarding caring for her father and children with an ease that amazed her. She discovered that, while her choices in a complicated situation might be limited, her attitudes, behavior, and her expectations of herself were within her control in any situation. In therapy, her main task then became the discovery that she could change all situations. Life's choices were no longer something imposed on her; even when she met what she felt as obligations, she still retained her power.

Beth's sense of external pressure is typical of female clients. All are likely to be in some state of confusion and partial ignorance about themselves in relation to their culture and upbringing; they may not understand why old patterns of behavior no longer work, why they cannot choose new patterns easily, why other people important to them fail to understand what they feel, or why neither they nor others seem able to resolve anything without conflict and frustration. As a woman moves through the nine steps of the decision-making process, a therapist has to be able to match her movements with great subtlety, offering but not imposing a new perspective. If the therapist is routinely conscious that changes affecting women clients affect all of society and all women, then she or he can offer the needed sense of perspective and dimension through asserting the validity of options. The social dimension removes isolation from a problem; it reassures the client.

The therapist will also find the task of detecting the dysfunctional easier if her or his sense of the dimensions of change is fresh; this may be particularly important in the case of a single parent who is trying to be two parents and to maintain a traditional home environment, or that of a new stepmother of teenage stepdaughters who is trying to set up rules for behavior (e.g., about peers or sexuality) by which she grew up twenty years before, or that of a 65-year-old widow in conflict with her children because of her relationship with a man. In every case in which roles conflict, the task of the therapist is to ask which role is no longer appropriate and what prevents a new option from being used.

Therapy and Decision Making

In a world of change, successful therapy will display a series of characteristics which are easily discernible.

1. The therapist should *approach each client as though she were at a choice-point*—a point in her life where she faces a series of options—even if she fails to recognize it at the moment. Consciousness of choice enables the client's sense of available power to operate right from the start; *clarification of present and future options* is thus the primary task of the therapist. Because she is living in a position of conflict between her cultural training and her present needs, the client may accept or reject to various degrees what her socialization and habits demand of her. She may be dissatisfied with an old role or with a new role for which she lacks guidelines. She may know she needs help in exploring new options—or she may be reluctant to change or even to recognize that change is necessary. She may be angry, and her anger may conflict with her learned passivity, creating a complex of emotions and behaviors that makes the point of choice very obscure. In all cases, the patient therapist helps her to unfold her options in both practical and emotional terms.

2. *Clarification should take place* in a specific manner: *by a survey of the client's whole situation in life.* The issue or difficulty presented by the client is likely to be just one symptom of a broader condition of change, and it may or may not be the cause of current emotional and practical difficulties. Surveying the client's whole life situation enables the therapist to detect the less visible groundswell of change, and it enables the client to see herself as the center of her situation with the potential for control. Thus the clarification process can begin even with intake forms of the kind recommended in the work chapter (Chap. 6), and it can itself have an immediate therapeutic effect.

3. Clarification, however, is not enough. Since many women do not know their options, the therapist's third task is *expansion of options.* We frequently see clients who first reject, often strongly, the option which they ultimately choose. A client may have first heard of that option in a therapy session; more likely, the socialization process or her individual upbringing has prevented her from giving it the consideration it merits. In either case the therapist acts as the agent of change simply by suggesting serious consideration of all possibilities—rather than accepting only those which the client is already considering and between which she is probably unable to choose. Expansion normally requires the therapist also to give reassurance about the *revocability of choice.* The data show that few of

118

women's choices today are final and irrevocable, though they all have permanent effects. Revoking past choices and making new choices on an experimental basis (i.e., with the later option of revoking them) thus become important ways of functioning amid a world of change despite our desire for rest and permanence. With their tendency to neglect long-term planning, many women fail to recognize that, because women's roles vary according to the stage of life, a woman may vary her choices through time to make them appropriate for an altered life situation. This does not mean that, if Anne now chooses to divorce George, she can have George back if she changes her mind later; it does mean, however, that no choice of basic role is necessarily a lifetime choice and that Anne can, if she chooses, move in and out of the married state several times during her life. At the same time there is the reciprocal need to help a woman work out the *implications of choice*. Few people can see all the potential ramifications of a particular choice, whether it be to major in a particular subject at college or to end a 30-year marriage. The unrealized consequences often bring regret; realism lies in examining as many implications of a choice as feasible, a task which counselors must be equipped to manage.

4. Also basic to the therapist's task is helping the client *understand the process of change and choice* itself: exploring various roles, choosing a new role, moving into that role, relinquishing old roles, fully developing the new role, evaluating the changes, and getting ready for fresh choices. Emphasis on the process reassures and educates clients; it removes self-blame, decreases pressure, and equips the client to undertake her own "therapy" when faced with future choices.

5. The above process sounds time-consuming and perhaps too abstract, and I do not wish to be understood to recommend that therapists give clients little lectures on the subject of change; the art of the therapist lies in evoking perspective from the particular and in avoiding the tendency to overlay the individual with a generic label—the areas where counseling and therapeutic skills really emerge. The goal of therapy with a sense of change is rather to combat two tendencies which afflict today's counseling and therapeutic processes. First is the tendency to focus on a specific and very narrow subject; for example, considering whether a client should major in home economics or law solely on the basis of her grade point average. Too many counseling/therapy situations closely resemble the life crises that produce them; they proceed so quickly that choice has to be made on the most superficial of understandings. This is especially true when the problem presented by the client seems drably practical (e.g., child care, transportation, or the choice of major) and so susceptible to a quick solution. The easy solution may be the worst solution to the real problem, but unless the whole situation has been examined, nobody will know. The second damaging tendency in some of today's counseling and therapy, especially when it resembles psychoanalysis, is the reciprocal of the first: the process is too broad and too slow. *Good counseling and therapy for women should not take too long.* Because women tend not to have a sturdy economic base, they cannot afford much extra in the way of time and professionals' fees; counselors and therapists should recognize the need to practice differently with a group whose members are generally in a much worse financial

position than are most men. Women cannot afford to waste therapy and counseling time.

6. More important than the length and thoroughness of counseling is the special goal of counseling women: to *equip them to make choices independently*. Any therapist who becomes a "guru" to her or his clients is doing the cause of women a disservice—no matter how much she or he verbally endorses the cause of women—by encouraging the female dependency which is a basic source of women's inability to function. One cannot combat a cultural habit by becoming one of its manifestations. The goal of counseling women is to have a former client who now operates as her own agent for change, who recognizes her own choice-points, and who needs less help in choosing between options.

Sample Experiences

Figures 5.1, 5.2, and 5.3 contain some experiences aimed at enabling clients and therapists to see the process of change function. Each focuses differently on the two basic issues of process and role; each helps the individual study the specific matters which concern her while simultaneously encouraging her to see those matters in a broader perspective.

These experiences are presented in the format one would use for groups, but they can easily be adapted for use with individual clients. They can be used as an introduction to any specific subject matter, such as options in education, career, lifestyle, or situation. The therapist may function at will as a facilitator, lecturer, or therapist since the depth of the materials can vary according to the purpose of the occasion. The aim of all these experiences is to equip the client to see her particular situation as part of a long-term development and as susceptible to resolution. Their character is designed to present issues less as problems (and therefore associated with powerlessness) than as choices (associated with opportunity).

These experiences work with individuals at every stage of development. Women eager for change use them emphatically to lay out and study their choices and the forces in their lives; women reluctant to change find them an easy avenue into subject matter which they may find threatening. All clients have the opportunity to separate their individuality from the roles they are called upon to play; once this separation occurs, they can develop a sense of flexibility and power, working out both immediate and long-range implications of various choices without losing their sense of identity. Women normally find it reassuring to understand that they are in the midst of a process, because this removes the sense of crisis and inability to cope.

Opportunities to use the principles discussed in this chapter are inherent to these experiences. *Clarification* of options by identifying specific choice-points is their basic strategy. *Expansion* of options occurs quietly; clients think the unthinkable without having been scared by it. The experiences enable counselors to draw the distinction between thinking and doing and to encourage experimentation. By emphasizing lifetime stages and the *revocability* of choice, they emphasize the ability of the individual to play roles and to change roles; therapists can thus help clients develop a sense of individuality distinct from their various roles. The experiences also emphasize the dimension of time. New attitudes and behavior take time to acquire; the transformation process does not happen easily or suddenly—it does not happen at all unless the client pays attention to its basic nature rather than just to its confusing manifestations. By emphasizing generational and age differences, the experiences show an individual that she has the time to play many roles and to be many individuals during her life. Reciprocally, they emphasize the *implications* of present choices, so that neither the present moment, the present problem, nor indeed the present experience can be seen as an isolated event.

FIGURE 5.1.   Present Choices/Future Plans

Equipment:
   One roll of shelf paper.
   Five Wants and Needs Cards, labeled respectively "family life," "intimate life," "work life," "personal life," and "social/community life." (Card size: 8″ × 8″)

Preparation:
   Unroll enough of the shelf paper onto the floor so that it stretches across the room and mark it to indicate divisions at ages 20, 30, 40, 50, and 60.
   Give one member of the group the five Wants and Needs cards.

Process:
   The client physically moves along the life continuum depicted by the shelf paper while telling the group what were, are, and will be her needs and wants at each age in the five areas indicated on the cards.
   Other members of the group suggest other options or point out implications.

Example:
   At 32, Kay faces a major choice-point: whether to move geographically with her husband for the third time in eight years to a location which suits his needs and wants, a move that would severely interfere with her needs and wants. She is locked into this problem and depressed. She has little sense of where *she* has been in life and where *she* wants to go as an individual distinct from her husband.
   She begins to walk the life continuum, talking about the issues suggested by the cards. At 20 she describes what her wants and needs were then, tending to see them as shortsighted. At 30 she starts to describe the wants and needs she had in mind before the present situation arose, then moves on to outline the choices she could make now, thus comparing wants, needs, and the effects of various choices.
   At 40 she begins to fantasize about the consequences of her present choices; and at 50, by fantasizing about what she would like to have accomplished at that age, she sees the dimensions of her present choices. At 60 she emphasizes predictable widowhood and depicts clearly two 60-year-old Kays—one who has subordinated herself to her husband's needs and one who has not.
   Suddenly she returns to 30 and starts, as she calls it, "weeding out" choices, wants, and needs.
   Throughout the process, older and younger women have suggested ideas and asked questions, helping Kay to clarify and expand her idea of what she is and what she might

121

FIGURE 5.1 (continued)

become. Kay emerges with a clear idea of what her life will be like (a) if she moves with her husband, and (b) if she refuses to move. By the end of the experience she is thoughtful and energetic, and she is beginning to see that a series of options other than the two extremes lie in front of her.

Purpose:

The aim of this process is clarification and expansion. It focuses on two characteristics common among women: their tendency to focus on the immediate issue as the most important, and the inclination to allow others to make long-term decisions about their lives.

The goal is to have the client see herself as a whole and powerful person by expanding her view of herself through time and in several basic areas of existence. Group members go through a similar experience as they watch and help her process. The therapist need comment only rarely since the experience encourages the client to accept responsibility for her own situation now and in the future.

Physical movement (standing on the life continuum, considering each card in turn, slowly progressing across the room, causing the group members to shift, and so forth) is important to this experience since it becomes a metaphor for progress along the real life continuum, making change visible and concrete and facilitating fantasy and acting out.

FIGURE 5.2. The Generation Game

Equipment:

One pad of newsprint, 2 feet by 3 feet.

Felt-tip markers.

Preparation:

Place at least ten pages of newsprint paper on the walls of the room. (Extra pages will be needed for larger groups.)

The pages should be headed as follows:

1. An adjective that well describes a woman in her:

   20s   30s   40s   50s   60s   70s+

2. What I like (or liked) best about myself in my:

   20s   30s   40s   50s   60s   70s+

3. What I like (or liked) least about myself in my:

   20s   30s   40s   50s   60s   70s+

4. Life's most important events in my _____ were or will be:

   20s   30s   40s   50s   60s   70s+

5. The activity or situation I liked (like, will like) best in my _____ is:

   20s   30s   40s   50s   60s   70s+

6. The activity or situation I liked (like, will like) least in my _____ is:

   20s   30s   40s   50s   60s   70s+

7. The greatest rewards in my _____ will come (came, come) from being a:

   20s   30s   40s   50s   60s   70s+

8. The least rewards in my _____ will come (came, come) from being a:

   20s   30s   40s   50s   60s   70s+

9. The age I most look forward to being is: _____ ; because _____.

10. The age I least look forward to being is: _____; because _____.

FIGURE 5.2 (continued)

Process:

Have all group members complete all ten wall charts. Writing on them should take about 30 minutes, followed by about 15 minutes of reading what others have written. Break the group into pairs or trios and have them discuss whatever they wish concerning the wall charts. Have the group as a whole discuss the implications of the experience.

Example:

This experience works very differently according to the age grouping of the participants, and it reveals very clearly the generational effect pointed out by Troll (1975). In a homogeneous group, differences in past experience and present attitudes will be less than in a group with mixed ages, but they will still be present.

Elaine is a professional woman in her late 30s, apparently successful but lonely, very assured in manner and apparently aloof. At the beginning of the experience she comments that she is sure everyone will give the same answers and asks if that is the point. She is clearly surprised and somewhat perturbed by what the other people write. "There's more to all of you than I thought!" she says. "There's more to me than I thought!" replies another woman. In the small group she tries at first to talk about what all this means for women in general, but the others bring her back to what it means for her. "Oh, I admire myself," she says brusquely. Then suddenly she becomes teary-eyed. "But I want children. And I wasn't brave enough to write that up like you did."

Purpose:

The aim of this experience is to clarify satisfactions. It is difficult for us to see from where our real satisfactions have come, both in the present and in the past, and more so to anticipate whence they will come at various future life stages.

The experience enables participants to make bold and explicit comparisons, to acquire information about differences, and to get both individual and group feedback. The variety within a group automatically creates a spectrum of choices and expectations.

The experience also clarifies value judgments and their effects on the individual choice; and especially if the group contains a variety of ages, it contests the stereotypes one age-group holds of others even while it exposes them.

FIGURE 5.3. Choosing A Life-style

Equipment:

Three or four sets of Wants and Needs cards, labeled "family life," "intimate life," "work life," "personal life," and "social/community life." (Card size: 10" × 12")

The same number of sets of Activities Cards (8" × 10"). Each Activity Card simply notes an area in which adults function, and the areas can be selected as the therapist wishes. For example:

Work life: moving up in the working world; full-time work; part-time work; no paid work; retraining; self-employment; highly paid work; work without stress.

Social/community life: contributions to society; politics; community service; charity volunteering; women's groups; common interest organizations.

Home/family life: single; being a daughter; married; living with others; living alone; parenting; not parenting; widowed; divorced; life-long marriage; being a traditional wife; working head of household.

Personal life: physical activities; hobbies; spiritual life; social life; leisure activities; time alone; relationships with men; intellectual life; giving to others; relationships with women; self-care and self-nurturing; type of home.

FIGURE 5.3 (continued)

Intimate life: serial monogamy; monogamy; relationships with relatives; living alone; being a lover; heterosexuality; bisexuality; lesbianism; relationships with children.

Preparation:

Find three or four volunteers and give each of them a set of Wants and Needs cards and a set of Activities Cards. Divide the remainder of the group into small groups, each to accompany one of the volunteers. Provide considerable floor space for each volunteer and her group. Instruct each volunteer to lay out the Activities Cards on the floor under the headings of their respective Wants and Needs cards.

Process:

Once the cards are laid out, the volunteer looks at them as options. She takes each area in turn, and in essence spends 45 to 60 minutes selecting her options by rearranging the cards. Some cards she will remove; as she does, she should explain to her small group why she removes them and why she lets the others remain. She also starts arranging them in terms of priority to her. Finally she sees linkages between various activities and shifts the cards to indicate linkages, distances, or conflicts between the activities. At each point she explains to the group what she is doing and why. The group (and the therapist) question, comment, sort, and help her clarify. Finally the cards will form a diagram of her life; when the volunteer indicates that her arrangement is complete, she, her group, and the therapist may comment on the arrangement. (For example, "Family and social life seem close together, but intimacy sits off by itself." Or, "Work life and family life are on the same level, but there are fewer cards in work life.")

Normally it is easier to tell the volunteer to use the cards to describe her present situation, i.e., the options she is presently choosing. If time and interest allow, the volunteer can also arrange the cards to describe her future situation (one or five or twenty years from now); the two arrangements can then be compared.

Example:

Chris is dealing with a major decision about her work life. A medical technician, she finds herself trapped in a job she finds monotonous; but she can change jobs within her field only by moving to another town, which family life makes difficult. When she first lays out the cards, she places work life at the top and center and spends much time explaining her choices within it. Eventually the group urges her to move on to the other areas. She eventually chooses family life, organizes it internally without trouble, but cannot find the right place for it in relation to her work life. The group urges her to show linkages, which turn out to be conflicts, so Chris removes the work life cards, puts them at the bottom, and places family life cards top and center, professing herself satisfied.

However, when she is asked to lay out the cards a second time, the work life cards again emerge top and center—which causes Chris to express anger at herself. "Which of these cards are the most difficult to place?" asks a group member. Reluctantly, Chris chooses "full-time work" and "life-long marriage," rearranging all the cards to show that these are her two centers and that they are in conflict. Suddenly she writes a new card with her name on it, another with her husband's name on it, and lays them down as a bridge between the two areas of conflict. "It never occurred to me this way," she says in surprise. "I've always thought this was just my problem, but Gerry's right in there with me, isn't he? I wonder what he thinks?" Later she asks to borrow a set of the cards so that she and her husband can do this experience together.

FIGURE 5.3 (*continued*)

Purpose:

The aim of the experience is to help an individual look at her whole life at one time so that conflicts and linkages may become apparent at a glance. The act of rearrangement suggests various actions and gives a sense of potential for change. Since life-style is a matter of priorities, these are emphasized by the process. The absence of value judgments from the group or the therapist emphasizes the individual's own values and their relationship to her choices.

Summary

In a time of strong social change, a major task of therapy is to be quick and flexible—as individuals need to be when faced with a multitude of options. The basic issues in women's lives are not so complex that they cannot be understood, and a few simple techniques will enable therapist and client to begin the process of identification and decision making very rapidly. At the same time, counseling women requires a special art and special artfulness. Old patterns die hard; the realities of daily life press ruthlessly on women. Change is a constant in their lives; choice, a necessity. To do their female clients justice, therapists must be clear about the nature of women's place in contemporary society, aware and suspicious of their own attitudes towards women's place, clear about the overall situation of the individual client, and aware of their own influence on that situation through action or inaction. The therapist's role with female clients always includes an element of training with the goal of helping them become today's free and powerful women; but in a time of change we are all trainees, and the therapist's art lies in coupling imaginativeness with humility.

6

Women in the World of Work

The famous "bottom line" in our society is the ability to earn money, and there is much cheerful cultural propaganda to the effect that, at least in this respect, women are much better off than they were a decade ago. We know that equal pay for equal work is the law of the land. We see women working in jobs which were previously closed to them by law and custom. We hear of some women making what is good money by any standard. We know personally increasing numbers of women who are surviving on their own, and the husband who refuses to allow his wife to work has become an old-fashioned figure.

The truth, however, is rather different. Women are indeed working more, but they are still earning less than men. Although women have made gains in some professions and occupational categories and some earn as much as do men, nonetheless as a group they remain dramatically poorer earners than men and their economic vulnerability is much greater. What this means to therapists and counselors is the subject of this chapter and the next. It is all too easy for mental health professionals to ignore the economic dimensions of the female experience. Every time a woman makes a choice—to work or not, to divorce or not, to change jobs or stay in place, to go back to school or not, to flee a battering husband, to bear a child or have an abortion, to live alone or marry—that choice has economic consequences more crucial and more influential than those of a similar choice by a man. Greater economic vulnerability is indeed one of the characteristics of the female experience; the aim of the present chapters is to equip mental health professionals to understand what the "bottom line" means as a foundation, a basis, for all other choices in a woman's life.

126

The freedom to earn better salaries seems at first glance to have been one of the best effects on women of many of society's recent changes—the decreasing birth rate, smaller families, abortion, increasing divorce rate, and changing attitudes to women working, among others. The truth, however, is that women are working more because they have to: women stay single longer; divorce is more common; child support is mainly the woman's burden; one-half or more of all married women work. Less than one-third of today's homes retain the traditional pattern of the male as breadwinner and the female as homemaker. More women than men are now entering the job market for the first time, and the average woman will work for at least 25 years, probably longer (U.S. Bureau of the Census, 1980a; National Commission on Working Women Fact Sheet, 1979). In sum, work, not marriage, has become the single most important fact of women's lives.

But all these changes have not substantially benefited women in financial terms. On the average, women still earn less than 60 percent of the average earnings of men. When wives work, their husbands get much of the dividends; studies show that husbands of working wives worry less about money than they did and fail to do more at home, whereas the wife works harder and longer hours than before. When couples divorce, the children but not the money go to the woman. The average income of divorced women is less than half that of divorced men, even though three-quarters of them work. Alimony and child support? Over half of all divorced women receive neither (U.S. National Commission on the Observance of International Women's Year, 1976). And the greatest direct cause of lower earnings—intermittency in the job market—affects women much more adversely than it does men because women are expected to give up work for child rearing. (In 1978, according to the U.S. Bureau of the Census, 91 percent of young women expected to have up to three children.) These are the kinds of fact which these chapters emphasize.

Neither women nor therapists are likely to look at the brutal facts when it comes to the great emotional experiences of life, such as marriage, having a baby, raising children, ending a marriage, or widowhood. Ignorance of the factual consequences of choices is likely to be stunning. Most loving married couples, for instance, want to have a baby. Will they make their choice on the basis of knowledge or emotion? Will they consider that one out of every 2.5 marriages now ends in divorce; that as of 1976 it cost an average $56,000 to bring a child to adulthood; that having one baby removes a woman from the work force for an average of five years; that she will lose an average of $58,400 in wages by staying home to care for the baby until it turns 14; that her ex-husband will provide child support for (probably) less than three years; or that she will spend time, money, and energy earning even that little by working with unsympathetic courts and costly lawyers? It is certainly not pleasant to bring these matters to attention, but informed choice is the basic assumption of our society, and the therapist's task may be precisely to make a client face those brutal facts.

The following chapters deal with myths as well as facts. Myths are a vital part of the process by which we survive in society—they enable us to feel comfortable because we believe much of what everyone else believes within given social parameters (Janeway, 1974). What society as a whole believes, we too tend to believe—even if it is to one's own individual disadvantage. Thus women tend to use myths to discriminate against themselves, especially in the area of work and achievement. Studies later cited show that women tend to choose a general social comfortableness over personal achievement and that they tend to build certain unconscious failure mechanisms into their work because society's myths reward such failures. Many women come to believe that—or at least to act as though—discrimination against them is fair and proper. The following chapter reveals how myths about women and work affect a woman's choices: her own expectations and those of others around her; her guilts and the fears or angers of those with whom she lives and works; her extra burdens, which she and others may see as necessary baggage; and the internal barriers to progress and even survival which acculturation has built into the individual's belief structure.

Though less frequent and powerful than they were, external barriers still drastically impede women's working lives, no matter how subtly they function. Women face all the difficulties of the working world encountered by men, and more. Society requires women to be both workers and homemakers, even while it makes maintenance of both roles difficult. Most therapists (especially males) are blissfully unaware of these extra difficulties, thinking of them only in terms of getting the dinner on the table or the laundry done—matters in which the large-minded male is glad to help and for which he modestly takes due praise. If a woman still experiences difficulties with being a successful worker, then society, the male for whom she makes the home, and the woman herself are likely to blame *her* rather than, for instance, blaming the male-oriented and inflexible structure of the working world or blaming the prejudices towards males that cause bosses to think of working women's rights as concessions or even favors.

Finally, the chapters analyze the implications of which therapists and counselors should be made aware, and in this respect there should be a preliminary word of warning. First, a professional works with not just a woman but a woman of a particular age or generation. In terms of a woman's concept of her relationship to work, a woman in her 30s or 40s has different perceptions and needs from those of a woman in her 20s or teens, caused not by her age but by the time and culture in which she grew up. There are huge differences between a mother and her daugher in regard to life experiences and self-expectations. A woman who entered the labor force even as recently as a decade ago may have internalized beliefs about herself which seem ridiculous to a younger woman who has never known a time when equal rights legislation, the Pill, and divorce were unavailable. On the other hand, since different groups of women are changing at different rates, a grandmother may be more progressive than a teenager, depending on religious, economic, and geographic background or life experience. Counselors can have no single agenda when women and work are concerned, and they should be wary of selecting from these chapters only those facts which reinforce their present beliefs.

On the basis of the facts that follow, I personally cannot decide whether a woman ought to work or stay at home or whether she ought to try for a career or settle for a simple job—assuming she has some choice. Having a man take care of you brings a lot of advantages; taking care of yourself means a lot of effort. But of three things I am sure: if a woman has to work or chooses to work, she ought to get for her labor the best salary which the market will pay. If she chooses not to work or to work intermittently, she ought to know what the financial consequences will be. And whatever she chooses, her therapist or counselor should have the skills and knowledge to assist in making her choice meaningful and valid—that of a fully developed, well-informed, equal human being.

Today's Working Women

Some 59 percent of adult women (aged 18 to 64) are now in the labor market at any given time, and 52 percent of working women have children under 18 years (U.S. Women's Bureau, 1979a and 1979b). About 42 percent of today's labor force is female, their proportion having doubled over the last 25 years (U.S. Bureau of the Census, 1980a). Unlike men, women cluster in a few occupational areas. More than three of five women are in clerical, operative, or service jobs (compared with about three out of ten men). In clerical and service jobs, they are a majority, and almost so in sales (43 percent), operative (45 percent), and technical/professional (43 percent) jobs. In the technical/professional category their high proportion is misleading because they cluster in the lower-paying jobs (social workers, librarians, teachers, nurses), leaving the higher-paying supervisory jobs dominated by men (doctors, hospital administrators, administrators of social agencies and mental health agencies, schools, libraries). In the skilled crafts, in managerial and nonretail sales jobs, and in the executive category, women are severely underrepresented.

One must conclude that women have not yet attained the levels of power and reward that their contribution to the labor force warrants. Better educated and better rewarded than in 1900 they may be, but in relation to male workers they have scarcely advanced at all since 1900. In 1978, 45 percent of all women workers worked in only ten job categories, all of them with less pay and lower status than male jobs held: secretary, retail sales clerk, bookkeeper, domestic, elementary school teacher, waitress, typist, cashier, garment worker, and nurse. The pattern of 1900 dominates in the subordinate and service nature of these categories, all of which are dead-end jobs without prospect for material or career advancement but which do allow for intermittency (U.S. Bureau of the Census, 1980a).

Shifts have occurred in the data during the later 1970s; some job categories are showing the first signs of real openness to women, among them the skilled crafts, the professions (especially law and accounting), financial management, nonretail sales, and services (bartending, cabdriving). Despite legislation, however, the changes thus far are comparatively small. Their significance is not so much in numbers as in the fact that, as women move into these job categories, the jobs slowly lose their traditionally masculine stereotype and offer women greater promise for the future. Reciprocally, some men are moving into job categories such as librarian, elementary school teacher, typist, and telephone operator which then lose some of their traditional feminine stereotype. Both changes are the result of recent legislation removing employers' rights to discriminate on the basis of sex.

Characteristics of Working Women

The nature of the women who work has changed more than the nature of the work they do, and the picture emerging in the 1980s has the following characteristics.

Age

In 1920, the typical working woman was 28 and single, whereas in 1978 she was 34 and married. In 1900, the median age for female workers was 26; in 1940, 32; in 1945, 34; in 1950, 37; and in 1961 it reached a peak of 41, declining to 36 in 1978 because of the maturing of the postwar babies (U.S. Women's Bureau, 1979b). But our population is now again aging, our average age 30 as opposed to 27.9 in 1970 (U.S. Bureau of the Census, 1979e), so that most of our workers will be older from now on. One can reasonably predict that there will be no age span during which women can be expected to work or not to work. If half of all adult women are working at any given time, if 9 out of 10 women work for some period during their lives, if the average worklife of women is 25 years and rising, and if we can no longer predict that motherhood and marriage will remove them from the labor market, then we can have no valid expectation at all of the "appropriate" age for a woman to work or not to work.

Heads of Families

The numbers of late-marrying, separated, divorced, and widowed women are rising rapidly. The number of families headed by women has doubled since 1940; now they are one out of every seven. A woman who heads a family is more likely now to work as well; in 1978, 59 percent of female family heads were working, comprising one out of ten women workers. Female heads of families are becoming younger, their median age now 41.8, a drop of more than ten years since 1960 (U.S. Bureau of the Census, 1979a, 1979b). But the most significant data are economic, and they provide disastrous evidence of inequality.

A family headed by a woman is much more likely than a family headed by a man to be impoverished or to be much lower in income. One out of three lives at or below poverty level (Sawhill, 1976; U.S. Women's Bureau, 1979a). Black

130

women who head families are even worse off; one out of two are below the poverty level.

Education

Education still is a working woman's best friend. Women as a group are not quite as well educated as men. While a larger proportion of working women than of working men has completed high school (74 percent versus 68 percent in 1977), fewer have completed four years of college (14 percent versus 18 percent), and fewer go on to further education (U.S. Bureau of the Census, 1980a). This pattern is changing among younger women. A larger proportion of those under 35 than of those over 35 have completed high school, and though GED certification among older women is increasing, they are still significantly less educated.

The association between education and later income is strong. The more education a woman has, the more likely is she to work, to avoid unemployment, and to be in a higher-paid occupation. Working women without high school diplomas are concentrated in service and operative jobs, those without college degrees are primarily clerical workers, and two-thirds of those with college degrees are in professional/technical occupations (U.S. Women's Bureau, 1976; U.S. Bureau of the Census, 1980a). The current surge of women seeking better education and more training therefore shows their changing sense of economic probabilities.

Income

After a certain point, however, education benefits a woman much less than it does a man. A woman with a college degree can expect to earn about the same as does a man with an eighth-grade education. In 1977, the amounts were $12,656 for women in this situation versus $12,083 for men (U.S. Women's Bureau, 1979c; U.S. Bureau of the Census, 1980a). This surely is one of the clearest examples of what inequality in our society means. It is, however, only a particular manifestation of the inequality of rewards which work brings to men and to women. In 1977 the median income for all female workers was $8,618 (for white women, $8,787, for black women $8,385), while for men the median income was $14,626 (for white men, $15,230, for black men $11,053) (U.S. Women's Bureau, 1979c). The census bureau indicates that the gap between the sexes is actually widening, both overall and within the major occupational categories (U.S. Bureau of the Census, 1980a). Despite myth and propaganda, equal rights to our country's wealth are *not* a reality.

Economic Need

Women work because they need the money, not out of some abstract rivalry with men. The following description of all working women in 1977 is rather different from that implied by people who demean women's desire to work.

- 25 percent were never married
- 19 percent were separated, divorced, or widowed
- 10 percent had husbands earning less than $7,000
- 8 percent had husbands earning between $7,000 and $10,000
- 15 percent had husbands earning between $10,000 and $15,000

If we believe a family income of $10,000 as barely adequate, then 62 percent of women who work do so out of economic need. If our magic figure is $15,000, then 77 percent work out of economic need. When inflation and unemployment strike our economy, most of the remaining 23 percent do not feel they are working purely out of choice (U.S. Women's Bureau, 1979a).

Unemployment

Because the kinds of occupational category filled by women encourage transiency and intermittency, women are often believed to be better off than men when unemployment hits. In reality, unemployment rates tend to be higher for women than for men, especially for older women, and there is no statistical evidence to show that women are more likely than men to get employment preference (U.S. Women's Bureau, 1976b; U.S. Bureau of Labor Statistics, 1980a). Women also suffer through lack of education; the less education, the more likely is unemployment. Minority women have very high unemployment rates, and the highest rate of all is that of young minority women (U.S. Bureau of Labor Statistics, 1980b). Women have a special problem with unemployment; while men are likely to have held a job and lost it, women are much more likely at any age to be entering or reentering the labor force (Ferber and Lowry, 1976).

Marital Status

About 55 percent of working women are married and living with their husbands, though divorce is causing a rapid increase in the number of women heading households (U.S. Bureau of Labor Statistics, 1980a). Marriage still reduces women's lifetime earnings, though less seriously than it did earlier in the century or even in the 1960s; the major cause is the presence of young children in the home. Many women with preschool children stay home, reentering the labor market at the average age of 35 or when the last child enters school. This picture, however, is changing. The average age of marriage is increasing and the number of children is decreasing, which mean that women tend to leave the world of work for briefer periods. It cannot be assumed—as used to be the case—that having a child means the end of a woman's worklife even for a year or so. In fact, the greatest proportionate increase among working women has recently been among women of childbearing age. In 1978, one-half of married women with preschool children or with both preschool children and children under 18 were at work (U.S. Women's Bureau, 1979a; U.S. Bureau of the Census, 1980a).

While the average worklife of a man lasts 45 years and that of a woman 25 years, the gap has been closing slowly, and forecasts show that it will narrow dramatically in the next generation. Women's worklife patterns are shifting towards those of men despite marriage. This change has major implications for the structure of both individual families and the nation's economy; at present it is a basic and ill-understood factor in some of our fiercest social debates—birth control, abortion, day-care centers, divorce, credit availability, social security, and work conditions. Women are fighting for the right to stay at work one way or another. In the future it may be a major force for restructuring the work environment along lines better oriented to people than to machines.

Minority Status

The employment patterns of minority women are distinctive. More likely than white women to be working wives and mothers, they also have less formal education, lower incomes, and jobs in low-skill, low-paid occupational areas. More often are they heads of families. In sum, even more than do white women, minority women work because they have to and earn less for their work (U.S. Women's Bureau, 1979a). Overall, about the same proportion of minority women as white women are at work or in the labor market. In 1979, for instance, when some 51 percent of white women were in the work force, some 52 percent of black women and 47 percent of Hispanic women were also workers. Data for other minority groups are less clear; the 1970 census showed the following proportions: American Indian, 35.3 percent; Japanese, 49.4 percent; Chinese, 49.5 percent; and Filipino, 55.3 percent (U.S. Bureau of Labor Statistics, 1980b; U.S. Women's Bureau, 1977b). The effort to eliminate the differential between white and minority women in terms of earnings is a major task for the 1980s.

Further Data

The statistical service provided by the U.S. Women's Bureau of the Department of Labor is invaluable. A list of its publications is available from the U.S. Department of Labor, Women's Bureau, Washington, D.C., 20210.

But the most important data for any therapist to remember are those which show that work is both normal and necessary for women. Our most recent data (U.S. Bureau of the Census, 1980a) show that we had 42,028,890 women (over age 16) at work—slightly more than 50 percent of all our country's women. Widows contained the smallest proportion (22.4 percent) of workers because they tend as a group to be older. Some 47.6 percent of married women were at work, making the idea of the traditional breadwinner/homemaker family a nostalgic notion. Never-married women of all ages work—60.5 percent of them—suggesting major (and often missed) opportunities for career counseling. And perhaps most significant of all, 74 percent of divorced women, many with children to support, are at work, moving through the world as independently and productively as do men. The task of meeting the various and complicated needs of these women in relation to their work is one of the most important facing the counseling and therapeutic professions today.

Realities Facing Working Women

Working women meet with very little understanding of their special needs and problems. Because most men are acculturated to accept the pains of work as inevitable, and because they are sheltered for much of their lives by women's domestic care, they can rarely understand how different matters are for many working women. Since most bosses are male, working women with problems are lucky to find only their complaints, rather than themselves, dismissed. Women who do not work offer little support to those who do, since they see a job as something extra. Bland incomprehension is the most likely response from mother, friend, or husband, and it is likely to reduce the working woman to murmuring, as did the pallid hero of T. S. Eliot's "The Love Song of J. Alfred Prufrock," "That's not what I meant. That's not what I meant at all." Other working women normally prove her only or major source of support, the only people in her environment capable of understanding the implications of her choice of life-style. Among dual-career couples, for instance, the normal social network is based on people who are supportive of the working wife rather than of the working husband (St. John-Parsons, 1978).

Bald statements and bare facts may help raise one's level of understanding. Imagine, if you will, giving a young man the following advice as he starts his career:

> You will start at a lower salary than half the working population simply because of your sex. You will earn roughly half the amount others earn, simply because of your sex. Your job will probably offer you little advancement or change for the rest of your life. If you stay single, people will think there's something wrong with you. If you marry, you'll have two jobs: one at work and one at home; and you'd better not let either interfere with the other, or do one better than the other. By the way: stay young and handsome. That's the way bosses prefer their male employees. But don't worry too much. The laws against work discrimination are all in your favor now. There's nothing at all to stop you from doing whatever you want to do—other than your own fear, ignorance, incompetence, sexuality, and monthly hormonal cycle. And who knows what to do about those? After all, you *are* a man. And by the way—don't compete with the women in your field. They're easily threatened, and they've got a lot more power. After all, they're women.

The Double Workload

Our society still regards work as a male priority and perquisite. A man who wants to avoid spending time on an outside activity can still safely say, "Sorry. I'd love to. But I have work to do." The rest of life takes second place to a man's working obligations, to the point that (it is said) a corporation hiring a married man gets two employees for the price of one, his wife setting him free to be the ideal worker by taking over all the other tasks of existence. Even the women's movement recognizes the complexity that work brings to life with the wry slogan, "Every working woman needs a wife." But what in fact happens when a working woman is a wife and/or mother? Not work, but her feminine role, is her priority. Her husband is never expected to be the "wife" she needs.

The data show that when a married woman starts work, she drops none of her responsibilities for child care and household maintenance, and almost two-thirds of working women have child-care responsibilities. The data show that when a wife starts work, a husband does not increase his share of the household load. The most recent information showed that when wives started work their workload increased an average of 13 hours per week while their husband's workload actually decreased by an average 1.5 hours per week (Manpower Report to the President, 1975). It would not be just to blame individuals for this situation; for generations the culture has complacently said both that a woman's place is in the home and that her work is never done. Habit thus makes the injustice of the double workload invisible to both women and men. Both sexes probably grew up in a home where the mother did not go out to work or where, if she did, she also fulfilled the traditional feminine role at home. Most men therefore expect to marry, and most women to be, a "proper" wife and mother. Further, men tend not to regard household work as real work since it is neither paid labor nor pleasurable enough to be a hobby. The younger generation is fumbling towards a new system of equal labor, but for now a married working woman can expect to see her workload increase and her extra labor taken for granted.

Some of my clients have organized their households in an egalitarian fashion or have even reversed roles, and as a sidenote I should record their reports that the attitudes traditionally attached to "homemaker" and "breadwinner" turn out to be related almost entirely to function rather than to gender. The husband whose wife comes home unexpectedly late for a meal is just as upset as the traditional wife used to be. Wives tend to forget to carry out the garbage. Stopping off for a drink with the women or even taking time off for a morning coffeebreak are common events which startle the couple when they occur. Men taking care of the children get into trouble at work when they have to take the child to the doctor. Women too tired to play with the children when they get home from work cause and resent complaints just as traditional husbands did. My own conclusion from this is optimistic; if these emotions and events cannot be ascribed to weaknesses of the sexes, the stucture of worklife and homelife must be out of date and there is every possibility of change in those areas, no matter how slow.

Child Care

Our society still regards child care as the task of the woman, who will have to take care of them before and after work and to arrange for their care while she is at work. Sample studies show that seven out of ten preschool children are cared for by relatives or by nonrelatives in the home, though day-care centers are enlarging their small (one out of ten children) involvement (Manpower Report, 1975). School-age children are normally cared for after school in their own homes by either relatives or nonrelatives. In both cases, the mother is normally responsible for arrangements (delivery and pickup), training (of both children and care givers), and management decisions (location, selection, hiring, and firing of personnel). She *may* share responsibility for the cost, but many working women use the *larger* share of their earnings to pay for child care. The major support which relatives give to a mother who is a single head of household may be free child care.

Our society also regards a child's well-being as the task of the mother. If a child is ill, the mother is expected to stay home in preference to the father. If there are problems at school, mother will normally handle them. Mother will normally continue to get breakfast, lunch, and dinner, do the shopping and laundry, and arrange all extra activities. With such societally induced expectations, it is no wonder that working mothers feel harassed, nor that employers are nervous about hiring them, nor that some people oppose their going to work at all. As Susan A. Darley writes, "Women who seek to combine the traditional feminine role with a career are bound to be viewed as deviants within each of their role-reference groups" (Darley, 1976, p. 96). Again, however, the problems are function-related, not gender-related. Men who head households without wives have the same complex roles and report the identical anxieties and difficulties. If they have thus far received less societal disapproval, it is probably because their numbers are smaller: 1.5 million male compared to 8 million female heads of household (U.S. Bureau of the Census, 1979a).

As the extended family vanishes, the problems of child care will increase. There is no easy solution. Some couples avoid having children altogether. Others find egalitarian alternatives: redividing household work, alternating functions, sharing jobs, finding shift work or flexitime jobs, and so forth. But our discrimination against women's work shows in the normal solution wherein the task of child care rests squarely on the woman; its effect increases women's anxiety and encourages them into either intermittency or unimportant jobs rather than careers. The choice seems fairly clear. If women are to go to work (as most do), and if the "traditional" family is to remain in force, then the extra burden will rest on the wife; she will not have equal rights. If, on the other hand, the woman is to receive equal rights, then husbands and the work environment will have to change.

Dual-worker Couples

The dual-worker couple is becoming the norm for American marriage, and child care is by no means its only problem in attempting egalitarianism. In 1978, the traditional pattern of male as breadwinner and female as homemaker survived in only 34 percent of American marriages (U.S. Bureau of the Census, 1980a), and inflation is lowering that percentage rapidly. The main reason for a dual-income family is the need for money, though women's desire to work also plays an important role.

But is a dual-income family the same as a dual-career family? In the latter, the work of one would be as important as the work of the other member of the couple, and the difficulty of reaching and maintaining this state is considerable. Both people may earn money, but can they both have the career or work history and prospects they each wish? This matter is especially important to women. Within the family money normally determines power, and since men usually earn more than women, any clash between careers tends to be resolved in favor of the man. Conflict lessens if the woman merely "takes a job," preferably one which can be replaced by another job at another place or at a different time. However, if a woman chooses to have a career—with all the subsequent need for stability, progress, and planning—life for the couple grows complicated. Some of the complications are the choice to be made if one partner is offered a better job in another town, the increase in personal relationships brought to a woman through her work, the new demands on her time and energy, the division of interests stemming from work and the sharing of those interests, and ultimately the degree of autonomy for the woman which a couple can permit in view of the traditional roles they learned in their childhood homes.

Research into these issues is just beginning. At the moment it seems that the woman experiences the most pressure because of her acculturation (and his) to the role of the woman as homemaker. Current thought, however, is that the effects on husbands are equally stressful; both men and women lack role models from previous generations for this situation. There is a great difference for a man between accepting the extra income which his wife brings in and accepting the extra autonomy which a real career demands. It may be that the irrational attitudes common among husbands of wives who are newly committed to careers (especially in middle age) may be the result of their internal conflict generated by previous acculturation rather than of a simple antagonism to women.

Intermittency

As mentioned previously, a major problem for women's work is their pattern of intermittency, principally due to child rearing. The desire of women to work seriously causes problems to both partners in a marriage: will they or will they not have a child? It also causes problems to employers: precisely what are "fair" provisions for maternity leave? But child rearing is not the only cause of women's characteristic intermittency. Usually among professional and dual-career couples, the need for the husband to make a geographical move for the sake of his career will cause the wife to give up her job (Poloma and Garland, 1971; Standley and Soule, 1974). This makes sense when the male has the greater earning potential, as in most cases (Gillespie, 1976), but it also has the effect of preventing the woman from ever catching up. She loses security, promotion, and a record of stability. Finally, myth has it that women's intermittency is caused by their frailty. This is false. The absentee rates due to illness and injury of both women and men are almost identical (U.S. Women's Bureau, 1974).

Economic Inequality

Women workers typically earn less than do men, regardless of skill, training, and experience, if not in any single job then at least over a lifetime. The differential has always been there, has increased since the 1950s, and has not decreased in the 1970s (U.S. Women's Bureau, 1979c). Statistically, the major reason is the clustering of women in the lower-paid occupations, but the inequality is not just a statistical artifact. Sex-role stereotyping limits women's opportunity at the time of hiring and placement, reduces their chances for advancement, and restricts their mobility within an occupation, especially their upwards mobility. Women fare badly even in managerial and administrative jobs, either because men feel insecure about promoting them and do not evaluate them adequately or because women limit themselves—all of which processes may be unconscious as well as conscious, and which function even in the presence of Affirmative Action legislation. Though education helps, even women with doctorates and equal credentials earn less than do men and hold less decision-making authority within an organization.

Change seems to be making women "the new poor" as more of them head families alone. One out of three female-headed families lives at or near the poverty level, compared with one out of thirteen male-headed families (McEaddy, 1976). In 1978, the average income for female-headed families was $9,412, compared with $20,629 for husband-wife families (U.S. Bureau of the Census 1980b). Comparative youthfulness may worsen matters. The median age of female heads of families dropped from 50.5 in 1960 to 41.8 in 1977 (U.S. Bureau of the Census, 1979a). In 1975, one of 10 female heads of family was under 25, compared with one of 25 in 1960 (McEaddy, 1976). But divorce is the leading cause of their poverty. Compared with an earlier generation, a young woman is 2.5 times more likely to be divorced in her early 30s while her children are young, and in 1979 a divorced woman's income was only two-thirds that of a divorced man: $11,000 versus $16,500 (U.S. Bureau of the Census, 1980b).

A fairly typical case is that of a waitress who sought career counseling. At that time Teresa, a Hispanic woman, was 28, had two children (aged 10 and 11), and had been divorced over a year before. Both she and her husband had worked while married and built up a middle-class standard of life, though they were by no means wealthy. Not having finished high school, Teresa was used to working in low-skill jobs and her income was a family extra. Shortly after divorce, her income became the family's sole means of support; she received no alimony, and her former husband paid child support for only three months before leaving the state. Within six months Teresa had lost both house and car because of payments she could not meet. As a waitress she earned about $2.50 (illegally low) per hour plus tips, without benefits, so that she had to pay her own medical insurance. Her children stayed with her mother until she came home from work. Teresa wanted to work on the line at an automotive plant, where she would have a take-home check of $225 per week plus benefits; this she saw only as a start. Anticipating remaining a single head of family, she wanted to develop a full career for herself, but she had to get the manufacturing job immediately in order to survive. Thus she faced two enormously difficult tasks: meeting short-term needs and planning a long-term future, and she had to act quickly. (Like many, perhaps most, women in this situation she did not want to go on welfare.) Her plight, her previous ignorance, and the desperation of her need are all familiar.

The phrase "displaced homemaker" now so frequently used to describe women like Teresa describes only a shadow of their situation. They are refugees, suddenly deprived of their standard of living, their future, and their home, thrust without baggage into an alien world. If there is no property to be divided, no-fault divorce eliminates alimony, and child support is fragile—half of all divorced women receive neither alimony nor child support (Griffiths, 1976). If young, the woman is likely to have children and to lack time and money to plan a long-term future. If older (the divorce rate for women in their middle years has doubled since 1968), she may be entering the job market for the first time or may possess outdated or rusty skills; the decline from her previous way of living may better be described as a plunge which brings psychological disaster. The realities of this group of women are sufficient to demonstrate the economic inequality between women and men in terms of both present situation and future opportunity. The truth is that the most likely way for a woman to acquire as large a sum of money as a man might reasonably expect to earn is still through inheritance and life insurance.

Internal Barriers to Women's Achievement

During the process of sex-role socialization, many women develop characteristics which become barriers to their achievement. These are crucial to career counseling because, without either client or counselor realizing it, these characteristics determine the questions raised and the ideas accepted by the client. A female has grasped the essentials of her sex role before the age of three, and her subsequent experience of family, school, church, community, peer groups, and the media help her internalize them completely. Many "feminine" characteristics are adverse to achievement at work. Studies show that women tend to engage in less long-term planning than do men, to be unclear about their wants and needs, to depend on others to make decisions, to gain self-esteem through the achievements of significant others, to nurture others at their own expense, and to mistrust their ability to determine their own futures. To remain feeling fully feminine, women often lower their aspirations, expect less of themselves than do men, and experience more confusion than do men regarding the importance of achievement in their lives. Some scholars believe that as a group women

139

systematically avoid success (Horner, 1972). Others see them as dominated by the fear of deviating from their sex role (Bem, 1977). Regardless of details, most women experience more internal conflict about career achievement than do men.

To say that women impede their own achievement is not to blame the victim. Both men and women acquire behaviors, attitudes, and values which the culture says is appropriate to their gender and which come to seem "natural" and "normal" because they are so familiar (Bem and Bem, 1970). By the time they reach adulthood, both females and males have internalized very complex messages about work and gender; they now move into institutions and systems which are themselves generated by the same sex-role stereotypes (Smith, 1968). Our institutions for education, technical training programs, media, community organizations, political structures, family structures, and work environment are all based on stereotypes so forceful and widespread that we cannot see them any more than we can see oxygen in the air (Blaxall and Reagan, 1976; Westervelt, 1975; Zellman, 1976). All women seeking career counseling are the products of a lengthy learning process.

Sex-role stereotyping affects several very important choices:

1. The specific occupational choices women make or do not make
2. Their career patterns over a lifetime
3. The aspirations and achievement behavior of women at work

What is well termed the "female sex-role ideology" (Bem and Bem, 1970) inevitably involves career options and choices at every age (Patterson, 1973). For instance, Lipman-Blumen (1972) found its effects on adolescent females; the extent of a young woman's sex-role ideology clearly determined the level of her educational aspiration—and lowered that level. Lipman-Blumen (1972) also found that women who espouse the "vicarious achievement ethic"—that is, the belief that women should achieve success vicariously through their husbands—had lower educational objectives for themselves. In sum, the female sex-role ideology sends a message we think of as typical of heathens and ignorant ancients: girls are not as valuable as boys. Success and achievement are masculine attributes, and to strive for them is unfeminine (Tangri, 1972; Baruch, 1976). Indeed, the successful woman is a deviate (Tresemer, 1974; Deaux, 1976; Illfelder, 1980). She may find good quality work devalued, and success will bring at least some negative consequences (Horner, 1972; Romer, 1977). Even other women do not highly value a woman's success, with the result that her motivation must come almost entirely from within (Altemeyer and Jones, 1974; Goldberg, 1968; Bardwick, 1977; Bunker and Seashore, 1977).

The result is that women tend to channel themselves into educational and job choices where they feel safe because society tells them these choices are feminine (Farmer, 1978; Illfelder, 1980; Fitzgerald and Crites, 1980; Fetters, 1975). This is the major reason that career counseling for females should be different from that with males. A man may experience some kind of psychological difficulty if he wants to fail; a woman is likely to be in trouble if she wants to succeed. Women's achievements do not get the same rewards as do men's (Deaux, 1976). An achieving woman experiences conflict between her roles (O'Leary, 1977); the outer world will lessen that conflict for a man, increase it for a woman.

Women use several unconscious behaviors to lessen the conflict between the need to achieve and the need to play the traditional feminine role. At work a woman may adopt a stereotypical role for the sake of the security it provides—mother, pet, sex object, or iron maiden (Kanter, 1979). Or she may attribute her success to luck rather than competence, and in the process block reinforcement for present efforts and future performance (Feather and Simon, 1973; Frieze, 1975; Deaux, 1976). She may modify her work behavior to suit the reactions and expectations of others, especially of males she perceives as hostile to competitive and assertive women (Rosen and Anesheusel, 1976). She may conceal her achievements or give credit to others, or she may downplay what she has achieved. One of my acquaintances received a raise which made her income larger than her husband's; she told him only at income-tax time, and then only because she had to. A woman may conceal achievements even from herself. One working mother received an award for performance on the job and actually forgot to tell her family. Other women prefer not to achieve directly at all, suppressing their own talents in order to play Adoring Wife or Stage Mother. Perhaps the most stressful (and currently widespread) solution is to play Superwoman, to be both the perfect worker and the perfect homemaker in return for rewards which a man might regard as negligible (Kundsin, 1974; Scareto and Sigall, 1979). Although the Superwoman avoids reproach for inadequacy at both work and home, the stress is enormous.

Scholars tend to see all these choices more as a function of situation than of personality: which role brings the greatest reward to the individual? This approach may be especially useful to career counselors. For example, Condry and Dyer (1976) recommend looking at the barriers to female achievement "in terms of the social feedback received as a consequence of playing one or another social role," and they emphasize examining the conflicts in feedback from "different roles played at the same time." Using this approach, a career counselor can help a client clarify and improve her feedback and thus her roles. This is actually in harmony with that important cultural message women receive which warns them to weigh carefully whatever they strive for in order to calculate the odds of becoming a loser. This approach takes that message and converts it into a positive direction.

Other cautions about female motivations to achieve must be kept in mind. One very important fact is that not all women fear success or lack achievement motivation. As Frieze (1975) points out, there are wide variations among men in achievement, and since women are just as heterogeneous, the same is probably true of them. Hennig and Jardin (1977) study successful women. Fitzgerald and Crites (1980) point out that even in the original studies by Horner (1972) and Tangri (1972) not all the women feared success equally or emphasized vicarious achievement to the same degree. Government data show that many women are successful, and many successful women report no conflict with their sense of femaleness. But the question must be, how many and at what price? The norm and the tendency, especially among women coming to career counseling, is some degree of conflict.

There is a second caution. Most of the previously mentioned studies deal with educated women heading for professional or technical jobs: the middle class and the majority race. What is happening with those who go to work right after high school or training programs outside higher education—who amount to 80 percent of working women? Not enough research is available to give us secure knowledge about them, but several books give great insight. Nancy Seifer's *Nobody Speaks for Me* (1976) provides much information as to differences created by minority status, class, age, and occupational status. Louise Howe's *The Pink Collar Worker* (1977) is an excellent introduction, as is Cynthia Harrison's *Working Women Speak* (1979). Black women, who are the largest minority group in the work force, display different characteristics from white women (see Chapter 10).

If women generally achieve less than do men in the world of work, the root cause is our society's view of what is feminine. Society sees the characteristics of a successful person as male and those of a subordinate person as female. Women are expected to inhibit aggression and assertiveness, to be passive with men, and to nurture others, while men are expected to be assertive and independent (Kagan, 1964). In these circumstances it is almost impossible for a woman to feel thoroughly feminine and to succeed. Thus in our work structure women tend to service and help others and to assist males who are active, assertive, and successful. Men tend to appear in positions which require people to supervise, manage, and make decisions. If either sex tries to switch roles, it is likely to be seen as deviant. It just happens that men's sex-role socialization prepares them for the more powerful and rewarding jobs.

However, one should emphasize the acquired nature of all these "male" and "female" qualities; they are not natural but habitual, not a destiny but an accident of acculturation. They can therefore be changed. If it is true that to choose to be fully feminine is to choose economic insecurity, then, for the woman who wants to achieve, the only avenue is to see that her feminine characteristics can be used or abandoned. And the most important role a career counselor can play may be to help women clients to remove their internal barriers to development—or at least to surmount them.

External Barriers to Women's Achievement

In holding their place in the world of work, women experience all the difficulties encountered by men, and more. The basic problem is that the rules of the workplace assume that being a worker is by far the primary role in a person's life, and since society has seen men as the most important workers, the rules are designed to suit them. Even the rules of the family and the home are designed to shelter the male as worker. The effect is that the power and structure of the world of work are male-dominated, male-operated, and a reflection of male values and needs. This is not always the result of prejudice against women, but it is the effect of the close identification between "male" and "work" (Vetter, 1975).

This state of affairs is so obvious that we hardly notice it. For example, when employers hire a married male, the expectation is that his wife's domestic labors will make his time maximally available to the employer; but when they hire a married female, they have no parallel expectation of her husband. Or another example: professionals expect to channel most of their energies into work for most of the day, the year, and their lives, to the point that most males arrange their entire being on this assumption. It would suit many professional women better, however, to work seriously only part of the day, the year, or their lives, so that they would have time for their other role as homemaker, but employers see this approach to work structure as unserious, amateurish, or simply impossible. Further, ambitious males work and are rewarded for working even longer hours; but how can a woman who is already spending those longer hours fulfilling her other role possibly increase the hours she spends at the employers' work? Her only choice, if she is as ambitious as a man, is to give up or delegate her other role.

Good jobs and the career paths that lead to them are rarely interruptible; the steady upward path is the route to achievement, and few careers allow (as does an academic sabbatical) for a leave of absence. A woman who interrupts her work to have and rear a child slips back. Thus women who wish to occupy both of their roles tend toward low-paid jobs where they are replaceable (such as secretary) or they reluctantly fall behind their peers. The only acceptable interruptions to work are the regular allowances of vacation and sick leave. Anyone, female or male, who tries to move in and out of a job or career for whatever reason will almost certainly pay a price; and the price is higher for women, especially in regard to the effects of seniority rules. What is true of the lifetime career is also true of daily labor. Despite the growth of flexitime, as yet few jobs allow workers to set their own schedules, no matter how useful this would be to the person who takes care of children.

What this means to women is clear: they must choose not to work or not to have children, or to fill both roles at the same time, or to work part time at low wages, or to work intermittently. Few men would happily face these choices, yet most women do. These are the extra external variables which women face, external barriers to work which most men do not encounter. (I speak here in terms of norms. Research shows that many men find the "normal" work pattern intolerable. Interestingly, many such men openly regard themselves as mavericks and are seen by others as deviant.)

Additional barriers face a woman entering the job market. For instance, hiring habits place most women in low-paying jobs where they compete with other women rather than with men for higher-paying positions—out of six secretaries, one can become an executive secretary; out of ten canners, one can become a forewoman, and so on. How many executive secretaries or forewomen later become executives? And vice versa, how many executives started work as secretaries or operatives? In the job categories where women tend to cluster, advancement is very limited. Clerks can become supervisors of other clerks, but they will not receive the on-the-job training that would make them full-fledged administrators; this waste is often rationalized by reference to the myth of women's higher absentee rates and lower reliability (U.S. Women's Bureau, 1974). Blatant discrimination still exists. In one large accountancy firm, for instance, there are auditors, all of them male, and clerk auditors, all of them female and all receiving lower pay. The justification is that auditors have to travel and women do not want to travel; the justification thrives even though female clerk auditors repeatedly apply for promotion. When I discussed this situation with the chairman, he solemnly explained to me that women ought to stay at home to take care of their families and that the single women only wanted to find potential husbands among their travel companions, which might lead to divorces. Clerk auditors, on the other hand, he said, could not be paid as much as auditors, because the justification for higher pay was the work done while on travel status.

Thus a great many women work at jobs for which they are overqualified. Women have to trade off advantages; many accept low pay, dull work, and lack of advancement in return for the freedom to enter and leave the job market when they have to. Then—simply because they view their work life as inevitably discontinuous—they accept the devaluation of their work and their selves, and they come to accept their low pay and lesser satisfaction as both palatable and understandable. Eventually the external barriers become internal barriers; these women come to believe that their work is the only work for which they are really qualified, no matter how poor their opinion of their male supervisors' ability may be.

Family structure also discourages women from working seriously and persistently. Our society's basic belief is that the mother of young children ought to stay at home; but if she cannot *afford* to stay at home, we still make only gestures toward helping her. We complain about the expense of "welfare mothers" but criticize them for neglecting their children if they do work. Though the government provides some child-care facilities for low-income women, the subject is politically controversial and a national network of such facilities is noteworthy for its absence. Private child care is expensive; it either deprives the woman of much of her earnings or it takes away the freedom of her relatives. Almost the sole help our society provides working mothers takes the form of laborsaving devices, for which they themselves pay. Statistics show how women combine the roles of worker and homemaker; they spend an average of more than 25 hours per week on household tasks and child care (Hedges and Barnett, 1972). It is small wonder that many young women find singlehood, childless marriage, or fewer children the preferable alternatives.

Collectively, counselors can work to change labor practices and the community's degree of support for family life through community action and legislation. Individually, counselors will find other barriers that confront women are their direct professional responsibility, such as policies or traditions of the educational institutions within which many counselors work which produce in women graduates significant gender-biased differences in occupational expectations. The sex bias in elementary and secondary education has been thoroughly documented concerning textbooks and other media (U.S. National Commision on the Observance of International Women's Year, 1977a), curriculum offerings and requirements (McCandless, 1969; Berstein, 1972; Trecker, 1971; Levy, 1973; Saario, Jacklin, and Tittle, 1973), vocational counseling (Thomas and Stewart, 1971; Friedersdorf, 1970; Abramowitz, 1975; Pietrofesa and Schlossberg, 1970; Harway, Astin, Suhr, and Whiteley, 1976; Yanico, 1978), and testing (Birk, 1974; Tittle, McCarthy, and Steckler, 1974; Ahrons, 1976; Fitzgerald and Crites, 1979). All students are subject to sex-role stereotyping about work expectations, and much of it comes from counselors themselves.

Sex bias in secondary schools affects women more than it does men because many fewer women continue their educations. In 1978, 60 percent of all working women had a high school diploma and nothing more, compared with 50 percent of men; 14 percent of women, compared with 18 percent of men, had a four-year college degree (U.S. Bureau of the Census, 1980a). There are signs that our society intends to tackle sex bias at this juncture tangentially. The Manpower Administration and the Women's Bureau of the Department of Labor sponsor an outreach program in connection with the Women and Work Incentive Program wherein, by working with trade unions and employers, they encourage women with less education to enter the skilled trades. The point, however, is surely that a remedial approach should not be necessary. The task of removing sex bias should have been undertaken in the schools, and counselors are among those who should see that it is done.

Post-secondary education is almost entirely male-dominated and male-operated. According to the National Center for Education Statistics, in 1977–1978, 74.6 percent of full-time college faculty were men, and the average annual salary for women was $17,604 compared with $23,447 for men (Women's Educational Equity Communications Network Newsletter, 1979). Both two-year and four-year colleges show sex bias in admissions practices, in conditions for financial aid, rules and regulations, curricula, student services, and faculty and staff attitudes (Westervelt, 1975). Traditionally, universities take women's work expectations less seriously than those of men. If they are beginning to change, it is only the result of a combination of anti-discrimination legislation (Title IX of the Education Amendments of 1972, Title VII and Title VIII of the Public Health Service Act of 1971) and their need to find a new reservoir of prospective students in an era of declining enrollments. Technical programs especially retain informal sex quotas or reject a higher proportion of female than of male applicants, particularly if the program leaders believe that women will have more difficulty than will men in finding future jobs in the area (Hooper, 1973).

Admissions policies affect women adversely by means of age restrictions and age bias, the difficulty of transferring credits, or reluctance to accept a prior pattern of part-time or intermittent study—all more likely to affect females than males because of their differing patterns of life. The discrimination here may be termed "accidental," as it often is with financial aid. In the latter case, if aid is restricted to full-time students, if no child-care costs are taken into account, if no policy exists for staggered or deferred payment, if work–study opportunities are limited, then women as a group are affected much more quickly than are men—especially older women with family responsibilities. The males in charge of admissions and financial aid are most unlikely to be aware of this problem. Women also reasonably complain that classes, professors, and study resources have schedules that ignore women's special needs and that universities fail to provide child-care facilities for parent/students (Westervelt, 1975).

The major problem in higher education is traditionalism. Colleges and universities for the most part seem out of date in regard to the current trend towards equality for women; older women returning to school often report that they are expected to have the life-styles of young males, for whom the system was designed. There is a pervasive failure among faculty and staff to abandon traditional attitudes toward women as women and women as students, hence the general inability to respond to their special needs. Women frequently report that faculty and staff fail to encourage their career goals and aspirations, often forcing them into an obedient hypocrisy which has little to do with education but is geared toward getting grades and degrees. Sex stereotypes also drastically influence academic and career counselors (who in turn complain that they cannot influence the faculty). Formal and informal sex discrimination affects women's job placements both during and after education. Complaints that male faculty see women students primarily as sexual beings are common, but the major problem may be the absence or low proportion of female faculty who can act as role models and leaders (Westervelt, 1975). Affirmative action is working with extraordinary slowness in equalizing representation among faculty. One report, for instance, recently pointed out that at Cornell University the proportion of male faculty declined from 92.4 percent in 1971 (when its Affirmative Action Program began) to 91.7 percent in 1979, a rate which would equalize the number of female and male professors by the year 2395 (The *Spokeswoman*, 1980a).

The number and nature of degrees awarded shows a pattern of inequality. In 1976–1977, women earned 46 percent of the bachelors' degrees and 47 percent of the masters' degrees (an increase of seven percent since 1930), and in 1975–1976 they earned 21.3 percent of the doctoral degrees, an increase from 14.3 percent in 1970–1971 (National Institute of Education, 1977b; Ott, 1977). The areas in which women and men earn doctorates are very different. Of the eight major discipline divisions, their proportions are roughly similar in only the social sciences and the biological sciences. In other areas the differences are as follows: in education, women 30.6 percent and men 19.1 percent; in engineering, women 0.7 percent and men 12.3 percent; in foreign languages, women 6.1 percent and men 1.9 percent; in letters, women 12.7 percent and men 6.6 percent; in the physical sciences, women 4.5 percent and men 13.3 percent; in psychology, women 9.9 percent and men 5.5 percent (Ott, 1977). Women with doctorates are unlikely to earn as much as do men with doctorates. They start at roughly the same salary, but within five to six years the men earn an average of $18,700, the women an average of $16,400, while after 22 to 23 years of experience (using 1973 data) men earned an average of $27,100 and women an average of $21,800 (Centra, 1974).

Shorter post-secondary education suits women better. In programs lasting one to two years, women in 1970 earned 55 percent of the engineering and science degrees and 69 percent of the nonscience degrees. In programs lasting two to three years, their proportion dropped sharply, to 38 percent in science/engineering and 47 percent in nonscience. This kind of information should be very useful to career counselors; it is the reason for the Vocational Education Bill of 1976, which requires each state to hire staff to help end sex bias in vocational education. It may be that males waste time and money on longer programs, though these generally lead to better employment and higher pay; but regardless of the merits of different educational patterns, the data show a clear differential between the developmental routes of women and men. Here, as in all other educational areas, our post-secondary structure is based on sex discrimination.

The Obligations of the Counseling Profession

In a recent survey conducted by the National Commission on Working Women, working women cited inadequate career counseling as one of their major complaints (Harrison, 1979). In 1976, Congresswoman Martha Griffiths commented, "Women are confined to low-paying jobs by virtue of their educational level, the type of counseling they receive, and society's unwillingness to accept the real reasons why women work." Thus the counseling professions, indicted, have certain responsibilities that are less a matter of preference than of professional obligation.

To Know the Law

The most immediate obligation of any mental health professional counseling women on the subject of work is to know what forms of discrimination against working women are illegal, so that suspected injustice may be investigated with the help of a lawyer. Statutes differ from state to state, so no detailed guide can be given here. Many rights also rest on decisions made by state courts, again preventing summary here and possibly necessitating legal help. The Equal Rights Amendment to the Constitution would greatly simplify the equalization process, though it would inevitably produce further detailed interpretations by the courts; but at the federal level there has already been a sequence of legislation which, though neither coordinated nor comprehensive, addresses the basic areas in which discrimination formerly prevailed. That sequence of legislation is as follows:

1. Equal Pay Act of 1963, with Amendments in 1972 and 1974.
2. Title VII, Civil Rights Act of 1964, as amended by the Equal Employment Opportunity Act of 1972.
3. Age Discrimination in Employment Act of 1967.
4. Executive Order 11246 (effective Oct. 14, 1968), as amended by Executive Order 11375.
5. Public Health Service Act of 1971, Title VII and Title VIII, as amended.
6. Education Amendments of 1972, Title IX, as amended.
7. State and Local Fiscal Assistance Act (Revenue Sharing) of 1972.
8. Civil Rights Act of 1968, Title VIII, as amended in 1974.
9. Equal Credit Opportunity Act of 1974, with amendments effective 1976.

This legislation does not seek advantages for women, only to remove disadvantages stemming from custom, habit, and existing law. Each item of legislation has been interpreted by the courts and is being implemented by federal agencies. In some cases, where the need for equality has brought with it the need for affirmative action, women have been given positive advantages by regulation or requirement (as in government contracts); since these change and develop at irregular times, detailed legal information will have to be specially sought. Generally speaking, women are now protected by federal legislation against discrimination in the areas of pay, employment, education, health, age, race, credit, and housing. Since, however, these laws have to be implemented by courts issuing rulings, agencies issuing regulations, and state legislatures changing laws, one cannot assume that the battle has been won. Details of the laws have not been decided, many laws are poorly enforced, and women are often ignorant of their rights or unwilling to insist upon them. Mental health professionals cannot assume that clients know their rights or that other people are charged with seeing that those rights are ensured.

Some excellent sources of information about the various laws and regulations affecting women are available.

1. "Federal Laws and Regulations Prohibiting Sex Discrimination" (detailed display poster), Women's Equity Action League, 733 Fifteenth St. N.W., Suite 200, Washington, D.C., 20005. $1.25 each.

2. American Civil Liberties Union, *The Rights of Women*, 1973.

3. Publications of the Women's Bureau, Employment Standards Administration, U.S. Department of Labor, Washington, D.C. 20210.

1975 Handbook on Women Workers, Bulletin 297, 1975.

"A Working Women's Guide to Her Job Rights," Leaflet 55, 1978.

"Brief Highlights of Major Federal Laws and Orders on Sex Discrimination," 1978.

"State Labor Laws in Transition: From Protection to Equal Status for Women," 1976.

4. Ross, Susan D., *The Rights of Women: An American Civil Liberties Union Handbook*, Discus Books published by Avon, New York, New York, 1973.

5. *To Form a More Perfect Union: Justice for American Women*, Report of the National Commission on the Observation of International Women's Year, 1976. For sale by the Superintendent of Documents, U.S. Government Printing Office, Washington, D.C. 20402. $5.20 per copy.

To Understand Women's Work Needs

Assuming that a professional has a basic understanding of the law of the land, her or his next obligation is to understand in depth the career and vocational needs of women as a group. This is not a simple task; knowledge of facts and comparative freedom from myth is essential—and difficult to obtain. Working within institutions as most of us do, influenced from childhood by theories and traditions based on male models, we all find the route to fairness difficult. This *may* be impossible for a male counselor and will certainly require much more effort on his part; it will be difficult enough for a female counselor. If only by virtue of having a job, education, career, income, knowledge, experience of the working world, and so forth, even the female counselor will differ from most of her clients in ways she must understand if she is to avoid having unrealistic expectations. The client's needs concerning work will not be the same as those of the counselor, and it is the counselor's obligation to detect the differences.

Only the knowledge of women's special work needs will enable a mental health professional to treat a woman as though she is not a failed man. Women have different expectations and aspirations and problems, and the overlap between women and men in these areas unfortunately only confuses the issue by blurring the much greater disparity. Because women receive different treatment from society (starting in childhood), because they are rewarded for different behavior, because they are haunted by different role conflicts, because they have never learned the skills and games which mean success for men in the economic sphere, they invariably have much to learn about work and career in order to catch up to men, and they have to learn under much more difficult circumstances. The lessons learned from our culture never vanish completely from the subconscious underbrush. They fade fitfully, perhaps slowly, perhaps by means of a sudden realization, but their eradication requires persistent effort by both women and counselors. It is easy to say that we do not regard women as different from and inferior to men; it is much harder to act as though we regard women as different from and equal to men.

The realities a woman experiences in the working world and in the rest of her life are experiences she shares with many other women and with very few men. Her choices in education, training, job, and career will be subject to influences different from those affecting men's choices and they will have different consequences economically, socially, politically, and psychologically. At the moment, career counseling for women is more complex than that for men, if only because change in society makes it an area where the counselor can take nothing for granted, where habits and routines must be questioned in the light of the facts.

The professional's own values must be called into question. Let us take an example. One well-known study (Matthews and Tiedeman, 1974) shows that there is a sharp drop, between junior and senior high school years, in the degree of commitment to a career which females display. If counselors are working with this age group, what should they do about that finding? Go along with the existing trend, preparing young women for the life they think they want? Actively combat the trend? Comply with it but ameliorate it by small homilies and rescue missions of individuals? Exhort the school as a whole to change its orientation and curriculum? Change the individual student's internal values? Provide passive understanding and support for the client's free choice? Offer education and information alone? Threaten the student by means of dire predictions about her likely future? Any of these is possible. None is meaningful unless the professional understands long-term consequences, likelihoods for the future, and pressures on the present.

To Help a Client Widen Her Options

Statistics and studies cited in previous sections show that women tend to narrow their options and often remain relatively passive in regard to work and income. The professional's obligation is to contest the narrowing and to activate. As a result of counseling, the client should view both herself and the world differently; as far as women and work are concerned, the difference should be measurably less passivity (and probably conventionality) when the woman chooses or changes training, career, education, job, or vocation, when she identifies her "proper" wage or salary, or when she is affected by one of those major events that disturb the life of a person who is both worker and homemaker.

Perhaps the most important area in which a client's perspective needs widening is her judgment of the purpose and seriousness of work. Society, and women, tend to believe that work is not really as important to a woman as it is to a man. Even sophisticated feminists are sometimes startled to find in themselves the small and unconscious expectation that sometime a man will be there to "take care" of them, even though they know that to be irrelevant to their work lives. If a woman marries, she will still work—before she marries, while she is married, and after the marriage ends. Her income will be necessary to her, and it may be essential to her family, with or without spouse. To make as much money as does an equivalent male, she will probably have to work harder or better, train more, and plan at least as well. In sum, to rely on others to take care of her is to risk placing herself and her children in a state of economic and psychological disaster. Despite all this, Juliet may continue to cling to the hope of Romeo. The myths are powerful, pervasive, and attractive; a client may listen and disbelieve. Thus the counselor's obligation is to insist at every stage of a woman's life that there are other choices, other ways of seeing herself now and in the future.

We are now talking about survival, not just happiness and self-fulfillment. Working women, according to the studies, may indeed be happier and healthier than nonworking wives; but before we discuss mental health we must deal with economic well-being, which remains the base in our society for many other sources of contentment or dissatisfaction. We are dealing with the rights of women simply to participate equally in the world of money, to earn during their lifetimes as much as they need and deserve.

To Attend to a Client's Rights

Neither women nor their counselors feel comfortable about asserting rights. Too few women insist upon their legal rights to equal pay, equal treatment, and equal opportunity, never considering asking for understanding of their special needs even when merited, and professionals are uneasy about being seen as militant. However, especially if counselors work for institutions funded by public money, it is clearly their responsibility to inform their clients of that to which they are entitled under law. It is not a matter of militancy but one of professional and civic duty. One article on the subject (Pendergrass, 1975) points out that this may involve the professional in handling requests for legal advice, assuaging depression and anxiety about the value of a woman's work, advising women with a good suit who do not wish to file or those with a poor suit who do wish to file, and supporting a plaintiff during a case. This may occur at any of several stages: when the client recognizes the problem, when she decides to act, when data or support from officialdom or the public are needed, when it becomes important to speak up to the responsible administrator or to keep detailed records of proceedings, or when an institution reacts either overtly or covertly. An adequate knowledge of processes and resources, as well as of the client, is an obligation of the counselor.

Where sex discrimination is overtly at issue, professionals often cannot judge how far their obligations to the client extend. Do they stop with psychological support or go as far as activism? Is there a conflict between their role with the client and their role as an employee? Should they help soothe or activate the client? Should they anticipate or react? Much will depend on personal judgments and on the specific type of counseling which is taking place, but despite all the possible confusion, the very least obligation of the counselor is to assert meaningfully the client's right to equality. The entire subject deserves careful thought from the professional, not a hasty decision of any kind.

That last sentence, indeed, might serve as a summary of all a counselor's obligations to female clients in this area. The process of counseling women requires constant self-questioning, and there is some truth to the rueful joke that counseling a working woman is almost as hard as being one. Given the general facts of women's situation as workers, given the individual fact of this client's existence, what should the client do and what should I do? What are the ramifications? Where does my responsibility begin and end? What do I do with what I know? Since these are the kinds of question which good counselors ask in any situation, in that sense the process of counseling women is not basically different from that of any counseling. The extra obligation is simply to understand that the realities of working women's lives make the counseling process that much more complex.

Figure 6.1, a fact sheet summarizing the changes in women's work lives, may be used by therapists to help their clients see the dimensions of change within which they live.

FIGURE 6.1. Counselor's Fact Sheet on Major Changes in Women's Work Lives

The life-work patterns of women are changing dramatically today. Here are some important facts you must be aware of:

- With the rising levels of educational attainment and career expectations, today's women differ dramatically from their mothers and grandmothers.
- Women are playing an increasingly important role in the U.S. economy. They comprise 40% of the civilian labor force today, as compared to 29% in 1950, and 20% in 1920.
- Today, over half of all women 18 years and older work outside the home in paid employment.
- Women work, on the average, 25 years outside the home in paid employment. This is an increase from 15 years in 1950 and 9 years in 1920.
- The average life expectancy for a woman today is 75 years, compared to 71 years in 1950, and 55 years in 1920. Women today outlive men by approximately 7 years.
- The typical worker in the United States today is 34 years old and married. The predominance of younger single women as workers earlier in the century is no longer true.
- The majority of women workers today are married and living with their husbands.
- The average age for re-entrance into the workforce today is 35 years old, when the youngest child enters school full-time. Many women re-enter the working world at this time, and remain until retirement age.
- Increasing numbers of women are not leaving the workforce for child rearing, but are planning their work lives around this responsibility.
- Unmarried women and married life-long working women have identical work life expectancies as men—from 40–45 years.
- Rising divorce rates and the increasing numbers of families headed by women have made working an economic necessity for significant and ever-growing numbers of women.
- Add facts to this list relevant to the clientele and population you as a counselor serve.
- _____
- _____
- _____

7

Career Counseling

Combining the information presented in the preceding chapter with the model for client change presented in Chapter 2, we derive a suggestion for a counseling approach specific to the career needs of women and some techniques which career counselors may use; these are the subject of the present chapter. Adequate rewards and satisfactions from work are a *basic* need for women. Women as a group are not clear about how to realize these needs, and both they and various perplexed institutions are turning more frequently to the profession of career counseling for solutions, even though that profession itself is too often ill-prepared to deal with the problem. The principles and techniques in this chapter are intended to assist career counselors in proceeding toward the fulfillment of those needs.

The Goals

The basic objectives of career counseling are as follows:

1. To destroy the myths, especially the internalized myths about women and work, that lead women to limit their own choices, plans, and fulfillment as workers.
2. To provide women with both the perceptions and the skills they need to overcome—on their own—both the internal and the external barriers to their advancement.
3. To provide services and support which will help women function effectively in a male-dominated environment.

These objectives are in addition to other counseling goals because the needs of women are different from those of men. They require a substantial restructuring of many existing counseling programs, but they are not in conflict with the existing goals of the career counseling profession. It is their absence, however, in existing programs which makes many women clients angry to the point of stridency, and these objectives should therefore seem only the minimal goals of a good program. They are simply the means of updating a profession which has fallen sadly and harmfully away from its obligations.

Sexism in Present Approaches

It should come as no surprise to learn that sexism pervades the discipline of career counseling. Though different research studies say it in different ways, all agree that women are the victims of inadequate and/or biased counseling, that when a counselor looks at a female student she or he sees a female rather than a whole person. Bias has been documented in the counseling process, in vocational tests, and in career information (Medvene and Collins, 1976; Harrison, 1979; Fitzgerald and Crites, 1979; Donahue and Costar, 1977). Both female and male counselors exhibit bias against women entering traditionally male occupations (Thomas and Stewart, 1971; Pietrofesa and Schlossberg, 1970). The only clear difference between female and male counselors in this matter is that males seem less accurately informed about female attitudes and occupational alternatives, so that female counselors may be marginally more realistic about issues and more supportive of women clients (Bingham and House, 1973). However, it is thought that the women's movement of the 1970s may be having the effect of widening the differential.

Counseling Tests

The area of testing shows how sex discrimination affects counseling. Authors of test instruments are becoming increasingly more aware that discrimination can unconsciously bias their questions and interpretations, and a substantial effort to remove that bias is taking place. Take, for example, three inventories widely used by career counselors:

1. The Strong-Campbell Interest Inventory (SCII, 1976) revised the admittedly biased Strong Vocational Interest Blank (SVIB, 1966). SVIB had one version for women and another for men. SCII—vulgarly called "the Unisex Strong"—combined all questions into one instrument, eliminated sex-specific questions, and modified sex-related vocabulary. Counselors use it under the impression that it is free of sex bias (Fitzgerald and Crites, 1980), whereas it is currently under revision in a further attempt to make it genuinely nondiscriminatory and better suited to the needs of women (Crites, 1978).

2. The Kuder Occupational Interest Survey (KOIS) developed a new format and leaflet during the 1970s because the previous format used masculine pronouns throughout, separate occupation-based criterion groups for females and males, and separate occupational and college-major scales in the leaflet. Though the new KOIS reduces the number of gender-linked items and gives more freedom of choice in its occupation lists, the controversy over its suitability for women continues (Fitzgerald and Crites, 1980).

3. The Holland Self-Directed Search creates major problems for women and minorities (Harway et al, 1976; Crites, 1978). Its limited choice of interests and abilities influences the outcome against them because white males have more opportunities to develop those interests and abilities.

Efforts to improve these inventories are of course praiseworthy, but the old versions are widely used and large numbers of present counselors have been trained with them. Their effect thus seems to be a limiting rather than a widening of women's career options and a reinforcement of traditional female career patterns (Fitzgerald and Crites, 1980). Fortunately, the number of revisions and new instruments is growing; the Schiffer checklist (Schiffer, 1978), the Zytowski evaluation method (Zytowski, 1978) and the Prediger and Lamb (Prediger and Lamb, 1979) self-check system for sex balance within the counselor's own population all seem likely to prove useful. New materials such as the Vocational Exploration and Insight Kit (Talbot and Birk, 1979) are being studied and tested, and new models for career planning by women which do not rely on interest inventories are being developed (O'Neil, Meeker, and Borgers, 1978). Counselors interested in avoiding bias in their testing need to be alert to both the old and the new in this area, with the major principle that the offering of a full range of career options should be their goal.

The guidelines for career interest inventories promulgated in 1975 by the National Institute of Education provide a primer of elements for which a counselor should examine any instrument. In the inventory itself, suggest the guidelines, the same form should be used for women and men unless separate forms are empirically validated as nonbiased; scores for all occupations should be given for both women and men; item pools should either reflect experiences and activities equally familiar to both sexes or should balance activities familiar to each sex; either occupational titles should be gender-neutral or both male and female titles should appear; and the generic "he" should not appear. In the technical information, the description of criterion and norm groups should include sex composition; criterion and norm data should be updated every five years; and the test's validity for minority groups should be investigated. Interpretive information should be affirmative, pointing out that environmental and cultural factors affect one's vocational interests and choices, that all jobs are appropriate for qualified people of either sex, and that the myths about women and men are based on stereotypes. (Further details of considerable importance appear in Harway, et al, 1976, pp. 137–138.)

Developmental Theories

The best-known career development theories now taught are inadequate, inappropriate, and counterproductive for women, essentially because they assume a similarity between female and male career development that does not exist. They disregard the effects of socialization on the lives of women. They ignore the internal and the external barriers blocking women's career development. They ignore the vocational and developmental tasks wherein women vary from men and which require different theoretical formulations (Patterson, 1973; Osipow, 1975; Fitzgerald and Crites, 1980).

The four general theories of vocational development usually taught—those of Roe, Holland, Super, and Ginsberg—all illustrate the problem. Though all are useful, they all explain career development as though it were the same for everyone, ignoring the special factors affecting women (and other minorities).

1. Roe's Personality Theory of Career Development rightly emphasizes the impact of socialization by focusing on personality and childhood experiences, but it fails to deal specifically with the great difference in the socialization of women as a group and with the results of socialization in women's career choices.
2. Holland's Theory of Vocational Behavior at least recognizes that it has limited application to women and acknowledges the differences between the developmental tasks of women and men, but it fails to present any specific approaches that would respond to those tasks.
3. Super's Vocational Theory fails to account for the way in which women develop their vocational self-concept and is therefore of limited use. Since women do not have as wide an exposure as do men to different careers and since they are strongly socialized against considering some of them, Super's emphasis on developmental events tends to keep women restricted to the traditionally female careers.
4. Ginsberg's Vocational Development Theory conceptualizes both sexes as having the same developmental tasks and goals, ignoring the mass of research that shows varying developmental tasks for both sexes and minority groups.

Thus all four theories have limited usefulness with women because they are based on male patterns and needs (Holland, 1966; Falk and Crosby, 1978; Fitzgerald and Crites, 1980).

Research has shown that we need theories better suited to the special needs of women as a sex. Where the career development of women is similar to that of men, existing theories are useful. Where the development of the two sexes is dissimilar, they are not only useless but destructive, leading counselors to ignore important and even critical differences. Fortunately, work has begun on better theories; Zytowski's Theory of Career Development for Women, developed during the 1960s, uses the female life cycle as its framework. Psathas' Theory of Occupation Choice for Women emphasizes the crucial relationship between sex and occupational choice in influencing women's entry into and movement through the working world.

However, there are major problems with both of these theories. Zytowski presupposes that the homemaker role is the basic life role for a woman, from which work and career are departures. Since this is not only a form of sexism but also does not apply to numerous women, his theory loses usefulness. Zytowski also assumes that women are free to choose among career patterns, thus ignoring the restrictions that typify their lives. Finally, he assumes that the roles of homemaker and worker are mutually exclusive, which renders his theory irrelevant for approximately half of all women. Psathas, on the other hand, grounds his theory firmly in the social context of women's vocational choices. The problem with his theory is that it has an exclusively middle-class perspective and emphasizes a developmental track and a variety of options which are simply not available to many working women.

Thus we have six major theories of career development, each of which has a limited use with most women, some of which are dangerous. Counselors should use all of them with discretion and even skepticism, aware of their sex bias and socioeconomic prejudices. At all costs, a counselor should not *assume* that any theory is appropriate for a particular client, especially when dealing with women from racial and ethnic minorities. No satisfactory construct for women's career development exists, and it is perilous to make do with the nearest reputable substitute. One has to use the existing theories for whatever they are worth, remaining aware that any of them might be hazardous to this particular client's well-being and future.

Attitudes

Career counselors need to develop certain habitual attitudes towards women clients if they are to achieve their goals. These attitudes are hardly revolutionary, but they are the minimal requirements to meet the needs of women specifically during this particular time of rapid change.

1. *Discover the facts about this particular client.* The need for this attitude is so obvious that its statement is almost embarrassing, but the truth is that very few people bother to examine an individual client's situation and nature to the necessary depth. To work with a client on the basis of a randomly presented self-report or as a "sample" of a subgroup is as risky as it is frequent. To work with a woman solely on the basis of the information one would collect about a man is equally risky. Rather, it is necessary almost to diagram the individual's past and present situation by examining in depth such matters as her family situation, income, education, work experience, preferences, and values. The aim of the process is to determine precisely what are the real as well as the perceived needs of this woman as she enters counseling.

2. *Encourage acknowledgment of the realities of working women's lives.* Because of acculturation, it is wise to assume that a woman client will in at least some respects be unrealistic about and ignorant of the realities of working women's lives. None of them will know as much about the subject as a good career counselor should. They are likely, for instance, to be unrealistic about money, marriage, and child rearing. They are unlikely to have the habit of long-term planning. They may have romantic illusions, and they almost certainly do not recognize their self-imposed limitations. The necessary counseling approach is to emphasize reality and require a positive response to it.

3. *Reassure the client that her situation is "normal."* Women usually bring more than their proper share of anxiety and guilt to counseling if they are having some problem about work. When problems or doubts arise, women tend to blame themselves. Counselors need to reassure them that their anxieties are legitimate, their guilts understandable, their situations similar to those of other women, and that the sources of their concerns are not just personal inadequacy. This kind of counseling often works by connecting the general realities with the individual situation.

4. *Reassure the client that her problem has solutions.* Optimism may be one of counseling's best gifts. Because women take on extra loads and responsibilities as a matter of duty, they tend to become frustrated and discouraged when they cannot solve their problems all on their own, and they tend to feel inadequate or hopeless. The assertion by the counselor that special techniques and materials to help them do exist surprises many clients.

5. *Start dealing with specifics as soon as possible.* Because women's work choices are highly complex, women clients often tend to see their problems as too large to be soluble. Breaking their problem into parts and handling one part at a time, though not an infallible technique by any means, helps to clarify the situation and gives clients a sense of power, which may be their greatest overall need.

6. *Have the client accept responsibility for her own situation.* Counselors should avoid making women's choices for them; this would perpetuate the cultural pattern that hobbles women in the first place. The counselor's task is to create awareness within the client, to present facts and alternatives, and then, most important, to train her to make a knowing choice. That choice may well be one which the counselor would not make; but it is more important that it be the client's own and therefore, in the long run at least, more likely to be right.

Stages of Career Development

Three stages in a woman's career development emerge as those at which a counselor is most likely to have some usefulness. A woman may be in any one of these stages at any age, and she may be in more than one of them at the same time. Detecting precisely where a client is may indeed be one of the counselor's most

158

productive tasks if it results in the client moving up from one form of work to another more rewarding.

Choosing a Career Pattern

When a client is choosing a whole career pattern, whether her first or a new pattern, counselors correctly emphasize any or all of the following matters.

1. To overcome the tendency of women to cluster in low-paid, dead-end, traditionally feminine occupations, good career counseling surveys the wide variety of job opportunities now available, insists that very few or no occupations are gender-dependent, and encourages the client to consider occupations which require greater skills and responsibility and which offer more reward and opportunity.

2. In terms of time and commitment, the work lives of the two sexes are coming to resemble each other much more closely. Good career counseling for women therefore emphasizes long-range and in-depth planning, not just finding a job or developing a single skill.

3. Legal rights are useless if unknown; many clients are unaware of recent legislation which protects their right to work. Good counseling informs and ensures that clients know who will help if they encounter illegal discrimination.

4. To redress past discrimination, federal and state programs exist with the intention of training women to enter the nontraditional occupations; clients rarely know of their existence. Good counselors have the duty to stay informed, especially regarding material supplied by the Women's Bureau of the U.S. Department of Labor and by means of periodicals like *The Spokeswoman*.

5. From the outset, career counseling should endeavor to remove both external and internal barriers to women's work equality by facilitating nonstereotyped decision making, encouraging self-exploration, providing a broad spectrum of options, and emphasizing long-term economic needs.

6. Intake forms, inventories, and testing instruments which contain any element of sex bias should be avoided.

7. Counselors should scrutinize their own institutions for subtle manifestations of sex discrimination (e.g., a situation in which all clerical workers are female and all supervisors male). If the institution itself fails to act as a model, its hypocrisy will affect clients adversely.

8. If a counselor learns of a source of active discrimination within the community, state, or region, she or he should consider what may be done. If the discrimination is illegal, then counselors should take action without hesitation.

9. For dealing with racial and ethnic minorities, special training and a specific environment is necessary, not just desirable. Many counseling institutions fail to attract minority-group clients who most need their services, often for reasons which can be quickly identified and altered.

10. Because so many older women are entering the work force, age bias within

the job market—and in the counselor—is a major issue. Counselors should receive special training against it, and they should be alert to age bias in their environment. Its presence in clients should also be investigated, since it is perhaps the major influence on the choices about career made by older women. (By "older women" one may mean women as young as their mid-20s; in other words, anyone past the usual age for beginning a career.)

Entering or Reentering the Working World

One quickly forgets what it was like to start work, and if one has never left the work force for an extended period, it is impossible to know personally what it is like to resume work. These failures of empathy prevent counselors from responding to some of the major needs and anxieties of clients.

1. Most potential workers need help in acquiring the skills needed in getting a job: writing a résumé or filling out a job application, being interviewed, searching for a job, communicating effectively, and so forth. In addition, women need help in perceiving and overcoming the self-imposed limits on their expectations. They may also need help in identifying and overcoming external barriers—employers' habits in interviewing, hiring, or placement, for instance—since they do not have the experience to know what is happening.

2. To expand clients' horizons, workshops and role models are invaluable. Clients do not know what to expect; discussions with experienced workers from a variety of fields can have dramatic effects on clients' attitudes towards what they themselves might achieve. Role models can be essential in discussing the potential of their work, describing how they trained for and found their jobs, giving tips and warnings about what to expect, and so on. They help clients overcome anticipatory fears and they lower the level of shock when the client starts work. They can provide a measure of the limitations of a particular occupation and suggest alternative tracks.

3. Counselors can negotiate with placement offices to ensure that women and men have equal opportunity with interviews, that the work environment meets women's special needs (e.g., adequate sanitary facilities), and that steps are being taken to reduce any antagonism toward women among existing workers.

4. Counselors should be ready to work with the frustration experienced by the many women who cannot find occupations or jobs commensurate with their abilities. They can provide both practical and emotional alternatives, and they can especially help clients move from docility or powerless anger towards openness and productive energy.

5. Legal rights again require emphasis at this stage. Counselors should be able to equip a client with methods of responding, for example, to interviewers who ask illegal questions about their plans for marriage and child rearing and to show her different ways of dealing with a prospective employer's concern about her degree of commitment to a career or her mobility within a business.

Functioning Effectively at Work

There are at least two distinct levels of "functioning" in the world of work: daily and long-term. Either or both may be a client's problem, and a counselor's time is eventually better spent working with the long term. This is not to derogate the effect of daily problems on workers' lives at all; it is rather to say that the counselor's task is to keep them in perspective and context. (On daily matters, many useful books directed to women now exist, with more created every month. Directing the client to read them on her own also serves the purpose of encouraging her sense of autonomy.)

1. Life span planning is the most comprehensive approach to long-term functioning at work, and it is one which most women have not considered. Comprehensiveness is especially important because of the several roles which any woman is likely to balance at different times in her life. Life span planning helps to give them a sense of flexibility and of the variety of options which they will have at different stages. In connection with career counseling, its purpose is to help them evaluate and re-establish their work goals.

2. Support systems are important to all workers. Women tend to have narrower and smaller support systems than do men, and they tend to orient these supports less toward achievement at work. Counseling programs can thus usefully establish support groups and networks which, on the one hand, help clients deal with short-term problems and needs and, on the other, encourage them to expand their horizons.

3. Power structures are not entities with which women are usually comfortable, though working men almost automatically orient themselves towards them. Counselors can help women workers understand and exploit the power structures within the working environment, whether these structures are formal or informal, and they can actually teach those who wish how to interact with them through the kinds of behavior that include or exclude one from membership. Males tend to intermingle or parallel their social and business relationships at work while women tend to separate them. Understanding male behavior creates an option for women that may turn out to be essential to their advancement.

4. All workers need to know how to deal properly with conflict, confrontation, negotiation, collaboration, alliance building, and compromise. Though some women are extraordinarily skillful in these areas, most need special training (usually by means of games and simulations) at least in adapting their existing skills to the new situation. It is not clear why this should be so, but important reasons for their needing these skills include their minority status within male-dominated institutions, their tendency to be kept in subordinate and powerless situations, and their isolation (especially if there are only a few women co-workers). Most males become comfortable with these skills during childhood, particularly through team sports.

5. Dual-worker marriage normally weighs more heavily on the wife than the husband. Many techniques exist for handling daily problems resulting from the

homemaker role which she is expected to fulfill; in this case counselors will find a productive link between the daily and the real long-term problem, which is whether she and her husband see her work as less important than his. The management of multiple roles is an area where career counselors can legitimately function when one of the roles is that of worker.

At all three of these stages of women's relationship to work, career counseling needs to be subtle and imaginative. The truism that a career counselor deals with a whole person, not just a working person, is more true of women clients than of men. Males tend to subordinate private life to working life, lowering at all costs the amount of trouble they have with work. Females' multiple roles make such ruthlessness difficult. Women and men in general perceive their relationship to work differently. Men assume not just that they will work but also that they have a right to work, that they have a right to the best work for them, and that their work rights should be expected. Women know that they need to work, but they think much less often of their "rights." They take work they do not like, they do dull work with less resistance, and they lack a strong concept of work rights. They are more easily imposed upon, which is a quality well in line with the feminine stereotype to which they have been conditioned. In career counseling, they usually find the examination of external and internal barriers fascinating and stimulating. Their self-esteem rises, and they gain the vital sense of being able to change matters that concern them.

Techniques

Inevitably, what one says in sections such as the preceding sounds too general, like an exhortation, whereas it should result in fairly straightforward changes of counseling technique. Thus the following section tries to give samples—by no means all-inclusive—of the kinds of techniques which fit the ideas recommended.

Facts About the Client

Where intake forms, inventories, and tests are used, they should be both thorough and free of sex bias. They may legitimately expand beyond subjects directly related to education, training, career needs, and work experience in order to uncover some of the multiple roles the client is filling. Clients may find this intrusive, and for this and other reasons a format which encourages the client to scrutinize her own situation and specify her own needs from a variety of options is desirable. In essence, this format begins the counseling process and starts the client on the path of taking responsibility for her own choices. A checklist prepared from the stages in career development, above, can be appended to the usual forms which collect standard personal data. During and after the interview, the counselor needs to assess the facts about the client's needs and situation in a systematic manner.

Destroying Myths

The best possibility of destroying a myth is through presentation of fact rather than argument. Indeed, rather than arguing a client into facing reality, counselors may find her stubborn preference for a certain myth provides vital clues to her genuine difficulties stemming from acculturation or her situation.

Several methods for providing a client with facts and then detecting whether the myth has been slain may be used. Of central usefulness can be a fact sheet distributed to all clients. Counselors may assemble their own, or they may use an existing fact sheet such as that entitled "The Myth and the Reality" provided by the Women's Bureau of the Department of Labor. Another effective technique, especially in groups, is to ask the clients to record their own beliefs about women and work and then cooperatively find out whether they are true or not; the counselor and printed materials act as resources. This has the advantage of moving the client toward self-analysis and accepting active responsibility for her own knowledge.

It is wise to avoid propaganda as well as argument—which is one advantage of using an independent printed source—but it is also necessary to evoke an active response from the client to determine whether or not she believes what she has read. One method is to have her identify the ways in which two or three of the myths affect her own attitudes and those of significant others in her life. Another technique is to have different members of a group argue for and against a myth. If a counselor identifies a particular myth as having special force for a client, it is useful to note it and to make use of it as a checkpoint during subsequent counseling.

Presenting the Facts

Some quick and easy method of presenting the facts about women's working lives is necessary, especially since many clients are not eager to spend much time reading about the subject. On the other hand, it is again wise to let the client study the facts on her own. The U.S. Women's Bureau publication "Twenty Facts on Women Workers" can provide the information for assembling a basic fact sheet. Add facts of relevance to the clientele and population served. Special patterns of black, Hispanic, Asian American, Native American, older women, rural women, etc., can be found readily (see listing that follows).

The client's response to the facts is more important than the facts themselves. Counselors should use the fact sheets to show the client how to analyze the impact of the realities on her own situation as a potential or current worker. This process is especially important when a young woman is entering the job market or when a woman is faced with two or three different choices for the future, including divorce or child rearing. Individual women find different facts of greatest personal importance, and they draw diverse implications for them. Their avoidances are also significant and should be noticed; and counselors should constantly be wary of following their own agenda rather than that of the client.

For the purpose of assembling facts, the following sources are useful:

1. Publications of the Women's Bureau, U.S. Department of Labor, Washington, D.C. 20210.

Minority Women Workers: A Statistical Overview, 1977
Economic Responsibilities of Working Women, 1979
Why Women Work, 1978
Employment and Economic Issues of Low-Income Women, 1978
A Woman's Guide to Apprenticeship, 1978
20 Facts on Women Workers, 1979
A Working Woman's Guide to Her Job Rights, 1978
American Indian Women, 1977
Women of Puerto Rican Origin, 1977
Mature Women Workers: a Profile, 1976

2. Publications of the U.S. Bureau of the Census, especially *A Statistical Portrait of Women in the United States*, 1980 (Current Population Reports, Special Studies, Series P. 23, No. 100). U.S. Government Printing Office, Washington, D.C. 20402.

3. Publications of the National Commission on Working Women, Center for Women and Work, 1211 Connecticut Avenue, N.W., Suite 300, Washington, D.C. 20036. Especially *An Overview of Women in the Workforce*, 1979.

4. *To Form a More Perfect Union*, Report of the U.S. National Commission on the Observance of International Women's Year, 1976, U.S. Government Printing Office, Washington, D.C. 20402.

Breaking the Mold

To make successful choices about work, women need to break the mold formed by tradition and out-of-date expectations of themselves which are dangerously irrelevant for today and tomorrow. The pace of change has accelerated in the economic world, and every worker can expect changes which she or he cannot anticipate. Whole occupations vanish or appear, retraining is mandatory, and the number of job changes and career changes one can expect is increasing.

Life planning. An introduction to life planning or life–work planning is the central technique for helping a woman break the mold. Many individuals and organizations have developed various approaches to life planning. The process may be done by a counselor working with an individual or with groups, and it may take one, two, or three days in a workshop, or may spread over several weeks as the woman or group concentrates on different areas. The life-continuum experiences in Chapter 5 (Present Choices/Future Plans and Choosing a Life-style)

164

are useful in this process. Unfortunately, many life planning materials are not designed specifically or exclusively for women. Counselors should therefore use them *only* in conjunction with the factual materials on women's lives, lest they reinforce unrealistic expectations.

Few women have undertaken long-term life–work planning and, in a sense, a client's ability to do it is a test of whether or not the counseling process has helped her. Its thrust is to counteract her tendency to see life's major events as inevitabilities and to reinforce her ability to make individual choices. Since women tend to believe that someone or something else always determines what happens to them in the long run, they also tend to live in the here-and-now. Self-direction over time is not a traditional part of the female role ideology, so women do not usually see themselves as controlling events or taking an active role in their own lives; they tend to react rather than to act. In their study of successful career women, Hennig and Jardim (1977) found that the presence or absence of the ability to plan for the long term was a significant variable. While most women aspiring to high positions in management showed little understanding of long-term goals, analysis of the personal and professional lives of 25 career women who made it to the top showed long-term planning as one of their most important characteristics. The same, one suspects, is true of women who succeed in work at any level.

"What do you want to be doing five years, ten years, and twenty years from now?" This simple question, in my experience, reveals a major difference between women and men. Men are usually comfortable with the answer (though not all of them, of course). Women are usually stunned by the question. They have difficulty even fantasizing where they might be, as though they see no future over which they have control. Goals set five or ten years before and seemingly then forgotten appear, upon examination, to have been achieved. But equally important are the immediate effects of planning. Counselors who provide the right technique will conserve a client's energy, help her organize priorities and gain a sense of control, and above all help her to see immediate choices as part of a continuing life process. This in itself is breaking the mold.

Goal Setting. Goal setting is as important to the same end as is life planning. The need to be realistic is important to women, contesting the sex-role stereotyping that encourages them to be passive and romantic. Counselors will find it productive to encourage them to think in terms of three types of goal: short-term, intermediate, and long-term. Realism comes from specificity.

Good materials specially designed for women exist in the area of goal setting.
1. Osborn, Ruth H., M.M. Parks, A.O. Smith, and H.O. Wolle, *Developing New Horizons for Women: Career Development for Employed Women*, New York: McGraw-Hill, 1976. This is a well-organized combination of manual and workbook aimed at self-understanding and self-evaluation, decision making, matching education and career, career evaluation and entry, ultimately life span planning.

2. Scholz, N.T., J.S. Prince, and G.P. Miller, *How to Decide: a Guide for Women*, New York: College Entrance Examination Board, 1975. This workbook aims at increasing women's ability to apply systematic decision making to their changing needs. Included are sections on women and power, assertion training, risk taking, and confidence building, along with emphasis on the actual process of making decisions.

3. Farmer, Helen S., *Guided Inquiry Group Career Counseling*, Urbana, Ill.: Illinois Union Bookstore, 1975. This well-structured manual clearly presents a six-step process for making educational and career decisions, working at some depth—but not specifically aimed at women.

4. Farmer, Helen S., and J.E. Backer, *New Career Options for Women: a Counselor's Sourcebook*, New York: Human Sciences Press, 1977. This has two companion volumes: *A Selected Annotated Bibliography* and *A Woman's Guide* intended for clients rather than counselors. Together the three comprise the most comprehensive presentation on career information for women, covering everything from legal rights to training and educational programs.

5. *Nonsexist Career Counseling for Women: Annotated Selected References and Resources, Part I and Part II*, WEECN (Women's Educational Equity Communications Network), San Francisco, Ca.: Far West Laboratory, 1978. This is a carefully annotated bibliography of a broad range of nonsexist materials for career counseling of women.

6. *Counseling Women for Life Decisions*, ERIC Counseling and Personnel Services Clearinghouse, Ann Arbor, Mich.: ERIC/CAPS, 1980. This is one of the *Searchlight* series resulting from a computer search of sources cited in ERIC's two indexes: *Resources in Education* and *Current Index to Journals in Education*. Most sources are articles.

7. Fisher, C., and F.D. Rhome, *Women: Working it Out*, Bloomington, Ind.: Indiana University, 1979. This *Study Guide* and accompanying program is aimed specifically at women returning to work or entering the job market after being homemakers. It covers all basic information, sources, and processes. The program is a series of eight half-hour television shows, accompanied by a study guide obtainable from: WTIU Channel 30, Radio-TV Building Room 210, Indiana University, Bloomington, Ind. 47401.

Women at Work

A woman at work is likely to have more difficulty than will a man in preserving the balance between her two roles as breadwinner and homemaker. This section covers the areas in which counselors most often can be of assistance to women during this phase.

Separating Crisis from Confusion. Before a working woman comes to counseling, she will normally have spent much time and energy in trying to solve her problems herself. Her state of confusion may itself have resulted in a crisis; she may decide on a divorce or on giving up her job or in some way running from her problems as an escape from the confusion. The task of the counselor is to help her decide what is crisis and what is more general confusion, thus setting the basis for problem management by becoming specific and gaining perspective.

Clarifying Long-term Versus Short-term Goals. A short-term problem (e.g., husband accepting a job offer in another locale) is likely to cause a woman to give up the search for long-term development. The task of the counselor is both to help in the search for long-term and short-term solutions which do not conflict *and* to see that the client maintains a sense of general direction even if the short-term solution is unsatisfactory.

Dealing with Injustice. Women are often treated unjustly, and they know it. The results of perceived injustice are anger and frustration, and the counselor needs to help affected women channel their emotions into constructive decisions for the future. Hidden anger especially needs to be confronted and released or it is likely to turn into self-condemnation or the decision to give up long-term effort.

Managing Multiple Roles. Management of time, delegation of responsibility, and the finding of outside resources are all areas in which a counselor can help a woman make decisions that will not damage her role as worker or her roles as wife and/or mother. Also much neglected is the need for a woman to have time for herself apart from her roles; women will readily sacrifice this essential need unless helped to discover that they have rights as individuals and that their lives can be organized to keep those rights. Most of a woman's choices in this area are severely practical. An excellent source of information and ideas for both married and single-parenting women is G. Norris and J.A. Miller, *The Working Mother's Complete Handbook*, New York: E.P. Dutton, 1979.

Allowing for Mobility. Women's work lives are often geographically interrupted by the career needs of spouses or the educational needs of children. The woman normally handles not just the logistics of such a move but also the problem of retaining her own career. The major task of the counselor is to help the woman retain some sense of control over her own destiny as a worker or, if she does not want to move, to help her deal with the relational issues involved so she may preserve her sense of identity.

Balancing Dual-worker Marriages. The major issues presented here arise from the following factors: inequality of earnings; comparative satisfaction with the job and needs for promotion; the commitment of time to work versus each other; greater freedom outside the home for the wife; child care, especially during emergencies or trips away from home; money management; and organization of social life. The central matter in which a counselor can help is in assuring that responsibilities for home and family are equally divided so that the woman has as many opportunities for development as does her husband. Among several good books on the topic, the following are recommended: R. Rapoport and R. Rapoport, Editors, *Working Couples*, New York: Harper Colophon Books, 1978; and C. Bird, *The Two-paycheck Family*, New York: Simon and Schuster, 1979.

Intermittency. Since the tendency to interrupt one's work life is more characteristic of females than of males, counselors can help women to counteract the sense of inferiority or unimportance which is likely to develop. Whether the cause of intermittency is a free choice by the woman (as in planned pregnancy) or a choice mandated by her role (such as a geographical move), she needs to (1) recognize that intermittency will impede her economic progress and development of skills, and (2) engage in long-term planning to minimize any damage to her career or self-concept.

Seeking Role Models. Most women workers need broader horizons and a clearer view of advancement. The counselor can help clients look for role models among women in her place of work or in her field or ensure that she meets role models from elsewhere through workshops and networking. The role models should be appropriate and realistic, ordinary persons with whom clients can identify, not necessarily "stars." Especially useful are women who have both made progress at work and managed the homemaker role.

Building Networks

Women are socialized to restrict their network building to areas and people connected with family, homemaking, and child rearing, whereas men learn to do it in connection with work. To extend their networks into the work world is therefore one of women's most important steps toward equality. Networks are a form of support system, not necessarily highly structured, most often informal groupings, alliances, and contacts. They represent knowledge and access to knowledge and power. Working women have networks which are usually restricted; they belong to other people's networks and are used by them. (In some cases, men think it is as important to relate well to a secretary as to her boss.) Women belong to trade organizations, professional groups, caucuses, and commissions which are formal networks, and they work and live within touching distance of dozens of informal work and personal networks. Many of the most important male networks exclude women or relegate them to lowly positions; many networks function around women without their being aware of them at all.

Networks are meant to be used, and this is the major problem women have with them; they tend to confuse using a network with using people. They think of using a network as self-serving, which acculturation forbids them as females, instead of seeing that networks exist precisely as exchanges for mutual benefit in areas of information, ideas, contacts, favors, strengths, and opportunities. At the same time, women seem to be good at maintaining those networks to which they do belong through social contacts, telephone calls, letters—the famous "personal touch." Thus the art of the counselor must be employed twofold: to overcome a client's uneasiness about using networks, and to show her how to translate her existing skills into building work networks. This may be as simple as keeping a card file of names and telephone numbers.

Networking has recently become a very important phenomenon within the women's movement as working women seem to provide each other with the support they do not receive from others. Two new books provide excellent guides to the subject; Welch (1980) is excellent for beginners because it emphasizes the reasons for having networks and the basic principles and psychology involved, including the crucial warning that one does not have to like the people who belong to one's network. However, her book tends to concentrate on the ambitious and career-oriented woman rather than on all working women. Kleiman (1980) deals with networks in a larger variety of fields, including one's personal life, and its information is more specific and comprehensive. Counselors should examine both books and recommend them according to the individual client's needs.

Power and Influence

Networking is one way of attaining power in one's work life, and power is an entity with which women do not usually feel comfortable; rather, they may not see that they have the right to say they want it or to go after it directly. Yet greater power is precisely what equality will mean. Power means many different things, but basically it is of only two kinds: power over oneself and power over others. One needs a share of both kinds of power in order to survive in the world of work. Making a deliberate choice of career or job, for instance, or planning a work pattern to last a lifetime are both forms of power over oneself. Moving out of the powerless, dull, and dead-end occupations means willingness to assume power through leadership, authority, and responsibility over and for others. The skills which bring greater financial and psychological rewards in the world of work— managing, supervision, decision making—all involve the use of power, no matter how delicately. Women may feel reluctant to face the issue of power but, if they want success or even security in their work, they have to do so.

Power results from the interaction of internal and external factors. Career counselors can help in two distinct ways; they can make women aware of the factors that bring or dissipate power, which is largely an educational action, or they can help women study their own relationships to those factors, which goes deeper into the individual's psychology.

To deal with the sources of external power, the best course is to recommend one of the many books about institutional structure and dynamics. They exist in a variety that offers something for people at every level of interest. More individually, the counselor can recommend that a client draw up a chart of her own organization's power structure (which will not be the official organizational structure). By using this chart, she should seek to identify the individuals who make the decisions about (1) distributing human resources, (2) budget, and (3) rules, regulations, and policy. On this basis the counselor can work with the client to determine how she can become part of the power structure. (Few people ever examine in detail the entire structure of the organization within which they work, yet experts note that this knowledge itself is one of the main routes to power.)

Internal power is a much more complex matter; it is derived from one's sense of self in relation to the rest of the world and is so drastically affected by sex-role stereotypes that some feminists suspect the dispersal or veto of female power to be a major male goal. A career counselor has the opportunity to help a client look at herself in relation to power: how much she wants, how much she has and where, and how comfortable she is with the idea. She needs to consider herself in relation to terms such as leadership and supervision; she needs to examine whether she is capable of giving orders (especially to men) and of making decisions for which men will hold her responsible, particularly if those decisions are wrong. The basic problem for women is that our socialization process considers different styles of exercising power as appropriate to females and males. Males are expected to use power styles known as concrete, competent, and direct; females are expected to use those known as personal, helpless, and indirect (Johnson, 1976). Fortunately, the culture is not absolutely rigid in this matter; but women can have trouble when they try to shift styles, trouble with their feelings about themselves and trouble from others. The reason that assertiveness training (popular because it shows women one way of becoming more powerful) has ended up disastrously for many women is that it emphasizes a change of power style without altering the sense of self—with the result that opposition to or failure in assertiveness causes a decline in self-confidence. Further work in developing a sense of internal power is probably the proper realm of therapy rather than of career counseling.

There is, however, a middle ground where career counseling is doing a great deal of excellent work: the area of improving skills and behavior as a worker. Methodology in this area consists of a series of techniques and attitudes which affect the sense of self: how to make decisions; how to supervise; how to present oneself (e.g., dress, posture, speech); how to communicate verbally and nonverbally; how to influence others; how to manage negotiation, confrontation, and conflict; and how to use alliances, collaboration, and competition. Many organizations have produced materials and offer workshops in these matters which counselors may use. (Noteworthy are those of the National Training Laboratories, P.O. Box 9155, Rosslyn Station, Arlington, Va. 22209, and those of University Associates, P.O. Box 26240, San Diego, Ca. 92126.) One strong note of warning should be sounded; most of the materials and workshops in these subjects are intended for a male audience, designed by men, and conducted by men. Women participants in such workshops sometimes report frustrating, irrelevant, or even offensive experiences. Counselors are wise to investigate carefully whether the materials and workshops have been specifically designed with women in mind; to enable them to do this, two books dealing with the relationship between sex-role stereotypes and the environment are invaluable: *Beyond Sex Roles*, edited by Alice Sargent (1977), and *Exploring Contemporary Male/Female Roles*, edited by Clark Carney and Sarah McMahon (1977). *Women, Money and Power* by Phyllis Chesler and Emily Jane Goodman (1976) will give counselors an excellent background in the entire subject of women and power, ranging from the individual to the political. *Freeing Ourselves* (Collier, 1982) is a manual for a workshop dealing with these issues, one of whose units deals specifically with "Women and Power."

Conclusion

Career counseling for women is too often given only incidental importance. The materials in this and preceding chapters have shown that, in fact, it is essential and exciting. The changes occurring in relation to women and work are not taking place fast enough—data disseminated by the 1980 World Conference for Women show the continuing inequality between women and men in the world of work. Worldwide, women make up 50 percent of the whole population and 33.3 percent of the official labor force; they perform, however, for 66.6 percent of all working hours. In return for their labor, they receive 10 percent of the world's income and own less than 1 percent of the world's property.

8

Women and Their Bodies

Therapists can no longer afford to accept or reject issues related to women's bodies as purely personal or narrowly psychological. Only if the therapist is aware of the social and cultural dimensions of an issue can therapy set the larger goals which the issue requires, such as

- counteracting the myths which cause women to think of their bodies as obstacles to full development as human beings
- helping women accept responsibility for decisions about their bodies
- encouraging women to develop their whole selves by appreciating their bodies, by caring for, enjoying, and owning their bodies in many different ways.

The goals may be obvious, but each has immediate and even legal ramifications. For example, how much advice may a therapist give about nutrition without infringing upon the forbidden area of "medical opinion?" What opinion may a therapist express about medication, especially tranquilizers, prescribed by a physician? When counseling a teenager, how far may a therapist's advice differ from that of the parents? What should a therapist advise concerning proceeding to bring a charge of rape—or incest? When does a therapist intervene in a case of wife abuse, and what form should that intervention take? Cultural dimensions are inherent in all these questions, and they are not easy to face.

In these circumstances the only viable goal is to have a woman reach the stage where she can make her own choices; the therapist must first equip the client with enough knowledge to make a responsible choice and then ensure that the client's environment is free of outside pressures which would take that choice from her. The therapist needs to be equipped with objective information of whatever kind is needed to avoid or contest the subjective, and she needs to combat actively the cultural influences which determine her own views. The goal of having a woman experience her own power from and over her body means that the therapist must avoid any stance which would reduce the client's sense of autonomy. This chapter examines the various aspects of uniquely female experiences from this point of view.

Attitudes Toward Female Physiology

Our culture has more powerful attitudes about the major events connected with female physiology than about parallel events in the life history of males. The uniquely female physiological events occur in three stages. First is pubescence, marked by menarche, the beginning of menstruation. Second is childbearing, including menstruation, pregnancy, childbirth, and lactation. Third is menopause, signaling the end of the childbearing capacity. Our culture associates these events with the major stages of a woman's life: becoming a woman, becoming a wife, becoming a mother, and declining as all three. There is considerable pressure for a woman to fulfill her various physiological potentials on schedule; and if she does not fulfill them, for whatever reason, she will earn disapproval. No such direct association between physiology and status occurs in relation to men.

Also in a manner which is not applied to men, the culture associates women's major physiological events with aberration or weakness. Unlike some cultures, we do not overtly associate menarche and menopause with witchery, nor do we overtly regard menstruating women as unclean, segregating them and limiting their contacts with men, food, utensils, and the community. In our culture the ritualistic drama is muted; but it still exists. What is the source, for instance, of the "embarrassment" men experience when explaining menarche to a boy or girl? Why is it the subject of amusement, shame, or fear? Why do we routinely avoid intercourse during menstruation or associate the menstrual period with unpredictable emotionalism? Is this experience or myth? Why is it routinely accepted that their monthly cycle creates an instability in women which makes them unsuitable for responsibility, while emotional patterns in males are not recognized?

Our culture has long seen a pregnant woman as in acute need of protection; encouraged to cease activity, work, and responsibility for anything but her baby's well-being, she is seen as a vessel for another person rather than as a person herself. She may be overprotected or indulged to the point of absurdity; she may find herself restricted and confined in a manner no nonpregnant person would tolerate. When she reaches childbirth and lactation, she will be hidden away as though she were doing something wrong. Childbirth is associated with an unrealistic degree of pain and danger, and lactation with sexual modesty—neither association having much to do with the facts or the needs of the situation, and neither of them created for the convenience or pleasure of the woman.

With menopause, "that time of month" turns into "that time of life." We are conditioned to expect and tolerate every kind of irrationality from menopausal women; this becomes an avenue for our dismissing them. One scholar, currently working, has found no explicit mention of menopause in any major literary works. The same scholar, however, finds a definite association in literature between middle age and dangerous or crazy women, whereas all the warm, witty, wise, and worshiped women are post-menopausal.

Our culture does not draw similar parallels between men's capacities and their physiological lives, perhaps because the major female events are more obvious, perhaps because they are more important to the race, perhaps because ignorance is still enough to breed fear and myth, or perhaps because of a power struggle between the sexes (Fee, 1975). Though the traditional response to the uniquely female physiological experience often has the kindest of intentions, it is still a form of bigotry. If education promulgated a better understanding of the facts and normality of the female experience, women would function better and more comfortably in our culture; but thus far our culture actively prefers myth.

Menstruation

The process of puberty is basically the same for both sexes. Hormones regulated by the hypothalamus bring about a rapid acceleration of growth, the appearance of secondary sex characteristics, and maturation of the reproductive system. In the female, menarche marks the beginning of the reproductive life. Menstruation is simply the method by which an unfertilized ovum (egg) passes out of the body. Ova mature in the follicles of the ovaries at the normal rate of one approximately every 28 days and during ovulation pass from the ovary through the fallopian tubes to the uterus, whose interior (stimulated by estrogen) grows, thickens, and receives an extra blood supply. The ovarian follicle, which produced estrogen, now produces progesterone which causes the uterine glands to secrete substances to nourish the embryo if fertilization has taken place. If fertilization does not take place, levels of both estrogen and progesterone drop, the uterine lining crumbles and, along with the unused ovum and some blood, leaves the body through the vagina. A miraculous process, perhaps; but widespread and profound ignorance has long made it seem more like an embarrassing illness.

Many women may experience discomfort in connection with menstruation at some time in their lives. Menstrual discomfort or dysmenorrhea is of two kinds: spasmodic or congestive. Spasmodic dysmenorrhea is associated with severe cramps, acute pain in the lower abdomen, and possibly nausea on the first day of menstruation; it is not uncommon. Congestive dysmenorrhea is associated with dull aching in the abdomen, water retention, mild nausea and constipation, headaches and backaches, perhaps breast pains, and some irritability, tension, depression, or lethargy. These symptoms may result from a progesterone deficiency which brings about sodium retention and potassium depletion (Boston Women's Health Book Collective, 1976). Not all women experience all these symptoms, and the same woman may or may not experience them at different times. Evidence suggests that the expectation of premenstrual tension and depression may increase the likelihood of their occurrence, whereas many women report an absence of depression (Paige, 1973; Seiden, 1976). In sum, it should be emphasized that dysmenorrhea is an occasional side effect, not an inevitable accompaniment, of menstruation.

The Woman's Health Movement tends to believe that our culture too often equates dysmenorrhea with menstruation, overly protects menstruating women, and therefore overly inhibits women's behavior. As one recent text states, "The sooner it is understood by everyone that menstruation is a routine physical occurrence and dysmenorrhea an unpleasant side effect that can usually be controlled, the sooner women will be able to find relief and get on with their lives" (Cooke and Dworkin, 1979, pp. 323–324). Menstruation is in fact a sign of good general health and normal functioning; menstruating women can do anything they would normally do. Nor does the increased emotionality associated with the premenstrual syndrome incapacitate them. Indeed, research on the subject finds no definite evidence of any set of behaviors connected with the menstrual cycle (Paige, 1973; Parlee, 1975; Seiden, 1976). The basic problem is that comparisons with nonmenstruating persons (females as well as males) show that they too go through periodic changes which may well be cyclical and may also include moodiness and emotionality. Before making realistic generalizations about the menstrual cycle, therefore, we need more research into all daily and longer-span rhythms. Reviewing all the studies of the effects of the menstrual cycle, Seiden found that only about 50 percent of women reported any irritability, anxiety, and/or depression at the time, though for undetermined reasons the results of the studies varied widely. There is also evidence that "menstrual symptoms" are determined by diet as much as by menstruation (Seaman and Seaman, 1977).

Our culture's attitudes would improve with education to counteract the tendency to consider menstruation an ailment or, worse, "the curse" which previous generations familiarly named it. The attitudes which have characterized our society—ignorance, embarrassment, shame, mockery—can hardly be called desirable or justified, but they will continue if we do not make better efforts at proper education of both females and males (Unger and Denmark, 1975; Whisnant and Zegans, 1975). In this respect the attitudes of women themselves are probably the key determinant. Women have special obligations to be honest and frank—as mothers to their daughters, and as mothers, wives, daughters, sisters, or lovers to their men.

Fertility Control

Many societies have made a woman's right to control her childbearing potential a political matter. Though many cultures allow freedom of choice, seeing no legitimate state interest in the matter, others have seen the state interest as over-riding personal interests (Gordon, 1975). Recent spectacular examples of societies which saw women's bodies literally as vehicles for the national interest have included Italy under Mussolini, where the duty and main purpose of women was seen as the bearing of large families, and Nazi Germany, where "the Aryan race" was strongly discouraged from exercising fertility control while other ethnic groups were forced into it. Complex relationships between fertility control and economic structure have existed; states apparently tend to permit birth control among the richer classes but not the poorer. Almost all societies practice some form of fertility control, either by contraception, by abortion (or even infanticide), or by legal limitation of intercourse; many religions have made it a principal issue in doctrine.

Controversy over freedom of choice in the United States is fairly recent. Prior to 1873, both abortion on request and the sale of contraceptives and abortifacients were legal. The national legislation against obscenity promulgated in that year by the famous moralist Anthony Comstock included all fertility control devices and information—an interesting and, to this day and age, absurd connection. The recent removal by the judiciary and legislature of government barriers to free choice of fertility control is a return to proper bounds of state interference with individual freedom.

Two factors have principally determined the amount and nature of fertility control in the United States: (1) religious and moral beliefs and (2) the safety and efficiency of contraceptive devices. Thanks to the work of Margaret Sanger and her colleagues in the early years of the century and to the long-term efforts of the Planned Parenthood Federation, information about fertility control has never been completely unavailable in America, even under the Comstock laws. Since World War II, medical advances have brought about inevitable legislative changes that enhance the legality of choices which millions of women and men were already making. As can be seen in the changes during the last decade, which have made displays of contraceptive devices a feature of the pharmacist's counter, there has been a strong tendency to shift this subject from the domain of morals to that of medicine. This has brought about a major change in the issues about fertility control; while an active debate continues regarding whether pregnancy should be a matter of choice or biological destiny, this has become a tangential issue for millions of people. The propriety of various contraceptive methods and devices now deals less with morality and more with their appropriateness for the overall health of women and families. Males are increasingly expected to assume as much responsibility for contraception as do females. Well-being of body and mind is the major concern. In medical terms, all current methods of fertility control have disadvantages; any therapist needs to be well informed since each disadvantage has important implications for the well-being and future of clients. (For details, see Kane, 1977; Boston Women's Health Book Collective, 1976; and Seaman and Seaman, 1977.)

For therapists, the central issue concerning fertility control may well be the matter of choice. Many fertility control devices are dispensed only through physicians; any physician is likely to prescribe according to his purely medical beliefs rather than as a result of careful investigation of the individual woman's situation. Women and men would be well advised to visit an organization specializing in dispensing advice about fertility control before or in conjunction with seeing a physician, for the mission of such organizations as the Planned Parenthood Federation is precisely to provide full information in a manner that will promote free and responsible choice. Many people believe that a woman should visit a female physician in preference to a male physician on the grounds that a woman is more likely to understand the personal issues of each method. Since our culture still tends to place primary responsibility for fertility control on women, the comparative degree of responsibility shared between a woman and a man may need to be raised by a therapist. Here the issue is clearly less medical than psychological and, therefore, a suitable subject for counseling. The short-term and long-term implications of any choice need examination; personal comfort, health, long-term consequences, sense of responsibility, side effects, and many other matters need discussion of a kind that is difficult to obtain outside the counseling situation. Fertility control is still not easy; choice is more complex in this area than ever before.

Abortion

The debate over free choice reaches its zenith over the subject of abortion. Should choice be legal or illegal? Should abortion be supported, ignored, or punished by the state? Should choice be controlled by physicians or by women themselves? Some women have always undergone abortion, often at enormous risk when it was illegal. In 1973, the United States Supreme Court made abortion legal during the first three months of pregnancy but set limits on free choice, and religious opponents continue to fight bitterly against free choice. Public opinion generally supports abortion under such extreme circumstances as when pregnancy threatens a mother's life or when the fetus is damaged or the pregnancy is a result of forcible rape or incest; but religious and other groups oppose abortion even in these circumstances, believing that from the moment of conception a woman's rights yield to those of the fetus. At the opposite extreme, some proponents believe that neither the state nor the medical profession should have the right to interfere with a woman's free choice to terminate a pregnancy.

In fact, few women dismiss abortion lightly. It is almost always a major crisis in a woman's life, and one which demands a quick decision. According to Shusterman (1976), the three most common reasons for abortion are that the woman perceives herself as unable to care properly for a child, that her family situation is highly unstable, or that she has a heavy commitment to activities outside the home such as education or work. Since such matters involve a woman's whole life-style, she is likely to see them as more than adequate reasons; others may not agree, and still others do not care. According to Shusterman, the most frequent causes of unwanted pregnancy are failure of the contraceptive device (one-third of all cases), denial of the possibility of pregnancy or rationalization after intercourse without contraceptives, and misuse or simple fear of contraceptives. Shusterman found that most women seeking abortions were at either end of the age range for fertility: younger than 25 or older than 35.

Myths surround the subject, and therapists would be well advised to study an annual summary of information published by the Center for Disease Control, *Abortion Surveillance*, even though its data appear two years after the event. For example, 1975 data show that women obtaining abortions tend to be white, young, unmarried, early in pregnancy, and overwhelmingly without other children—a pattern very different from the stereotype in the public mind. Since 1972, the proportion of women having to travel to another state for an abortion has dropped dramatically; the number of deaths due to abortion has been halved. The various methods for removing the fetus from the uterus are described succinctly in *Our Bodies, Our Selves* (1976) in terms which an ordinary individual can understand. Dilation and evacuation seems to be the safest of the three leading methods for first-trimester abortion (*Women and Health*, Women's Equity Action League (WEAL), Aug., 1977, p. 5).

Two main crisis points at which a therapist may need to intervene usually accompany abortion. First, obviously, is the time of choosing whether or not to abort. The safest and easiest period for abortion is during the first twelve weeks, both legally and medically. Abortions occurring between twelve and sixteen weeks are more difficult, but the risk is medically acceptable. After twenty weeks, abortion requires a major surgical procedure with mandatory hospitalization. The decision is thus one which should be made quickly; but it must also be made carefully, for both ethical and psychological reasons. Abortion is normally a major life event which may precipitate important reassessments and powerful emotions—the second crisis point. If a therapist can work with a client both before and after the abortion, there is a much better prospect for her mental health.

When at the point of deciding whether or not to abort, clarification is the client's primary need. Abortion is not usually a solitary decision; a woman seeks—or decides not to seek—the advice of significant others, a process which involves a re-evaluation of her relationships. The choice is thus made within an environment which may afford a great variety of problems; within this environment the therapist may be the only neutral agent available to help a woman decide her own values and measure the importance of others' pressures. If the client decides to proceed with the abortion, the therapist's task is to assure that she acts prudently, utilizing all medical safeguards. The event is physically and psychologically stressful, and a woman needs support from as much of her environment as possible. After abortion, reactions vary widely. A recent study of women who had had therapeutic abortions showed them relieved and happy for the following few months (Adler, 1975), but that condition depends greatly on the social environment and on the significance a client attaches to the event. If either the message from the environment or from the client's own value system is that abortion is a crime or a sin to be atoned, then the woman is likely to feel guilt at having taken control over her own body. Simple regret is more probable than not, though it is likely to be mixed with the more positive feelings of relief. A physiological disorganization similar to postpartum depression affects some women. Others may be angry with themselves, with society, or with people close to them, depending on the nature of the experience.

During a group session, one client was completing work related to her fears about having a child when suddenly another, Sue, began to cry, at first softly, but then with wrenching grief from deep inside. When I asked her what was happening, she burst forth, "I feel so guilty. I had an abortion and now I see nothing but reminders of how bad I am. You think you want a baby, Lois. I could have, and I didn't, and I can't forgive myself! I watch TV and see babies and feel guilty, I go to church and hear about the importance of life and feel guilty, I look at my sister with her children and feel guilty. Everywhere I turn I am reminded of what I did and how selfish and bad I am." Another woman asked why, feeling that way, she had had an abortion. "Bob and I decided not to have a baby until he finishes his education," Sue replied. "Because then I could stop working and be the real mother I've always wanted to be. I'm on the pill and it should be safe, and I've gotten pregnant twice and had two abortions while on the pill. Don't ever trust it! You can't trust anything!" Then she began to sob again, then to cry very deeply, and I encouraged her to let her body go into whatever position it took naturally. She curled up on the floor, and with my hand on her abdomen I guided her deep breathing as she wept for some five or ten minutes, sobbing, "I'm bad, I'm bad." As soon as the crying began to subside, I started saying, "No, you're not—no, you're not—no, you're not." She looked up into my eyes and said, "I'm not?"

Then we began to talk about her decisions: how she had been taught at home and church to honor human life; how she could not tell her parents what she had done twice; and how she feared for her relationship with Bob. As we talked softly, other group members moved near and touched her and spoke of their fears of the same thing, of their support for her choices, of her courage at having done what she felt she had to do. Eventually, to integrate the range of emotions through which she had moved, I had Sue sit in front of each woman in the group and tell her that she had had two abortions and why. As she moved on, the awful secret came to seem less and less sinful. Two weeks later, she told the group that she had told her parents, who had offered her understanding and love rather than the scorn she had feared. "We still have another year of school to go," she said. "I just hope I don't get pregnant again."

All these emotions provide opportunities for therapists and counselors to function, but it would be as unwise for a professional to emphasize negative emotions as it would be to take an entirely moralistic stance for or against the abortion. A much larger opportunity for therapy exists at this period; the most common, almost universal, reaction of clients to abortion is increased thoughtfulness. Women tend at this time to re-examine their values and choices, their relationships with men and their families, and their attitudes toward themselves and their functions. One way or another, with ease or difficulty, they have taken responsibility for their bodies; the power generated by making that choice generally helps them become more willing to learn about their bodies, their sexuality, their attitudes towards birth and birth control, their degrees of dependence or independence regarding men, their images of themselves. Abortion counseling, in other words, is not only a matter of making repairs but an opportunity for building a new structure.

The poignancy of the situation appears in the following two poems:

It is somehow easier
to accept the killing
when i consider it a birth—
the birth of me—
that potential for life had to be
sacrificed
in order that i might live
at that point i too felt dead
but now i have never
NEVER
felt more alive.

*

It was a hauntingly selfish act.
And yet maybe the most
Generous thing I could do.
Everything considered.

g.v.o. 1977

Childbirth

Even childbirth is as much a cultural event as a personal event. Because humans rely on learning rather than on instinct, individual attitudes and practices vary according to culture; our culture overdramatizes childbirth, exaggerating its dangers beyond any point justified either by mortality rates or the actual experience of pain and effort. Most women form their attitudes toward childbirth on the basis not of accurate information but of myths about the experience gathered from novels, films, television, and family tales; and their attitudes can determine the nature of their own experience. Even labor pains, for example, have been shown to vary due not just to such physical variables as the size and positon of the child or the nature of the obstetrical procedures but also to previous learning and other less measurable psychological forces.

During the last 50 years culture has made childbirth practices in the United States abnormal. In most cultures today childbirth takes place in the home, and its supervision has historically been the responsibility of women; foreigners tend to regard our physician-dominated, hospital-centered practices as unusual. They are unusual even in terms of our own history. As recently as 1938 a majority of American childbirths took place in the home (Brack, 1976), and many people still alive were born in their parents' bed, attended by a nurse, midwife, or doctor, with the other family members in the next room. Since mortality and illness rates are not necessarily lower with hospital births than with home births, many people believe that our present practices are the result of the expansion of the male-dominated medical profession and the patterns of industrialization. While increased medical knowledge made a larger role for physicians probable, urbanization and better transportation joined with economics and the exclusivity of physicians to encourge the dominance of hospitals. Unfortunately, I believe, childbirth then came to be considered a medical crisis rather than a natural event, one wherein the woman is mysteriously transported away from home and family, tended, even guarded, in a manner with ritualistic or priestly overtones (Ehrenreich and Ehrenreich, 1971; Robson, 1973).

Many women believe that the physician/hospital approach is dehumanizing and overly controlling. The search for technical impeccability, they believe, has led to practices which are psychologically harmful to both mother and child. By taking precautions against what might go wrong, by standardizing as necessary that which is only sometimes necessary (Seiden, 1976), physicians unintentionally foster the attitude that childbirth is a dangerous and exclusively physiological event; whereas Hazell (1969) and others in the women's health care movement affirm that pregnancy, labor and delivery are states unto themselves and are by no means illnesses. More than one theorist asserts that many physician/hospital practices are harmful to the psychological and perhaps the physiological well-being of mothers and children (e.g., LeBoyer, 1975), but the medical needs of childbirth mean that one cannot do without trained medical assistance. One way or the other, childbirth has therefore become a sociological as well as a physiological tussle.

Whether a woman chooses the physician/hospital model or an alternative childbirth method (e.g., home birth), the role of a counselor is reasonably certain: to see that her choices are well informed and to help her maintain a sense of power and joy. Only a specially trained counselor can give any advice at all regarding technical matters concerning delivery. (The best introductory guides to the subject are in Cooke and Dworkin, 1979; Boston Women's Health Book Collective, 1976; and Romney and Gray, 1975.) But counselors can help women make their own choices, and they can also deal usefully with the family and work environment. Practical matters may need resolution—the cost of hospitalization, when to cease or resume work, help with care of the newborn and other children, and any of the regular concerns of life which may be complicated by childbirth. In particular, the counselor can bring about the involvement of others with the childbearing experience. In very few cultures is childbirth a solitary experience, and most contemporary approaches emphasize companionship and support.

181

Since physician/hospital procedures have tended to neglect the psychological dimension almost entirely, and since they do not do the best job in providing information and dispelling fears, many women join voluntary groups run by experienced women, helping each other regain the control that comes from knowledge and the joy that comes from sharing. Nurse midwives are an excellent source of information and support (Ehrenreich and English, 1973). The International Childbirth Education Association and The Association of Psychoprophylaxis and Obstetrics provide formal classes in childbirth and parent education. Both organizations offer support to parents electing both traditional and nontraditional childbirth experiences.

Most important, the child's father should be involved when possible, attending the same childbirth-preparation class, reading the same books, learning the same exercises and breathing techniques, and eventually serving as coach during childbirth. (In the absence of a father, another woman can fill many of these roles.) The reports of many women and men jointly involved in the birth process indicate important, long-term gains in the father's sense of ownership, his degree of cooperation with childbearing, and his respect for the mother. From the viewpoint of a woman's sense of power, educated childbirth in any of its various forms is superior to the traditional physician/hospital procedures. The goal in prepared childbirth is a mother informed about and often in charge of what is happening, using the help of others, in touch with herself (mind and body), and anything but a passive object. Women who experience educated childbirth report feeling freer sexually, more independent emotionally, and more confident as mothers. In conjunction with a physician, women can use midwives, support groups, "open" delivery rooms, or lying-in centers. The principle should be that the woman has the maximum amount of choice available and that she is not sacrificed to the convenience or theory of others.

After Childbirth

The first weeks of the mothering process are normally stressful and tiring, a period when a woman needs considerable support. If she lacks support from husband and family, her sense of inadequacy is likely to increase as she tries to function in a new role in addition to her other roles.

We call the most visible forms of stress *postpartum depression*, which affects about half of all new mothers for periods varying from hours to weeks and ranging in severity from mild anxiety to psychosis. A mild depression setting in between the second and fourth days after delivery is usual and similar to that experienced by many surgical patients. Some mothers experience frightening dreams without depression, or fantasies about suicide or the baby's death. Other emotional symptoms include confusion, insecurity, and shock; feelings of inadequacy and inability to cope with the new life are also common. Fear that the marriage will deteriorate affects some mothers. In conditions of such stress, child abuse may begin even with the newborn.

We know surprisingly little about the causes of postpartum depression; they seem to be a mixture of physical and psychological factors. Among the physical factors may be hormonal imbalance, shock similar to that of postoperative shock, the dramatic reduction of estrogen and progesterone following childbirth, and thyroid malfunction. Socially induced stress arises from the conflict between expectations and reality. Facing society's ideal of motherhood as a glorious and absorbing experience when she is fatigued and no longer pregnant, a woman may lack the energy implied by society's ideal, begin to blame herself and to feel inadequate, and doubt her ability to live up to the ideal in terms of love and care. When education about child rearing is absent, ignorance and inexperience lessen the mother's ability to take responsibility and often lead to anger. Especially in the absence of good support from a family, internal conflict feeds upon itself and leads to depression. Husbands sometimes desert their wives at this time, fleeing from the new situation; or they may flee psychologically while remaining physically—accepting no responsibility for child care, showing little interest in the baby, and paying no special attention to the woman's needs.

This is an area where counseling seems to have a growing importance as young couples become more isolated within our society. Education and counseling for both parents may be desirable for a period of weeks with the counselor serving almost as a monitor. Counselors need to be wary of one parental characteristic frequent at this time; feeling the need to live up to society's expectation that they will be good and loving parents, some couples deny their own feelings of inadequacy. As a result, they may consciously or accidentally conceal evidence of real inadequacy; others who may recognize what is happening—parents, relatives, friends—may be reluctant to criticize poor child rearing practices. The extreme result can be child neglect and child abuse. The counselor can monitor this situation realistically by using a checklist of objective criteria about the infant and child-care habits, including such matters as number of hours of sleep, feeding amounts and frequency, diaper arrangements, and presence or absence of others in the home. Many pediatricians use such checklists.

Support groups of other mothers can be of great help. The mother's psychological state also needs monitoring; some genuinely feel the uncontaminated joy expected by society, but many feel uneasy, inadequate, or panicky. To avoid increasing these doubts, the counselor's basic stance should be: "Of course you are doing a good job as a mother, and of course it's not a bed of roses. What bothers you and how would you like to change it?"

The basic issue is similar to that apparent in other aspects of a woman's life: she is acquiring a new role. She has a whole new set of behaviors; her relationships change both in practical terms and in terms of what others expect of her and what she expects of others. The counselor's task is to aid in the transition through clarification of the adjustments to old roles that need to be made and, perhaps, to help the woman change her expectations of this new role in the light of reality. She has to juggle what she wants to do as a spouse, as a mother, perhaps as a worker, and—the role most often neglected—as an individual with needs of her own. She has to eliminate some past activities and expectations. She must delegate some tasks, learn to manage her time differently, change the structure of the family, and perhaps deal with fresh conflicts within the family triad or among siblings. She also has to find time and motivation for self-care.

Breast-feeding provides examples of deeper conflicts which may arise at this time. While most mothers find breast-feeding a pleasant and fulfilling experience, those who do not are likely to feel that there is something wrong with them; and those who cannot breast-feed may feel inadequate, uncaring, or unloving. Both of the latter groups report feeling "betrayed" by their bodies. Some women feel ambivalent or embarrassed about breast-feeding because they are used to thinking of their breasts solely in sexual terms. Because society likes the image of the mother who breast-feeds, those who do not are likely to feel abnormal, inferior, and unfeminine. The truth is, of course, that bottle-feeding also benefits the child through the amount of contact and loving and that these benefits are the most important. To help a client see this truth, the counselor needs to help the woman separate her image of herself from the stereotype provided by society and her own socialization. The La Leche League, now over twenty years old, provides mother-to-mother information and support to women desiring to breastfeed. Encouraging a woman to contact her local chapter can provide the client with essential support and encouragement.

Many of us are reluctant to "interfere" with a mother's privacy after childbirth, believing somehow that it is such a natural process that the woman will respond and function "naturally." That may have been the illusion created when families were large and close and stable, but it is a totally unrealistic expectation in a world where young women may well never have seen any child rearing at close quarters. Even childbirth has been affected by change in the family structure and the multiplicity of women's roles. Nothing about it is "automatic;" everything is a matter of learning. When this learning has not yet taken place or when a situation suggests that improper learning dominates, the counselor has an important function.

Women and Breast Cancer

Childbirth practices are an example of the widespread failure of the medical profession to come to terms with psychology as a whole and with feminine psychology in particular. Neither nurses or doctors are at ease with the psychological reactions of patients to illness or treatment, and many seem ignorant of or contemptuous toward even the most elementary principles of human relationships. At no point in her medical history can a woman safely expect understanding from her doctors, and in certain matters she cannot trust them to make the right decision on her behalf. The problem of trust is worsened by two disparate factors. First, a woman has to trust medical professionals as diagnosticians and mechanics during some of the most critical events in her life, even though she knows that the profession may not concern itself with her psychological well-being. Second, the medical profession often internally relegates women to secondary importance, with the result that male domination of the profession forces a woman to entrust all her major health decisions to men. The woman patient is thus doubly vulnerable because of her acculturation—which makes it difficult for her to question the advice of doctors *and* to make demands on men.

Mastectomy provides an excellent example of the harm that can be done. A peculiar form of the fear of cancer which we all experience affects women dramatically: fear of mutilation of the breasts. It is a realistic fear; one-fifth of all female cancer is breast cancer. (Cervical cancer is the second most common cancer for women.) The customary treatment has been radical mastectomy—removal of the entire breast and adjacent musculature with disfiguring results. All too often, women are in the vulnerable position of being asked to make an immediate decision regarding surgical intervention without sufficient time and information about alternatives and choices.

Fortunately, this situation—which faces a woman with the very image of her passive and powerless feminity—seems likely to change. In 1979 a meeting of experts sponsored by the National Institutes of Health and the National Cancer Institute recommended: (a) that radical mastectomy should no longer be the standard treatment for local breast cancer, and (b) that there should be a lapse of time between the biopsy of a suspicious breast tissue and a mastectomy (Kasper, 1979). Radical mastectomy having proven no more effective than less disfiguring procedures, recommended surgery now would leave muscles intact and reduce the amount of disfigurement and incapacitation. Counselors and therapists have the responsibility to encourage women to investigate the various treatment modalities and to choose a physician accordingly.

This entire situation stresses the extent to which women must work with their physicians and the overwhelming importance for a woman to take responsibility for her own body. No man, I suspect, can understand the significance of breast surgery to a woman. Faced with a radical mastectomy, she knows that her only escape from death is mutilation of that part of her body which she had identified since childhood with womanhood and since puberty with sexuality and attractiveness. (The only male equivalent would be surgical removal of the penis or testes, though the parallel is inexact.) With our culture's emphasis on the sexuality of breasts, women receive both great pleasure from them and a considerable part of their sense of identity. Widespread publicity about the need for early detection of breast cancer—six out of ten breast cancers metastasize within a month after detection of the tumor—has encouraged women to examine their breasts regularly and has therefore increased the sense of prospective betrayal by their femininity.

The fear of mutilation and sense of distrust in femininity take various forms. My own mastectomy clients reiterate the following themes: fear of loss of sexuality and loss of sexual attractiveness to spouses and others; fear of recurrence; depression and anger aimed at self or the physician; lack of ability to plan a future. Researchers indicate that the prevailing fears are those of recurrence of the cancer, loss of attractiveness, and self-blame. This last occurs because of our culture's tendency to blame the victim of an illness as somehow responsible for that illness. It is often connected with the feeling that the woman has done something specific to bring about the breast cancer—abandoned religious training about sexuality, for instance, or had a secret affair. These are powerful psychological issues, and most commentators (Asken, 1975; Ervin, 1973) believe that the emotional suffering after a mastectomy is much greater than the physical pain.

Hospitals now provide special counseling services for mastectomy patients while they are in the hospital, but in my experience many women live the trauma of a mastectomy for months and even years. During this period the therapist has several clear goals: providing emotional support, producing information to counteract myths and combat old rules, and helping the client to accept that she is not the cause of her ailment. Re-evaluation of one's life, facing life after having faced death, is normal after a trauma of this significance; a woman may at this time be open to help in setting new goals for her life, whether those goals be long- or short-term ones. Relationships change and the therapist may want to work with the entire family, especially the spouse or lover, so that all may justly appraise the new situation. Fluent communication is essential since most women are aware that their anxieties are "unrealistic," no matter how real. The American Cancer Society will provide materials, advice, and sometimes special counselors for mastectomy clients; they sponsor the Reach to Recovery program which uses former mastectomy patients as teachers. Support groups for former patients are present in many areas and provide the ongoing communication and nurturing the environment may lack.

Therapists have a major opportunity to be of value both before and after breast surgery. Help in practical matters, such as in choosing a physician or a procedure, can be given without intruding upon medical territory. Clarification of anxieties before and after surgery is an important counseling service. Reappraisal of self and life situation after surgery may be crucial. Abandonment of elements of sex-role socialization that attach far too much importance to the breasts may have to be undertaken. The marriage of one of my clients, a 36-year-old named Shirley, began to break up immediatedly after her mastectomy; she came to me filled with grief and terror. Most of her reactions were due to a frightening sense of isolation caused mainly by the attitude of her husband, Mike, who seemed suddenly to have shut her out of his life as though she were to have no part of their future. "It's not just that I feel unclean," said Shirley, "but I feel like I don't really exist. It's like he was tellng me over and over again, 'You're dying, you're dying.' I *think* he's frightened of me, but he says that's ridiculous, and that makes me terrified." Mike came to a therapy session; he seemed a very cold man, unwilling to express himself. What he said during the first session indeed seemed to indicate disgust for the change in his wife, but one statement gave hope: "I know me," he said. "It takes me time to get used to things." In the second session, I asked him to close his eyes and imagine the surgical scars on Shirley's chest which he was unwilling to look at in reality. Then I asked him, still with eyes closed, to touch the real scars with his fingertips. He did so reluctantly, but when he did, Shirley began very gently to guide his hand; and with eyes still closed he began to cry, then to sob. "I was so afraid," he said. "I love you so much." This story has a happy ending—Mike's breakthrough enabled Shirley to make hers. Fear vanished swiftly when confronted with a combination of love and communication, and the mastectomy became their problem instead of hers alone.

Sexuality

The sexual revolution heralded in the 1960s has been in progress for at least 60 years; it is no passing fad. Its continuance is guaranteed by the importance of sexuality to the sense of self; as women expand their concept of self and their rights as individuals, their sexual behavior will necessarily change. The sexual revolution is also supported by economic changes; as women grow economically less dependent, there is a series of effects on marital status and life-style which inevitably involve women's sexuality. In analyzing the 3,019 questionnaires collected for *The Hite Report* (1976), Hite found three forces encouraging women to retain traditional sexual attitudes: habit; fear of the loss of love; and economics as embodied in the marriage tie. None of these is an immovable object, whereas female sexuality is proving itself an irresistible force.

The female sexual revolution will necessarily grate against monogamous, child-oriented, heterosexual traditionalism; so narrow have been the bounds of traditional sexuality that almost anything is a variant; and every variant is an assertion of the individual against the norm. Every assertion of individuality is an expression of power—and the body power expressed by free choice in sexuality is the most basic power of all. It is small wonder, then, that feminine sexuality is continuously at the forefront of social controversy. The degree of change is exaggerated by the characteristics of traditional sexuality, wherein a woman's sexuality was subordinated to and openly regarded as weaker than that of a man. Women were not thought to enjoy sex unless they were wicked. Their sexuality was a necessary instrument for male pleasure, whether within or outside of marriage, to be exploited physically or in fantasy. Women were considered to be sexual only so they might stimulate and capture men—and, of course, as a necessary avenue to the production of children. When women start to consider sexuality for the pleasure it gives to them, when they choose more than one lifetime partner, or when they prefer another woman or a vibrator to a husband, the reversal is so complete that shock is the inevitable response.

The affirmation of their sexuality by women is a basic rupture of the chain that has bound their bodies to ownership outside themselves. Claiming ownership of their own sexuality means accepting responsibility for fertility control by any preferred method, claiming the right to choose between giving birth and having an abortion, understanding the lifetime processes of human reproductive systems, and overhauling their relationships with others. Accepting sexuality means coming to terms with all of our bodily processes—indeed, confronting them instead of submitting to them. If women wish to appreciate their sexuality, then they are likely to oppose many long-standing beliefs and practices, such as the myth of vaginal orgasm, and to allow themselves the freedom of sexual expression in such ways as enjoyment of clitoral stimulation, the use of mechanical aids to bring climax (orgasm), and the refusal of orgasm in favor of whole-body sensual pleasure. Female sexuality becomes something which a woman herself—rather than spouse, lovers, religion, the law—covets, owns, and controls.

Perhaps the issue of pornography, which most men fail altogether to understand, best demonstrates the profundity of this change. Even simple pornography such as that promulgated by male-oriented magazines, beauty contests, and "cheesecake" photography is likely to offend and irritate many women. Brownmiller (1975) well expresses their feelings: "The gut distaste that a majority of women feel when we look at pornography, a distaste that, incredibly, it is no longer fashionable to admit, comes, I think, from the gut knowledge that we and our bodies are being stripped, exposed and contorted for the purpose of ridicule to bolster that 'masculine esteem' which gets its kick and sense of power from viewing females as anonymous, panting playthings, adult toys, dehumanized objects to be used, abused, broken, and discarded" (pp. 442–443). Brownmiller's analysis of the reasons for male interest in pornography may be incomplete, but her sense that the display of female sexuality for the delight of men weakens and debases women is unmistaken. Women increasingly insist that either "cheesecake" and pornography be eliminated (not, I think, a likely event) or male sexuality be treated exactly the same way. Either solution is an attempt to assert equality, to even the balance between male and female.

The keynote of contemporary approaches toward sexuality, as far as therapy is concerned, must be the acceptance of individuality. Norms are no longer pervasive, tradition no longer predictable. The spectrum of sexuality has broadened, and it is unwise for a therapist to assume that anyone is or should be at any particular point of the spectrum. Great variations exist due to membership in various economic or ethnic groups, to religious values, family patterns and attitudes, and even to geographical location. Especially important is the generational effect, from which few women escape. Younger women who grew to maturity after the most recent wave of the sexual revolution, which includes the development of the contraceptive pill, will have values and attitudes different from those of their mothers and grandmothers, who in turn will differ from each other. During the last twenty years the ready availability of birth control devices, the longer periods for which women remain single, the increase in the divorce rate, and changing social attitudes in general have given young women a degree of sexual freedom almost certainly not available to their mothers. Attitudes differ even more; that which is a right and a pleasure to a younger woman is likely to have been at best a source of anxiety to her mother; to her grandmother it may have been no entity at all, certainly not one within her control or primarily for her own pleasure. If we tend to see older women as asexual, this may well be a result of traditional acculturation—and how they have thought of themselves.

The frequent conflicts over sexuality which occur between young women and their mothers or grandmothers are the result of cultural change, not of wickedness, decadence, conservatism, or narrow-mindedness in the individual sense. A vital role for the therapist in matters of sexuality is to help women see this generational difference for what it is and to enable not just mothers to understand daughters, but to encourage daughters to understand mothers. Each therapist and each woman needs to respect every other woman for wherever she is on the spectrum. This certainly does not mean ignoring the existence of the spectrum, for younger women have to make choices and older women may want to make new choices. The therapist's task is to help a woman who wants to explore all her sexual options; to free her of rules or behavior which make her uncomfortable, whether conservative *or* revolutionary; and to encourage her to respect herself and other women regardless of sexual orientation and/or preference.

Generational differences are not always paramount. Many women in or beyond their middle years want and need information that has become available since their youth—with the intention of changing their views on sexuality. This may be especially true of the increasing numbers of divorced or widowed women in our society who find themselves in need of a new sexual life-style. As one of my clients put it, "I know I have new freedom sexually now that I'm out on my own again, but I keep trying to use the rules I learned back in 1946 and that is ridiculous! My daughter, at twenty, is much better off than I am. I'm all boxed in with my old rules and values, and I don't know how to get out." Reciprocally, many women try to practice the "new sexuality," feel very uncomfortable with it, and need to be reassured that they are not failures because they are not "modern."

Fortunately, the generations are still capable of being kind to one another, and that kindness is a force by which they can set each other free. One client, a woman of 55, found an unexpected source of support and had an invaluable learning experience initiated by her young adult daughter. Divorced after 34 years of marriage, she had been ready to reconcile herself to sexual inactivity, but her daughter challenged this choice. She bought her mother a vibrator and taught her how to use it; to help her mother feel easier about her body, she took her to nude beaches; and then she encouraged her to have sexual relationships with men again. The mother was surprised and a little embarrassed; but she felt fortunate, for the habit of children is to say nothing about the sex life of a widow or divorcee even when attention is given to other aspects of their lives. The same sequence of learning can take place between a middle-aged daughter and an aged mother. There is, for instance, no reason for a daughter to chide her mother for forming sexual relationships with fellow residents in a retirement center.

Traditionally, the only respectable choice of a woman without a husband has been to ignore her sexuality and to permit others to ignore it. Statistics show that this situation is unlikely to endure; females outnumber males in the population, and divorce is more common. Men tend to find women of increasing age less sexually attractive, leaving large numbers of sexually active women unnoticed. Under these circumstances, it is likely that we will see a situation similar to that thought to have existed after the slaughter of ten million men in Europe during World War I; more women turned to relationships with other women, to serial and transitory relationships with men, and to self-stimulation.

Flexibility may be the quality most required of individuals in this fluid cultural situation. Men have conscious and unconscious fears and hopes about women's sexuality, and many men are threatened by changes in the situation that they grew up to expect. Regardless of male fears, the mass of women are not changing independently of men but in relationship to men; both sexes will have to undergo a series of adjustments and new discoveries. Neither sex will easily adjust to a change in ownership of women's bodies; it will take time to arrive at a new cultural consensus. Almost all an individual can do in such a situation is accept the reality of variety, contrast it with the confines of one's cultural environment, and make an individual choice. Here the therapist can play a major role, helping the individual client discover where she fits among the charts and tables presented by Kinsey, Hite, and others to demonstrate the variety among women in their pleasures, needs, patterns, wants, and choices.

Menopause

Both women and men, as they grow older, go through a period of declining reproductive activity known as the climacteric. In women this is marked by menopause. Just as menarche marked the beginning of her ability to reproduce by starting menstruation during pubescence, a woman ceases to menstruate at the time of menopause. After two or three decades of ovulation, the ovaries slowly become less capable of responding to the stimulus of hormones from the pituitary. Fewer ova are released, and the cyclic production of progesterone is interrupted, causing estrogen levels to fall. The lining of the uterus ceases to thicken, and menstrual bleeding changes its pattern and eventually stops.

The woman's system has to go through a major readjustment. Without the regular cyclic process of estrogen and progesterone, the pituitary generally overreacts by producing excessive amounts of these hormones, creating an imbalance whose most important feature is a decrease in the amount of estrogen. Since estrogen influences the nourishment of breasts, uterus, vagina, smooth muscle, and skin, the fall in estrogen levels is associated with such signs of aging as the loss of muscle tone and skin elasticity. The "hot flash" is caused by the hypothalamus responding to falling levels of estrogen. Vaginal infections become more likely since lower estrogen levels are associated with less acidic vaginal secretions. A whole range of other physical problems (e.g., insomnia, palpitations, vertigo, nausea, loss of appetite, backaches) *may* be related to menopause, but no direct link has been established; by no means do all women experience these symptoms, and there are other possible explanations. The overall physical change, however, is enough to give one a feeling of ill health at times; and menopause continues through enough years to make the concurrence of other unrelated ailments almost inevitable.

People also associate menopause with emotional symptoms: moodiness, irritability, nervousness, depression, instability in personal relationships, and others. However, it is now much less fashionable than even a decade ago to assume that menopause is the cause of such experiences; many women experience none or few of them. These symptoms are also emotionally associated to any major physical event, including those experienced by men. Finally, there are sufficient social and psychological influences occurring at the same time which may account for them.

The age at which menopause occurs is a difficult period for many women since it is a period of marked decline in the physical attributes for which men have valued them and they have valued themselves. (Menopause may occur at any time from age 35 to 60; the average age is 47. Its duration is from two to ten years.) Many women at this age are discovering that their status in life was derived from ancillary sources: the appearance of sexual attractiveness, the ability to produce children, and resemblance to society's norm for "beauty." Biology has lent the woman power; it has not come, as she had probably thought, from her "self." As this realization comes to her, she must become more individual and rely less on fortuitous support from the race and society. Thrust into individuality, she is called upon to use resources which she is likely to have let lie fallow for many years; the task is difficult and causes emotional upheaval. Further, society combines with biology to deprive her of support at the time she most needs it—her physiological change is seen as a decline. She can no longer fulfill society's major expectations of her, to be sexually stimulating and to bear children. With the major problems of mating and child rearing now over, she has more time and space—and fewer people who need her. Though she still has 20 or 30 good years of life ahead, society sees the "important" events of her life as over; the status she gathered as a wife, mother, and homemaker is now of little more use than the gold watch of retirement is to a man. While a male is considered to be in his prime during these years, little is expected of a woman of the same age. If she becomes emotionally disturbed by this change, that very disturbance is used to belittle her further. The causes of emotional disturbance at the time of menopause are thus similar to those at menarche, less physical than social; society does not see women of this age as worthwhile or even necessary.

Individual women at the age of menopause have always managed to escape the

191

fate of their peers; and there are many whole (though small) cultures which reward the postmenopausal woman with increased status and power, so we may legitimately conclude that the association between "menopause" and "decline" is not inevitable. Only some of the characteristics of menopause are biological; the individual woman with good counseling can overcome even those. The crucial needs at this time seem to be the ability to relinquish outmoded roles and the power to become more instrumental in the world. The vast majority of women will find little purpose in trying to remain primarily sex objects and mothers, so good therapy will help them put those roles behind them and find satisfactory replacements. This process is intensely pragmatic. A woman depressed because her role as mother is no longer available (the "empty nest syndrome") mainly needs help in finding some other outlet for her emotions and skills; and whether that outlet is paid work, unpaid work, or merely filling hours of idleness, the basic problem is to have her realize that she does have the skills for a new role.

Increasing numbers of women at the age of menopause enter or reenter the job market, where—especially if they have not been lifelong workers—they will face the practical problems of work life. If a woman has lost her mate, she will possess a very different economic and social status whose parameters she will need to describe closely. She will face some new manifestations of discrimination, such as being passed over in favor of younger women for jobs which were not available to her when she was their age. As all people must, she will have to face the resentment of no longer being young, discover that maturity and competence are not necessarily rewarded, and find herself outmoded in skills; but counseling should show her that these emotions are not uncontrollable generalities of menopause, the inevitable lot of all women, as much as they are practical problems capable of solution when divided into their components. In other words, the woman client needs to be shown where her own power now lies.

At the time of menopause, a woman basically has only two choices. She may, sooner or later, accept society's message about the value of menopausal women and submit herself to being put on the shelf. Or she may see that she can pursue opportunities to develop her personhood which, when they were given to her earlier, she overlooked in favor of fulfilling societal expectations. She can now undertake the development of her physical, social, emotional, and intellectual abilities which she earlier neglected in favor of subordination. Menopause is thus merely a signal of the need to re-examine and recreate coincident with maturity and preparatory to aging. In and for itself, it is an event of small significance. Many therapists suspect, indeed, that some women tend to use menopause as an excuse to avoid the new task of maturity. If everything can be blamed on physiological inevitability, then there is nothing that the woman can do except remain as passive and powerless in front of her body's development as she has been. Menopause thus becomes an excuse for avoiding development rather than for undertaking it. Therapists should be wary of the same attitude in themselves since they too will share the societal stereotypes that tend to present menopausal women as "finished" and to lump the remaining decades of their lives under the rubric of old age.

Sexuality and Aging

Older women are not asexual. The withdrawal of sex hormones during menopause has only an indirect effect on sexual drive and behavior (Masters and Johnson, 1968). While both women and men experience changes in sexual physiology with aging, both sexes respond basically as they did before and remain capable of orgasm, though frequency and intensity decline (Williams, 1977). Though women over 65 are less concerned with sex than they were when younger, many still seek out and respond to sexual encounters, report erotic dreams, and are capable of multiple orgasms (Kaplan, 1974). Most studies support the idea that the sex drive of women is more stable than that of men and less susceptible to the effects of aging.

Yet the data show that sexual activity in older women is less frequent and ends earlier than it does in men. Why? The key factor is apparently the opportunity for regular sexual expression, which is related to the availability of partners (Williams, 1977). Here the brute facts of divorce, widowhood, and discrimination against the aging are more than usually brutal. Since the ratio of men to women declines dramatically with age and since the remaining men tend to be either married, gay, or more interested in young women, the "double standard" governing men and women can go into full operation. Because men are valued more for what they do than how they look, they can remain sexually "attractive" and active longer than can women (Sontag, 1972). Since there are fewer men than women among the aging, men find it easier to obtain sexual partners.

In fact, many women experience an increase in sexual energy during and after menopause. Free from the fear of pregnancy, often having more time now that child rearing is over and economic stability is achieved, those who have worked out the frictions of the marital relationship often experience a sexual flowering. If opportunities with partners shrink, masturbation may become a more important source of sexual release (Masters and Johnson, 1968). On the other hand, women may use aging as a reason for avoiding sex. For instance, a woman who regards intercourse as a sinful act permissible only for purposes of reproduction is likely to lose all interest in sex. A woman who has been ashamed of her body all her life is now likely to be more embarrassed by the signs of aging and to be less sexually active. But these are attitudinal factors, not biological; the way a woman feels about herself and her body is likely to be the main determinant.

Older women may not want to raise the issue of their sexuality, especially with a younger therapist, yet it may need to be raised because it is so closely related to loneliness, low self-esteem, and depression. There are two comparatively easy avenues toward the subject, each important in its own right. First, techniques to reawaken the clients' sense of the body should be used: self-massage, massage, yoga, personal adornment, dancing, and exercise are among the possibilities. Second, greater socialization and an open search for companionship should be encouraged through participation in various groups and activities. Older women are not likely to be interested in the kind of search for a mate which a younger woman might undertake; nor are they likely to be anything but embarrassed by the rituals of youth. However, these are not the only alternatives to solitude, and any attempts which the woman makes to expand out of the sexually passive and socially limited role into which the socialization process casts the typical older woman ought to be explored and encouraged.

Further Reading

We now have several excellent sources of information about the subjects of this chapter, each with a slightly different viewpoint and with substantially different information. The following are recommended:

1. Boston Women's Health Book Collective, *Our Bodies, Our Selves*, New York: Simon and Schuster, 1976.
2. Cooke, C. W., and S. Dworkin, *The MS Guide to a Woman's Health*, Garden City, N.Y.: Doubleday, 1979.
3. Diagram Group, *Women's Body: an Owner's Manual*, New York: Paddington Press, 1977.
4. Seaman, B., and G. Seaman, *Women and the Crisis in Sex Hormones*, New York: Rawson Associates, 1977.
5. Williams, J. H., *Psychology of Women: Behavior in a Biosocial Context*, New York: Norton, 1977.

9

Abuse of Women's Bodies

One of the common reasons that prompt women to enter therapy is any of the forms of bodily abuse to which they subject themselves or which others inflict upon them. The mental health professions are only beginning to develop a professional attitude toward these abuses; their delayed response may be related to the fact that therapists deal with only the individual case, whereas the causes for widespread abuse of women's bodies seem to be societal, reflecting the general powerlessness of women.

Physical Abuse by Others

The American family unit is characterized by an abnormal level of physical aggression (Hindman, 1979). While any family member may be the target of violence, women are particularly vulnerable. A random sample of 2,143 couples showed that some 50 to 60 percent had acted violently toward each other, and almost always had the man physically attacked the woman (Straus, 1976). The data on violence led one researcher to conclude that "women really are twice as safe on the street as in their own homes" (Sterne, 1976, p. 61).

Wife beating is present in many American marriages, but our society has not yet decided that it is a major problem, or even intolerable. Physicians, for instance, are legally required to report injuries resulting from domestic violence against children but not that against wives. Police intervene reluctantly because of embarrassment, feelings of inadequacy, and anxiety; according to the Federal

Bureau of Investigation (FBI), intervention in domestic disputes brings about 27 percent of police deaths while on duty. In the court system, neither the criminal nor the civil courts respond effectively, each court tending to shift responsibility to the other (Eisenberg and Micklow, 1977). Prosecutors who encourage women to file charges often do so reluctantly because there is a high probability that the charges will later be withdrawn. Shelters and safe environments for women escaping from brutality are just beginning to appear. Neighbors, friends, and family are often afraid to intervene, if only because the violence may then be directed toward them. Thus, in many ways children and animals are better protected against violence in the home than are wives. Even though most cases of wife beating are not reported, those reported outnumber cases of reported rape three to one. According to the FBI, 25 percent of all murders result from family disputes, and one-half of domestic murders were spouses killing spouses. Physical abuse is a daily reality and fear for literally millions of wives.

The causes of wife abuse are complex. Woolley (1978) finds four categories of direct causes: (1) rage and frustration caused by seemingly insoluble problems from all possible sources; (2) alcohol or drug use, though drunkenness is often the excuse rather than the reason for violence; (3) difference in status, such as the husband having a poorer education or a lower income than has the wife; and (4) fear of the woman's dependence on him with which a man may feel unable to cope, such as when his wife becomes pregnant. But the indirect causes which give males psychological and practical permission to abuse females are much more complex, and the interested therapist should read in its entirety the analysis of the cultural and individual factors outlined by Straus (1976). Whether wife abuse is a method used by the culture to preserve male dominance or whether it occurs because women are physically, psychologically, and socially less powerful than are men has only recently become a subject of debate. (See Brownmiller, 1975; Langley and Levy, 1977; and Martin, 1976.) Experts expect an increase in wife beating because, as one speaker at a 1976 Conference on Battered Women put it, "Battering is an attempt to put and keep women in their place. It happens whenever a man perceives that a woman . . . is stepping out of her role" (Leghorn, 1976).

In remaining ambivalent about wife abuse, the health professions reflect the historic American attitude that what a man does in the privacy of his own home is nobody else's concern, a belief which encourages us to ignore, underestimate, or develop false explanations for the battering of women. The following list contains many of the mitigating explanations of the data widespread in our society. None of the following statements is true.

Myths about Wife Abuse

1. "Wife abuse is a pathological act committed only by men who are severely mentally ill."

2. "Most men are brought up to believe that violence toward a woman is wrong."

3. "Wife abuse occurs almost entirely among the lower classes and the less

educated or among certain ethnic groups, because such treatment of women is a traditional part of their cultural system."

4. "Wife abuse is an isolated act occurring only once or twice in the course of a relationship."

5. "Women actually want to be dominated physically and behave in ways intended to aggravate men so as to induce violence."

6. "A wife needs to be corrected occasionally. Correction clears the air."

7. "Striking a woman is not real violence, which occurs only if a weapon is used or the woman is beaten unconscious."

8. "If a husband strikes a wife, she probably drove him to it."

9. "Wife abuse is a private problem, not a crime, and it must be dealt with by the family, not outsiders." [U.S. National Commission on the Observance of International Women's Year, 1977f]

All these myths thrive solely because our culture sees wives as subordinate to husbands and women as subordinate to men. Many women accept abuse as their natural lot; they may see it as normal because it existed between their parents. They may see it as "deserved." They may be ashamed and embarrassed by the private matters that preceded the abuse. They may be terrified. Most often, they have not the slightest idea what to do about it, and they usually cannot find anyone to whom they can turn for help. But our society tends to blame women themselves for the violence to which they are subject; if they put up with the abuse, it is assumed that in some strange way they like it. As Erin Pizzey points out, this creates an intolerable dilemma: "In reality [women] stay and put up with it because they have nowhere else to go. Because they stay and put up with it they are assumed to like it and so they are blocked from finding somewhere else to go" (1977, p. 37).

Why do women put up with it? Certainly not because they choose to be abused or to incite violence or because they enjoy or deserve it. One study found three basic reasons why abused wives accept their situation: (1) the less severe and less frequent the violence, the more likely is the wife to remain; (2) the more she was abused as a child, the more able is she to tolerate abuse from her husband; and (3) the fewer material resources and less economic power she has, the more likely is she to stay (Gelles, 1976). In sum, the overwhelming reason for battered wives staying with the men who batter them is that they either have or see no alternative.

Physically abused women—women who are powerless, or believe themselves to be powerless, to change their situations—are therefore excellent candidates for help from therapists. The role of the therapist is to halt the physical abuse by helping the client find an alternative as quickly as possible. If the situation has a quick practical solution such as finding a shelter, then psychological problems should wait; physical abuse is not a postponable problem and even a short-term or partial solution can bring about dramatic changes in some clients' orientation.

Norma Jean, an intelligent 23-year-old, was married two years and had an 8-month-old baby when she came to therapy wanting "to work on myself because I think I'm messed up and I have to grow up." We began with figure: what did "messed up" mean? It meant not cleaning the house properly, not being a good mother, going home every month to spend a few days with her parents, and managing money poorly, all of which were connected with a poor self-image. But Norma Jean arrived for her second session with a bruise under her left eye and a cut on her mouth; I immediately asked how that had happened. She said she had fallen while cleaning the top shelf of a closet and was okay. Although I was suspicious, we continued to work on what she presented that day, mostly her sense of inadequacy. However, the following weekend she telephoned. She was crying, and I could hear her baby daughter wailing in the background. "It's not right," she said. "All this mess is *not* my fault. He's been hitting me again, and it's not right. He's gone out and I had to call you because you're the only one I can trust. What can I do?" Questioning her, I found out that an incident like this— Bob hitting her in a rage and leaving in the car—happened often. I told her she should leave immediately. She argued. I insisted, gambling on the authority she had granted me. She had neighbors whom she trusted; I told her to pack up the baby's essentials and go to them while I called the Women's Shelter. I told her about the shelter, got the neighbor's address, and within 30 minutes Norma Jean was on the way to the shelter in a car driven by the shelter's staff. I met her there so that her transition to a safe environment would be easier and to help her deal with the guilt which she was experiencing. Hers was a story familiar at community agencies: an abusing husband who blamed her for his abuse.

Norma Jean stayed at the shelter for several weeks, even though this was her first visit; with the experience of other women to guide her, she decided to move back home to her parents and file for divorce, which she did. She also participated in a group therapy program run by the local women's center to help abused women determine what was external and what internal in the pattern of abuse to which she had submitted. Such active intervention by a therapist is risky, gratifying, often unsuccessful—and essential in the case of abused women. As Norma Jean later told me, she called me because she had to get out and could not do it alone.

Whatever the sequence of therapeutic activity, experts agree that it should include the following steps:

1. Help the client work out the practicalities of leaving her situation. Clients are likely to possess children, to lack money, and to have isolated themselves from family and friends. They may need somewhere to go immediately in order to get away from the home situation, but without help from family and friends, they may not know or consider community alternatives; they may also feel that practical considerations are in themselves reason enough to stay in the home and continue to be abused. The ability to refer to other community resources is therefore crucial to a therapist's role.

2. Deal with the client's reluctance to discuss the matter. Embarrassment, shame, humiliation, and loyalty to the spouse make such reluctance typical, and the client may have other beliefs which prevent her from feeling the proper indignation and freedom. She may believe that a certain amount of violence from

husbands to wives, or from "him" to "me," is natural and right. She may not know that other wives are not physically abused, seeing her own situation as usual. She may believe that she deserves to be abused, especially if she was also abused as a child. Feelings of guilt, sometimes connected with real "misbehavior" on her part, may silence her. Many clients accept physical abuse as so much a part of their lives that, coming to therapy for other reasons, it does not occur to them to mention that they are being abused. The therapist should be prepared to take the first steps toward breaking this silence that confines the client.

3. Help the client confront the reasons she stays in an abusive situation. Use of the list of myths provided above is an effective device for providing information, and most abused women believe at least some of those myths as a result of their acculturation to the passive female role. Other reasons are usually more individual; the client may believe that the situation will right itself after a particular event has happened. Her church, her family, or her peers may be telling her that she ought to stay "for the good of the children." She may not know that community shelters or legal protection exist. She may believe that, if she leaves, the husband's violence will worsen and she will still be without protection. Finally, she is likely to be so psychologically as well as physically battered that her initiative of any kind has succumbed to fear. In all cases the therapist acts as a source of reality.

It should be emphasized that the combination of practical and psychological difficulties in these situations makes it nearly impossible for an abused wife to take initiative on her own. The habits of a lifetime, the experience of months or years, and the terror of the coming evening may combine to make individual rebellion impossible. The therapist acts as the first of several agents who will provide an environment in which change becomes possible: community organizations, women's groups, the legal system, and the family and friends. Indeed, once the abuse has been stopped, the therapist's work may well have just begun. The abused wife experiences the powerlessness of women in one of its most extreme forms, and the only real repair lies in her regaining a sense of her full autonomy and right to exercise her own power.

Rape

Rape is sexual intercourse which occurs forcibly and against the victim's will. Force includes duress or intimidation but not necessarily physical violence. Rape terrifies and degrades its victims to a degree which its technical definition is incapable of conveying; it threatens body and psyche in ways not present in other kinds of violent crime, creating an enormous sense of powerlessness and anger that is extremely long-lasting. The experience is something which most men are incapable of imagining.

Myths about rape abound in our culture; many of them stem from male sexual fantasies. The best source of factual information to contest these myths is *Rape*, published by the U.S. National Commission on Observance of International

199

Women's Year (1977d). The commission's materials show, for instance, that rape is anything but an impulsive act of erotic passion—some 71 percent of all rapes are planned in advance. Rape typically falls into two distinct categories: assault without forewarning ("the blitz"), and the "conned victim" approach, wherein the woman is talked into placing herself in a situation where she is vulnerable. Rapists are not members of an insane, threatening-looking subspecies who are recognizably dangerous; any man may be a rapist, and the rape may occur anywhere. While most victims over 18 years of age are raped by strangers, many know the rapist (who may be a friend, relative, or husband), and children are likely to know the assailant, who has picked them out.

Women are not, as men often claim, "asking for it." Anyone can be a victim. Women from all races, classes, and economic backgrounds become victims; Rape Awareness in Miami (U.S. National Commission on the Observance of International Women's Year, 1977d) reported their ages as ranging from two months to 85 years. Seductive or provocative dress is not a prerequisite to rape, nor is being in "the wrong place." Rapists go where women are, not vice versa. According to the U.S. Law Enforcement Assistance Administration (1979), the typical victim is young, poor, and unmarried; the highest risk groups are women aged 16 to 24 and women from racial minorities. In the 26 cities studied, the most dangerous hours were between 6 PM and midnight, and the most dangerous places were streets, parks, and other public places. A vast majority of victims sought to protect themselves, usually by fighting back and/or crying out. Of all reported forcible rapes, 51 percent resulted in the arrest of the assailant, but many rapes go unreported. Minority races reported an estimated 76 percent of actual cases and white women 62 percent.

Rape is always accompanied by some violence or by the immediate threat of violence: choking, beating, brutality, forcible penetration, the use of a weapon. Murder or disabling injury is always an immediate prospect to the victim, and if women do not always resist rape, it is because assertive reactions may provoke worse harm. The normal psychological consequences are similarly serious; they include a generalized fear of men, fear or uneasiness about all sexuality, guilt, decreased sense of independence and fears of being alone, loss of trust in male–female relationships, loss of self-respect, nightmares, and suicidal impulses. Any or all of these consequences may last for years. From the viewpoint of a man who hates women, rape is the perfect crime.

Rape victims normally need supportive counseling, but therapy may vary widely in source and duration. Some need professional therapy of a fairly deep nature; others gain what they need from special programs such as feminist groups, crisis intervention centers, task forces on rape, and community rape prevention and treatment programs. Extremely important is support from family, friends, and community officials from the very first moment of contact with the authorities; the nature of the original contact with the police may be critical. Immediate treatment by a physician is essential, both to examine the victim for injuries or disease and to provide medical evidence in case of need. Emotional support at this time is just as important as the medical examination, and as the woman moves out into her general environment again, continuing support is probably necessary. One experienced rape center recommends that a hospital counselor see the victim when she first comes to the hospital and then make follow-up calls 48 hours later, two weeks later, and six weeks after the attack to determine the need for therapy, since long-term effects are often delayed (Clark, 1976). Rape centers report that women deprived of social and emotional support may take years to recover. Many therapists find clients who have carried the trauma of rape within them for years after the event, never telling anyone of their burden of guilt or shame, sure that they will meet with reproach or disbelief if they "confess."

Counseling rape victims involves three general phases; because the trauma of rape is so great and has different effects on its victims, it is likely to trigger unexpected disturbances. The first phase is *catharsis,* and the role of the therapist at this time is to listen and to believe. The woman needs an environment in which she can discuss anything she chooses regarding her rape, even if it seems foolish to her. Feelings of humiliation, shame, and guilt may well come first: "I should not have been so stupid as to be there!" "I should have known better." "How could I let him con me like that?" One client, who had had car trouble on the highway and was raped by the man who stopped to help her, first assured me that she should have been smart enough to find someone else to help her; then she expressed guilt about her ignorance of car maintenance, since she might have fixed the trouble ahead of time. Equally frequent and forceful is the desire to avoid having other people know that one has been raped. Underlying this guilt, of course, is the internalized myth that a woman is in some way responsible for having been raped, the belief that the crime is the victim's fault. Anger will also arise at some stage in therapy; the anger must be expressed if recovery is to be made, but it should not be forced by the therapist, only supported. One client drew a rough picture of her assailant on a large sheet of paper, stabbed it with her pen until it was tattered, tore the drawing into small pieces, then burned the pieces, saying over and over again, "I want to kill him—he doesn't deserve to live—I'll destroy him the way he tried to destroy me!" This was symbolic "magic," of course; but like most magic it was very useful in restoring the magician's sense of power.

Such emotions may well recur, especially if a trial ensues and the victim meets with the coldness of the criminal justice system. Having relived the rape for the benefit of her family, the police, her attorney, and her therapist, she must now relive it in public and in the presence of her attacker. She needs support at the trial, if only in the shape of the therapist's presence in the courtroom; and she needs more support afterwards to deal with further shame, guilt, and anger until the event is substantially behind her.

The second phase of therapy is *creating support* from others. Because of their feelings about rape, people who normally provide support for the victim may be useless, or they may be unable to employ basic human skills. Anyone in the victim's environment may have archaic attitudes about rape and therefore do her harm. Therapists obviously must familiarize themselves in advance with the system which the community provides for dealing with rape victims so that they may give advice regarding proper procedures and the right people to contact. Essential is a knowledge of community organizations and individuals specially trained to deal with rape victims, whether they be associated with the police or with feminist groups. Therapists should be able to provide the client with some advance knowledge of what to expect in the community and to help the client set up necessary contacts.

The third phase is _rebuilding trust_ in one's self, one's environment, and in one's personal relationships. Many clients experience a sharply increased fear of moving around in the world again. Fear of the environment in which the rape occurred (which may even have been her own bedroom) may generalize itself. Some clients are afraid to go shopping, to live by themselves, or to take a trip alone. They feel that they cannot trust themselves to make sensible decisions and that they need more or less constant supervision. This, of course, is a drastic loss of autonomy; a woman expressing such loss needs help in turning her unreasonable fear back into appropriate caution. Similarly, she must learn to trust people—especially men—again, to rebuild individual relationships and her general relationships. The more that people around a victim can be open, supportive, and accepting, the more rapidly can a victim rebuild—but people's insensitivity in this area is equaled only by their embarrassment. The therapist, then, may need to work with the victim's husband or lover, her friends, and her family; in addition, for the woman herself, support groups made up of other victims are by far the most useful technique. Rebuilding may be accompanied by reevaluation. Because rape is traumatic, it often prompts a change in values and life goals or life-style, with the result that it may be the beginning of a longer therapeutic process.

A raped woman will probably be a weakened woman. As with any victim of violent crime, she is likely to feel powerless and in need of protection; the pseudosexual nature of this crime, when abetted by a woman's previous cultural conditioning, makes consequent disturbance to the personality structure even more severe. Good therapy, however, can help a rape victim do more than restore herself to what she was; it can provide her with the avenue to greater strength and a stronger sense of self. Women are often criticized for supposed "antagonism" to males, yet recovery from rape often helps a woman create the degree of assertiveness about her own rights as a female which is the base of that so-called antagonism. In this respect, Susan Brownmiller's analysis of the cultural environment of rape should be recalled by every therapist:

> Once we accept as basic truth that rape is not a crime of irrational, impulsive, uncontrollable lust, but is a deliberate, hostile, violent act of degradation and possession on the part of a would-be conqueror, designed to intimidate and inspire fear, we must look toward those elements in our culture that promote and propagandize these attitudes, which offer men, and in particular, impressionable adolescent males, who form the potential raping population, the ideological and psychological

encouragement to commit their acts of aggression without awareness, for the most part, that they have committed a punishable crime, let alone a moral wrong. [Brownmiller, 1975, p. 439]

In addition to Brownmiller's classic book on the subject of rape, therapists will also find the following useful: Felicia Guest, *To Comfort and Relieve Them: A Manual for Counseling Rape Victims*, available from Reproductive Health Resources, 1507 21st St., Suite 100, Sacramento, CA 95814; and the National Center for the Prevention and Control of Rape, a division of the National Institute of Mental Health, an excellent source for training materials, information, and technical assistance and a potential source of funds.

Abuse by Addiction

One form of abuse of the female body, a widespread and increasingly prevalent form, is carried out by women themselves—addiction to alcohol or other drugs. No matter how much society in general and other individuals in particular encourage women to abuse addictive substances or fail to discourage them from abuse, the eventual refusal to continue an addiction must come from the individual herself. Addiction therefore poses, in especially dramatic terms, the question raised throughout this chapter: how does a woman make her own body a locus of power and self-esteem? And how does a therapist assist her to take control over her own physiological destiny?

The issues of addiction are so complex that there is not space here to summarize them all adequately. Addiction counseling has developed into a field which requires a therapist to have special knowledge and skills and, perhaps, a special temperament. In this field a little knowledge is a dangerous thing; it can lead to egregious errors if the therapist is not specially trained. This section therefore summarizes only enough information to indicate the complexity of the field and its basic dynamics from the viewpoint of this chapter. References to enable therapists to expand their knowledge independently are included.

Alcohol Abuse

The most widespread and damaging form of drug addiction is the abuse of alcohol, a substance used by four-fifths of the population with comparatively benign effects but by a substantial minority to the great harm of themselves and others. How large is that minority? Officially we say that there are 10 million "alcoholics" in the country, about 10 percent of the adult population, but there is a recent trend to estimate that at any given time 20 million people may be "in trouble with alcohol." In addition, each alcoholic affects adversely the lives of three or four other people. Rated officially as the country's third largest public health problem, alcoholism has long-term debilitating effects on a greater proportion of the population than does any other ailment.

What proportion of the population with drinking problems consists of women? We do not know. Tradition held that women could not have drinking problems. A decade ago experts believed that females made up 20 percent of the alcoholic population. That figure is currently regarded as conservative, and some estimates now range as high as 50 percent of the alcoholic population, 5 million women, or one out of every 20 females (Homiller, 1977; Sandmaier, 1977). Many believe that alcoholism is now becoming as much a female as a male problem, others that for various cultural reasons its extent among women has been hidden. Recent reports show that at treatment centers women are steadily increasing their numbers so that the ratio of men to women is growing more equal; but experts also point to the generally greater willingness of women than men to accept the need for help (Wilsnack, 1977). Despite the confusion, it is inevitable that a significant proportion of the women in any therapist's clientele is likely to be in trouble with alcohol.

What of the depth and duration of their addiction? The onset of alcoholism is gradual, the dependency long unnoticed, and its cessation usually quite difficult. It generally begins with social drinking, and it *usually* ends not just with sobriety and controlled drinking but with abstinence; members of Alcoholics Anonymous like to refer to themselves as "recovering alcoholics" and to use the analogy of a permanent disease. One of the most pernicious features of alcohol as an addictive substance is that it is socially approved to the extent that most people are unwilling to see alcohol addiction as a likelihood for themselves or for others, though to a trained diagnostician the symptoms are fairly obvious. We lack social norms, and this makes it easy to move from reasonable to unreasonable consumption of alcohol—and to addiction.

The patterns of female alcohol addiction have similarities with those of men—and significant differences. A recent statement by a leading scholar shows the newness of realizations in this field:

> Much of the research conducted on women and alcohol in the past six years has had this same focus: demonstrating that women alcoholics are indeed different from men alcoholics. I believe that we have finally won that battle, made that point—that men and women alcoholics differ in some major respects. And it was an important point to make, since for many years researchers have been studying only men but generalizing their conclusions to women—or assuming that treatment programs developed primarily for men would be equally effective for women. However, it seems to me that it is now time for a second phase in research on women and alcohol, time to shift our attention and energy from how men and women drinkers may differ to how women drinkers differ *among themselves*. [Wilsnack, 1977]

As summarized by Wilsnack, the major differences between the patterns of alcoholism among women and among men are as follows. The male typically develops his excessive drinking during his 20s, the woman during her 30s (Lisansky, 1957; Rathod and Thomson, 1971). Once they begin, women's alcohol problems develop much more rapidly than do those of men (Lisansky, 1957; Curlee,

1970; Elder, 1973; Beckman, 1977) with the result that both sexes typically enter treatment during their 40s. Of particular importance to therapists, women alcoholics much more often than did men related the onset of their drinking problems to an external life crisis: divorce or marital problems; death of a parent or spouse; obstetrical or gynecological problems; the menopausal time of life or the departure of children from the home (Lisansky, 1957; Curlee, 1969; Wilsnack, 1973; Beckman, 1977). This affects therapy deeply. If true, changes in these external factors or changed attitudes toward them may greatly aid recovery, but Wilsnack points out that women may only feel more need to rationalize their addictions in terms of external events. Men drink more often and more heavily than do women. Women more often drink alone and at home. The symptoms of alcoholism in women entering treatment are often less obvious because they are less severe (Horn and Wanberg, 1973). Women alcoholics tend to show less self-esteem than do men alcoholics (Beckman, 1977), and once in treatment usually progress more poorly than do men. This leads some people to support the general societal view that women alcoholics are in some way "sicker" than male alcoholics; but the differences are much more explicable in terms of our failure to study the particular problems of women alcoholics and develop treatment programs specific to them (Sandmaier, 1980). Finally, female physiology shows certain specific connections to drinking patterns: the stages of the menstrual cycle, levels of estrogen, the use of oral contraceptives, and most dramatically the fetal alcohol syndrome, all of which create gender-specific differences between men and women.

The most interesting difference between male and female addiction lies in its etiology, which seems directly related in part to sex-role expectations. Unfortunately, we do not yet know enough about the relationship between alcoholism and sex-role identification or conflict to make realistic generalizations. One school of thought maintains that the entry of women into the wider world, with increased socializing, stress, and "masculinization," increases the amount they drink and the frequency of problem drinking. Women's liberation, in other words, makes them as likely as men to become enslaved to alcohol. Another school maintains that the increased independence brought about by abandonment of the traditionally feminine role *decreases* the likelihood of alcoholism; indeed, alcoholism is more likely among women fulfilling the traditional feminine role of housewife. A third approach reconciles the previous two by stating that any conflict between the actual sex role and the preferred sex role increases the likelihood of a drinking problem. The most recent research shows the causes of female alcoholism to be rooted in the social roles of women. The "research indicates that the culturally defined set of behaviors demanded of women actually engenders much of the pain and conflict that push women toward abusive drinking" (Sandmaier, 1980, p. 89).

Can we erect models for female alcoholism and its treatment which differ from those that apply to men? Only to a very limited extent. There is simply not enough knowledge about either the etiology of alcoholism or the nature of

205

women who drink. There are, however, two points which the therapist should remember.

The first is that society tends to see a drinking woman in much less favorable terms than it does a drinking man. One praises a man for being able to hold his liquor well; the same phrase reflects disapproval of a woman. We see female alcoholics as somehow "sicker" or less normal than male alcoholics, a dim but powerful relic of the nineteenth-century view of the woman as the angel of the hearth and not susceptible to the earthly sins that plague men. This view has very damaging practical consequences for women (Homiller, 1977). Alcoholic women have lower self-esteem than do alcoholic men (Lisansky, 1957; Curlee, 1968; Blane, 1968). The rate of marital instability, divorce, and separation among women alcoholics (two-thirds are divorced) is higher than among alcoholic men; the result is that women more often than men lack such support, emotional and financial, as may be provided by a spouse. For every ten wives who stay with an alcoholic husband, one husband remains with an alcoholic wife (Fraser, 1973). There is a significant lack of treatment programs for women, and an even greater lack of trained role models to act as their therapists (Homiller, 1977; Schultz, 1975; Fontaine, 1975). In sum, the story of inequality continues through alcoholism as through other aspects of women's lives.

The second point is that the feminist approach to alcoholism therapy seems likely to be productive for men as well as women. Maxfield recently summarized this approach: "A feminist approach is a whole-person approach. It considers all aspects of a woman's existence and recognizes the interrelationship between physical and psychological health. It takes into account that, because of their still unequal position in society, women's experience of reality and their conceptualization of this reality differs from that of men. It is also a social change approach: it takes a dynamic view of historical development and requires faith that the present situation can be changed. Faith in change is also an important element in the treatment of alcoholism" (Maxfield, 1979). Sandmaier (1980) takes this point even further, suggesting that female alcoholism is linked to women's "powerless social condition" and that improvement in the area cannot be great without "far-reaching changes in women's status in society." In my own experience, certainly, the sense of powerlessness which women generally experience is magnified and almost parodied in the powerlessness both sexes experience in the face of alcoholism.

Abuse of Other Drugs

Drugs other than alcohol fall into three categories. Illicit drugs, such as heroin, are those proscribed by law for any but the narrowest medical uses. Prescription drugs are those controlled by law, with physicians and pharmacists as authorized distributors. Over-the-counter drugs are those available for public purchase according to the individual's will, with some legal control over their quality and the manner of their advertising. In all three cases, most of the "pushers" of drugs are male. In all three categories, high financial stakes and outrageously high profits for the sellers are a major factor. Despite the existence of the Controlled Substances List—which makes an attempt to classify and illegalize drugs according to their health risks—the legality or illicitness of a drug does *not* depend on the degree of health risk, though in general physicians are given control over those which have the most dramatic and immediate adverse effects on health. It is not scientific fact but social habit that makes cigarettes and alcohol available over the counter while heroin and marijuana are illegal. And the existing control system does not work well. Illicit drugs are available if one has the money and life-style to acquire them. Prescription drugs are so widely used and many of them are so ruthlessly addictive that the situation is a national medical scandal.

Most users of licit drugs are women. Some 60 percent of psychotropics, 71 percent of antidepressants, and 80 percent of amphetamines are prescribed for women (McConnell, 1978). About 80 percent of women alcoholics use other drugs as frequently as they use alcohol. What is responsible for this imbalance between the sexes? Is it the greater weakness of women, some genetic or psychological need to be dependent on something external for their state of mind? A recent major report prepared for the National Institute on Drug Abuse blames not the psychology of women but the image of the psychology of women which is possessed by physicians: "[The physicians'] lack of sensitivity can be traced to their medical education, where little emphasis is placed either on problems which have implications for the health of women or on alcohol and drug abuse. Physicians are taught to treat symptoms, rather than to identify underlying problems, and are conditioned to believe that women are not as psychologically 'sound' as men, are inherently more dependent and likely to have emotional problems" (Chambers, Inciardi, and Siegal, 1975). Advertisements for sedatives, tranquilizers, and mood-altering drugs, says the NIDA report, "portray women as anxious, depressed, in need of a medical 'crutch' to deal with their problems, and thus reinforce the tendencies of physicians to prescribe such drugs for those problems." In my own experience and that of my clients, physicians especially tend to prescribe medications for the symptoms of uniquely female experiences such as menstruation, pregnancy, and menopause. According to NIDA, 80 percent of prescriptions for the mood-altering drugs are written by general practitioners, obstetricians, gynecologists, and others without special training in psychopharmacology, and only 9 percent by psychiatrists. As far as I can tell, if a troubled woman seeks the advice of a physician he is likely—in effect, if not intent—to see the woman and not her life situation as being at fault and to remove the symptom of her ill-content, not the cause. Physicians are not trained, and on the whole are inadequate, to be counselors of women. Female physicians are for the most part conditioned in precisely the same manner as are males.

No therapist can afford to rest happy once she or he has made a referral to a physician, especially if the client has a problem with any kind of drug. There are too many horror stories to ignore: underdiagnosis, misdiagnosis, cross-addiction, multiple prescriptions, poly-drug abuse, and total failure to respond. Furthermore, many of the mood-altering drugs reduce clients to the status of zombies, relieving the temporary pain but also rendering the client incapable of reason and growth. Psychiatrists themselves have become increasingly cautious about the use of drugs because of the incredible growth of psychopharmacology during the last decade or so. We have come a long way since Miltown® was introduced in the 1950s. At present 14 percent of the adult population uses Valium® , now known to be a highly addictive drug with withdrawal symptoms that *may* be as bad as those of heroin; yet Valium® is no longer widely used even in connection with psychotherapy. While psychiatrists are growing increasingly skillful at determining permanent chemical supports for use in counteracting mental illness reflective of some form of chemical malfunction in the body or mind, they are also increasingly loath to use ordinary mood-altering drugs as a routine component of therapy or alone. In sum, the power of a physician to prescribe drugs is simply not the right way to restore to a woman a sense of her own power.

A therapist needs to estimate the proportion of clients who may need some kind of temporary or enduring chemical support; that proportion will vary according to the nature of the clientele. In my own practice the extent turns out to be less than 5 percent. At a public mental health center, I have been given estimates as high as 20 percent; but the proportion also depends on personal opinion. I have seen mental centers with as many as 90 percent of their clients taking some form of mood-altering drug, the prescriptions being issued under physicians' standing orders. One needs to investigate whether there are alternatives to chemotherapy. A client in a state of crisis may benefit from temporary chemical support, but she may benefit more from a good session of active therapy. A client in a state of continuing stress may benefit from drugs; but she may also benefit more from changing her daily physical habits. In sum, a therapist can properly contest the public's willingness to accept prescription drugs by pointing out the alternatives, specifically because the danger of psychological and physical dependency is so very great. Finally, one needs to determine who will prescribe the drugs. If I suspect that drugs would be useful for any reason, I make a referral to a psychiatrist for an overall evaluation, even though this is an extra cost to the client; and I choose a psychiatrist who is well trained in psychopharmacology and whom I personally know to be cautious and careful. Either from the psychiatrist or from me, the client receives a full explanation of the purpose and limitations of the drug, emphasizing the danger signs of dependency and the side effects so that they may alert themselves and, if necessary, me. This is precisely so that the client will still have control over her own body and will not have the illusion of *needing* chemical support when it is not in fact necessary. I also ask the client to compile a list of all drugs, whether prescription or over-the-counter, and the amounts of alcohol which she is likely to consume so that she can make her own choice regarding which she will use.

During recent years the trend to encourage prevention and self-care has benefited therapists by providing clients with a substantial alternative to the passivity of drug use. Many clients today prefer, for instance, a regular schedule of physical activity (running or jogging, yoga, aerobic dance, racquetball, or stress and relaxation exercises). With addicted persons, this has the added benefit of breaking up the social habits and companionships which encourage addiction. The aim, in the phrase of Glaser (1976), is to create a positive addiction. Another alternative is to use the services of a well-trained nutritional expert, who can design a combination of diet and vitamin/mineral supplements for the individual. There is increasing evidence that nutritional changes make a difference, but the area is full of poorly trained true believers; one should select only a well-trained and academically qualified expert. The advantage of both physical exercise and attention to nutrition is that they encourage a woman to take charge of her own well-being. She uses the help of others, but the power is her own.

Implications for Therapists

The model for change presented in the opening chapters of this book suggests the effect of physical abuse of any kind upon a client. The body is the basic source of personal power, and if it is subject to abuse by any external agent, the psychological consequences will be serious.

One of the important diagnostic steps for a therapist, therefore, is to ascertain the extent and nature of any physical abuse to which the client herself or others may be subjecting her body. Some therapists use either a part of the intake interview for this purpose or short-form screening tests such as the Michigan Alcoholism Screening Test. Others make the data part of the client's self-evaluation, believing this to be a much more important therapeutic tool as well as a more accurate diagnostic technique. No evaluation should be moralistic or disapproving, since these qualities conflict with the goal of therapy by reducing the client's sense of power, making her depend on another's judgment, and lessening her long-term responsibility for her choices.

An important therapeutic act is the destruction of myth, which usually arises from the inaccurate data provided by the culture. Particularly important is the myth that the victim is alone responsible for the abuse she experiences, since this joins with women's tendency to internalize myths about women and results in an intolerable and destructive guilt. For accurate and timely information about a particular form of abuse, referral to specialists is the best technique. Therapists need to know all the community agencies and individuals specially trained to deal with abuse of various kinds. It is impossible for a single therapist to be equally well-informed in all areas of abuse.

The main task of the therapist is to encourage the client to accept responsibility for her own body. A sense of "ownership" may be the ultimate goal of counseling which deals with body issues. At the basis of the Women's Health Movement is the desire to have women accept responsibility for their bodies instead of simply handing them over to the medical profession or others. As long as the medical profession, for instance, or the criminal justice system is dominated by males with outmoded views of the nature of women, women will receive little encouragement to be anything but passive (Rochelle, 1977; Martin, 1976); whereas in all areas of bodily abuse, passivity is the greatest danger.

Therapists can also help clients to use and appreciate their own bodies, thus enhancing their sense of body power. Many women are so intimidated by physicians that they need to practice how to communicate purposefully with them. More basically, many women need to abandon the bodily habits of posture, musculature, breathing, voice, and stance that indicate powerlessness and to experience the powerful alternatives, especially in groups. Self-appreciation is a form of power. Most of the attention which women give to their bodies has the goal of making others enjoy them; women need training in how to care for their own bodies for themselves instead of for men or for other women. Finally, exercise provides good avenues for experiencing and expressing body power. Unlike men, most women prefer noncompetitive exercise, but therapists may also legitimately encourage women to try some form of competitive exercise if only for the experience.

The sense of body power as human and healthy and a woman's rejection of all forms of physical abuse will never result from after-the-fact restraints on male power or the availability of abusive substances. It will arise only from women themselves; those who do not develop a sense of the right to their own bodies will always be vulnerable to outside attack. Body power has social, economic, and legal ramifications great enough that any change in women's attitudes to their bodies may create shock. Particularly, women's current attempts to exchange powerlessness and submissiveness for an internal sense of body power and enjoyment are causing reactions which range from surprise to disgust and rage. But a woman must develop a sense of body power and body rights if she is to develop a sense of total self. Helping a client to own her own body and refuse to submit it to abuse is as important a therapeutic action as any therapist can take.

10

Minority Women and Women in Poverty

Tolerance holds our society together; intolerance riddles it. We discriminate against racial and ethnic groups. We distrust the poor and uneducated or those whose sexual preferences differ from our norm; we are uneasy with the aged. We have hung a mirror on the wall and the mirror tells us that the fairest American of them all is male, young, and well-off, with all limbs intact and faculties clear, white of skin, and filled with only respectable lusts. The further from that image one's reality is, the more discrimination one experiences. Fortunately, our society does not like discrimination; we do not think it right that being a female should be a burden, nor that being poor or black or different in any other way from that ideal image should be burdensome. So we encourage some people in our society—among them therapists—to make those burdens lighter. That is the subject of these last chapters: how therapists can work effectively with women who live under double or triple burdens of discrimination.

The women's movement began among middle-class white American women and most of the mental health profession is white and middle class; but most of America's women are not white and middle class. Should the mental health profession make special efforts to bridge that gap? My own belief is that, in therapy and counseling, equal treatment may be unfair; the profession should put extra strength on the side of women with special burdens. Much of that strength should flow through female counselors and therapists. The individual woman owes some of her strength to women's collective strength: to the history of where we have all been, where we all are now, and where we are trying to be in the future. To limit our struggle for equality only to those who are superficially like us is to make the eventual loss of that struggle inevitable. We need to be concerned not just that one of us can acquire success, power, or wealth but that others unlike us can develop as much as possible—that a woman born and raised in poverty may have the money to raise her children better or choose an abortion if she wishes; that a woman aging and seen as "unattractive" may have an equal opportunity for jobs by which she can support herself; that the woman who speaks English badly, or she who is sightless, or she who is not very intelligent has the right to overcome the prejudice against her disadvantage.

As is well known, there are two schools of thought regarding whether a mental health professional can really help a client who is very different from the professional in sociological terms. One school holds that differences are unimportant and emphasizes shared humanity and professional skills. The other school maintains that such an emphasis is misleading and dangerous. It is more difficult to counsel women who live with burdens one has never personally experienced, even though one has much in common with them in other areas; one needs special information and training if one is to deal with them systematically or in depth. For instance, a job counselor who has always led a middle-class life cannot easily comprehend the financial factors that determine a poor woman's choices; a young woman cannot comprehend the weight of the different values one develops with middle or old age; a white therapist cannot fully anticipate the reactions intrinsic to being from a minority race or ethnic group. Experience in working with numbers of women suffering under an extra burden is invaluable but not alone sufficient; reading and knowing the research data help at best to make one know that she or he doesn't know enough. Where a woman's extra burden is an important therapeutic or counseling issue, the best course is to hand the task over to a specialist.

Even writing about women suffering from double or triple discrimination is difficult; it is hard to be aware of one's own ignorance or acculturated discriminatory attitude. The danger of being patronizing is great, as is the risk of being out of date. Most of the minority groups discussed here now have their own viewpoints and spokeswomen. The groups are not homogeneous, and they do not agree with each other. Readers may therefore find the contents of these chapters cautious. They include only those groups with whom I have personally worked in some numbers over the years (aging women, black women, lesbians, and lower-class women) or those about whom there exists respectable research data (women from several ethnic minorities and female offenders). I have made fewer recommendations than usual about ways to proceed, and where they appear they have been confirmed by my own experience. Otherwise, I have restricted myself to presenting information on the lives of these groups of women and to presenting sources of training materials specifically developed for working with a particular group. At the same time, women with extra burdens cannot be seen only as samples of those burdens. Because they are also women and people, the issues and techniques discussed in other chapters also apply to them.

Sex and Cultural Discrimination

Women from several cultural groups suffer discrimination due to their racial or ethnic heritage which is different from and worse than that experienced by white women. The four most distinctive groups are black women, who make up 12 percent of the total female American population, Hispanic women (6 percent), Native American (.035 percent), and Asian-American (.06 percent). These women suffer from the obvious discrimination represented by racial prejudice directed against them by outsiders and from discrimination within their own groups due to cultural expectations which do not agree with those of the norm of American society. In a few ways, they also benefit more than do white women from experiences unique to their cultural heritages—which in some degree compensate for the greater hardship they experience in our culture.

Minority women do not constitute a single block with common characteristics. Not only is each of the four cultural groups very different from the others but each group also differs considerably within itself. Obviously not all minority women live in poverty; they are not all poorly educated and culturally deprived. They do not all live in urban slums on welfare, heading their households without much help from men. Assimilation to the middle-class norm may not be occurring with the rapidity for which some seem to hope, but many minority women from all cultural groups live middle-class lives and come from middle-class backgrounds.

However, it is to the statistical norm that this chapter must address itself, as provided by the data about work from the U.S. Bureau of the Census (1979c, 1979d, 1980a).

Some 5 million minority women (53.3 percent) work, a higher proportion than that of white women (49.5 percent) but lower than minority males (74.1 percent) or white males (78.6 percent). Their unemployment rate is higher than that of any other group: 13.1 percent versus 6.2 percent for white women, 10.9 percent for minority males, and 4.5 percent for white males in 1977. Unemployment introduces a dangerous instability into their lives, but the data hardly support the popular image of "masses" of minority women on welfare. When they work, however, it is for much lower returns. The median income for minority women in 1977 was $6,611, which was 94 percent of the median income of white women, 73 percent of that of minority men, and only 54 percent of that of white men, even though in years of education the four groups were almost identical. The reason is that most minority women work in service or low-paid clerical jobs. Only 44 percent of minority women hold white-collar jobs, compared with 63 percent of white women (U.S. Bureau of the Census, 1980a; U.S. Women's Bureau, 1977b).

Work is a normal expectation for minority women, not a choice. About 42.4 percent of minority woman workers are married, another 28.6 percent divorced, separated, or widowed. Of those with children under six years of age, 58 percent

213

are workers; of those with children between six and seventeen, 67.3 percent are workers. Their incomes are usually crucial to the family's well-being. Approximately 36 percent of minority families are headed by women—and of these one half are below the poverty level. In other words, the minority woman who heads a household endures the worst economic plight available in our society. When she works, she may not be much better off than when unemployed. It is small wonder that such women need a disproportionate share of our social services (U.S. Bureau of the Census, 1979a; 1980a; U.S. Women's Bureau, 1977b).

The U.S. Commission on Civil Rights (1978) indicates some of the deeper patterns of discrimination against minority women. Their skills are likely to be less developed by the educational system. Once educated, they can expect lower returns than do other groups in terms of both earnings and choice of career. They will have less access to better jobs—better in terms of stability and prestige as well as monetary rewards. Their opportunities for promotion and wage increases will be fewer, and they may have lower earnings despite equal work. This in turn means that they will spend more of their income for housing and food, they will have less desirable housing and worse choices of where to live, and they are much less likely to own their own homes. Such patterns of economic discrimination are one of the major reasons for the existence of Affirmative Action programs and Manpower Training programs.

The economic vulnerability of minority women blunts many of the tools a professional might use to help a woman find a better life. How much change can a minority women make in her life? How many risks can she safely take? Will the change be worth it in terms of rewards? The U.S. Commission on Civil Rights resolutely points out the importance of money to well-being; diet, appearance, entertainment, and health are all dictated by economic status. If a high proportion of income goes to basics, then one cannot think of recreation, travel, education, or a change of residence as an option. If one is constantly protecting her economic situation—on a daily, not even a weekly basis—then how free is she to join in the range of activities that promote a sense of self-worth? If there is a male breadwinner in the picture or in prospect, then how many chances can one take in regard to independence? Is there the slightest need to wonder why many clients among minority women are passive, distrustful, or skeptical? Is a middle-class therapist likely to be aware of, for instance, the damaged health brought about by poor diet; the resentment caused by material oppression; the distrust caused by having to fight to cling to the economic borderline; or the lack of optimism induced by the constant disappointment of the group as a whole?

If, however, the professional belongs to the same minority group as the client, she or he is more likely to share the same cultural expectations—and these expectations could work to the woman's disadvantage. Many of the original cultures of minority women valued males more than females, especially in economic terms, often to the point of being patriarchal. All minority cultures have a long history of deprivation in terms of education, employment, and, worst, expectations. Out of these patterns emerge the generic stereotypes that damage both the client's and the professional's ability to respond to the individual: black women are "aggressive and matriarchal;" Asian-American women are "docile and submissive" or "exotic, sexy, and diabolical;" Native American women—do they have personalities or needs at all?

The task for a professional is complex. On the one hand she or he has to respond to the client's cultural identity; she is a woman, she belongs to a particular cultural group. She may have different cultural values, language skills, attitudes towards society at large, expectations, and, perhaps above all, pressures from her living environment to which she must respond. On the other hand, professionals have to see the client as an individual who is not the *victim* of her cultural heritage and who will almost certainly depart from the norm and the stereotype in a number of ways—who is much more than just another minority woman.

Two special issues require mention. The counselor's task is to help the individual client develop herself as an individual, particularly in terms of economic advancement; but two studies show that these goals may be in conflict with the cultural values among which the client lives. A recent review of career counseling studies found that lower-class persons from all ethnic backgrounds typically and perhaps unrealistically perceive fewer options in their environment than do persons from the middle and upper income classes (Farmer, 1978); they are skeptical that change is possible or will work out for the best. Further, as a group minority women seem likely to feel a strong bond to the family and a strong sense of responsibility to that family. The goal of developing their independence and their potential is likely to be seen as in conflict with their cultural values (Hart, 1977). The false idea that a woman must choose between herself and her family is thus a more forceful and prevalent reality for minority women than for majority women; they cannot resolve any conflict because from the start they see the conflict as irresolvable.

Minority women are not likely to use mental health services to the extent that they might. One review of the literature (Padilla and Ruiz, 1976) shows that mental health agencies cause some of the underusage. Their location is inaccessible or difficult without private transport, they are not bilingual, they are too expensive, they assume that all clients are free to give time and money for mental health in the manner of the middle class. Cultural stereotypes also undermine counseling agencies; Sue (1977) shows how many counselors are so bound by class and culture that they choose techniques and goals which are wildly inappropriate for their clients. Padilla and Ruiz (1976) studied psychotherapists and found them holding cultural stereotypes toward minority groups that guaranteed the failure of counseling, i.e., negative attitudes toward them and social distance from them. The bonds of class and culture create misdiagnoses with a frequency that is little short of scandalous, through basic misunderstandings which may be induced by such minor matters as mis-hearing, mispronunciation, and the use of the wrong word. A comprehensive study by Sue (1977) found not only that cultural minorities underuse mental health services but also that Asian-American, black, Hispanic and Native American clients terminated counseling at a rate of approximately 50 percent after the first interview compared with 30 percent for Anglo clients. This probably shows their good judgment. It also shows that the basing of counseling and therapy on middle-class characteristics is unfair, that equal treatment in counseling may be discriminatory.

Several special models for approaching the minority group client have been developed and are listed in a latter section of this chapter. The four steps recommended by Sue are basic and essential:

1. Have a knowledge of minority group cultures and experiences.
2. Separate clearly and explicitly the generic and particular characteristics of counseling in general and of the different theories of counseling.
3. Compare these characteristics to see which are consistent, conflicting, or new.
4. Choose that approach which will best enable you to work with a culturally different client.

There is also a basic need to respond to the femaleness of a woman client. Westervelt (1975) finds several factors which tend to lower the educational achievement of minority group women. Most matters—such as low income and status, poor elementary education, geographical and political isolation—apply to both males and females. But the worst influence belongs to women alone—the effects of cultural values which determine the feminine role to be subordinate and unassertive and which are thus counterproductive to educational achievement. Herein lies the special need to treat women in minority groups differently from minority men, despite the validity of the overall goals for both sexes.

In spite of all the differences in culture and habit which impede my own professional work with minority women, I find them alert to the issues that dominate their lives. Awareness often lies just under the surface; what is lacking is a structure in which the women can formulate and articulate their awareness. I therefore use two basic principles. Working on my own awareness as much as theirs, I encourage them to identify their own problems rather than letting me do that job for them in terms of my own structure, and I start work with them distinctly on their own terms. However, to avoid being passive, I also emphasize change in any area and then help the client examine the ramifications of that change. Whether in education, therapy, or counseling, I have found that the only ultimately viable goal is consistent control of elements of her own values and life by the client— regardless of any well-intentioned agenda I might have for her.

Black Women

Many black women see the discrimination against them as blacks to be worse than the discrimination against them as women. Research has not yet told us whether they are right or whether, like other women, they tend to underestimate the amount of discrimination their femaleness brings them, perhaps even wrongly attributing some of it to discrimination against their race. The data do

216

show, however, that the two sources of discrimination reinforce each other. In many areas black women are worse off then black men.

Black women routinely undergo an experience of life which very few white women can begin to comprehend. Whether in terms of oppression or of deprivation, they have been "kept in their place" sexually, economically, and psychologically. During slavery, their situation was worse than that of black men in the sense that they lacked sexual control over their bodies and ownership of their children. Emancipation set them free to drift among the economic substrata, still the victims of discrimination. Even in terms of where they live, what work they do, what protection they may count on, which economic roles they may fulfill, black women remain as a group less free than white women. At the same time, some commentators suggest that there have been important compensations; Gutman (1976) argues that both during and after slavery a resilient and vital family network provided a basis for solidarity, self-esteem, and independence within the black community which was of particular benefit to women. Angela Davis believes that because the perquisites of traditional femininity have never sheltered black women as much as white women, they are readier at developing and using survival skills. Several studies show that black women experience less conflict with their men when they develop themselves economically. Most commentators remind us that when any racial identity becomes a positive rather than a negative force, as is happening in the black community, it becomes a source of strength for the individual. In sum, the pattern of disadvantage for black women is bad but may not be all bad. Identity as a black can help rather than hinder one's identity as a woman.

The therapist dealing with black women may be frustrated at the particular strength with which the message to "keep in your place" as both blacks and women operates. Chafe (1977) has depicted the structure of powerlessness which typifies the black community. First comes physical intimidation and fear, the most extreme form of social control. Second is white domination of black economic status; the highest status jobs within the black community (e.g., teachers, ministers, civil servants) depend far too often on the ability to please the white power structure. Third is psychological domination by whites over the limit of black aspirations. Expectations communicated verbally and nonverbally by other persons both black and white heavily influence that goal to which a black person will aspire. Fourth is the control exercised by the black community over itself in self-defense—the training given, often unconsciously, in how to adapt to the needs of survival. As blacks, and as women, black women have constantly been ordered to "stay in their place" to the point that individual clients may be psychologically unable to consider alternatives offered by a counselor whether in regard to education, career, marital status, residence, or any other choice.

Historically, only a small proportion of black women has ever had the luxury of free choice. By far the majority of blacks are forced to live in the worst areas of every community, given the poorest educations, limited to the worst-paying jobs, subjected to the poorest housing, the worst health care, and consistent violence.

217

If racial terrorism has decreased, it has been supplemented by urban violence. If economic deprivation has lessened, poverty remains much more characteristic of the black community than does the middle-class way of life. Black women also lack advantages possessed even by deprived and oppressed white women. Since white women have been distributed widely throughout the economic structure, they have always had role models who offered viable alternatives, and white women live intimately as individuals with the social group which does have the most power—white men. If they cannot achieve power directly, they can approach it vicariously through better economic status, greater protection, and indirect gratification. In sum, it is hard to argue that white women as a group are worse off than blacks as a group, and it seems likely that black women are in the worst position of all. Small wonder, then, that black women place racial discrimination ahead of sex discrimination as the cause of their plight. As Maya Angelou (1970) has pointed out, the black woman going through the normal human stresses of adolescence and adulthood is also caught in the crossfire of white prejudice, black powerlessness, and masculine pride, a combination hardly likely to generate a sense of freedom and well-being. It is not strange that many black women regard white women with suspicion or resentment and keep them at a distance. As one client said to me, "You don't have to deal with black men. I have to deal with them and all their prejudices *and* with white men and all their prejudices. And with you—I should have just your problems!"

The differences can result in therapist/client interactions with more than a trace of the absurd. As a career counselor in the early 1960s, I was angry that the rigid white prescription regarding sex roles had kept me for so long from developing as a worker. Many of my black clients, however, resented the *lack* of traditional, rigid sex-role prescriptions, which made their men expect them to work and deprived them of the "luxury" of being only a suburban homemaker. I resented the powerfulness of white men as men; my clients often resented the powerlessness of their males as blacks. Added to this was their uneasiness about their association with me as their first intimate contact with any member of the dominant race. Where I saw myself as perilously powerless in my part of the structure, they saw me as dangerously powerful because I held any part in that structure. Good will was simply not enough to overcome these unconscious conflicts.

At the same time we must be wary of allowing ourselves to accept stereotypes which present black women as inevitable victims. Historically, black women have had more access to white society than have black men. In 1970, one in ten black women workers held a professional position (Gump and Rivers, 1975). Just as the civil rights movement seeks to turn black anger into black pride, there is evidence that discrimination can provide the basis for unusually high motivation. Epstein (1973) studied a group of black professional women. Characteristically, this group had felt almost no ambivalence about choosing to pursue a career. As children they tended to have received encouragement and support from their families and to have felt special. As models they tended to have mothers who were "doers," many of them professionals or semiprofessionals, almost all of them playing important roles within and without the family. Their family backgrounds were either middle class or stressed middle-class values, and the famous Protestant work ethic had been influential. In adulthood they were self-confident and had a higher than normal regard for both themselves and for other black women professionals. The conventional marriage/homemaking prescription was less important to them. They had typically not been pushed to marry by their families. Once professional, they had less opportunity to marry except for marrying "down." As a group they had the lowest fertility rate of any group, but they were less anxious about their children than were other groups and made use of the extended family for child care.

If some black women differ from the majority of blacks, they also differ from the majority of white women in constructive ways. Several studies suggest that many black women may not discriminate against themselves as badly as do many white women. Data analyzed by Weston and Mednick (1972) suggest that black college women fear success in intellectually competitive situations less than do white college women and that they do not believe to the same extent that intellectual mastery will lead to rejection by the male. Beckett (1976) surveyed research comparisons between black and white attitudes to women's working and found, for instance, that black women have more confidence in their ability to combine career and family than do white women, that black men are more likely than white men to approve of this combination, and that, if the men do not approve, the women are less likely to be influenced against work by that disapproval. While black families express a more traditional ideology about the family and sex roles than do white families, in fact they show more egalitarian behavior than do whites. Finally, Beckett suggests, black men and women express more confidence in themselves as workers than do whites, and black children perceive their parents as more effective than do white children.

At this point I should warn against reading any research conclusions in this field too easily. All studies are complicated by the mixture of race and gender, and by the state of rapid change in which we find ourselves. For instance, results of studies on the fear of success in college women changed dramatically between 1968 and 1971, first because the original studies concentrated on white women, then because differences between white and black women vanished as white women diminished their fear of success (Mednick and Puryear, 1976). Another study (Brief and Aldag, 1975) on attitudes towards work showed that certain attitudes were shared by black males and females but not by all males or all females, meaning that a generalization claiming attitudes were based on sex failed to respond to differences based on race. And even if a finding is accurate, what are we to make of it? Murray and Mednick (1977) make a point very significant to therapists and counselors. We do not know, they point out, whether a black woman's drive to achieve has an intrinsic source (self-aspiration) or an extrinsic source (responsibility to family and race). In this situation, a professional cannot know which source dominates without exploring the individual's attitudes.

As research progresses, stereotypes are crumbling rapidly. Smith (1977) suggests that whites too often see differences as deficits. In fact, the evidence suggests such matters as the following: (a) the black family structure is not unstable, is not customarily headed by women and matriarchal in authority, does not routinely possess children lacking in discipline; (b) there is no significant difference between blacks and whites in self-concept; (c) black language patterns are different from but not inferior to white language patterns. Another study undermines the stereotype of the macho black male. Giving a sex-role questionnaire to black and white college students, O'Leary and Harrison (1975) found that blacks were less prone than whites to sex-role stereotype and to devalue females.

But the stereotype that black women have more power than do black men is also the subject of current debate. In a powerful book about the civil rights movement, Wallace (1979) denies the myth of black women as superwomen and accuses black men of chauvinism. She suggests that a major failure in the efficiency of the black movement has been the refusal of black males to fully involve black females and suggests that black females have had less of a role as activists than other authors (e.g., Beale, 1970) suggest. Far from being the dominant and egalitarian person of myth, Wallace suggests that the black woman has become "a social and intellectual suicide," both misled and distrusted by black men. Whether Wallace is right or wrong, her book is important because it has caused the first real debate over the causes of the plight of black women: white racism, black sexism, or economic exploitation in what mixture? One remembers the observations of scholars such as Mack (1971) that the power structure in marriage is determined more by economic and social class differences between the partners than by other factors, which shows that this particular debate is crucial to black women in sorting out all the major features of their lives, both economic and relational. Do they indeed, like white women, suffer conflict between their roles as women and as workers, despite stereotypes suggesting the contrary?

My own experience also is that mental health professionals—because of stereotypes about sex, race, and class—view white women more optimistically than they do black women. Let us first then emphasize the positive: that black women develop invaluable traits of self-reliance, independence, and a sense of responsibility; that black families show egalitarian tendencies; that black women do not particularly suffer from low self-esteem; that sex-role stereotypes affect their economic choices less adversely than they might. Jeffries (1976) advocates just such a positive approach in order to counteract the pessimism counselors tend to display; seeking a client's strengths on which to build is always a good approach to counseling and therapy. However, shallow positivism can easily become mechanical and insulting; it also renders some counseling concepts useless, especially if the aim of the client is to discover and overcome the real obstacles to her achievement. Positivism, if it is shallow, cannot help black women find the role models they need in the working world nor can it combat the tendency of black women to lower their expectations of themselves on the grounds that blacks as a group, and women as a group, get too few rewards to make the effort worthwhile. This tendency—which manifests itself in such seemingly trivial matters as refusing to get to work on time, answering a business telephone too casually, or refusing to attend an evening class because it contains too many whites—has sources in emotions and stereotypes far too strong for mere positive urging to contest.

Professionals have to perceive black women as participants in a series of struggles: that of blacks, that of women, and often that of the poor. In an apt contrast, LaRue (1974) terms white women "suppressed" and black women "oppressed." This has two important implications for professionals. First, they have to see a black woman's struggle as partly, and perhaps primarily, the struggle of all blacks. Second, they cannot use white women as models for black women. Many black women see their goals as very different from those of white women; LaRue suggests that this is right, on the grounds that to identify with white women is to reject the strength of black revolutionary history. Many black women see women's liberation as a force that could divide them from their men. In relationship to their men, a black woman may be, suggests Beale (1970), the "slave of a slave," but for that very reason she may not be able to feel sympathy for the women's movement until it becomes antiracist, anti-imperialist, and even anti-middle class.

Nonetheless, therapists and counselors can still work with black women as women in many areas. For example, a study by Jackson (1975) showed that black women have very positive aspirations for their children—in contrast to the stereotype of the apathetic and irresponsible welfare mother. Those aspirations have become, in the work of some counselors, a major force in helping black women overcome overwhelming odds against job achievement. Many black women deal with strong conflicts between the practical demands of their roles as breadwinner and homemaker, and they lack knowledge of social agencies, cooperative organizations, and sources of help which can ease such matters as transportation and child-care costs. Psychologically, the frequently healthy self-concept possessed by black women encourages imaginativeness on the part of the counselor; they possess survival skills the professional may lack. Years of working with impoverished black women taught me that they often have an (sometimes antisocial) ingenuity which my experience had never given me, but they frequently did not know how to apply it effectively to make *progress* economically; our sessions became a collaboration in the most genuine sense, specifically an alliance between women. Like white women, black women need to expand their vision of themselves as able to achieve a wider variety of goals; in that process they will come upon the obstacle of their female sex-role stereotype. The stereotype may well be different from that of white women, but the task of overcoming it is the same.

Hispanic Women

"Hispanic" is a general term for Spanish-speaking persons and those with Spanish surnames. Hispanics form the second largest minority group in America, an estimated 12 million, and are expected to become the largest due to high immigration and fertility rates. Generalizations about Hispanics are usually inaccurate and may be offensive, for they are just as diverse as Anglos—their only main similarities stem from a general Spanish cultural heritage, including language and religion. Some Hispanic families have been "American" for generations, longer in fact than most whites. Others live in parts of the United States which are Hispanic (e.g., Puerto Rico). Others come from Central America, South America, the Caribbean, Mexico, and even Spain, and they bring different national heritages with them; they may be recent immigrants or not. Those from Mexico (Chicano/Chicana) are the largest group, those from Puerto Rico the second largest. According to recent estimates, most of the 7.2 million Chicanos live in the southwest, most of the 700,000 Cubans in Florida, and most mainland Puerto Ricans in the northeast, especially New York (*Time*, 1978). They include people with wealth and middle-class skills, impoverished urban residents with only survival skills, aristocrats who settled the southwest and owned it, island blacks, Spanish-Indians from rural villages—they are a score or a hundred different groups. The message for mental health professionals is the same in regard to all minority groups: emphasize what is "minority group" about a client only in so far as it is true and significant.

Data about Hispanics are limited and distorted because they include a large number of recently impoverished immigrants. With that caveat in mind, and with the extra warning that English is a second language for Hispanics, the following generalizations may prove useful. Hispanics are the least educated minority; some 40 percent have completed high school, compared with 46 percent of blacks and 67 percent of Anglos. They have completed an average nine years of schooling, but about 25 percent have completed less than five years. Only 2.2 percent of those aged 25 or over are college graduates (Padilla and Ruiz, 1976). Because the Hispanic culture offers a vital alternative to the general culture, Hispanics tend to live in enclaves where they remain at the bottom of the economic ladder. Though there is a small Hispanic upper class and a growing middle class famous for entrepreneurship, 27 percent of Hispanic families (compared with 16.6 percent of non-Hispanic families) earn under $7,000 a year, and their unemployment rates run steadily higher (*Time*, 1978). This is the classic pattern of an ethnic group which has recently immigrated. The tendency to live in Spanish-speaking enclaves deprives Hispanics of equal access to education, housing, and health care as well as to jobs, but there are strong signs of upward mobility. The group shows conflicting impulses towards assimilation with the larger society and preservation of original ethnic or national identity, so that one can make few predictions about any given individual (Ruiz and Padilla, 1977).

In 1978, women made up 51 percent of the Hispanic population, or about 6 million. They were younger than the national norm: 22.8 years. Their median education was less: 9.9 years. A higher proportion was married (59.5 percent), but 18.3 percent were separated, divorced, or widowed, and 20.3 percent of Hispanic households were headed by women. About 45.4 percent of Hispanic women worked, comprising 38 percent of all Hispanic workers. Their unemployment rate was high (11.6 percent), and their incomes desperately low; in 1977, $3, 669 per year compared with $7,797 for Hispanic males and $10,607 for Caucasian males. Of those women with children under age six, 25 percent worked, and of those with children between six and twelve, 44 percent worked. More than 72 percent were clerical, service, or operative workers, and 11 percent were in administrative, managerial, or professional jobs (U.S. Bureau of the Census, 1979c, 1980a; U.S. Bureau of Labor Statistics, 1980a).

The largest single group was made up of Chicanas or Mexican-American women, 81 percent of whom lived in urban areas. In 1977, 46.2 percent of them earned less than $5,000. Of the 18.8 percent of families headed by Chicana women, 46 percent were below the poverty level. Chicano families are normally very strong patriarchies, as are their community's economic, political, and social structures. The role of the female is precisely defined: supportive, subordinate, and uncritical within the family. The Chicana is raised under the close control of her parents and male relatives, and marriage makes her subordinate to her husband and male children. The family unit is more important than its individual members. A Chicana who tries to make use of the freedom and opportunity available to women in the larger society has three choices: adopt the traditional feminine sex role as rigorously as possible, thus indicating her continued subordination; choose dual roles, thus preserving the traditional structure in one part of her life while filling other roles away from home; or abandon her culture to identify with what is essentially middle-class non-Spanish behavior.

Even when Chicanas move into the broader culture, they tend to retain Hispanic values. Kinship ties, for example, remain more important than individual wishes. One interesting study (Carrillo-Beron, 1974) compared Chicana and Anglo women to determine whether they saw differently the degree of control exercised by them over their own lives. The Chicanas saw the family as exercising significantly higher power over them than did the Anglos. Another study comparing Chicano and Anglo college students, male and female aged 18 to 24, all middle class, showed the Chicanas to possess the most traditional attitudes of all groups in regard to the family, including the strongest support for strict child rearing, domination by the father, and faith in supernatural authority. The author's conclusion was that the degree of adherence to conformity and submission to authority was higher among Chicanas than any other group, including Chicanos (Ramirez III, 1967). The Chicana choice would thus seem very difficult. Adherence to the traditional sequence of a woman's life (virgin, wife, mother) guarantees subordination, but attempts at liberation guarantee disapproval from their culture and also identification as lower class or uncultured (Nieto-Gomez, 1976).

The consequences of this choice are little understood by outsiders. Chicanas have a high drop-out rate, for instance, but this means not that they undervalue education so much as that they cannot preserve their heritage in an alien educational environment, especially when practical and economic difficulties are great and when the rewards of completion may seem small compared with those offered

223

by family and culture. Their question must sensibly be: is it worth it? Their response to the women's movement may be similar; "liberation," they may feel, offers them less than what they have, and when this doubt is added to the racism they experience, they may well choose to oppose the women's movement. Current opinion is that the more customary track of a Chicana wishing to defeat the stereotype of herself as a passive and dependent figure is to retain her outward feminine traditionalism in a labor force dominated by males and non-Hispanics and to achieve success purely by individual capability (Cruz, 1976). Can a professional recommend any other choice safely? Certainly not unless she or he has a deep understanding of its consequences.

The second largest group of Hispanics, Puerto Ricans, are full citizens of the United States; they frequently move between the island and the mainland and tend to retain their distinctive culture in either place. Full citizenship, however, has not brought full acceptance (Christansen, 1977), and Puerto Ricans justifiably resent treatment by other Americans (especially employees of the federal government) as foreign or inferior. In 1978, females were 54 percent of the almost 2 million Puerto Ricans living on the mainland, thus comprising 16 percent of the Hispanic women in the United States or 1 percent of all women. With a median age of 22.4 years, 56.4 percent were married and only 10.6 percent divorced, showing the commonwealth's cultural and religious preferences. However, 1976 data showed 35 percent of Puerto Rican households headed by women as contrasted with 12 percent for the whole population at the time. About 62 percent of those households lived in poverty. About 32 percent of Puerto Rican women worked, compared with 45 percent of all Hispanic women and 49 percent of all women at the time. Of the working women, 27.3 percent were operatives, 34.4 percent clerical, and 11.9 percent service workers, while 12.2 percent were unemployed (U.S. Bureau of the Census, 1979c, 1980a; U.S. Women's Bureau, 1977c).

Moving to the mainland brings to the family a severe cultural shock, especially in the form of challenges to the dominance of the father. In the commonwealth the norm is for the father to be undisputed head of family and for family members to subordinate individual needs to the whole; but in New York the tendency is to disperse and for the young to show greater independence. Economic need may propel the mother into the work force, where she bears the brunt of discrimination and where her lack of ease in the English language deprives her of self-confidence (Hart, 1977); but observers suggest that Puerto Rican women are well equipped to survive. In their culture the woman is often the center (as distinct from the head) of the family: educator, motivator, adviser, even provider. That tends to make her persevering, ambitious, determined, independent, and able to achieve academically (Christansen, 1977). We do not have the data to prove this suggestion, and it sounds suspiciously like another form of the Superwoman myth. The general pattern of Puerto Rican women in our society is the same as that of all women—deprivation and clustering in traditionally female occupations. Part of the cause may be racism; part of it is also sexism.

Our knowledge of other Hispanic groups is even less than our knowledge of the two largest. We know that stereotypes about one group do not apply to other groups. We know that Hispanic women pick their way through a chaos of sexism, racism, and deprivation that renders the experience and advice of most professionals irrelevant. Their sources of strength lie in the family and in the clarity of their sense of value as women in the family, both of which bring them into conflict with the broader society. Yet their economic deprivation, and the fact that living in a broader society implies that transition is taking place, mean that they have need of counsel. Traditionally, outsiders have helped new American immigrant groups to make the transition into the majority culture. The situation therefore demands that interested therapists and counselors receive special training.

Asian-American Women

In 1973 there were 2 million Asian-Americans (about 1 percent of the total population), mostly concentrated in the state of Hawaii or a few urban enclaves, with extended families located in otherwise alien communities. One skirts racism in lumping Asian-Americans together as a single group. People of Chinese and Japanese origin predominate, but the category includes Koreans, Indians, Pakistanis, Vietnamese, Thais, Indonesians, Malaysians, and Pacific Islanders including native Hawaiians. Each subgroup has its own strong and distinctive culture, and their only real link is the racism they encounter in the larger community.

Our information about them is woefully inadequate. Their levels of achievement are generally higher than those of other ethnic groups, especially in the case of Japanese and Chinese, but we do not know why they succeed or whether they have succeeded in their own terms. An unusually high proportion of Asian-American women (51 percent) work, and these figures do not include those who work without pay in family businesses. Asian-American women are better educated than are blacks, Hispanics, or whites, yet they still congregate in clerical jobs as secretaries, bookkeepers, salesclerks, though to a lesser extent than do other groups, and their income is slightly below the national average. As a group, Asian-American women work consistently, and they do well (especially the Japanese Americans) though not as well as do men or whites. Those born overseas do less well; illiteracy in English is a serious problem so their work is likely to be menial (Hart, 1977). War brides have not done well at assimilating into the majority culture. Their divorce rate is high, and they continue to need help in adjusting (Kim, 1977). One sample study showed over 20 percent of Asian wives of military men now heads of household (Hart, 1977), but opinion seems to be that the younger generation of Asian-Americans is doing much better.

Most Asian cultures define the female and male roles clearly, support male development, and subordinate the female (Fujitomi and Wong, 1976). But social changes and greater wealth are allowing some women to develop freely, especially among the upper classes. American immigration policy also encourages entry by women likely to succeed, so that it is not unusual to meet foreign-born as well as native-born Asian-American women who have moved with great success in the American culture. They may benefit from strong family traditions, such as shared child rearing within the extended family resulting in less interference with a woman's career, but Fujitomi and Wong (1976) assert that, like other minority women, Asian-Americans have to contest sexism within their own cultures as well as racism in the larger culture. Strict loyalty to the family, strict self-control and discipline, multi-generational living arrangements, and a dislike for open competitiveness especially on the part of women are all factors which differentiate them from the broader culture. These factors may well cause conflict if their occupations call for them to be assertive as a solitary individual or require high visibility with the public, which contradicts their acculturation to modesty and moderation. Finally, generational differences are growing within all Asian-American subgroups and are becoming a source of concern which may bring the younger generation into counseling and therapy.

Native American Women

Smallest and poorest of our minority groups are the Native Americans. According to the 1970 census, there were 388,210 Native American females (outnumbering males), of whom some 230,000 were age 16 or older. Only 35 percent were in the labor force, and one-third had no incomes. For those with incomes, the median was $1,697, compared with Native American males, $3,509. They worked in service jobs (26 percent), clerical jobs (25 percent), operative jobs (19 percent), and professional/technical jobs (11 percent). More than one-third had graduated from high school, but only 10 percent had attended college. The half of Native American women living in urban areas had better educations and incomes than those who lived on reservations (U.S. Women's Bureau, 1977b; U.S. National Commission on the Observance of International Women's Year, 1976).

Few generalizations about Native American women are valid. Approximately 789 tribal entities exist within the United States, and they differ widely from each other. Hart (1977) sees them as offering three cultural alternatives: the traditional, in which adherence to tribal religion and original cultural patterns is the main effort; moderate, in which the cultural heritage is making adjustments as a whole to the main culture; and progressive, in which white beliefs and modern values replace the traditional. In addition to racism from whites, Native Americans must struggle within the dominant culture to retain their ethnic identity; and within the general Native American culture they must make decisions about their tribal identity. In addition, the paternalism of white society, represented by the Bureau of Indian Affairs, is another problem. Until recently, the BIA had a policy of taking children to boarding schools during the school year for four to twelve years (Witt, 1976). Nurturing children in the home is of course a major means of cultural survival, and Native Americans are searching for an educational policy that will reinforce tribal beliefs and allow each tribe to express its own nature. Native American values are often in sharp conflict with those of the dominant culture: living in harmony with the natural world; lack of time consciousness; concern for giving rather than accumulating; respect for age; cooperative government; and others. It may be fortunate, therefore, that English remains the second language for about one-half of Native American women.

Some scholars maintain that Native American women cannot be comprehended at all from a white sexist viewpoint. As a whole, Native American societies encourage individual freedom within the tribal life, and some tribes have been matriarchal, matrilineal, and matrilocal (Witt, 1976). Some tribes allow or encourage their women to be authoritative, while others prefer them not to be conspicuous as decision makers (Holyan, in Hart, 1977). Christensen (1975) states that Native American society has not and does not restrict its women by structured role delineation. Racism and economic repression concern the tribes and the women more than does inequality between the sexes. The preservation of the family and the tribe, and more control over political, educational, economic, and social decisions, are more important.

Yet Native American women are worse off than their men. Since they are the center of family well-being, they deal with the poor health, diet, living conditions, and educational problems of the family unit. Where females had power, they have lost it, as among the previously matriarchal Iroquois (Wallace, 1973) or the Seneca (Jensen, 1977). A recent study of the Sioux found the women worse off than white women and Sioux males in terms of almost every possible psychological criterion (Bryde, 1970). Despite government efforts, health care is worse among Native Americans than in any other group, and infant mortality rates are high (Witt, 1976). Alcoholism is endemic and epidemic, with all the ensuant stress on family and tribal life—75 percent of Native American suicides are alcohol-related, almost three times higher than in the general population (Frederick, 1973). Some 42 percent of Native Americans, twice the national average, drop out of high school (Chumbley, 1973). In sum, the responsibility of Native American women for the homemaker role subjects them to the worst stresses of Native American life. Whether or not they need special help as women seems a moot issue in light of such problems. Anything a professional does which has a positive effect will improve the lot of the Native American woman.

Further Reading

Obviously, work with women from ethnic minorities is a highly specialized field. The following list of printed sources is no more than an introduction, but each source contains further bibliographies.

1. "Asian Americans: A Success Story," Special Issue, *Journal of Social Issues*, 1973, 29 (2).
2. "Counseling the Culturally Different," Special Issue, *Personnel and Guidance Journal*, 1977, 55 (7).

3. "Counseling Across Cultures," Special Issue, *Personnel and Guidance Journal*, 1978, 56 (8).
4. U.S. National Commission on the Observance of International Women's Year, *Workshop Guides, 1977: Older Women; Female Offenders;* and *Sexual Preference*.
5. "Counseling Women," Special Issues II and III, *The Counseling Psychologist*, 1976, 6 (2) and 1979, 8 (1).
6. Padilla, A.M., and R.A. Ruiz, *Latino Mental Health: A Review of Literature*, Washington, D.C.: Government Printing Office, 1976.
7. Women's Educational Equity Community Network, *Rural Women and Education: Annotated Selected References and Resources*, San Francisco: Far West Laboratory, 1978.
8. Women's Educational Equity Communication Network, *Hispanic Women and Education: Annotated Selected References and Resources*, San Francisco: Far West Laboratory, 1978.
9. "Resources for American Indian/Alaskan Native Women," *WEECN Network News and Notes*, Spring, 1980.

Following is a list of organizations that focus on the concerns and welfare of minority women. They are an excellent source of information for professionals.

1. *Asian-American Women.*

Organization of Chinese-American Women, 3214 Quesada St., NW, Washington, D.C., 20015; Pauline W. Tsui, President, (202) 227-1967. Established in 1977 to promote the equal participation of Chinese-American women in all aspects of life in the United States.

2. *Black Women.*

Alpha Kappa Alpha (AKA), 5211 South Greenwood Ave., Chicago, IL, 60615; Ann Mitchem Davis, Executive Director, (312) 684-1282. The oldest black college-based sorority in the country which sponsors educational programs including career counseling, leadership training, and financial aid.
Black Women's Employment Project, NAACP Legal Defense and Education Fund, Inc., 10 Columbus Circle, New York, NY, 10019; Jean Fairfax, (212) 586-8397. Project specializes in litigation on behalf of black women workers.
Black Women Organized for Action, P.O. Box 15072, San Francisco, CA, 94115; Eleanor R. Spikes, (414) 387-4221. Focus is on action upon issues that affect black women including workshops on health, the media, and job skills.
Commission on Higher Education, National Council of Negro Women, 1346 Connecticut Ave., Washington, D.C., 20036; Francelia D. Gleaves, (202) 638-1961. Focus is organizing black women to examine and improve the situation they confront in colleges and universities across the country.
National Hook-up of Black Women, Inc., 2021 K. St., NW, Suite 305, Washington, D.C., 20006; Sharon Tolbert, Executive Dir., (202) 293-2323. A

communications network for black women dedicated to improving the status of the black community and black women.

3. *Spanish-speaking Women.*

Association of Latin-American Women, P.O. Box 7523, Oakland, CA, 94601; Lisa Gonzales, (415) 562-4338. Major goal is to develop leadership skills among Latinas and to work towards improving the Spanish-speaking community.

Chicana Rights Project, Mexican American Legal Defense and Educational Fund, 501 Petroleum Commerce Bldg., 210 N. Mary's St., San Antonio, TX, 78205; Patricia M. Vasquez, (512) 224-5476. A resource agency for combatting patterns and practices of discrimination against Mexican-American women.

Chicana Service Action Center, 2244 Beverly Boulevard, Los Angeles, CA, 90057; Francisca Flores, (213) 381-7261. An agency established to give women the opportunity to upgrade employable skills, establish vocational goals and improve basic educational skills.

Mexican-American Women's National Association (MANA), P.O. Box 23656, Washington, D.C., 20024; Gloria Lopez, (202) 254-8127. MANA was organized to provide a national forum by which Chicanas can impact on national issues of concern to them.

National Chicana Foundation, 2114 Commerce, San Antonio, TX, 78207; Deuvina Hernandez, (512) 224-7528. Major focus is research and the application of research in areas of concern to Mexican-American women.

4. *Native American Women.*

North American Indian Women's Association, 720 East Spruce St., Sisseton, South Dakota, 57262; Hildreth Venegas, President. A nonprofit educational association established to promote the improvement of education, health and family life of North American Indian people.

Women in Poverty

In the United States, we would like to deny the existence of a class structure, but the data will not allow us. The richest 5 percent of our families receive 16 percent of our country's total family income, while the poorest 20 percent of our families get 5 percent of the total family income. According to the U.S. National Commission on Civil Rights (1978), this ratio has remained constant since 1947. We are reluctant even to admit that a lower class exists; it contradicts the American Dream, denies the vision of a land of freedom and opportunity, and frightens us. We can understand a person being temporarily poor, but the existence of people who live poor all their lives—the true lower class—flouts our expectations as Americans. We see them as not only poor but also immoral, as associated with crime, violence, alcohol and drug addiction, prostitution, and (the worst sin of all) lack of willpower. Their welfare costs us too much; we have handed their problems over to the government, and we want the government's employees—including therapists and counselors—to deal with those problems so that we will not have to worry about them.

Sociologists detect the existence of our lower class through any of a long series of variables. A well-known analysis of variables by Kahl (1957) detected five classes in America and drew a useful distinction between the lower class and families with low incomes. According to Kahl, our upper class consists of 1 percent of our citizens, the upper-middle class of 9 percent, the lower-middle class of 40 percent, the working class of another 40 percent, and the lower class of 10 percent. Several variables identify them, but a recent analysis by Hacher (1975) is of special interest to our purposes. Hacher sees the main distinction (aside from income) between the working class and the lower class as being the female-centered family. Dividing poor families into "stable" and "disorganized," she sees the presence of a functioning husband/father as the main distinction. In stable families, the male's job is likely to be menial and seasonal and his pay low, but he still tries to fulfill the traditional male role—though he may use physical coercion to do so. Disorganization appears when the paychecks of wives or children grow large enough for them to assert independence. Hacher believes that lower-class males have only their physical strength and their ascribed superior status as males by which to maintain dominance, making their authority easy to undermine and their departure from the family likely. The family which then emerges as mother-dominated loses one breadwinner, making it even more vulnerable to poverty.

The strong correlation between women and poverty supports Hacher's hypothesis. Between 1970 and 1977 the number of poor families headed by women rose by 35 percent, while the number of poor married-couple families declined by 18 percent (U.S. Bureau of the Census, 1980a). In 1978, although only 14.4 percent of all family heads were women, 49 percent of all poor families were headed by women. One out of four families headed by white women were poor, but more than one of two families headed by black women were in poverty. In 1977, poor people aged 65 or older included 960,000 men and 2.2 million women. In 1976, the unemployment rate among all women heading families was 9.8 percent; among these heading poor families, it was 25.6 percent. In all, *two out of three poor people are female* (U.S. Bureau of Labor Statistics, 1980b; U.S. Bureau of the Census, 1979a, 1980a; U.S. Women's Bureau, 1977a, 1979a).

Many kinds of people make up the lower class, but we find them hard to see. They may be workers (full-time or part-time), housewives, heads of families, living alone, welfare recipients or fiercely independent, white or minority group, urban or rural. They may live in rural shacks, city shanties, nursing homes, government-built high-rises, flophouses, trailer parks, vacant lots, or the streets. The much-maligned "War on Poverty" during the 1960s was our first major attempt to find and do something for them. We have only recently discovered the existence of poor rural women, who live without social or educational services, without contacts with the outside world, and without amenities, transport, or health care—living in regions where myth tells us all is freedom, neighborliness, and nature's bounty. We make stop-and-start efforts at helping mobile immigrant agricultural women, who work harder than do their men and live lives of almost unremitting deprivation. We are taking a first look at elderly women, nearly twice as likely as men of the same age to be impoverished; as of September, 1979, their average income was $255 a month from retirement benefits compared to $325 for men (Social Security Administration, 1980). Inflation is pushing a whole new group of young women who are full-time workers beneath the poverty level, as is divorce.

Our judgments about the lower class tend to be more moralistic than sensible. If we see a prostitute, we see an immoral woman rather than one who lacks job skills and wants money. We complain about welfare "queens," but we blame welfare mothers for not taking better care of their children. We assume that in some fashion people are poor because they do not want to be otherwise, though the reality is the opposite. Freedom of choice, for example, is simply not a lower-class assumption; lower-class persons see fewer options in their environment than do middle-class persons (Farmer, 1978), and their perception is quite accurate. To arrange and pay for child care, transportation, appropriate clothing, or special training are minor matters for the middle class but very difficult for the lower class, whose enclaves lack every kind of facility including food stores and offer only low-paying jobs for which the poor compete with the poor. The very idea of "career choice" is a middle-class (and male) idea. If the researchers are right in claiming that career choice is determined mainly by social class and by whom one knows (Duncan, Featherman, and Duncan, 1972), then lower-class people will choose lower-class jobs because these are all their environment offers and because they have no adequate role models or friendships outside their own class. There is no sense in our becoming irritated with them for failing to make choices which do not exist or blaming lack of moral fiber for what is quite obviously lack of opportunity and incentive.

With the marginal exception of television, therapists and counselors are often the only real bridge out of the lower class, which explains the growth and importance of social work as a profession. But social work can be itself damaging. A prominent lower-class trait is to perceive whatever happens to them as a result of what others do to them rather than to their own choices or efforts. Welfare and many other government programs emphasize subordination and dependency, thus increasing the impression that power belongs to others rather than to oneself (Farmer, 1978). That sequence is worse with women, among whom acculturation already encourages a female sex stereotype antagonistic to self-assertiveness. The mental health profession must therefore be wary to avoid that same pattern. The goal of encouraging clients to take charge of their own lives and change their own environment from their own efforts is at its clearest when working with lower-class women. Professionals must exploit, for instance, the strengths latent in ethnic communities in order to find appropriate role models and support systems.

The instinct for upward mobility needs to be encouraged, but not just in material terms so much as in the ability to control one's own decisions. One has to provide information, stimulate self-motivation, offer skills, develop self-confidence, and seek for psychological clarity.

This inevitably leads a good professional into two forms of activism. First is the kind of activism usually called "outreach." The client most in need of help from therapy and counseling, it seems, may be the least likely to come for such services in the first place. In a study of urban women, Lopata (1973) made the point neatly in regard to education; the less educated a woman is, Lopata found, the more likely she is to be isolated from social contacts and therefore the less likely to know about educational opportunities. Thus an educational program which uses only passive recruitment will never reach the people who most need it because they will never hear about it and/or never see its application to themselves. Hence, says Lopata, active recruitment is the only reasonable alternative. As another example, a recent unpublished study of a high-rise public-housing project showed that there were two main reasons for the presence of so many nonfunctioning appliances (such as stoves and air conditioners): (1) people did not know to whom (among many employees) they should report the malfunction; and (2) they thought they were supposed to wait until they were asked. A simple system of "asking" solved the problem. Illiteracy programs found a third example. Illiterate people were actually eager to learn to read; they did not know where to go to learn. We are dealing here with a population that is ill-informed and—particularly because it includes many older women—trained to be docile and passive, which is the meaning of seeing others as having more power than oneself. Outreach is therefore a therapy and counseling essential.

The second kind of activism is more complex. It is not that obvious kind of activism in which the professional battles on the client's behalf against bureaucracy, violence, discomfort, exploitation, or evil—though that of course is often enough necessary—but the kind that trains the client how to fight the battles for herself. As various self-help and community action programs have shown, this is not easy; but as others have shown, it is far from impossible. The needs of lower-class women are severely practical; they are also profoundly psychological. Both elements need to be faced by professionals. Some lower-class problems can be solved only by outsiders, others only by insiders, still others only by collaboration. The art of counseling and therapy is to judge precisely what mixture appears in any given situation, and to develop the appropriate response. No matter how unskilled lower-class persons may be in terms of middle-class values, abilities, and knowledge, there is always a level at which they are running their own lives, and the proper counseling and therapy aim is to raise that level.

11

Older Women, Lesbians, and Female Offenders

Age

All women experience the double discrimination brought by aging. As Pauline Bart (1975) writes, "This is not a good society in which to grow old or to be a woman, and the combination of the two makes for a poignant situation" (p. 351). These are the poignant voices of some of my clients:

I'm getting old. I'm 33!

It's too late for me. I'm 50, and it's too late to start over. I wish I was 30 years younger and had all the choices you young women have.

I wasted my youth. I dropped out of school to get married and have babies, and I helped Ron run the business. Now we're divorced and I've got the kids—and a dumb job. No money, and I'm tired all the time. I'm 38. I feel old. Ugly. Finished.

I'm only 68. I'm a widow now, and I want to figure out what to do with the rest of my life.

All of us suffer the pangs of growing older, but women more than men suffer from pain *and* discrimination on account of age since our society prefers youth and beauty and tends to identify the two. This is not a meaningless generalization; men hire women because they are young and pretty—for jobs which have nothing to do with youth or beauty. They marry them for the same reasons. Women have to fight against being thrown on the scrap heap for reasons which do not apply to men or in circumstances in which men have more options and defenses. Our discrimination against older women is so pervasive that a woman's anxiety about aging has become a matter for joking, while a man's preference for young women is a matter of pride. Aging is natural and inevitable; we have come to accept discrimination against women because of age as equally natural and inevitable. Women discriminate against themselves in regard to aging, either by fighting it and denying it or by converting the healthy acceptance of the aging process into the internal message that nothing can be done about it—consignment to that dreaded scrap heap is inevitable.

Older clients represent a challenge to mental health professionals; a much younger counselor may tend to condescend or dismiss, to be too brusquely positive, or to react indifferently to a woman's anxieties about aging, with the result that the practical consequences of age on a woman cannot be seen. Poor therapists respond negatively to a woman's aging; they automatically limit the options they present. They restrict or dismiss what they hear because they regard it as inappropriate to the woman's age and tell a woman she ought or ought not to do something solely because of her age. Even good therapists may fail to see the gifts maturity brings, neglect the limitations or preferences that accompany it, or require thoughts and actions which a more mature person's life-style makes difficult. Therapists tend to assign too little or too much importance to age, either ignoring or overemphasizing it; by doing so, they exaggerate the impact of age on all the other women's issues which a client presents. This is an area in which mental health professionals seem, as a group, to find it most convenient to do nothing or to proceed in error rather than to work effectively.

Age Stereotyping

We all know of our society's bias for or against various age-groups but scholars have only recently begun to study it, probably for the reason advanced by Simone de Beauvoir in *The Coming of Age* (1970): "When we look at the image of our own future provided by the old we do not believe it: an absurd inner voice whispers that *that* will never happen to us—when *that* happens it will no longer be ourselves that it happens to. Until the moment it is upon us, old age is something that only affects other people" (p. 13). Fear is widespread—fear of wrinkles, the first grey hair, expanded waistlines, receding hairlines, of loss of hearing, sight, health, and energy, of ugliness in the eye of the beholder, and eventually of death. Fear leads to avoidance, even of knowledge about the subject of aging—except in all those private moments when it is our most earnest preoccupation. Our avoidance leads to bias against age in others; whether we applaud a woman for "having the courage to admit her age" or allow her to get away without stating it, we are admitting our discrimination. Our stereotype of age and women is simple—it's a bad combination.

Like all stereotypes, age bias distorts our perceptions of ourselves and others, our judgments, and the decisions we make. While different ages obviously differ, we tend to react to a specific age not because we *observe* it to be different but because we *assume* it to be different. Age bias works against the young as well as against the old; it works against all of us at all ages. Troll (1976) describes three different forms of age bias. *Age restrictiveness* affects everyone of any age by accepting certain behavior as suitable only, or primarily, to a certain age (e.g., one should marry between ages 20 and 31). A person not engaging in that behavior at that age, or engaging in it at another age, is seen as abnormal. Under *age distortion* the behaviors or characteristics of a certain age-group are perceived inaccurately. The behavior of middle-aged women is explained away as "menopausal;" juveniles are described as eager to learn or young people as energetic, regardless of the actual behavior of any individual. Until 1978 even the nation's laws presumed that all persons older than 65 should retire. *Age-ism* presents a whole age-group negatively—all young people are rowdy and high on drugs, all middle-aged people are dull, or all old people are nags. All forms of age bias are a form of bigotry in which we all engage. The question for therapists is whether their own age biases affect their clients negatively.

Women and Age Stereotyping

So strong and pervasive is the double standard for women and men in regard to aging that we tend not even to be aware of it until we experience it personally. For instance, our society sets the age limits for the major events of life earlier for women than for men; women are expected to lose their "attractiveness" sooner, to end their major responsibilities (child raising) earlier, and to decline in prestige as attention-worthy much sooner than are men. Since a woman is expected to marry and have children at an earlier age than is a man, her youthful development goes towards "home" at the very age a man's goes towards "work"—though this enduring cultural bias seems to be shifting as women postpone marriage and child rearing. But can a similar shift occur in the accepted alliance between youth and female beauty? Society sees women as sexually attractive at younger ages than it does men, but their attractiveness is perceived to dim earlier (Troll and Schlossberg, 1971). By middle age women are viewed as less physically *and* psychologically appealing than are men, and a complex series of reactions to old age commences (Neugarten and Guttman, 1968). A man ages into responsibility and esteem; a woman out of them. Age distortion assumes that women must be miserable, must have already fulfilled their main functions in life, and must be irrational or undesirable for hormonal reasons.

Society's attitudes are in strong contrast with what seem to be the facts and may even be based on value judgments aimed at demeaning women. Theorists of adult developmental stages (e.g., Levinson, Gould, Troll, Neugarten) currently report that in fact, starting around middle age, males tend to become more oriented to the internal world, the family, and relational virtues while females become more oriented to the external world and achievement. Thus society's value judgments falsely emphasize woman's role as the bearer of children or try to make that single phase of her life more important than all other phases put together. This is a largely unconscious effort to reward women only in a narrow range of the spectrum of their activities and for a brief period of their life span. The attempt thus to limit women by age stereotyping seriously damages them. Sommers (1974) writes:

> Sex and age discrimination are a poisonous combination because employers look for qualities in most female employees which have no bearing on the job per se, but which reflect their own or community prejudices. One such prejudice is that a woman should be pretty (i.e., young) for certain jobs such as bank teller, airline hostess, or receptionist. Yet such work could be done just as adequately by a woman 40 or over, and a reentry woman at that. [P. 7]

The biological differences between women and men caused by aging are not enough to justify the double standard. While some aging changes affect women only, the explanation of variations in aging lies less in gender than in external factors (such as nutrition, climate, exercise, genetic inheritance, stress) and in perception (creases in a man's face are more likely to be seen as "attractive"). As with the aging process as a whole, the biological differences are less important than are our attitudes. Most physical changes are identical or parallel in women and men; the ratio of body fat to total weight increases, as do the connective tissues and fibers between body cells, while there is a gradual loss of muscular strength and of elasticity in skin and blood vessels. (For details, see Williams, 1977; Troll, 1975; and Bishof, 1969.) But a woman going through these changes departs much further than does a man from the norm of "attractiveness," which is entirely a matter of societal attitude.

As another example, society gives greater weight to women's loss of the capacity to reproduce. The biological difference here (usually during the 40s or 50s for women, much later and more gradual for men) does not explain the different weight which society attaches to the event in women and men. The villain here is sex-role stereotyping. Society's esteem has very little to do with a man's reproductive capacity and, even though it flows more easily to decorative males, surprisingly little to do with his sexual attractiveness. A plain, childless male can still fulfill his sex-role stereotype satisfactorily; we are not so kind to a similar woman, whose loss of reproductive capacity also deprives her of several essential features of her sex-role stereotype revolving around that capacity. To the extent that a woman values herself or is valued as a sexual partner and mother only, she suffers more from biological aging. The climacterium of the middle years affects everyone in the form of a dramatic change in physical appearance (Troll, 1975); men ride out the change more easily than do women, though it is not easy for either sex. Men's advantage is twofold: after the change they are still seen as attractive, and they are more likely than before to be seen as mature and wise. They remain workers and leaders, thus continuing to fulfill their sex-role stereotypes.

This is the reason that the "myth of menopause" is so important to the women's movement. We know that, while most women experience some discomfort or disturbance during the climacteric, only 10 to 15 percent have either physical or emotional problems serious enough to need medical help (Shafer, 1970), and many take the whole process in their stride (Neugarten, 1977). At the same time, we are discovering more evidence for the existence of a parallel male period of disturbance whose symptoms and effects may be just as serious and widespread though less obviously physiological. Thus most contemporary theorists believe that the source of menopausal problems for women lies less in the biological process than in the loss of the sex role most strongly rewarded by society. We shall probably soon conclude that the sexes are more alike than unlike. The true import of the myth of menopause is that it serves to demean and devalue women just as they enter their years of greatest maturity and achievement, just as they are freed to enter a broader world and to compete more with men on male territory.

The Plight of Older Women

Age stereotyping affects women drastically in many areas of their lives. Especially if a woman has committed herself to the role of sex object, wife, and mother, she reaches what Sommers (1974) aptly calls "mandatory retirement" while her husband is still in his prime; and since women actuarially outlive men, the traditional woman is likely to spend her later years alone and poor. No woman can count on a man to support her or keep her company as she ages. Divorce, widowhood, and men's tendency to marry down in age make that inevitable. Although women greatly outnumber men after age 65, there are twice as many grooms as brides of that age and older. About one out of every four divorces occurs after eighteen or more years of marriage, and the resulting displaced homemakers have to create a wholly new way of life at a time when their self-esteem is lowest and their vulnerability to age bias reaching a peak (Sommers, 1976).

Work is the key issue for the three million women who are currently in this demographic category. Since our society and government do not regard homemaking as a job, they are ineligible for unemployment benefits. Not having "worked," their skills are rusty and their self-confidence in the work force low. Competing with women who are younger and more attractive, they are ready to take low salaries and dull jobs. They come from all parts of the social spectrum— some are former recipients of Aid to Dependent Children whose children have left home, while others are former wives of professional men, who stayed home as their husbands built careers. Speaking as head of the NOW Task Force on Older Women, Sommers (1974) points out that elderly women on fixed incomes have replaced derelict males as the principal customers for meals distributed by charity. "If gross inequities between the sexes did not exist," she asks, "why are so many of us poor when we grow old?" As they age, she suggests, women are punished for fulfilling the roles that society assigned them when young. Thus the ability to earn a decent salary at the earliest possible age is a woman's main protection against age bias. Whether they depended on a man's income when younger, or held low-status, poorly paid jobs, older women (and especially older minority women) have

237

less job security and fewer retirement or disability benefits than do men and than they need.

As women age, therefore, they need to acquire and improve their job skills. Counseling centers can help greatly. At least fourteen states have so far established special programs to help women over age 35 in various ways; at least two states, California and Maryland, have funded centers to aid displaced homemakers in writing resumes, job placement, and survival skills. The needs of aging women vary greatly; some require training in job skills, others need placement, most of them have to upgrade their existing skills. A woman who has always lived alone is likely to need a whole new support system as she ages. A woman newly living alone and accustomed to having a man take care of "things" may need help with the whole range of individual practical survival. But it should be emphasized that these women already have many valuable skills which merely need development and expression. The facts show that older women have lower absenteeism and better performance rates than do younger women, and maturity and experience are likely to provide them with skills that younger women have not yet acquired. The art of counseling and therapy is to determine where their superiority will win them extra rewards rather than to allow them—by falling into competition with younger women—to become the victims of age bias.

The Generational Effect

Different generations have undergone unique life experiences, especially during recent decades of swift social change, and they have coincidentally developed attitudes quite diverse from those of prior generations. This is what Troll (1975) aptly terms "the generational effect," and it is of major importance to counselors. For example, women born during the second decade of the century tend to have rural or immigrant backgrounds and grew up at a time when a high school education was not essential. Because of the Great Depression of the 1930s, they may have married and had children late and they may have worked for the first time during World War II and/or lived without affluence as young people. After the war they retreated with joy to the new wealth of suburbia, though many remained in traditional "women's work" jobs which they were grateful to have. They seem a tough generation but one which accepted sex discrimination as legally and psychologically natural, though as they now reach retirement, they are growing active in organizations such as the Gray Panthers and the NOW Task Force on Older Women. The women of the next decade, the 1920s, grew familiar during childhood with the kind of improvisation caused by want resulting from the Depression. As youths, they were involved with World War II, then joined their elders in producing the postwar baby boom and suburbia. Restricted by a succession of events beyond their control, they made affluence important—and also the values delineated in Betty Friedan's The Feminine Mystique (1963).

The women born in the 1930s were children during the war. Their menfolk were absent in service to the armed forces; then many of them enrolled in college under the G.I. Bill. They all grew up into the affluence of the 1950s. They married young, had children early, and were a "traditional" group; but in their mature years they felt the influence of the women's movement and the civil rights movement. Many of them have now become independent as our changing social structure shifted its foundations during their middle years, and they are characteristically a bridge generation regarding values and life-style. Women born in the 1940s grew up taking modern affluence for granted: the bomb, television, the contraceptive pill, appliances to save labor, and the time, money, and technology to experience international travel and recreation. Apparently more free from outside pressures than were their predecessors, they grew diverse quickly; they were the energy behind the social revolutions of the 1960s and 1970s, the famous "youth culture" which declared people over 30 untrustworthy. Now over 30 themselves, and still affluent in choices and belongings, they continue quieter revolutions in values and life-styles.

Their children and those of the next decade's parents will be different in ways which may only partially be foreseen. Accustomed to diversity and surrounded by richness of choice and substance, the coming generation of young women will probably show more independence and self-sufficiency. At least partly because of the women's movement, they will have more self-respect and engage less in vicarious achievement. They will expect to work and to build different kinds of marriage and family, and they will explore a wider variety of roles, taking for granted the efforts of previous generations to free them from inequality. One hopes that they will find many of the problems covered in this book irrelevant—though they will still bear within them the heritage of the past.

Therapists will find that the generational effect has two major impacts on their work. First, clients will share some values with their generations rather than with their sex. This will create expectations, conflicts, and reactions which differ largely because of a client's age-group, and the therapist will have to be alert to those differences. The various generations may use the same words, but the words may have different meanings; they will experience most of the same life events, but their reactions and needs will vary widely. "Divorce," for instance, is both a term and an experience which means such dissimilar things to each of the generations that they can hardly communicate with each other about it. With apologies to Gertrude Stein, a rose is a rose but not the same rose. This difference will create the second effect on the work of therapists by affecting them as individuals. They cannot be sure that they are discussing the same rose as is the client from a different generation—or the same divorce, "work," "anxiety," "significant relationship," or the same "future." Too little research has been devoted to the effect of a generational difference between professional and client, but therapists should be aware that if young people complain that the older generation does not understand them, so do older people know that the young do not understand them.

The generational effect therefore could become disastrous when older women enter therapy and counseling. Probably they will encounter therapists in entry-level jobs and therefore much younger than themselves. The first person they meet at a mental health or counseling center can determine their entire future in the program—by misdirecting them, misjudging them, by simply failing to understand the real nature of their problems, or by "turning them off" just by being themselves. Add the generational effect to age bias, and older women face a perilous situation when they come to counseling and therapy—one which is the therapist's responsibility to prevent.

Problems for Therapists of Older Women

Their own age bias is the first problem facing therapists of older women. Using a test to measure age bias among counselors, Troll and Schlossberg (1971) found that more than half of them could be considered age biased. (Female counselors were generally less age biased than were male counselors.) This age bias affects older clients most adversely. A survey of all studies (Troll and Nowak, 1977) reveals that the professionals most likely to work with older women view them as rigid and slow to respond to treatment, and a survey of the health care personnel from whom older women most seek advice (physicians, nurses, social workers, physical therapists, dentists) shows them to think the same (Coe, 1967). Thus no obligation of professionals working with older women is stronger than the need to confront their own age bias, for the expectations it creates in them are almost certain to defeat their efforts.

To confront one's own age-ism means to cease perpetuating the view of the aged, or just of older individuals, as "them." We must eliminate this detachment from our own future—this is one area in which counselors and therapists must exercise both empathy and sympathy deliberately and for their own good as professionals. The experience of aging is a major problem for almost everyone; the therapist can only benefit as both professional and individual if she or he pays close attention to the client's experience of it. Of particular importance is a therapeutic response to the anger which many older women feel, anger which too often lies repressed in the form of depression or fatigue. In the face of societal promises unkept, opportunities lost, and a world that declares them obsolete, older women are justified in feeling angry; and they can find a great source of energy in the venting and using of that anger for their own purposes rather than against themselves.

Another problem for therapists is to work with, rather than against, the generational effect, especially when they are helping an older woman to restructure her life. This is a complex task. An older woman needs new skills and new roles; she has to face new concerns, issues, concepts of womanhood, and different approaches to matters such as sexuality. She has to abandon old myths. At the same time, however, she cannot think or feel the same way as a woman from a different generation; she cannot totally become the New Woman. Therapists should not try to impose values on an older woman but to evoke a response to those values from her probable strengths. Older woman need to be asked more than told, encouraged more than challenged, and invited rather than organized.

The basic task, one should remember, is to help a client feel better about herself and make her own choices; and in the case of older women this means turning their attention to their strengths rather than to their weaknesses, to their credits rather than to their debits. A healthy new self-concept will allow them to view maturity as a new process of becoming themselves, in both psychological and physical terms. Freer from the limited self-concept to which they were socialized, they will see themselves as whole persons rather than as formerly pretty girls serving out the remainder of their term. In this regard, both the values and the respect of the other generations can be a major benefit and incentive.

Finally, the therapist will face the problem of activism. As the National Organization of Women points out, the present dual attack on discrimination against both sex and age has a very high potential for social change. Professionals cannot simply operate a placement service; therapists dealing with older women are likely to find themselves drawn into conflicts with employers, regulations, legislation, and the bureaucracy simply because these constitute the web in which dual discrimination catches older women. The therapist's own organization will also need scrutiny. The basic questions must be asked: do older women have the counseling, the therapy, the training programs, and the work which they need and deserve? One must also remember that equality of opportunity with younger women is not necessarily fairness. The situation of a woman of 22 who enters a doctoral program is not the same as that of a woman of 52 entering the same program, simply because one will be 26 and the other 56 when they finish. What should a counselor do? Advise the older woman not to go for her doctorate? Tell her that, like it or not, she has to follow the same course as all other students—or jolly her along with cheery words? Seek to have the institution design a special doctoral program, or an equivalent, for older women? Stay silent or forcefully remind her about the effect of not working for four years on her Social Security benefits? Encourage her in her preference to take this program, or work with her to ascertain her real needs and objectives and then seek some better way of meeting them? The choices are not easily made; activism is not just a matter of marching in a demonstration. A good counselor or therapist may have almost as much difficulty in choosing as does the older woman.

Older women face a series of traps; one of these traps is the popularity of youthfulness. *Time* magazine recently caused offense by writing an article called "In Praise of Older Women" in which almost all the women named were in their 30s, the oldest 46. A second is the stereotype of women rendered harmless by old age, whereas Margaret Mead warned our culture about a future of activism caused by what she called "PMZ" or Post-Menopausal Zest. A third trap is middle age, wherein a woman feels herself left out of both youthful activities and those for senior citizens. A fourth is sexuality. Should she: chase men; sit at home and wait, pining; forget the whole subject; use a vibrator; enter a gay relationship; or pay for sex the way middle-aged men do? A fifth is intimacy. If the children and husband all leave home, how is she to structure a social life and create friendships? A sixth is the future; not just the greater imminence of death, nor even the proximity of old age, but how to make meaningful the years between now and then. A seventh is the failure of young persons to understand, and the older woman's reluctance to "impose" on people who are busy with their own lives. One could make the list longer—the failure of males her own age to be sensitive, mature, or interested; the fear of women her own age that she is a threat or a warning; neglect from children and family; physical and financial abuse by family; marriage or nonmarriage; a dead-end job or no job at all, among other possibilities. And then, perhaps, the cruelest trap of all, which was pointed out to me by one of my clients. "I look at other women my age," she said, "and in the same boat, roughly speaking. And they're happy! and energetic! and successful! Why aren't I?" There is no doubt whatsoever that aging is a gratifying experience for many people, who vow that the old adage about life beginning at 40 is completely true. Good therapy will help a woman to avoid all the traps and discover the truth in the truism.

Lesbians

Sexual preference is one of those matters over which our culture's attitudes are in a state of rapid transition, and lesbianism is a subject about which neither academic researchers nor the heterosexual world know enough to avoid debate and disagreement. Research has given more attention to male than to female homosexuality, and much research is quickly outdated as society's attitudes and behavior change and as the attitudes and behavior of lesbians change. But lesbianism remains a burden because it is not generally accepted as a legitimate sexual preference. Choosing a gay life-style has negative consequences for both females and males, and there are adequate reasons for lesbians to feel, as some do, that they are one of the most persecuted minorities. As women, they usually work in low-paid jobs earning less money than do homosexual males; and unlike most homosexual males, a large number of lesbians have children to support, having found their sexual preference late. Indeed, many lesbians feel that they have more in common with heterosexual females than with homosexual males, their sexual orientation being only one factor in their generally discriminatory environment. In one way they tend to be worse off than heterosexual females; they lack the benefits that stem from attachment to men. To learn precisely what are the privileges and assumptions of a heterosexual woman, one writer suggests trying to experience life for a week as though you were a lesbian. Imagine your life as economically and emotionally dependent on women rather than on men. Tell everyone—family, roommate, fellow workers—that you are a lesbian, and then watch their reactions. Socialize only with women, especially when walking on the street or going out at night. The writer suggests that the experience will teach you that "self-loving and independent women are a challenge to the idea that men are superior, an idea that social institutions strengthen and enshrine" (U.S. National Commission on the Observance of International Women's Year, 1977e, p. 4).

Definition of Lesbianism

To overcome society's discrimination against homosexuality, therapists need a definition of lesbianism which contains no element of discrimination. Alfred Kinsey's attempt at such a definition by means of a heterosexuality–homosexuality *continuum* established a healthy direction for the field by emphasizing the range of sexual behavior through which humans move; but many scholars believe that the Kinsey Scale concentrates too much on purely sexual behavior. Martin and Lyon (1972) originated the following widespread definition: "A lesbian is a woman whose primary erotic, psychological, emotional and social interest is in a member of her own sex, even though that interest may not be overtly expressed." However, some heterosexual women dedicated to the women's movement feel that the definition is inadequate because it can be interpreted as applying to them. In its study of *Sexual Preference*, the U.S. National Commission on the Observance of International Women's Year (1977e) described a lesbian as a woman whose sense of self and energies center around women; who is woman-identified; who commits herself to other women for political, emotional, physical, and economic support; to whom women are important; and whose sexual energies center on women. All these definitions have the virtue of freedom from moral judgment.

Lesbianism is not abnormal. Former estimates were that the percentage of exclusively homosexual females in the population was very small (about 1 percent), but recent research reports that these estimates are far too low (Martin and Lyon, 1972; Clark, 1977; Bell and Weinberg, 1978). Because of social disapproval, self-reporting is notoriously unreliable on this subject; and the concept of a continuum of behavior suggests that, although many people may have homosexual experiences, few of them may think of themselves as homosexual. As long ago as the 1940s, among women aged 20 to 35 one in five single women and one in ten married women reported having had a homosexual experience (Kinsey, Pomeroy, Martin, and Gebhard, 1953). The Institute for Sex Research, founded by Kinsey, estimated that homosexuals account for 10 percent of the population (13 percent of the males, 5 percent of the females) using as a definition of homosexual anyone who has had more than six sexual experiences with a person of the same gender. The National Institute of Mental Health Task Force on Homosexuality estimates that 10 to 12 percent of the adult female population has had some overt homosexual experience (Gebhard, 1972). Surveying slightly more than 3,000 women, Hite (1976) found 8 percent reporting a preference for sex with women and another 9 percent identifying themselves as having had sex with both women and men. For whatever reason, the numbers discovered by researchers have steadily increased.

It seems likely that more women are having some lesbian experiences or becoming (at least for a time) exclusively lesbian. This could be the result of the sexual revolution, the surplus of females in the population, the women's movement, lowered anxiety about self-reporting, postponement of early marriage, increasing divorce, and a host of other factors. Regardless of cause, its result is to remove lesbianism from the realm of the abnormal. Lesbians come from every economic class, educational level, age, religion, and geographical locale. Some are single, some married, divorced, separated, or widowed, and many have children. Lesbians are diverse in life-style, visibility, and behavior, and they differ as much as does any other group in political and social strategy. In this sense, the statement by Martin and Lyon (1972) that "the lesbian is every woman" is perhaps the most useful definition of all for a therapist; it emphasizes that lesbians, like everyone else, are people as well as sexual entities.

Sex-role Socialization

The sexual preference for the same sex which lesbians feel obviously brings them into external conflict with societal norms. A problem for some lesbian clients arises when they internalize society's censure of their departure from the norm of the feminine sex role. Thus both external and internal pressures can make lesbian life quite difficult, and clients may express the sense of pressure at both the conscious and the unconscious levels. Childhood causes sex-role socialization to influence lesbians as it does all women, and their later sexual preference causes them—like other women who do not fulfill some part of the sex-role stereotype—to develop conflict between different portions of themselves which they resolve in various ways. Their acculturation as women may cause their self-concepts to be particularly vulnerable to external disapproval. Conditioned as females to be sensitive to acceptance or rejection by others, they may translate a negative social response to their sexual preference into an internal comment about their self-worth. This dynamic should be in the forefront of a therapist's consciousness when a client has problems with lesbian inclinations.

Because the lesbian life-style requires the individual to adopt some combination of traits regarded as traditionally feminine or masculine, lesbians have to challenge feminine sex-role behavior to some extent; and to that same extent they have to learn to define themselves independently of society's reactions—similar to women who depart from the sex-role stereotype in other ways. For example, tradition accepts female sexuality mainly for the purpose of bearing children, and to choose not to associate sex with procreation is to that extent a "deviance" from the social norm. Another example of "deviance" is the choice not to live with and to depend economically on a male, which contrasts with the expectations of the feminine stereotype. More generally, Abbott and Love (1972) suggest that lesbians as a group differ from many heterosexual women in being unafraid to develop qualities of independence, self-actualization, strength, and intelligence which—regardless of sexual preference—bring a woman into conflict with her sex-role stereotype. Therapists need to understand that these deviations have to do with sexual preference only incidentally and with departure from the sex-role stereotype primarily—since to that extent the problems lesbians experience are the normal problems experienced by any individualistic woman.

The conflict between sexual preference and sex-role socialization shows up in the kinds of difficulty which Riddle and Sang (1978) suggest many lesbian women experience intrapersonally. Negative elements of her self-image may cause a lesbian to struggle internally and/or externally with the female stereotype in the world of social, political, and economic choices. Moving through a predominantly heterosexual world for socialization and work, she may feel guilt about her sexual preference and have to suppress aspects of her sexuality. In developing intimate relationships with her lover, her children, or her lover's children, she may feel a unique kind of intrafamily stress regardless of whether she is openly, discreetly, or secretly lesbian. She may therefore live with a high degree of stress because few of her choices are automatic, run by the conscious and unconscious satisfactions of fulfilling the sex-role stereotype; deliberative choice is a quality which lesbianism necessitates, and this is a form of stress as well as a strength with which therapists need to work.

Differences from Heterosexual Women

Psychological research indicates that lesbians do not differ dramatically from heterosexual women in regard to mental health, well-being, and adjustment. One recent study, for instance, compared heterosexual and lesbian women in terms of scores from the Minnesota Multiphasic Personality Inventory (MMPI). The scores showed no major lesbian characteristics, no major differences in overall life-style, and no major differences in psychological adjustment on the MMPI total score. Subscores showed some differences: heterosexuals showed up as more extroverted on the hypomania scale, and lesbians as more masculine on the feminine/masculine scale (Oberstone and Sukoneck, 1976). A study comparing college women who have had at least some homosexual experience with those who have had none (Goode and Haber, 1977) made the important point that homosexuality and heterosexuality may not be discrete categories or even points along a continuum. Among their sixteen homosexually experienced respondents they found two general types. One group, according to the authors, will discontinue or curtail heterosexual intercourse and adopt a lesbian identity, if they have not already done so. The other group, however, suggests to the authors that homosexual contact may be one measure of the individual's degree of sexual activity and interest as a whole, including heterosexuality. This group was sexually adventurous and experimental and seemed to demonstrate that some women can comfortably create a bisexual pattern.

Differences between the women without homosexual experience and those with such experience was evident in the Goode and Haber study. Those with homosexual experience were less likely to be virgins, had started intercourse earlier and with more males, and were slightly more likely to have engaged in fellatio or cunnilingus. They were also more likely to have engaged in loveless sex with a male, to masturbate more often and enjoy it more, to fantasize more during sex, and to have daily sex more frequently as an ideal—suggesting a higher degree of overall sexual activity of all kinds. They were also less likely to enjoy fellatio and less likely to mention intercourse with a man as the source of their most pleasurable orgasms. Findings such as these demonstrate the current tendency of researchers to believe that attitudes toward sexuality as a whole are at least as important as attitudes toward heterosexuality/homosexuality in terms of behavior and satisfaction.

A lesbian's attitude toward males cannot be predicted on the basis of her sexual preference. Many lesbians have had some heterosexual experience; they also tend to be more heterosexually active during their lives than are homosexual males, entering same-sex relationships both several years later than do their male peers and after at least one heterosexual experience (Riddle and Morin, 1977; Oberstone and Sukoneck, 1976; Bell and Weinberg, 1978). Hite (1976) found that greater satisfaction from sex with another woman was only one factor in creating a lesbian preference. Other important factors were the sense of greater equality in a relationship with a female, the removal of dependence on males, and the desire to give up second-class status or to make a political statement in reaction against men. This again demonstrates the variety characteristic of sexual behavior and motivation.

Although our society (and some homosexuals) tends to group people together on the basis of their sexual preference, research evidence suggests that lesbians are more like heterosexual females than they are like homosexual males. Though the authors did not fully draw this conclusion, the recent Kinsey study of female and male homosexuals presents extensive data to support it. Homosexual females, according to this data, are described as much less likely than homosexual males to be promiscuous, to have had many sexual partners, to have sex with strangers, to separate sex from affection, to associate volume of sex with their sense of self-worth, or to see fidelity as a restriction on their independence (Bell and Weinberg, 1976). Both sexes, in other words, show the tendency to fulfill their sex-role socialization despite their preferences for sexual activity with the same sex.

The Extra Burden

The extra burden carried by lesbian women is not their sexual preference but the discrimination which that preference brings them. Discrimination from external sources needs to be removed; conflict caused by the internalized feminine sex-role stereotype would decrease if external disapproval declined. An open lesbian sexual preference is likely to bring harassment and contempt in many areas of life such as in housing, schools, work, community organizations, and within the family. This is all in addition to the lesbian's separation from the activities of the heterosexual majority, which she can enjoy only if she is willing to associate herself primarily with a male. The claim of lesbian women that they are subject to double discrimination—on account of their gender and on account of their sexual preference—is justified; both anti-homosexual bias and male domination of social structures make their lives more difficult. Their status as lesbians worsens their already low status as females, as is evident in the cases in which courts have reversed their usual tendency to award the custody of children to mothers on the grounds that these mothers were lesbians.

Our society is nonetheless increasingly comfortable with the concept of sexual freedom and freedom of sexual preference. More and more women want to explore their sexual natures without pressure from others either against or for any sexual preference. Among those women are lesbians, whose wish is straightforward: they wish to live their lives free from discrimination, seeking rewards and satisfactions equal to those of other citizens, able to choose women openly as their partners and to establish homes and families of the kind they wish. According to our country's constitutional intent, these wishes would seem to be rights just like the rights of males or heterosexual females. Therapists who see a lesbian preference as a sign of illness or maladjustment rather than as a source of discrimination should be aware that they are making a moral, religious, or emotional judgment stemming from their own acculturation, not a professional decision. A lesbian client must be able to discuss her total life and all her relationships without feeling disapproval.

Counseling and Therapeutic Approaches

Therapists accustomed to working with lesbian women emphasize the need to develop approaches free of heterosexual bias. A lesbian client may bring to therapy an issue closely connected with her sexual preference, one more closely related to her gender or individuality, or any mixture. Riddle and Sang (1978) emphasize the importance of defining the nature of the client's problem: is it a matter solely of life-style? Or is it a deeper emotional and psychological problem? They recommend providing the time and environment for the client to deal with any stresses or fears resulting from the lesbian life-style and helping the client to understand those emotions in a social/political context, so that she may measure the mixture of life-style and individual problems. This approach provides the essential separation between discrimination and personal sexual preference.

To overcome a therapist's own heterosexual bias, Clark and Berzon (in Clark, 1977) recommend special retraining for working with homosexual clients, whether female or male. Such training should include developing comfort with and appreciation of our own homosexual feelings, however slight; maintaining conscious awareness of the subjective reality of oppression which the client experiences; and working with the client as an equal, not an inferior. The objective of the training should include the ability to undo the client's negative conditioning due to social stereotypes of homosexuality; to decrease the client's degree of shame or guilt by supporting her feelings and thoughts; to help the client expand the range and depth of her feelings, especially affection openly given and anger expressed constructively; and to assist the client in developing a system of personal values by which she assesses herself rather than relying on society's values for validation. All these concepts are valid examples of good therapy which are in harmony with the individual's development as a woman.

In this anti-homosexual society, the therapist may be the only individual in the client's present environment—and particularly the only heterosexual—whom she can trust regarding the subject of her sexual preference. It is therefore incumbent upon the heterosexual therapist to affirm the viability of lesbianism or an orientation towards women. At the very least, therapists should be equipped to counteract the social myths about lesbians, and they should possess information about lesbian organizations, community service centers, literature, and legal rights which will enable the client to establish her own broader system of social support. Most experts recommend using the now extensive network of gay organizations as a referral source for information and consciousness raising. No therapist who believes that a homosexual orientation is a sign of mental illness should work with a lesbian client. In 1973, the American Psychiatric Association voted that homosexuality should not be considered a mental disorder, and in 1975 the American Psychological Association endorsed that opinion. Though the matter is still in debate due to attempts to reverse those votes, the debate should not concern a therapist. A therapist who believes that lesbianism is a form or sign of mental illness in itself should refer the client to someone who does not see sexual preference in such terms, remaining aware that even such a referral may seem a rejection to the client.

The conclusion of the authors of the recent Kinsey study of homosexuals has implications important to heterosexual therapists of lesbian clients. Their clearest finding, they report, is that homosexuality is not necessarily related to pathology. Thus, "decisions about homosexual men and women, whether they have to do with employment or child custody or counseling, should never be made on the basis of sexual orientation alone." That basic recommendation regarding therapists' attitudes is accompanied by a warning concerning values. "What has survival value in a heterosexual context may be destructive in a homosexual context, and vice versa," say the authors. "Life-enhancing mechanisms used by heterosexual men or women should not necessarily be used as the standard by which to judge the degree of homosexuals' adjustment. Even their personality characteristics must be appraised in the light of how functional they are in a setting that may be quite different from the dominant cultural milieu" (Bell and Weinberg, 1978, p. 231).

Finally, therapists should be wary of regarding lesbians as partially developed women. Militant lesbians claim that they are in fact more fully developed than are heterosexual women; although I personally find that claim more disruptive than useful, there is sufficient research evidence to demonstrate that lesbians attain as full a development and as much autonomy as any heterosexual woman. In love relationships, for instance, some lesbian couples show an equality in the sharing of power which is demonstrated by a closeness and satisfaction that many heterosexual couples would envy (Peplau, Cochran, Rook, and Padesky, 1978). Many heterosexual couples seeking equality in their relationships discover that autonomy and attachment are not mutually exclusive; studies such as the above confirm that lesbians are quite as capable as heterosexual women of developing themselves fully as both independent and loving individuals. The art of therapy is to enhance that development by removing a client's internal and external barriers in this area, just as in any other.

Female Offenders

Women identified as offenders by the criminal justice system may carry, from that moment on, as many extra burdens as any other group in our society. They face discrimination on at least four counts: as offenders, as women, normally as members of a minority group, and typically as persons lacking money and education. As a group, they are treated differently from men at all stages of the criminal justice system process, with the corrections system being particularly unfair to them. Inherent in the criminal justice system is the power of a series of individuals —police, prosecutors, judges, probation and parole officers, defense attorneys, jailers, and corrections staff—to make individual decisions in particular cases. To determine whether the sum of these decisions is a pattern of discrimination against women as women, one would need a long-term national study comparing the treatment of female and male offenders matched according to a series of variables, and such a study does not yet exist. Available data already show, however, the truth of the system's own complaint that the law does not know how to deal appropriately with women (U.S. National Commission on the Observance of International Women's Year, 1977b).

Women make up one of every five persons arrested, one of nine convicted, and one of 30 sentenced to jail or prison (Female Offender Resource Center, 1976). Their declining ratios in these stages of the process may suggest that any pattern of discrimination works in their favor, but in fact, if women are less likely than men to be subject to criminal justice action, it is because they are generally less heinous in behavior. Steadily, over the last 30 years, only one out of ten persons arrested for homicide, robbery, burglary, or assault has been female. In the best book available on the subject of women and crime, Simon (1975) suggests that this is because their extremely subordinate position in the intensely chauvinistic world of crime makes them less likely to be at the scene of a crime, to be involved in violence, or to be charged with a major offense. If they do commit a major offense, they tend to behave differently from men. Analysis of data from Washington, D.C., for 1974 to 1975 concerning women involved in violent crime showed them significantly more likely than men to have attacked someone they knew (82 percent), about equally likely to have used a weapon when they did attack (84 percent), but very much less likely to have used a weapon in a robbery (32 percent) or to have been arrested on felony charges (30.7 percent). Nationally, women comprised 14 percent of all those arrested for violent crime and 16 percent of all those arrested for any crime in 1975 (Simon, 1978).

The crimes with which women are most often charged are shoplifting and other forms of theft, drug use, and crimes of passion (Simon, 1975). A study of the jailed population found that about 80 percent of the women were there for disorderly conduct, drunkenness, prostitution, or minor larceny, and of the 20 percent charged with felonies, more than 40 percent were first offenders (Crites, 1976). Personnel in the criminal justice system believe that women are not generally as dangerous as men (Crites, 1976), are not usually the planners or organizers of crime, are not normally connected with organized crime, tend to be the users rather than the pushers of drugs, and most often become involved as ac-complices of a husband or lover (Simon, 1975). Arrested women tend to have fewer prior arrest records than men, and the typical offense history of those who do is one of multiple arrests for "victimless" crimes (e.g., prostitution, drunken-ness, disorderly conduct, and drug use). Rather than mirroring the typical male history of escalation from petty to serious crime as a life-style, most women show records of what Crites (1976) calls a "deteriorating life rather than a criminal career."

There has been a much-publicized increase in female crime during recent years, but the increase has occurred for the most part in white-collar crime and larceny (theft). Apart from the crimes which have been by definition totally female (soliciting and prostitution), men still greatly outnumber women in every crime category; but especially in embezzlement and fraud, women's proportions have recently risen sharply, and most of the recent two-thirds increase in arrests of women is in response to white-collar offenses (Price, 1977). Several explana-tions have been offered for this increase; it may be that women used to have less opportunity to commit crime since they had less opportunity on the whole (Price, 1977). It may be that both increased participation in the work force and increased need caused by divorce and inflation are the cause—and in this respect it is in-teresting to note that the typical female offender is young, poor, black, poorly educated, and has several children (Simon, 1975; Price, 1977; Crites, 1976). This is not the kind of person likely to have been encouraged into greater assertiveness by the women's liberation movement, the cause for the increase often suggested by men. While women's rise toward equality should probably show up in undesirable as well as desirable matters, a more likely effect of the women's move-ment has been to decrease the degree of "chivalry" which both their partners in crime and the police claim to have shown towards women in the past; and in the work place, if women want to be treated more equally as workers, they are also more likely to be "turned in" by employers or fellow workers when they do com-mit an offense.

Do arrested women receive differential treatment from the courts? A lower proportion of women than of men is convicted and a much lower proportion sent to jail—but the offenses they tend to commit are those for which conviction and imprisonment are unusual. Sample studies show that the courts treat women paternalistically except in cases of assault (Simon, 1975), that on the average they receive substantially lighter sentences than do men for the same offenses (Simon, 1978), and that they are less likely to be convicted and more likely to receive pro- bation if convicted (Frankel, 1973). But the data regarding convictions and sentences are highly unreliable, and practices vary drastically from state to state and court to court.

The usual explanation for differential treatment of women and men is judicial chivalry or naivety along with a degree of practicality in terms of resources; but other explanations are more likely. Prosecutors and judges do not treat less serious criminals as firmly as hardened criminals, and they believe that most women are not likely to be hardened criminals or repeat offenders of a serious crime. They also know that the effect of a severe sentence is much more severe on an impoverished mother. They are less likely to impose fines or imprison when it will harm the family unit by punishing the person who is responsible for both earning the income and caring for the children, and they are reluctant to increase the cost of crime to society by making the support of children a public cost. Thus some judges argue that a fine makes matters worse, that jail or prison should be used against a female head of household only if she is a very serious offender, and that the process of arrest and court processing is already a more serious punish- ment for a female than for a male. Almost anyone familiar with our court system will agree. Its lack of resources, its failure to respond to uniquely female needs both because of their fewer numbers and the excuse of equality under the law, and its almost total domination by male personnel make it a singularly unpleasant ex- perience for any woman.

Very few women go to prison, though we lack precise data. According to the Law Enforcement Assistance Administration, in 1977 there were 11,044 women in state and federal prisons, but the numbers held in county jails are unknown, especially those held before sentence or (particularly concerning juveniles) without conviction in correctional centers (Glick, 1977). Women are much less likely than men to be imprisoned. In December, 1970, state and federal prisons held 196,000 inmates, of whom 5,600 were female. In 1971, women were 18 per- cent of all persons arrested, 9 percent of those convicted, and 3 percent of those sentenced to a state or federal prison. In 1975, there were three federal institutions for women and 23 for men, 40 state institutions for women and 250 for men (Simon, 1975). (These data do not include status offenders—juveniles confined in "training centers" largely for lack of anywhere else to place them—whose situa- tion is special. See Female Offender Resource Center, *Little Sisters and the Law*, 1977.)

Imprisoned women are often called "the forgotten offenders" because of their small number and their comparative quiescence. Their prisons usually look bet- ter from the outside than do men's. More rural, they have fewer fences, towers, and guards than do male prisons. Inside they often tend to be less fearsome also, allowing women greater privacy and more freedom to decorate their space and themselves. Indeed, feminists have advocated creating male prisons or sexually

251

integrated prisons which have been brought up to the quality of female facilities, though others claim that the generally smaller size of female prisons is the differential factor. Imprisoned women seem to fare as well as do males, and in a few ways better; they have more comfort, shorter terms and higher probability of parole, and more visits outside prison. Occasional lawsuits and news stories reveal violence and degradation, especially in the matter of rape. But female offenders are nonetheless termed forgotten because the system fails to respond to the most important of their uniquely female needs. As a lawyer from the Southern Poverty Law Center put it, "As long as women have a couple of flowers and a clean prison, everything is seen as OK . . . because this is a male-oriented society."

Prisons fail to respond to basic elements of the uniquely female situation. It is known, for instance, that males are less likely than are females to visit a spouse in prison; but because women's prisons are fewer, they are less likely to be close to the inmates' homes, thus reducing the possibility for visits from other members of the family. (This is especially true of federal prisons since there are only three for the entire country.) The entire issue of the relationship between women and their children is badly handled by prisons, even though (unlike male prisoners) some 70 to 80 percent are responsible for their children (U.S. National Commission on the Observance of International Women's Year, 1977b). No prison can cope with the needs of a pregnant woman, and women's jails are less likely than men's to have full-time medical staff or adequate hospital wards. There is some evidence that institutions have prevented inmates from having legal abortions. In one state, women are leg-chained during childbirth and recovery in an outside hospital because state regulations require the chaining of all prisoners while outside the jail. Most prisons separate mothers from newborn children entirely, and some pressure them to put the children up for adoption. Many jails forbid visits by juveniles, and no prison allows children to live in (Armstrong, 1977; Simon, 1975).

Another major problem lies in prison services. In the first place, women's prisons lack services regarded as routine for men—counseling, recreation, libraries—which means that whatever slender opportunity for personal development exists in prisons is absent from women's prisons. Second, educational and vocational training programs are inadequate, out-of-date, and sex biased. If women receive job training, it is for the traditionally female occupations or even hobbies (e.g., cosmetology or flower arranging). Simon (1975) concludes: "Both in the types of work for which the men are being trained after they leave prison and in the work available to them in prison as a source of income, the opportunities for earning better incomes at a wider variety of jobs place the male inmates at an advantage over the women" (p. 76). A survey of inmates in two federal prisons compiled by the U.S. Women's Bureau found that 80 percent wanted more job training and 85 percent wanted more education than was available (Koontz, 1971). A survey of 6,000 offenders in community-based correctional programs by the American Bar Association found them reporting lack of job skills as their major problem, lack of education as their second (Female Offender Resource Center, 1976).

Once out of prison, women tend to stay out; only those with a history of drug use or serious arrest records tend to repeat. The major problems of life which brought them into prison in the first place may well have been worsened by their incarceration. The ABA survey found offenders reporting practical problems associated with child care and readjustment to family life as their third largest problem, while clearly neither their education nor job skills had improved. And, among the three-quarters of inmates who were mothers, the Women's Bureau found nine out of ten expecting to support themselves and a majority to support dependents after release (Koontz, 1971). For these reasons in particular the U.S. National Commission on the Observance of International Women's Year (1977b) found female inmates the best possible candidates for such correctional concepts as community-based residential and nonresidential programs, halfway houses, work release, training release, education release, and visitation by family and spouse. The goal should be better education, broader practical experience, meaningful rehabilitation, and increased family contact. We cannot sensibly take a subpopulation, declare it socially unacceptable, ignore it during its incarceration, worsen its problems, and then expect it to improve its behavior.

Good counseling and therapy could obviously improve the lot of female offenders in many ways. They are by no means irretrievably committed to a life of crime; they typically serve two to four years in prison. They are typically in their 20s and are single parents; they are eager for better education and job skills. The plight of their children is serious—when a father goes to jail, his wife cares for the children; but if she goes to jail, the children normally go to relatives or to social agencies. When mothers come out of jail, they need help with child care, job training, and education (U.S. Women's Bureau, 1977a). Much of their counseling may be related to practical matters, but it may also extend into fairly profound psychological issues. Society sends these women the message that they are bad women and bad mothers, but Glick (1977) found in a sample survey that they do not see themselves as worthless and indeed believe that they can change their lives for the better after release; this may mean that counseling and therapy have a good foundation on which to build.

Contact with offenders can take place at any stage of the criminal justice process—after arrest but before trial, after conviction, after sentencing, during incarceration, before or after release—but professionals should be aware that the criminal justice system itself is most unlikely to ask that counseling take place. Its personnel simply do not think in such terms, and it is up to the professions to initiate any program. Female offenders are a population in need of counseling and therapy. If they remain the forgotten offenders, the forgetfulness may be the fault of the counseling and mental health profession as much as it is of the criminal justice system.

Implications for Counselors and Therapists

Counseling women with extra burdens differs from counseling or therapy with other women only in that one needs extra strategies and skills to deal with the burdens. The main issue is still the client's perception of who controls her choices and actions—she or an outside source. As Sue (1977) describes, the lack of a sense of control over one's destiny is pervasive among persons of low economic status or minority social status; and according to Rotter (1966) the person who sees the locus of control as external believes that rewards flow from an external source (luck, chance, powerful others) rather than resulting from her or his own actions. Such an individual sees herself as powerless when confronted by events and circumstances. This is precisely the area in which most women need to work; but in the case of women with extra burdens, Sue points out that the perception of helplessness arises from real experience. Sex discrimination against females institutionalizes male power, and even institutions designed to help burdened women tend to make them feel more helpless by keeping control in the hands of the institutional structure.

In dealing with social institutions and the reality of everyday life, the normal reaction is to adopt the simple but profound strategy embodied in the celebrated Alcoholics Anonymous verse; we change what we can change, accept what we cannot change, and pray for the wisdom to know the difference. But the woman with double or triple burdens does not operate in this way. Losing the ability to discriminate between what she can and cannot control, she often tries to test her power only in unimportant matters and indirect ways, avoiding what she believes she "knows from experience" to be beyond her control. Choice eventually seems to be a delusion; and when choice vanishes, despair and anger are inevitable. The professional's task is to help the client realize that her perception is partly unreal —while acknowledging that, for a woman laboring under double or triple burdens, the perception may be close to reality. To experience power, such a client has to change both herself and her environment.

The professional's task is to work with her in both areas of change. To gain a sense of power, the client must change her values, her attitudes, her expectations, and her behavior, but these internal changes may not effect much if external forces such as institutions and individuals do not also change to increase her opportunities to experience a sense of power. Professionals can and must operate in both areas to achieve success with a client suffering from double or triple bias. Helping a client remove both internal and external barriers means functioning as both an internal change-agent and an activist. The task may seem too demanding, but the model for client change discussed in Chapter 2 suggests how it can be undertaken fairly comfortably—and, remember, a change which starts in one area of a client's life will start to radiate to all other areas. The model suggests four goals for a client. First, she must change the rules and expectations she has for herself. With burdened women, this is especially important in the matter of deciding where she does and does not have some power over her destiny. Second, she must learn new skills for taking control over her life. For burdened women, Shirley Chisholm provides the motto: "Nobody's giving power away. You go out and get it." Third, she must learn new communication styles. Burdened women in particular need to learn how not to communicate helplessness and how to communicate their real needs and wants. Fourth, she must build a positive self-concept. This will come only after success; and in the case of burdened women, some of that success may have to result from collaboration with activist counseling and therapy.

There is no sense in a professional's denying or ignoring that discrimination affects burdened women seriously, nor in acting as though a client can make it vanish simply by changing her attitudes and actions. Cognitive restructuring has to be honest and realistic; if not, one is simply blaming the victim by saying that all she needs to change is herself. Professionals need to work in areas in which there is some degree of real choice. In terms of attitudes, for example, a client can continue to accept society's valuation of herself and maintain her valuation of society, or she can choose more constructive valuations. In terms of communication, she can experiment with new ways of stating her needs to family, to fellow workers, to institutions, and to important individuals in her life. In terms of behavior, she can explore both within and outside counseling the differences between acting passively, assertively, and aggressively. Throughout, awareness of present patterns and of the existence of other patterns is the key factor, and this is an area in which counselors and therapists can function comfortably.

Change of this kind within the client will both cause and be reinforced by changes in the external world. At this point a professional may choose to become the client's advocate, and some counselors and therapists become adversaries of the system or institution that holds clients back; but the essential task of the professional is to collaborate with the client—to do things with her rather than for her. Three opportunities for activism are particularly important: the professional's own environment, the training and education structure, and the employment situation. The reasons for emphasizing the professional's own environment are the need to avoid hypocrisy, the importance of providing role models, and the greater power of the counselor or therapist within that environment. In the two latter areas—education and employment—counseling agencies, especially those with a psychological orientation, tend to accept the status quo; they do this even though the client's deficit in these areas which provide her with basic economic power will make it much more difficult for her to gain psychological power. One cannot expect clients to pull themselves up by their own bootstraps when they have no boots.

In the area of education and training, it can be harmful as well as ineffectual to encourage a client simply to enroll in a program or to refer her to an educational institution for that area of her counseling. She needs to make two distinct choices. The first is whether further education or training is right for her. In these days of declining enrollment, educational programs of all kinds are eager to take women students; and at the best of times they do not consider whether a student is making the right choice in terms of her own life history. They expect the student to have made that choice herself. The result may be many women students wasting time and energy in classrooms merely on the general theory that education is a good thing, whereas in fact they might be better off earning a living instead and making their own progress in the world of work. Counselors can help a client think through the issue of whether education—particularly more education—is indeed the right thing for her situation, age, skills, and needs, or whether there is a better choice. Assuming that she chooses education or training, her second choice is the nature and duration of the program. Generally speaking our educational structure is not designed for use by women, especially older women, and it is poorly suited to the needs of those on the borderline of poverty. A woman with extra burdens needs to chose her program carefully in regard to subject matter, cost, schedule, duration, and eventual effect on her economic well-being. Indeed, the traditional tendency to focus on just the talents and wishes of a prospective student may be harmful to burdened women. Acculturation will push them toward traditionally feminine spheres, and their reaction to discrimination will encourage them to make the least assertive choice.

The U.S. National Advisory Council on Women's Educational Programs (1976) has outlined the qualities desirable in an educational program for culturally deprived women. A good program will:

1. Not expect students to conform immediately to middle-class standards in terms of skills and behavior but meet them where they are;
2. Broaden their options rather than teach narrow skills, encouraging them to enter untraditional fields where economic returns are likely to be higher;
3. Build up their self-esteem consistently;
4. Be flexible in practical matters, such as making cost adjustments or providing financial aid, changing hours and location, providing child care facilities;
5. Respond to the psychology of mature women rather than adolescent or young women;
6. Operate in areas where there will be jobs;
7. Engage the students in planning curricula;
8. Make special, strong outreach efforts to contact the right target groups;
9. Build students' leadership and interaction abilities.

Unlike, for instance, most college programs, this kind of education is closely related to employment, and the linkage will draw good counselors into working also with prospective employers. In this regard, counselors can, for example:

1. Encourage employers to hire women suffering from extra burdens, especially by use of Affirmative Action guidelines;
2. Support legislation that provides better economic opportunities for burdened women;

3. Insist that communities and certain employers provide good day-care programs;
4. Deal with both individual and general problems connected with the employment and employees;
5. Assist women in building networks and leadership.

A counselor cannot safely assume that an employer has any understanding at all of the special needs of women employees, especially those with extra burdens. Unfortunately, one can assume that understanding will be lacking among supervisors and fellow workers. Even the training programs directly related to an employment situation will have staff without special training in the needs of the students.

Typical of the pattern was a training program with which I was associated, part of a large federal grant to train "welfare mothers" for jobs in construction which were not traditionally female. The program staff and trainers were either university personnel or employees of a training institution which had previously trained only men. They received no special instruction in the nature and needs of the students either as women or as impoverished women who head families. They gave them the same curriculum and similar living conditions to those the men received; and though they gave the women very good technical training, the program ended up reinforcing the sense of powerlessness and hopelessness from which it had intended to rescue them. The program took urban women into a rural area and provided them with almost no leisure activities, but scolded them if they stayed out late. For five days a week for twelve weeks, it took them away from their children—then penalized them if they had to stay home for a day to take care of the children's needs. The staff were all white, the participants mostly black; the staff were almost all male, and some were accused of exchanging grades for sex. A high degree of friction and incipient rebellion reinforced the trainers' stereotypes about women as inferior students and their prejudices against this "kind" of woman. Much of the friction came from the surprise of the staff to discover that adult women with families lead lives more complex than those of males, that they have different needs, and that they do not react well to authoritarianism and anger. The female members of the staff were all in positions where they could not influence staff attitudes profoundly, and they aroused anger by becoming the students' advocates. The aim of the program was ostensibly to find these women jobs and "get them off the welfare rolls," and the students showed their endorsement of this aim by the sacrifices they made to come to the program and by their hard work in it; but the program made minimal efforts to find the women jobs afterwards. Those who found jobs for the most part found them on their own or with the help of other agencies or, in some cases, through being chosen from the rest according to uncertain criteria. As a group, therefore, the trainees ended up knowing more but also feeling much greater frustration and powerlessness. From their viewpoint the program was marginally successful and unnecessarily unpleasant; but the official evaluation announced that the program was highly successful, its training goals having been achieved and enough placements made to justify its cost.

Many similar programs have failed, supporting the opinions that you cannot solve problems by throwing money at them and that we have a subpopulation that does not want to get off welfare. In fact, the programs too often fail because of the trainers, not the trainees. Conventional trainers may be startled to find, as in the program described, that students are upset because the schedule prevented their attending church with their children; but this is a real need, that of an adult woman, and one to which the program should have responded. Among the elements needed but usually missing in training programs for burdened women are the following:

1. Long-term career counseling and life planning;
2. Psychological counseling and/or support groups;
3. Communication skills for the working world;
4. Educational planning and development;
5. Family counseling oriented to persons who are both homemakers and breadwinners;
6. Leadership skills for responsible jobs, including within unions or professional groups;
7. Referral service to social agencies and information sources;
8. Alcoholism and drug addiction counseling;
9. Mental health services for dealing with personal relationships and the stress of adult life;
10. Staff awareness of the students as people rather than as just students.

All these elements should appear in association with education for adult women, whether the education deals with job skills or graduate knowledge, whether it is brief or long. To this end counselors will have to work with staff, and if possible with employers and co-workers, for the task of redesign is impossible for the trainees themselves.

A program whose goal is a woman able to take charge of her own life should display that goal in all its interactions; teaching should be by example as well as by precept. Working with adults means that one has to display as well as encourage such skills as planning, management of time and energy, decision making, clarification of values and communication, and networking. Women with extra burdens do not lack skills, but they do need development in new directions; for example, a woman who can weave her way skillfully through the welfare system may not be able to translate that skill into dealing with the working world. She may be unable even to fantasize the status and benefits of being a well-paid worker, and she will underestimate the number and complexity of the choices and changes that await her. She will perceive being "normal" and "middle-class" as a dream rather than as a potential reality. As another example, an older woman who has been away from the job market or education for some time will tend to blame herself for her lack of skills and will not know how to bring her maturity to her aid; trying to fit in with younger students, she may choose an educational track or job behavior which is in fact to her disadvantage. Generally speaking, when such women make mistakes, they tend to retreat unnecessarily and to see defeat where only rethinking is necessary. The "automatic pilot" of being young and upwardly mobile does not function well in burdened women.

When counseling or working therapeutically, it is hard to remember that change never occurs in just one area of a person's life. The development of a new work role, life-style, or self-concept requires the choice of new definitions and functions for the family, new relationships, new support systems, networks, social relationships, habits, institutions, and even a new identity. These factors are the same for anyone who makes a change; it is their particular form in the case of a burdened woman which professionals need to study closely. To accompany a person through change, a counselor or therapist acts as a bridge to the new identity. Women burdened by any of society's forms of discrimination have lost—or concealed—more of their individual identities than have most of us. The symptoms of the loss are deprivation in both material and psychological terms, less involvement or less successful involvement with life, and the emotions accompanying lack of control over one's life. These symptoms are not unique to women with extra burdens, but they are more pronounced among them. The goal of the professional is to conclude therapy with a client who sees herself as having the right to be as free as any other individual and the power to be so.

12

The Goals of Therapy
with Women

The final act of the therapist is to help a client decide when to end her therapy; in theory the decision should be easy. When the client decides she can function as an autonomous adult, when she shows no symptoms of deep, underlying disturbance, when her relationship with the external world has reached a degree of orderliness—these are all criteria which may determine when therapy should end. In practice the decision is more difficult. Because women's issues are complex and need to be worked out over time, women clients are economically profitable to therapists and, especially in the case of male therapists, they may also be emotionally profitable. One has the sense of being vitally helpful and important, and the point at which the therapist's involvement becomes an impediment to the client's further growth needs to be observed carefully. I am speaking not just of gurus who like disciples but of any therapist legitimately concerned about a client's well-being.

Several factors suggest that therapy with women should end at the earliest possible point. The cost of therapy can quickly exceed its dividends; women are economically needy as a group. In addition, prior conditioning of women to dependency can encourage transference to the therapist who, by responding in helpful ways, may increase the degree of dependence. Women's very willingness to explore themselves and to be adventurous and flexible can keep them in therapy longer than is necessary. Most of all, the primary goal of therapy with women is that they become autonomous; and with this goal in mind it is better that they test their autonomy from the therapist sooner rather than later.

The qualities which a woman seeks from mental health counseling are in many ways the obverse of what she brings to it; a summary from the viewpoint of a healthy woman suggests the kind of goal which client and therapist might have. The overall goal is mental health rather than mental discomfort, and that vague entity can be specified: for women as for men, economic power is the most effective means of guaranteeing survival, and a sense of one's own psychological power is the most effective means of sustaining mental health.

New Power over Emotional Lives

Every woman needs her own sense of psychological and emotional power to develop and live her life as fully as possible, and in my opinion this is the most important issue facing women today. Miller (1976) defines power as the capacity to implement, especially those abilities which one already possesses. Therapists, by this definition, do not give women power or even teach it to them; they help them to uncover it within themselves by experiencing control over their emotional lives and the power of making choices. They help them validate their feelings, ideas, and dreams, especially those which have been long suppressed. They encourage exploration of the full range of possibilities available to the client.

Power over one's own emotional life is of particular importance to women because of a peculiar cultural quirk. Unlike many other cultures, ours sees power as control over others rather than over oneself (i.e., technically we see power as dominion). Further, power over others has historically meant to control, to limit, and if possible to destroy the power of others. Power has always been defined as a matter of dominance over others, and it has always been a win-or-lose situation. This is essentially an aggressively male definition of power, and in our culture women have predominantly been the losers. Women have been taught not only to be powerless, not only to fear power in general, but also to fear what power they possess themselves. Thus the image of the witch, the sorceress, the seductress—all images of woman-power—are to be feared, scorned, and destroyed. All the "dark women" of literature were thus mysterious creatures, wicked because they sought to get what they wanted. Thus we teach all women that their emotional lives must be controlled and confined within acceptable and unimportant realms; and thus is instilled the discomfort with openly expressing power which almost all women demonstrate.

The great objection to the psychoanalytic label of "hysteric" for women has been its demonstration of male power to label women's emotions irrational. The claim that women are irrational, with the inherent suggestion that men are rational, is an easy way for a society that formally values rationality above all to ensure that women are not trusted with power and do not trust themselves. In this either/or of false polarities—either him or me, either the male or the irrational, either the good or the bad, either power over others or powerlessness over self—women have long been conditioned to find safety on the losing side. The logical alternative that one need not be a victim or victimize others, that power over

261

oneself and over one's own life is the desirable goal, has not yet become a feature of our culture, though it may well become a feminine goal.

In our culture, women have always been excluded from the white male aristocracy, that hierarchy in which a few have greater power than the many but in which almost all men have more power than almost all women; even those women at the top, though they may have the illusion of power, access to the ear of power, or derivative power in noneconomic matters, in reality have little direction or real power (Chesler and Goodman, 1976). Male power perpetuates itself in a variety of ways: sex-role stereotypes, status, ascribed expertise, control of the options and reinforcers in society, and ultimately brute force (Polk, 1974). One of the signs that the recent women's movement represents a real revolution, indeed, is that it has systematically been wresting exclusive control over these matters from males. In our society, white males control the important decisions over our collective economic, political, and technocratic resources (Terry, 1974). Control over resources is essential for freedom; and although women may have won the vote, they have not yet dominated one single legislature or important political or financial post. Our society routinely gives its most highly valued roles to males rather than to females, with the result that males have a monopoly on access to our society's entire range of resources (Lipman-Blumen, 1976).

For the present, however, women are stuck with the power styles assigned by the socialization process, and the contrasts between the styles assigned to women and to men are instructive. The basic styles regarded as appropriate for women are the personal, the helpless, and the indirect. By contrast, those for men are the concrete, the competent, and the direct. In the personal style, dependency on personal relationships is the keynote, power won through liking, loving, approval, and sexual influence; whereas men's concrete style is independent of relationships, winning power through such tangible resources as money, knowledge, physical strength, and control of institutions. In women's indirect style, they are encouraged to gain power through manipulation, sneakiness, the avoidance of confrontation, and any method which does not seem like power; the direct style of men calls for aggression, assertion, confrontation, negotiation, compromise, overt competitiveness, formation of alliances with explicit goals, and the resolution of conflicts through bargaining. The helpless style calls on women to win power through appearing incompetent; for men the call of sex-role stereotyping is to appear as unneeding as possible (Johnson, 1976). The personalities which emerge from the two sets of styles are vastly different, of course, as are the consequences. As Chafe (1977) explains, while being covert and manipulative wins women enough power to survive, the playing out of the stereotype perpetuates their general comparative powerlessness so that the overall system prevails and promulgates itself endlessly. The only escape is a change of style.

Style is no small matter when it comes to the expression and acquisition of power. Frieze and Ramsey (1976) point out an interesting effect of nonverbal communication: "Nonverbal behaviors which communicate low status and submission are precisely those crucial to attributes of femininity. . . . A woman who rejects these low status behaviors is often accused of being too assertive or aggressive." They found, for instance, that women are touched more than are men by both men and women, and since higher status persons have permission to invade the spatial boundaries of lower status persons, this sex-related difference is clearly a nonverbal establishment of superiority in position and rank. These findings are confirmed by Henley (1973), who found that men are much more likely to touch others and women more likely to be touched. Chesler and Goodman (1976) report that women are taught to smile much and to speak softly and deferentially as ways in which their body language routinely communicates deference, helplessness, and maternal concern; their dress, posture, and movements are likewise affected. Deaux (1976), finding that women prefer greater contact and less distance between them and other individuals while men prefer more distance and less contact, suggested that these factors display women's emphasis on affiliation, men's on dominance.

Examples are endless.* Their significance is in consistently demonstrating that the absence of power is built into "femininity," its presence built into "masculinity." Equally significant, however, is that by changing their styles women can consciously and quickly gain the experience of power. Change any item in their body language, for instance, and they will experience a visible change in their relationships, thus giving themselves an opportunity for both experimentation and positive rewards. They can gain an immediate sense of what it means to control oneself and to express feelings differently, and consequent motivation to generate new emotions in themselves. This, therefore, is an area in which therapists with the right skills can quickly produce vivid examples of what the client can expect from therapy: a new sense of control over one's emotional environment and an indication of what power means to the individual.

The changes in one client demonstrate what experimentation with power styles can provide. Amy at 24 had married a man just out of the army who was eager to finish his undergraduate education and to go on to graduate school. She had been delighted to meet him. A schoolteacher, she admitted that "though I was finally learning to live alone and like it, I was really just waiting for a man to come along." Having internalized the rule that says a woman needs a man to complete her life, she had waited for an external power to generate changes in her. Happily married, she moved to a university town where the only job she could get was as an unskilled laborer in a print shop. Her income was necessary to their support, and she was satisfied to be able to support Jim so that he would eventually be capable of providing her with the economic status, the home, and the children she wanted. As the years passed, things changed; Jim moved through school and Amy worked at whatever jobs she could, while growing steadily more grim. She came to counseling at age 31 because she hated herself. She felt miserable, isolated, frustrated, confused, and angry with herself "for getting myself into this

*For details, see Blaxall and Reagan, 1976; Bunker and Seashore, 1977; and Gornick and Moran, 1972.

mess." Her theme: "Why don't I want what he wants? If I can just hold out, my life will be better some day, but I can't hold out any longer." She expressed her self-contempt vividly by literally picking on herself, constantly pulling and pushing at her hair and clothes and face, and displaying fingertips raw with biting. Using metaphor, she explained that these mannerisms expressed the way she felt, pushed, chewed, and pulled by life.

Through therapy—which began as simple career counseling—she soon found that she had no clear goal in life. Before marriage she had wanted to be married, thinking that to sacrifice herself and take care of somebody would eventually get her whatever it was she wanted. This was a classic example of manipulative and indirect power seeking achievement vicariously. But if an external force fails to give us the power we expect it to, we become angry with the external force; and Amy was soon angry with Jim. "He knows what he wants," she complained, "and it's not what I want. How do I get him to do what I want?" In a women's group, she at first vastly enjoyed expressing her anger with her parents, her husband, and society, playing "poor little me" for all she was worth. The group would not let her get away with it; they challenged her: "What do you want?" She had no specific answers. Under pressure, she admitted that she had put and kept herself in a position of powerlessness; she grew angry with herself, at one stage banging herself violently on the forehead while asking others to stop her—a classic example of the powerless style.

The group then began a series of exercises in power styles in which they physically experienced different ways of expressing themselves. Amy was fascinated. Experimenting rapidly, she performed as an actress would; and when one of the new methods "fit" her, for the first time she became animated, cheerful, and full of energy. She began to use the different methods at home and at work. She began to communicate to Jim, her family, and friends what she wanted from life; she saw this as a very real risk because being a good daughter and wife and not putting any demands on others had been her basic rules. At this point we gradually realized that she had stopped biting her nails and pulling at her hair and face. She began to look energetic and to dress differently. At her request, Jim came to therapy privately and with Amy; the issue was that his need to finish an advanced degree at a school in California was not shared by her. She did not want to move again. Jim's reaction was shock. A gentle man, he said: "I feel that I've been walking over you for years. I had no idea. I feel terribly guilty for bringing you here in the first place. I've often thought it was a mistake for you. But I knew what I wanted, and I thought you did, too." She admitted that his assumption was fair, since she had always given him the impression that she shared his goals.

Eventually they agreed to separate even though they still cared for each other greatly. As long as she was with Jim, Amy felt she could not do what she had to do—invest herself in the basic task of becoming a whole and separate person. He went to California; she now has title to their house in the country and continues her job, in which she has been promoted and is growing skilled. She resists any affiliation with her family as well: "It's too risky for me right now. I need my own

264

time." She has maintained an elaborate support system among women and friends but will form no individual attachments: "I can't be us until I'm me." She feels that everything she does now is part of the process of self-definition, though she still finds it "much easier to say what is not me than what is me." She consistently receives what she regards as a major reward: "People who knew me two or three years ago literally don't recognize me now." The reason is visible; in appearance, manner, dress, voice, movements, and stance the former little brown wren, sometimes by dint of pure acting ability, is evolving into a proud peacock.

Expanded Choices in Behavior and Attitude

Almost without exception women coming to therapy are seeking expansion of themselves. This will often manifest itself in pragmatic matters: desire for a different job, a new lover, or a different or new education. It will often stem from dissatisfaction with present circumstances, which may be blamed. When therapists work with such situations, however, they grow accustomed to frustration; they put a lot of effort into solving old problems and suggesting new possibilities, all of which the client either rejects or only appears to consider. Deeper issues are involved and must be faced before the surface problems may be resolved. To state that a modern, androgynous women can transcend sex roles and choose whatever behavior is appropriate is no more than a slogan if it assumes that one can instantly overcome socialization as a female and respond in a manner that befits the situation. In fact, women need opportunities to experiment with a new range of behaviors, not just so that they may judge the validity of the behaviors, but so that they may have time to identify and overcome their habitual feminine responses. Expansion, in other words, is internal development as well as external achievement, and it may have to be leisurely.

The most difficult behaviors for women to own, explore, and test are those which their learning process has most firmly restricted. Nonetheless, clients have the right to expect that they will leave therapy with definite changes even in these most difficult areas, not just with surface advice, information, and exhortation. They need to know what it is like to be outwardly angry and yet see oneself and others survive. They need to experience fierce competitiveness, even if only in some basic form such as arm wrestling, against women and men. They need to see, feel, and hear the differences between autonomy and dependence and to do something difficult completely independently. They need to express feelings in confrontation instead of avoiding them with silence, kindness, tactfulness, or sympathy. They need to trust others' ability to survive and to trust themselves —to go against the group, to turn away from it, to neglect it, or to be unkind to it even if that raises a conflict of feelings. They need to experience taking a risk, however small, to be forceful instead of compliant, and to be direct and confrontive in pusuit of what they want or believe in. They need to nurture themselves in the ways they have given care and attention to others. And all this must be done, not just said; experienced, not just talked about. Therapy offers them a place where they can do at their own paces those things which they cannot do elsewhere, especially in those areas which have been most strongly forbidden to them in the outside world.

Both individual and group therapy offer a safe place for a woman to expand her behavioral and attitudinal range through experiencing any new feeling and exploring its consequences. Therapy should never simply say, "Go forth and do!" There are several practical reasons for this approach. The client will probably not be adept at any new behavior when she starts, and she will lack confidence. In the world, her new behavior may have disastrous consequences; even if it is successful, she will probably feel some guilt or discomfort about engaging in previously prohibited attitudes. Therapy provides for all these problems and offers security and support. If a woman explodes with rage in a woman's group, for instance, she is unlikely to be told, "Stop that!" More likely she will hear encouragement such as "Let it all out! It feels so good! I know!" or "I've felt exactly that way!" or "Okay, now what are you going to *do* about it?" In other words, she will be in touch with released energy rather than with released guilt.

The balance currently required of women is possibly greater than at any other time in their history. The many women who juggle roles at home and work simply cannot recklessly experiment; unusual or unfeminine responses might expose their economic vulnerability, wreck fragile relationships without purpose, or increase their stress and fatigue uselessly. Women cannot *easily* switch behaviors or *smoothly* expand. The world currently requires that they combine skills in interacting (home, family, intimate relationships) with skills in achieving (work, money, living alone). In one area they want to be sensitive, affectionate, reliable, appreciative, cooperative, and friendly; in the other assertive, enterprising, organized, rational, industrious, and forceful. It is possible for a woman to display both sets of characteristics, but inevitably there will be some leakage or overlay of one set into the other. Complete separation of the two—a split personality—is improbable and dangerous to the sense of self. Therapy offers the opportunity not just to experience polar opposites but to integrate, pair, or combine them so that the individual can choose the mixture with which she herself feels comfortable and whole. Therapy, in other words, should not push a woman off balance in the outside world; it should enable her to find what she needs to improve her balance. In that respect only will a client be genuinely able to expand her behavior and attitudes so that choices are not external to her—something she grabs at—but internal, flowing naturally from her.

Clearly Defined Self-boundaries

In Gestalt terms, the concept of separateness is essential to the healthy person. An individual's "I"-boundaries arise from a combination of experience with living and built-in capacities for handling new or intensified experiences. They may take various forms: body-boundaries, value-boundaries, familiarity-boundaries, expression-boundaries, and exposure-boundaries. Satir (1976), Polster and Polster (1973), and Perls (1969) all emphasize the contact boundary, that point at which one experiences the *me* in relation to the *non-me* and better defines both. The essence of this act lies in discriminating between the self and the non-self in the universe.

Women seem to have more difficulty defining their self-boundaries than do most men. Most feminist therapists find self-boundaries to be more permeable in women than in men to such forces as sympathy, love, empathy, sensitivity, and duty. Fortune seems to take hostages from women more easily than from men, and women stand ready to sacrifice their selves in order to redeem those hostages. The source of women's self-esteem is not achievement so much as it is being loved and lovable (Levine, Kamin, and Levine, 1974). Personal and indirect power styles mean that women find a sense of identity in being liked, approved, loved, and lusted after, which involve being vulnerable to others in two ways. First, a woman must be more aware of others' wants, needs, feelings, thoughts, and senses so that she may know how to win a favorable response. Second, if she fails to win that response, she is at the mercy of the other, less disclosed, person (Johnson, 1976). Either way, the nature of the other person tends to be more important than her own nature and experience, which to her appear less valid.

In Gestalt terms, women are overly focused on the wants, needs, thoughts, feelings, and senses of other people at any point in time; this means that they have no precise line which marks where they begin and others end. In every manifestation of the "I"-boundary they tend to be permeable and unclear. In the words of the Polsters, "All our lives we juggle the balance between freedom or separateness on the one hand, and entry or union, on the other. Each of us must have some psychological space within which we are our own masters and into which some may be invited but none must invade" (1973, p. 99).

Therapy aims precisely at helping a client to define where her balance lies, where separateness and union differ, where her own psychological space lies, where the point of invitation or invasion occurs, and where the contact points between our boundaries and those of the other exist. Contact is neither togetherness nor joining; it can only occur satisfactorily between two separate entities. (This is, incidentally, why a fully developed man prefers a self-actualizing woman, one he can admire and respect as well as love.) For contact to take place, the woman must perceive herself as a complete entity whose psychological space is as valid as that of the other; she must be aware that there is a difference, and not necessarily any relationship, between what is happening inside her and inside the other. This is precisely the kind of subject with which therapy is especially well suited to deal—through the participation of the caring but independent therapist.

The dynamics of retaining power are important for both client and therapist to remember: "If one person's freedom depends *exclusively* on another person *allowing* it, one loses one's own sense of the power she must exercise in protecting and defining her own psychological space from natural incursions on it. Envisioning a world where freedom to act is bestowed or guaranteed rather than *achieved* is, regrettably, wishful thinking, utopian and noncontactful" (Polster and Polster, 1973, p. 103). A loving couple who had come to therapy because of irritations with each other presented the same point in personal terms. "I want to shelter you," said the distressed husband. "What's wrong with that?" "But I don't *want* you to shelter me," the wife snapped, then paused. "But I would love to have you shelter my space." This seemed to me also to express well the healthy relationship between client and therapist, for it outlines where the adventure lies: in the contact, in identifying the points of separateness and union. To be always separate is not much more satisfactory than to be always dependent. To be both interdependent and autonomous is not an impossible state but the ideal, and one which a client can experience in the therapeutic relationship. She may then transfer that experience to the rest of her life so that work and family do not overwhelm her sense of self no matter how intensely she engages with them.

A confused client demonstrated this process well. Judith, age 35, was running out of patience with the traditional after 15 years of marriage. At 20 she had been delighted to marry a somewhat older man who made all the decisions and dictated what she had to do in order to nurture him. There had been some conflict when the births of three children distracted her, and much fatigue resulted from several geographical moves made to further her husband's career; but she had experienced no major unhappiness for years. By 35, however, with children aged 13, 11, and 9 developing their own lives, Judith's disillusionment and frustration were beginning to show. She persuaded her husband to "let me go to work" again as a secretary on two conditions: she would be home each day when the children got home from school, and she would not engage in evening activities with people from work.

At work she rejoiced in being "a separate person" for part of each day; she especially enjoyed "buying things with my *own* money." A very competent woman, she later applied for the job of office manager and got it. Trouble immediately arose because the company required her to take a two-week training program in another city. Her husband was irritated and accused her of breaking their bargain. Judith placated him, arranging for her mother to replace her in the home while she was away. The absence from home was a turning point; Judith experienced the pleasures of being a free individual. She did not, as her husband suspected, have a sexual affair. Her joy came from making her own decisions and winning the respect of teachers and co-workers. She returned full of excitement and eager to share her experience with her husband. He had been gruff on the telephone but now, instead of listening, he launched a tirade—the sum of which was, "Don't bring that women's lib stuff into this house! You're a wife and mother, and you've got everything you need right here." Judith's experiment in expanding her self-boundaries promptly collapsed.

She felt enormous guilt, believing every criticism that was flung at her. She accepted her husband's opinion of her and believed she had narrowly escaped becoming a bad wife and mother. So she overcompensated, redoubling her activities in the home and hiding everything she discovered about herself in the work environment. She did not realize that her marriage—in any real sense of the word—was deteriorating rapidly, not because of her work but because of the dishonesty to herself that her situation encouraged. When she became surly and irritable at home, especially with the children, she blamed herself and shut down her feelings. She became "like a robot the moment I enter the house. The very people I wanted to share my excitement with most, I can't talk to. I feel guilty and closed off about everything. I feel as if I am a machine that performs, smiles and performs—just a machine." But it was through work that she began to see the meaning of her danger and chose to come to therapy. "I'm scared," she said, "because as time goes on I find I'm shutting down even at work. I'm getting afraid to talk to *anyone* about what I'm feeling. I think I may be angry inside. I know I want to be treated as though I have something to say, but I'm getting to feel nobody cares." Concerning her marriage she could only say, "Perhaps I'm selfish and unappreciative. He's a good man. He gives me everything I need. He's not unkind."

In Judith's therapy we started with the task of finding out where others left off and she began. In group and individual therapy she began to see shades and options. She watched others define themselves by experimenting and tested herself cautiously. At work she steadily relaxed, willing to risk herself with people whom she could trust. At home she initiated change with her children, slowly refusing to be seen exclusively as mother/servant and teaching them to take responsibility for themselves. With much difficulty she then began in couples therapy to work on her relationship with her husband, whom she still loved, and she discovered what was to her a surprise: when she was quietly confident about something, instead of dependent and seeking permission, he responded well. There were occasional conflicts, but Judith began to hear what she had earlier called "tirades" now as "grumblings." Her husband, it seemed to her, wanted merely to know that she understood what she was doing and he was not in fact the chauvinist she had suspected. As she demonstrated confidence, he followed suit. There are still hazards to be negotiated, but it seems unlikely that this couple will regress permanently. Their relationship has changed, they both feel for the better. They have discovered that when two people try to be together it is simply more pleasant for *both* to know where each of them begins and ends. Judith has developed a signal which works for both of them. Whenever her husband says, "What you really mean is . . . ," they both stop talking about the subject until at least the following day. This sometimes makes them grind their teeth; other times, they laugh.

New Rules and Expectations

A random selection from a group's wall sheets, written as examples of rules from childhood which still affected group members, will demonstrate how forceful the inappropriate and outmoded rule can be:

Don't talk so loud. People might think you are mad at them.

Don't be angry at your father. Look at all he does for you.

Don't beat the boys.

Watch your language. You sound like a slut.

All men are that way. Just play it quietly and smile and you'll get what you want sooner or later.

A few tears can be very useful.

Keep your legs together. Nice girls don't sit that way.

Of course your brother should have more privileges. He's a boy and can take care of himself.

Each rule had its manifestation in current daily life. Written down, some of them seemed absurd; but for the most part their owners had to admit they still saw them as "true" or "right." Next the group explored messages which they found themselves giving to themselves repeatedly and which had originated at a much earlier age. For example,

I can't be angry at him. It isn't his fault that he was brought up to expect a wife to do the cooking.

I can't tell my mother to butt out. It would hurt her.

The kids must learn to come straight home from school. Who knows what might be happening to them?

Stay overnight? Oh, I couldn't do that!

The point of both exercises was soon understood by the group; they realized that they had very efficiently become their own "keepers." Internalizing these rules meant that they no longer needed external policing since they did such a good job themselves. They then began to realize that they did not need policing at all, for the enemy, if there had ever been one, had stolen away in the night. Their responses had been as outmoded as they were restrictive. (For more information and ideas, see Collier, 1982.)

Newness does not guarantee a rule's viability. New rules can become harmful "shoulds" if selected without regard to their appropriateness to the individual. Here are samples of new rules which various members of the same group indicated were pressuring them uncomfortably in the same manner as the old:

A woman should have a lifetime career.

A woman should be bisexual.

A woman should not have babies and get caught in that trap.

A woman should have nothing to do with a male chauvinist.

A woman should have an open marriage.

A woman should always be assertive.

This pantheon of rules derived from feminism caused a wild debate. Some women strongly subscribed to one or some of them, others were equally opposed. Out of the debate emerged the lesson: a woman can choose those rules which are appropriate to herself, not to women in general. The therapist made one rule of her own, taken from Gestalt techniques: when a generalization was made, the speaker had to substitute "I" or "you" wherever the instinct was to say "men" or "women." This made an absurdity of most generalizations or rules, and the point was clear. An adult operates healthily on the basis of those rules which suit her own life-style and values.

New Communication Styles

A woman has to learn new techniques to express new attitudes. If she wants to show she is angry, how does she do it nonverbally as well as verbally? Should she smile or not smile; look someone in the eye or look out the window; stand up straight or sit down behind a desk; say explicitly that she is angry about X or let the person figure it out? An infinity of details may need to be explored; valuable in this effort are such books as *Body Language* (Fast, 1970) and *Body Politics* (Fast, 1980).

The areas in which women especially need to improve their communication styles are direct statement of wants and needs, negotiation, conflict resolution, confrontation, and communication of one's own experience. Although new techniques will help, these matters are highly emotive; a woman sensing their affect may want to proceed further than simply learning techniques. The style of communication changes the message; though the words may be identical, the same message is not delivered with a posture of helplessness as is with a posture of self-confidence. Women must learn, therefore, to listen to themselves and to the message they are actually sending, to experience what their bodies are doing as they communicate, and to hear the tone of delivery; success in self-observation leads to achievement of inner clarity, and this is in the realm of personal growth rather than of technique.

Summary

The five preceding areas discussed in this chapter offer a myriad of observable criteria for determining mental health in women; observable criteria are what both clients and therapists most urgently need in order to determine when therapy has reached its limits. Whether one considers therapy something which cures illness or an aid to growth, no definition of health makes sense if it fails to include measurable behavior and self-reported comfort with such behavior.

Beyond this point it is difficult to say where the limits of therapy lie. Like stress, mental health is an entity which fluctuates, even among psychopaths and neurotics. Some people feel the need for therapy intermittently throughout their lives; others use therapy as a device to resolve problems and to continue growth, a time for concentration and new ideas. Still others use therapy only briefly or at one stage of their lives. There is no rule for determining which of these groups is right, because each individual will determine her or his own way of surviving in the world regardless of the therapist's opinion.

Measurements for Ending Therapy

Therapists need to diagnose a client's status as she nears the end of therapy in a way similar to that done when she began. Below is a checklist which can be used for this purpose; it is presented as a series of questions and is adapted from a checklist of goals for feminist counseling developed by Klein (1975).

1. Does the client still experience pain related to performing roles in the outside world, especially pain from reluctance to give up roles stemming from sex-role socialization?
2. Are her remaining signs of stress the normal consequences of changing herself and her life-style; does she understand the relationship between her new behavior and its consequences?
3. Does her self-esteem depend on the judgment and reactions of others (including the therapist) or has she established her own values?
4. Does she understand the degree to which her behavior and choices (past, present, and future) result from the internalization of sex-role stereotypes? If she chooses a stereotypical role, does she do so knowingly, understanding the consequences?
5. Can she express her full range of emotions effectively, especially in the areas of anger, power needs, and the balance between autonomy and interdependence?
6. In interpersonal relationships, does she see individuals as people or primarily as representatives of their gender? Is she capable of finding support and encouragement from women as well as men?
7. Do her choices of roles match her expectations of herself, especially in the areas of achievement and recognition?
8. Does she have enough skill in decision making and problem solving to decide which problems are soluble and which are not? Having made a decision, is she able to accept healthily any doubt or guilt which may ensue?
9. Is her degree of ownership over her body enough for her to (a) enjoy her sensuality, (b) manage her own sexual and reproductive life, and (c) avoid physical abuse by herself or others?

The therapist should have functioned as an agent of change in each of these areas. The change model presented in Chapter 2 suggests that a change in any one area will have been accompanied by a change in the others; evidence of a failure to change in one of them may be a sign that further work is necessary. Ultimately, the decision to end therapy may be determined by the answer to a single question: is the client now as capable as any adult of becoming her own change-agent? Regardless of the therapist's agenda, is the woman now in charge of her own life and capable of changing it to suit her own ends?

Mental Health for a Woman

We can sum up by stating that mental health is not an invisible entity which one purchases at a single time; it is a series of visible component parts which are carefully constructed into a functioning whole.

The woman who emerges from therapy as mentally healthy is identifiable by a series of characteristics:

1. She values herself as an individual and as a female rather than depreciating herself as a woman.
2. She chooses behaviors according to their suitability to her and to the situation, perhaps deliberately resisting conforming to female sex stereotypes but certainly not conforming to them unwittingly.
3. She consistently tends toward emotional, social, and economic self-sufficiency, striving for separateness and autonomy before seeking interdependence.
4. She blends autonomy with interdependence in the form of a selected number of deep relationships with others in personal and social activities.
5. She orients herself toward reality and realism, avoiding overreaction in favor of accepting herself, others, and the world for what they are.
6. She appreciates differences as much as similarities, preferring variety in herself and others to stereotypes.
7. She does not victimize herself, does not let herself be victimized, and does not present herself as a victim.
8. She enjoys the power of her emotions and her self and displays this power through vivacity and energy.
9. She takes risks and extends herself without placing too much emphasis on either success or failure.

The Therapist's Task

One of my own rules is that the therapist should use the concepts of androgyny and sex-role transcendence in working with both women and men. Feminist therapy has, I think, successfully identified the basic issues which almost inevitably arise when women move into new personal and cultural roles: adult autonomy, intimacy, power, anger, self-nurturance, and sexuality, among others.* Feminists have successfully identified the qualities which sex-role socialization inhibits in women and which need to be developed if women are to become full adults. Add to these the qualities identified as polarities by the theory of androgyny, so that the opposite of whatever exists can be identified and explored, and the therapist will have a more than adequate method with which to assist the confused client to organize her existence. As long as the shared goal is expansion, as long as there is a clear sense of transcending the sex role so that construction and rejection are at most temporary, then the therapeutic process will continue in a healthy manner and direction. There will also be a series of specific behaviors and attitudes by which the client can measure her own changes after experimentation. The relationship between therapist and client will therefore be as egalitarian as the process of growth requires.

Beyond this a programmatic approach grows dangerous, and a therapist can thereby do more harm than good. Unfortunately, not even the acquisition of full androgyny is a guarantee of success. Kenworthy (1979) has recently pointed out that, so sexist is our society, an androgynous man is still valued more highly than is an androgynous woman. A man today receives social rewards for departing from the male stereotype, whereas a woman still risks social penalties by behaving in a traditionally masculine manner. There is still a firm limit on what we can achieve as complete and powerful human beings, and there is no sense in a therapist's having or breeding illusions simply because they are "better" illusions than are some others.

The therapist's task is much more varied and challenging than that offered by any program. The ultimate beauty of the "self" is that it is inextinguishable and unique. It starts with a dab of raw material already showing those qualities acquired through inheritance; the basic constitution and mysteriously acquired roots of selfhood produce individuality in even the newborn. Basic needs, capacities, talents, anatomical equipment, and physiological and temperamental balances are already present, influenced by what we can only call prenatal and natal chance. This raw material grows rapidly into a recognizable "self" as, interacting with the world, it discovers its nature and that of forces outside it. We are calling aspects of the self instinctive, given, natural—to indicate their indestructibility. All this is potentiality, not actualization; while there are some roles which the individual can never fulfill, one does not yet know what one might become. Each is launched now into a personal life history. Each will develop—as what?

Some of our inner nature will depend on our species; more of it will be idiosyncratic. Much of what our psyches become will depend on extra-psychic influences such as family, culture, the environment, and accidents of time and space—and we will learn to complain that the universe has not done right by us. We will find that a human culture may inhibit or foster growth, as may a family, and that

---

*For further details, see Gornick and Moran, 1972; Franks and Burtle, 1974; Rawlings and Carter, 1977; Wyckoff, 1977; Pancoast, 1975; Miller, 1976; and Bernard, 1981.

growth depends not only on the environment but on ourselves. We are not just creations or inventions of society, which, as Maslow put it, can help or hinder a rosebush but cannot turn it into an oak. Nor are we, as clients, the inventions of a therapist. The client's responsibility in regard to therapists, as in the rest of her life, is to make them serve her purposes rather than serving theirs. The therapist's responsibility to clients is to recognize that the limits of therapy appear at the very edge, not at the core, of selfhood.

Bibliography

ABBOTT, S., and LOVE, B. *Sappho was a right-on woman: A liberated view of lesbianism.* New York: Stein and Day, 1972.

ABERNATHY, V. Cultural perspectives on the impact of women's changing roles on psychiatry. *American Journal of Psychiatry,* 1976, *133,* 657–661.

ABRAMOWITZ, S. I. Locus of control and self-reported depression among college students. *Psychological Reports,* 1969, *25,* 149–150.

ABRAMOWITZ, S. I., WEITZ, L. J., SCHWARTZ, J. M., AMIRA, S., GOME, B., and ABRAMOWITZ, C. V. Comparative counselor influence toward women with medical school aspirations. *Journal of College Student Personnel,* 1975, *16,* 128–130.

ADLER, F. The rise of the female crook. *Psychology Today,* 1975, *9,* 42–48 and 112–114.

ADLER, N. E. Emotional responses of women following therapeutic abortion. *American Journal of Orthopsychiatry,* 1975, *45,* 446–454.

AHRONS, C. R. Counselor's perceptions of career images of women. *Journal of Vocational Behavior,* 1976, *8,* 197–207.

ALBIN, R. S. Depression in women: A feminist perspective. *APA Monitor,* 1976, *7,* 27.

ALTEMEYER, F., and JONES, K. Sexual identity, physical attractiveness and seating position as determinants of influence in discussion groups. *Canadian Journal of Behavior,* 1974, *6,* 357–375.

American Psychological Association. Report of the task force on sex bias and sex-role stereotyping in psychotherapeutic practice. *American Psychologist,* 1975, *30,* 1169–1175.

ANGELOU, MAYA. *I know why the caged bird sings.* New York: Random House, 1970.

APPLEY, D. G. The changing place of work for women and men. In A. G. Sargent (Ed.), *Beyond sex roles.* San Francisco: West Publishing Company, 1977.

Bibliography

ARBUCKLE, D. S. *Counseling: Philosophy, theory and practice*. Boston: Allyn & Bacon, Inc., 1965.

ARMSTRONG, G. Females under the law: Protected but unequal. *Crime and Delinquency*, 1977, *23*, 109–120.

ASKEN, M. J. Psychoemotional aspects of mastectomy: A review of recent literature. *American Journal of Psychiatry*, 1975, *132*, 56–59.

ASLIN, A. L. Counseling "single again" women. *Counseling Psychologist*, 1976, 6, 37–41.

———. Feminist and community mental health center psychotherapists' expectation of mental health for women. *Sex Roles*, 1977, *3*, 537–544.

BAILYN, L. Accommodation of work to family. In R. Rapoport and R. N. Rapoport (Eds.), *Working couples*. New York: Harper & Row, 1978.

BARDWICK, J. M. *Psychology of women: A study of bio-cultural conflicts*. New York: Harper & Row, 1971.

———. (Ed.). *Readings on the psychology of women*. New York: Harper & Row, 1972.

———. Some notes about power relationships between women. In A. G. Sargent (Ed.), *Beyond sex roles*. St. Paul: West Publishing Company, 1977.

BARDWICK, J. M., and DOUVAN, E. Ambivalence: The socialization of women. In J. M. Bardwick (Ed.), *Readings on the psychology of women*. New York: Harper & Row, 1972.

BART, P. Depression in middle-aged women. In S. Cox (Ed.), *Female psychology: The emerging self*. Chicago: Science Research Associates, 1975.

BARUCH, G. K. Girls who perceive themselves as competent: Some antecedents and correlates. *Psychology of Women Quarterly*, 1976, *1*, 38–49.

BEALE, F. Double jeopardy: To be black and female. In T. Cade (Ed.), *The black woman*. New York: The New American Library, Inc., 1970.

BECK, A., and GREENBERG, R. Cognitive therapy with depressed women. In V. Franks and V. Burtle (Eds.), *Women in therapy*. New York: Brunner/Mazel, 1974.

BECKETT, J. Working wives: A racial comparison. *Social Work*, November 1976, 463–471.

BECKMAN, L. J. Alcoholism problems and women: An overview. In M. Greenblatt and M. A. Schuckit (Eds.), *Alcoholism problems in women and children*. New York: Grune and Stratton, 1976.

BELL, A. P., and WEINBERG, M. S. *Homosexualities: A study of diversity among men and women*. New York: Simon & Schuster, 1978.

BEM, S. L. The measurement of psychological androgyny. *Journal of Consulting and Clinical Psychology*, 1974, *42*, 155–162.

———. Psychological androgyny. In A. G. Sargent (Ed.), *Beyond sex roles*. San Francisco: West Publishing Company, 1977.

———. Sex-role adaptability: One consequence of psychological androgyny. *Journal of Personality and Social Psychology*, 1975, *31*, 634–643.

BEM, S. L., and BEM, D. J. Case study of a nonconscious ideology: Training the woman to know her place. In D. J. Bem (Ed.), *Beliefs, attitudes and human affairs*. Monterey, Ca.: Brooks/Cole, 1970.

———. On liberating the female student. *School Psychology Digest*, 1973, *2*, 10–18.

BEQUAERT, L. H. *Single women: Alone and together*. Boston: Beacon Press, 1976.

BERNARD, J. *The female world*. New York: The Free Press, 1981.

Bibliography

———. *The future of marriage*. New York: Bantam Books, 1973.

———. *Women, wives, and mothers: Values and options*. Chicago: Aldine, 1975.

BERNSTEIN, J. The elementary school: Training ground for sex role stereotypes. *Personnel and Guidance Journal*, 1972, *51*, 97–101.

BERZINS, J. I., and WELLING, M. A. The PRF Androscale: A measure of psychological androgyny. Unpublished manuscript, University of Kentucky, 1974.

BIRD, C. *The two-paycheck marriage: How women at work are changing life in America*. New York: Rawson, Wade Publishers, 1979.

BIRK, J. M. Interest inventories: A mixed blessing. *Vocational Guidance Quarterly*, 1974, 280–286.

BIRK, J. M., BARBANEL, L., BROOKS, L., HERMAN, M. H., JUHASZ, J. B., SELTZER, R. A., and TANGRI, S. S. A content analysis of sexual bias in commonly used psychology text-books. *JSAS Catalog of Selected Documents in Psychology*, 1974 (Ms. No. 733).

BLANE, H. T. *The personality of the alcoholic: Guises of dependency*. New York: Harper & Row, 1968.

BLAU, F. D., and JUSENIUS, C. L. Economists' approaches to sex segregation in the labor market: An appraisal. In M. Blaxall and B. Reagan (Eds.), *Women and the workplace*. Chicago: University of Chicago Press, 1976.

BLAXALL, M., and REAGAN, B. (Eds.). *Women and the workplace: The implications of occupational segregation*. Chicago: The University of Chicago Press, 1976.

BLOCHER, D. H. *Developmental counseling*, second edition. New York: Ronald Press, 1974.

BLOCK, J. H. Conceptions of sex role: Some cross-cultural and longitudinal perspectives. *American Psychologist*, 1973, *28*, 512–526.

BOHANNAN, P. The six stations of divorce. In J. M. Bardwick (Ed.), *Readings on the psychology of women*. New York: Harper & Row, 1972.

BOSMA, B. J. Attitudes of women therapists toward women clients, or a comparative study of feminist therapy. *Smith College Studies in Social Work*, 1975, *46*, 53–54.

The Boston Women's Health Book Collective. *Our bodies, our selves*. New York: Simon & Schuster, 1976.

BRACK, D. C. Displaced—the midwife by the male physician. *Women and Health; Issues in Women's Health Care*, 1976, *1*, 18–24.

BRIEF, A., and ALDAG, R. Male–female differences in occupational attitudes within minority groups. *Journal of Vocational Behavior*, 1975, *6*, 305–314.

BRODSKY, C. M. The pharmacotherapy system. *Psychosomatics*, 1971, *11*, 24–30.

BROVERMAN, I. K., BROVERMAN, D. M., CLARKSON, F. E., ROSENKRANTZ, P. S., and VOGEL, S. R. Sex-role stereotypes and clinical judgments of mental health. *Journal of Consulting and Clinical Psychology*, 1970, *34*, 1–7.

———. Sex-role stereotypes: A current appraisal. *Journal of Social Issues*, 1972, *28*, 59–78.

BROWN, C. R., and HELLINGER, M. L. Therapists' attitudes toward women. *Social Work*, 1975, *20*, 266–270.

BROWNMILLER, S. *Against our will: Men, women and rape*. New York: Simon & Schuster, 1975.

BRYANT, B. E. *American women today and tomorrow*. Washington, D.C.: U.S. Government Printing Office, 1977 (No. 052-003-00249-3).

Bibliography

BRYDE, J. F. *The Indian student: A study of scholastic failure and personality conflict.* Vermillion, South Dakota: Dakota Press, 1970.

BUNKER, B. B., and SEASHORE, E. W. Power, collusion, intimacy–sexuality, support: Breaking the sex-role stereotypes in social organizational settings. In A. G. Sargent (Ed.), *Beyond sex roles.* St. Paul: West Publishing Company, 1977.

BURCHINAL, L. G. Personality characteristics of children. In F. I. Nye and L. W. Hoffman (Eds.), *The employed woman in America.* Chicago: Rand McNally, 1963.

BURKE, R., and WEIR, T. Relationship of wives' employment status to husband, wife, and pair satisfaction and performance. *Journal of Marriage and the Family,* 1976, *38,* 279–287.

BUTLER, R. N. Ageism: Another form of bigotry. *Gerontologist,* 1969, *9,* 243.

BYLER, W. Removing children. *Civil Rights Digest,* 1977, *9,* 18–27.

CAMPBELL, A. The American way of mating: Marriage si, children only maybe. *Psychology Today,* 1975, *8,* 37–40 and 42–43.

CARNEY, C. G., and McMAHON, S. L. (Eds.). *Exploring contemporary male/female roles: A facilitator's guide.* La Jolla, Ca.: University Associates, 1977.

CARRILLO-BERON, C. *A comparison of Chicana and Anglo women.* San Francisco: R & E Research Associates, 1974.

CARTER, D. K. Counseling divorced women. *Personnel and Guidance Journal,* 1977, *55,* 537–541.

CARTER, H., and GLICK, P. C. *Marriage and divorce: A social and economic study,* second edition. Cambridge, Mass.: Harvard University Press, 1976.

CENTRA, J. *Women, men, and the doctorate.* Princeton, N.J.: Educational Testing Service, 1974.

CHAFE, W. H. *Women and equality: Changing patterns in American culture.* Oxford: Oxford University Press, 1977.

CHAMBERS, C. D., INCIARDI, J. A., and SIEGAL, H. A. *Chemical coping: A report on legal drug use in the U.S.* New York: Spectrum Publications, 1975.

CHESLER, P. *Women and madness.* Garden City, New York: Doubleday, 1972.

CHESLER, P., and GOODMAN, E. J. *Women, money, and power.* New York: Bantam Books, 1976.

CHRISTANSEN, E. W. When counseling Puerto Ricans. *Personnel and Guidance Journal,* 1977, *55,* 412–415.

CHRISTENSEN, R. A. Indian women: An historical and personal perspective. *Pupil Personnel Services Journal,* Minnesota Department of Education, 1975, *4,* 12–22.

CHUMBLEY, P. Social problems of the urban Indian. Paper presented at Workshop IV on Indian Suicide and Alcoholism, National Congress of American Indians, January, 1973, Phoenix, Ariz.

Civil Liberties Review. Quotes famous and infamous on women and their rights. May/June, 1977, 61.

CLARK, D. *Loving someone gay.* New York: New American Library, 1977.

CLARK, T. P. Counseling victims of rape. *American Journal of Nursing,* 1976, *76,* 1964–1966.

COE, R. Professional perspectives on the aged. *Gerontologist,* 1967, *7,* 114–119.

Bibliography

COLLIER, H. V. *Freeing ourselves: Removing internal barriers to equality.* Newton, Mass.: Education Development Center, 1982.

CONDRY, J., and DYER, S. Fear of success: Attribution of causes to the victim. *Journal of Social Issues*, 1976, *32*, 63–83.

CONNELL, N., and CASSANDRA, W. (Eds.). *Rape: The first sourcebook for women.* New York: The New American Library, Inc., 1974.

CONSTANTINE, I. L., and CONSTANTINE, J. H. Sexual aspects of multilateral relations. In J. R. Smith and L. G. Smith (Eds.), *Beyond Monogamy.* Baltimore: The John Hopkins University Press, 1974.

COOKE, C. W., and DWORKIN, S. *The Ms. guide to a woman's health.* Garden City, New York: Doubleday, 1979.

COOPERSTOCK, R. Sex differences in the use of mood-modifying drugs: An explanatory model. *Journal of Health and Social Behavior*, 1971, *12*, 238–244.

COPELAND, E. Counseling black women with negative self-concepts. *Personnel and Guidance Journal*, 1977, *55*, 397–400.

COSTRICH, N., FEINSTEIN, J., KIDDER, L., MARECEK, J., and PASCALE, L. When stereotypes hurt: Three studies of penalties for sex-role reversals. *Journal of Experimental Social Psychology*, 1975, *11*, 520–530.

The Counseling Psychologist. Principles concerning the counseling and therapy of women. 1979, *8*, 21.

COX, S. (Ed.). *Female psychology: The emerging self.* Chicago: Science Research Associates, 1976.

CRITES, J. O. Review of the self-directed search. In O. K. Buros (Ed.), *The eighth mental measurements yearbook.* Highland Park, N.J.: Gryphon Press, 1978.

———. Review of the Strong–Campbell Interest Inventory. In O. K. Buros (Ed.), *The eighth mental measurements yearbook.* Highland Park, N.J.: Gryphon Press, 1978.

CRITES, L. (Ed.). *The female offender.* Lexington, Mass.: Lexington Books, 1976.

CRUZ, C. Chicana. *Youth Authority Quarterly*, 1976, *29*, 23–24.

CURLEE, J. Alcoholism and the "empty nest." *Bulletin of the Menninger Clinic*, 1969, *33*, 165–171.

———. A comparison of male and female patients at an alcoholism treatment center. *Journal of Psychology*, 1970, *74*, 239–247.

———. Sex differences in patient attitude toward alcoholism treatment. *Quarterly Journal of Studies on Alcohol*, 1971, *32*, 643–650.

———. Women alcoholics. *Federal Probation*, 1968, *32*, 16–20.

DARLEY, S. A. Big-time careers for the little woman: A dual-role dilemma. *Journal of Social Issues*, 1976, *32*, 85–98.

DEAUX, K. *The behavior of women and men.* Monterey, Ca.: Brooks/Cole, 1976.

DE BEAUVOIR, S. *The coming of age.* New York: Warner Books, 1970.

———. *The second sex.* New York: Knopf, 1952.

DELANEY, D. J., and EISENBERG, S. *The counseling process.* Chicago: Rand McNally College Publishing Company, 1972.

DELK, J. L., and RYAN, T. T. Sex-role stereotyping and A–B therapist status: Who is more chauvinistic? *Journal of Consulting and Clinical Psychology*, 1975, *43*, 589.

Bibliography

THE DIAGRAM GROUP. *Woman's body: An owner's manual.* New York: Grosset and Dunlap, 1977.

DINKMEYER, D., and McKAY, G. *Raising a responsible child.* New York: Simon & Schuster, 1973.

DONAHUE, T. J. Counselor discrimination against women: Additional information. *Journal of Counseling Psychology,* 1979, *26,* 276–278.

DONAHUE, T. J., and COSTAR, J. W. Counselor discrimination against young women in career selection. *Journal of Counseling Psychology,* 1977, *24,* 481–486.

DOUVAN, E. Employment and the adolescent. In F. I. Nye and L. W. Hoffman (Eds.), *The employed mother in America.* Chicago: Rand McNally, 1963.

——. The single parent: Challenges and opportunities. In R. K. Lorring and H. A. Otto (Eds.), *New life options: The working woman's resource book.* New York: McGraw-Hill, 1976.

DUNCAN, O., FEATHERMAN, D., and DUNCAN, B. *Socioeconomic background and achievement.* New York: Seminar Press, 1972.

DWECK, C. S. Children's interpretation of evaluative feedback: The effect of social cues on learned helplessness. *Merrill-Palmer Quarterly,* 1976, *22,* 105–110.

DWECK, C. S., and BUSH, E. S. Sex differences in learned helplessness: Differential debilitation with peer and adult evaluators. *Journal of Developmental Psychology,* 1976, *12,* 147–156.

EHRENREICH, B., and EHRENREICH, J. *The American health empire: Power, profits, and politics.* New York: Vintage, 1971.

EHRENREICH, B., and ENGLISH, D. *Witches, midwives and nurses: A history of women healers.* Old Westburg, N.Y.: Feminist Press, 1973.

EISENBERG, S., and MICKLOW, P. The assaulted wife: "Catch 22" revisited. *Women's Rights Law Reporter,* 1977.

EPSTEIN, C. F. Positive effects of the multiple negative: Explaining the success of black professional women. *American Journal of Sociology,* 1973, *78,* 912–935.

——. *Woman's place: Options and limits in professional careers.* Berkeley: University of California Press, 1970.

ERIKSON, E. H. *Childhood and society.* New York: Norton, 1963.

——. *Identity: Youth and crisis.* New York: Norton, 1968.

——. The inner and the outer space: Reflections on womanhood. *Daedalus,* 1964, *93,* 582–606.

ERVIN, C. J. Psychologic adjustment to mastectomy. *Medical Aspects of Human Sexuality,* 1973, *7,* 42–65.

FABRIKANT, B. The psychotherapist and the female patient: Perceptions, misconceptions and change. In V. Franks and V. Burtle (Eds.), *Women in therapy.* New York: Brunner/Mazel, 1974.

FADEM, S. S. Facts and figures to help you put price tags on kids. *The Herald-Telephone,* Bloomington, In., January 18, 1980, 15.

FALK, W. W., and COSBY, A. G. Women's marital–familial statuses and work histories: Some conceptual considerations. *Journal of Vocational Behavior,* 1978, *13,* 126–140.

FARMER, H. S. Learning the guided inquiry procedure: The six steps of guided inquiry. In N. C. Seltz and H. V. Collier (Eds.), *Meeting the educational and occupational planning needs of adults*. Bloomington, In.: Indiana University, 1976 (ERIC Document Reproduction Service No. 143–885).

——. Career counseling implications for the lower social class and women. *Personnel and Guidance Journal*, 1978, 56, 467–471.

FARMER, H. S., and BACKER, T. E. *New career options for women: A counselor's sourcebook.* New York: Human Sciences Press, 1977.

FARRELL, W. *The liberated man.* New York: Random House, 1974.

FAST, J. *Body language.* New York: Pocket Books, 1971.

——. *Body politics: How to get power with class.* New York: Tower Books, 1980.

FEATHER, N. T., and SIMON, J. G. Reactions to male and female success and failures in sex-linked occupations. *Journal of Personality and Social Psychology*, 1975, *31*, 20–31.

FEE, E. Women and health care: A comparison of theories. *International Journal of Health Services*, 1975, 5, 397–415.

Female Offender Resource Center. *Female offenders: Problems and programs.* Washington, D.C.: American Bar Association, 1976.

——. *Little sisters and the law.* Washington, D.C.: American Bar Association, 1977.

FERBER, M. A., and LOWRY, H. M. Women: The new reserve army of the unemployed. In M. Blaxall and B. Reagan (Eds.), *Women and the workplace: The implications of occupation segregation.* Chicago: The University of Chicago Press, 1976.

FERSTER, C. B. Behavioral approaches to depression. In R. J. Friedman and M. M. Katz (Eds.), *The psychology of depression: Contemporary theory and research.* Washington, D.C.: V. H. Winston and Sons, 1974.

FETTERS, W. B. *Student questionnaire and test results by sex, high school program, ethnic category, and father's education: National longitudinal study of high school class of 1972.* Washington, D.C.: U.S. Government Printing Office, 1975.

FITZGERALD, L. F., and CRITES, J. O. Career counseling for women: Standards for counseling. *The Counseling Psychologist*, 1979, 8, 33–34.

——. Toward a career psychology of women: What do we know? What do we need to know? *Journal of Counseling Psychology*, 1980, *27*, 44–62.

FONTAINE, D. *A chance and a choice.* St. Paul, Mn.: Association of Halfway House Alcoholism Programs of North America, 1975.

FRANKEL, L. J. Sex discrimination in the criminal law: The equal rights admendment. *American Criminal Law Review*, Winter 1973, 469–510.

FRANKEL, M. M., and HARRISON, F. W. *Projections: Education statistics to 1985–86.* Washington, D.C.: U.S. Government Printing Office, 1977 (National Center for Education Statistics publication 77–402).

FRANKS, V., and BURTLE, V. (Eds.). *Women in therapy.* New York: Brunner/Mazel, 1974.

FRASER, J. The female alcoholic. *Addictions*, 1973, *20*, 64–80.

FREDERICK, C. J. *Suicide, homicide, and alcoholism among American Indians: Guidelines for help.* Washington, D.C.: National Institute of Mental Health, 1973 (U.S. Department of Health, Education and Welfare, ADM No. 76–42).

Bibliography

FREDERICK, V., FRETTA, N., and LEVIN-FRANK, S. Women mental health consultants: "Cutie pies or libbers?" *Psychiatric Opinion*, 1976, *13*, 26–32.

FRIEDAN, B. *The feminine mystique*. New York: Dell Publishing, 1963.

FRIEDERSDORF, W. W. A comparative study of counselor attitudes toward the further educational and vocational plans of high school girls. *Dissertation Abstracts International*, 1970, *30*, 4220–4221.

FRIEZE, I. H. Women: Expectations for and causal attributions of success and failure. In M. T. S. Mednick, S. S. Tangri, and L. W. Hoffman (Eds.), *Women and achievement*. New York: Wiley, 1975.

FRIEZE, I., FISHER, J., McHUGH, M., and VALLE, V. Attributing the causes of success and failure: Internal and external barriers to achievement in women. Paper presented at conference on *New Directions for Research on Women*, Madison, Wisc., 1975.

FRIEZE, I. H., and RAMSEY, S. J. Nonverbal maintenance of traditional sex roles. *Journal of Social Issues*, 1976, *32*, 133–141.

FUJITOMI, I., and WONG, D. The new Asian American woman. In S. Cox (Ed.), *Female psychology: The emerging self*. Chicago: Science Research Associates, 1976.

GARFINKLE, S. H. Occupations of women and black workers, 1962–74. *Monthly Labor Review*, 1975, 98, 25–35.

GARNETS, L., and PLECK, J. H. Sex role identity, androgyny, and sex role transcendence: A sex role strain analysis. *Psychology of Women Quarterly*, 1979, *3*, 270–283.

GEBHARD, P. H. Incidence of overt homosexuality in the United States and Western Europe. In J. M. Livingood (Ed.), *National Institute of Mental Health task force on homosexuality: Final report and background papers*. Washington, D.C.: U.S. Government Printing Office, 1972.

GELLES, R. J. Abused wives: Why do they stay? *Journal of Marriage and the Family*, 1976, *38*, 659–668.

GILBERT, L. A., and WALDROOP, J. Evaluation of a procedure for increasing sex-fair counseling. *Journal of Counseling Psychology*, 1978, *25*, 410–418.

GILLESPIE, D. L. Who has the power? The marital struggle. In S. Cox (Ed.), *Female psychology: The emerging self*. Chicago: Science Research Associates, 1976.

GILLIGAN, C. Woman's place in man's life cycle. Paper distributed by Center for Research on Women, Wellesley College, October, 1978.

GLASER, D. *Positive addiction*. New York: Harper & Row, 1976.

GLICK, P. C. *The future of the American family*. Washington, D.C.: U.S. Government Printing Office, 1979 (U.S. Bureau of the Census, Current population reports, Special studies, Series P-23, No. 78).

GLICK, R. M. *National study of women's correctional programs*. Washington, D.C.: U.S. Government Printing Office, 1977.

GOLD, D., and ANDRES, D. *Relations between maternal employment and development of nursery school children*. (ERIC Document Reproduction Service No. 135–461)

GOLDBERG, P. A. Are women prejudiced against women? *Transaction*, 1968, *5*, 28–30.

GOLDMAN, N., and RAVID, R. Community surveys: Sex differences in mental illness. In M. Guttentag, S. Salasin and D. Belle (Eds.), *The mental health of women*. New York: Academic Press, 1980.

Bibliography

GOODE, E., and HABER, L. Sexual correlates of homosexual experience: An exploratory study. *The Journal of Sex Research, 1977, 13,* 12–21.

GORDON, L. The politics of birth control, 1920–1940: The impact of professionals. *International Journal of Health Services,* 1975, *5,* 253–277.

GORNICK, V., and MORAN, B. K. *Women in sexist society.* New York: Signet, 1972.

GOULD, R. L. *Transformations: Growth and change in adult life.* New York: Simon & Schuster, 1978.

GOVE, W., and TUDOR, J. Adult sex roles and mental illness. *American Journal of Sociology,* 1973, *78,* 812–835.

GRIFFITHS, M. W. Can we still afford occupational segregation? Some remarks. In M. Blaxall and B. Reagan (Eds.), *Women and the work place.* Chicago: University of Chicago Press, 1976.

GROSSMAN, A. S. Women in the labor force: The early years. *Monthly Labor Review,* 1975, *98,* 3–9.

GUMP, J. P., and RIVERS, L. W. The consideration of race in efforts to end sex bias. In E. E. Diamond (Ed.), *Issues of sex bias and sex fairness in career interest measurement.* Washington, D.C.: Department of Health, Education, and Welfare, 1975.

GURIN, P., and EPPS, E. *Black consciousness, identity, and achievement.* New York: Wiley, 1975.

GUTMAN, H. G. *The black family in slavery and freedom, 1750–1925.* New York: Pantheon Books, 1976.

GUTTENTAG, M., SALASIN, S., and BELLE, D. (Eds.).*The mental health of women.* New York: Academic Press, 1980.

GUTTMAN, D. Female ego styles and generational conflict. In E. L. Walker (Ed.), *Feminine personality and conflict.* Monterey, Ca.: Brooks/Cole, 1970.

HACHER, H. M. Class and race differences in gender roles. In L. Duberman (Ed.), *Gender and sex in society.* New York: Praeger, 1975.

HALL, D. T. Pressures from work, self, and home in the life stages of married women. *Journal of Vocational Behavior,* 1975, *6,* 121–132.

HAMLIN, D. E., Hurwitz, D. B., and SPIEKER, G. Perspectives: Family violence. *Alcohol Health and Research World,* 1979, *4,* 17–22.

HAMMER, S. *Daughters and mothers: Mothers and daughters.* New York: Signet Books, New American Library, 1976.

HANSON, R. O. Maternal employment and androgyny. *Psychology of Women Quarterly,* 1977, *2,* 76–78.

HARE, N., and HARE, J. Black women in 1970. In J. M. Bardwick (Ed.), *Readings on the psychology of women.* New York: Harper & Row, 1972.

HARKNESS, C. C. *Career counseling: Dreams and reality.* Springfield, Ill.: Charles C Thomas, 1976.

HARRAGAN, B. L. *Games mother never taught you: Corporate gamesmanship for women.* New York: Rawson Associate Publishers, Inc., 1977.

HARRISON, C. *Working women speak: Education, training, counseling.* Washington, D.C.: National Advisory Council on Women's Educational Programs, 1979.

HART, D. Enlarging the American dream. *American Education,* 1977, *13,* 10–16.

Bibliography

HARWAY, M. Sex bias in counseling materials. *Journal of College Student Personnel*, 1977, *18*, 57–63.

HARWAY, M., and ASTIN, H. S. *Sex discrimination in career counseling and education*. New York: Praeger, 1977.

HARWAY, M., ASTIN, H. S., SUHR, J. M., and WHITELEY, J. M. *Sex discrimination in guidance and counseling*. Washington, D.C.: National Center for Education Statistics, U.S. Department of Health, Education and Welfare, 1976.

HAUN, L. E. *A study of U.S. counselor educators by sex* (The Commission for Women 1973–74 Report Summary). Washington, D.C.: American Personnel and Guidance Association, 1974.

HAVIGHURST, R. J., and NEUGARTEN, B. L. *Society and education*, third edition. Boston: Allyn & Bacon, Inc., 1967.

HAWLEY, P. What women think men think: Does it affect their career choices? *Journal of Counseling Psychology*, 1971, *18*, 193–199.

HAZELL, L. D. *Commonsense childbirth*. New York: G. P. Putman's Sons, 1969.

HECKMAN, N. A. Problems of professional couples: A content analysis. *Journal of Marriage and the Family*, 1977, *39*, 323–330.

HEDGES, J. N., and BARNETT, K. Working women and the division of household tasks. *Monthly Labor Review*, 1972, *95*, 9–14.

HEFNER, R., REBECCA, M., and OLESHANSKY, B. Development of sex-role transcendence. *Human Development*, 1975, *18*, 143–156.

HEILBRUN, A. B., JR. and THOMPSON, N. L., JR. Sex-role identity and male and female homosexuality. *Sex Roles*, 1977, *3*, 65–79.

HENLEY, N. M. Status and sex: Some touching observations. *Bulletin of the Psychometric Society*, 1973, *2*, 91–93.

HENNIG, M., and JARDIM, A. *The managerial woman*. Garden City, New York: Anchor Press/Doubleday, 1977.

HINDMAN, M. H. Family violence: An overview. *Alcohol Health and Research World*, 1979, *4*, 2–11.

HITE, S. *The Hite report: A nationwide study on female sexuality*. New York: Macmillan Publishing Company, Inc., 1976.

HOLLAND, J. L. *The psychology of vocational choice*. Waltham, Mass.: Blaisdell, 1966.

HOLMES, D., and JORGENSON, B. Do personality and social psychologists study men more than women? *Representative Research in Social Psychology*, 1971, *2*, 71–76.

HOMILLER, J. D. *Women and alcohol: A guide for state and local decision makers*. Washington, D.C.: Alcohol and Drug Problems Association of North America, 1977.

HOOPER, M. E. *Associate degrees and other formal awards below the baccalaureate, 1970–71*. Washington, D.C.: U.S. Government Printing Office, 1973 (National Center for Education Statistics).

HOPKINS, J. H. A comparison of wives in dual-career and single-career families. *Dissertation Abstracts International*, 1977 (University Microfilms No. 77-16, 583).

HORN, J. L., and WANBERG, K. W. Females are different: On the diagnosis of alcoholism in women. Proceedings of the First Annual Alcoholism Conference of the National Institute on Alcohol Abuse and Alcoholism, June, 1971. Washington, D.C.: Department of Health, Education and Welfare, 1973, 332–354.

Bibliography

HORNER, M. The motive to avoid success and changing aspirations of college women. In J. M. Bardwick (Ed.), *Readings on the psychology of women.* New York: Harper & Row, 1972.

HORNEY, K. *Feminine psychology.* New York: Norton, 1973.

HOWE, L. K. *Pink collar workers: Inside the world of women's work.* New York: G. P. Putnam's Sons, 1977.

HUNGERFORD, N., and PAOLUCCI, B. The employed female single parent. *Journal of Home Economics,* 1977, 69, 10–13.

HUNT, J. G., and HUNT, L. L. Dilemmas and contradictions of status: The case of the dual-career family. *Social Problems,* 1977, 24, 407–416.

IGLITZEN, L. B. A child's eye view of sex roles. In *Sex-role stereotyping in the schools.* Washington, D.C.: National Education Association, 1973.

ILLFELDER, J. K. Fear of success, sex role attitudes, and career salience and anxiety levels of college women. *Journal of Vocational Behavior,* 1980, 16, 7–17.

JACKSON, R. Some aspirations of lower class black mothers. *Journal of Comparative Family Studies,* 1975, 6, 171–181.

JANEWAY, E. *Between myth and morning: Women awakening.* New York: Morrow, 1974.

———. *Man's world, women's place.* New York: Delta Books, 1971.

———. The weak are the second sex. In U. West (Ed.), *Women in a changing world.* New York: McGraw-Hill, 1975.

JEFFRIES, D. Counseling for the strengths of the black woman. *Counseling Psychologist,* 1976, 6, 20–22.

JENSEN, J. M. Native American women and agriculture: A Seneca case study. *Journal of Sex Roles,* 1977, 3, 423–441.

JOHNSON, C. L., and JOHNSON, F. A. Attitudes toward parenting in dual-career families. *American Journal of Psychiatry,* 1977, 134, 391–395.

JOHNSON, M., and SCARATO, A. M. A knowledge base for counselors of women. *The Counseling Psychologist,* 1979, 8, 14–16.

JOHNSON, P. Women and power: Toward a theory of effectiveness. *Journal of Social Issues,* 1976, 32, 99–110.

JOHNSON, R. W. Relationships between female and male interest scales for the same occupations. *Journal of Vocational Behavior,* 1977, 11, 239–252.

KAGAN, J. Acquisition and significance of sex-typing and sex-role identity. In M. L. Hoffman and L. W. Hoffman (Eds.), *Review of Child Development Research.* New York: Russell Sage Foundation, 1964.

KAHL, J. *The American class structure.* New York: Rinehart & Company, 1957.

KANE, F. J. Iatrogenic depression in women. In W. Fann (Ed.), *Phenomenology and treatment of depression.* New York: Spectrum, 1977.

KANTER, R. M. *Men and women of the corporation.* New York: Basic Books, 1979.

KAPLAN, A. G. Clarifying the concept of androgyny: Implications for therapy. *Psychology of Women Quarterly,* Spring 1979, 3, 223–230.

KAPLAN, H. S. *The new sex therapy.* New York: Brunner/Mazel, 1974.

KASPER, A. S. Breast cancer: Alternatives to radical mastectomy. *Spokeswoman,* 1979, 9 (14), 5.

Bibliography

KENWORTHY, J. A. Androgyny in psychotherapy: Will it sell in Peoria? *Psychology of Women Quarterly*, 1979, *3*, 231–240.

KENWORTHY, J. A., KOUFACOS, C., and SHERMAN, J. Women and therapy: A survey of internship programs. *Psychology of Women Quarterly*, 1976, *1*, 125–137.

KIM, BOK-LIM C. Asian wives of U.S. service men: Women in shadows. *Amerasia*, 1977, *4*, 91–115.

KINSEY, A. C., POMEROY, W. B., MARTIN, C. E., and GEBHARD, P. H. *Sexual behavior in the human female*. Philadelphia: W. B. Saunders, 1953.

KIRK, W. Where are you? Black mental health model. *Journal of Non-White Concerns*, 1975, *3*, 177–188.

KLEIMAN, C. *Women's networks: The complete guide to getting a better job, advancing your career, and feeling great as a woman through networking*. New York: Lippincott & Crowell, 1980.

KLEIN, M. H. Feminist concepts of therapy outcomes. *Psychotherapy: Theory, Research, and Practice*, 1976, *13*, 89–95.

KLERMAN, G. L., and WEISSMAN, M. M. Depressions among women: Their nature and causes. In M. Guttentag, S. Salasin, and D. Belle (Eds.), *The mental health of women*. New York: Academic Press, 1980.

KOONTZ, B. *Public hearings on women and girl offenders*. Washington, D.C.: Commission of the Status of Women, November 4, 1971.

KRONSKY, B. J. Feminism and psychotherapy. *Journal of Contemporary Psychotherapy*, 1971, *3*, 89–98.

KRUMBOLTZ, J. D., and THORENSEN, C. E. *Behavioral counseling: Cases and techniques*. New York: Holt, Rinehart & Winston, 1969.

KÜBLER-ROSS, E. *On death and dying*. New York: Macmillan, 1969.

KUNDSIN, R. B. (Ed.). *Women and success: The anatomy of achievement*. New York: William Morrow, 1974.

LADNER, J. A. *Tomorrow's tomorrow: The black woman*. Garden City: Doubleday & Company, 1971.

LANGLEY, R., and LEVY, R. *Wife beating: The silent crisis*. New York: E. P. Dutton, 1977.

L'ARMEND, K., and PEPITONE, A. Helping to reward another person: A cross-cultural analysis. *Journal of Personality and Social Psychology*, 1975, *31*, 189–198.

LA RUE, L. The black movement and women's liberation. In S. Cox (Ed.), *Female psychology: The emerging self*. Chicago: Science Research Associates, 1974.

LE BOYER, F. *Birth without violence*. New York: Alfred A. Knopf, Inc., 1975.

LEGHORN, L. Social response to battered women. Speech given at Wisconsin Conference on Battered Women, October, 1976.

LEVINE, S. V., KAMIN, L. E., and LEVINE, E. L. Sexism and psychiatry: Theory and review. *American Journal of Orthopsychiatry*, 1974, *44*, 327–336.

LEVINSON, D. *The seasons of a man's life*. New York: Alfred A. Knopf, 1978.

LEVY, B. Sex-role socialization in schools. In *Sex-role stereotyping in the schools*. Washington, D.C.: National Education Association, 1973.

LEWINSOHN, P. M. A behavioral approach to depression. In R. J. Friedman and M. M. Katz

Bibliography

(Eds.), *The psychology of depression: Contemporary theory and research.* Washington, D.C.: V. H. Winston, 1974.

Lewis, M. There's no unisex in the nursery. *Psychology Today*, 1973, 46–49.

Lipman-Blumen, J. How ideology shapes women's lives. *Scientific American*, 1972, *226*, 34–42.

——. The implications for family structure of changing sex roles. *Social Casework*, February 1976, 67–78.

——. Toward a homosocial theory of sex-roles: An explanation of the sex segregation of social institutions. In M. Blaxall and B. Reagan (Eds.), *Women and the workplace.* Chicago: University of Chicago Press, 1976.

Lipman-Blumen, J., and Tickamyer, A. R. Sex roles in transition: A ten-year perspective. *Annual Review of Sociology*, 1975, *1*, 297–337.

Lisansky, E. S. Alcoholism in women: Social and psychological concomitants. I. Social history data. *Quarterly Journal of Studies on Alcohol*, 1957, *18*, 588–623.

Lopata, H. Z. The effect of schooling on social contacts of urban women. *American Journal of Sociology*, 1973, *79*, 604–691.

——. *Widowhood in an American city.* Cambridge: Schenkman Publishing, 1973.

Lowenthal, M. F. Psychosocial variations across the adult life course: Frontiers for research and policy. *Gerontologist*, 1975, *15*, 6–12.

Lowenthal, M. F., Thurnher, M., Chiriboga, D., and associates. *Four stages of life: A comparative study of women and men facing transitions.* San Francisco: Jossey-Bass, 1976.

Lunneborg, P. W. Sex and career decision-making styles. *Journal of Counseling Psychology*, 1978, *25*, 299–305.

Lyman, H. B. Changes in self-image of divorced women taking single again course, 1976 (ERIC Document Reproduction Service No. ED 136–158).

Maccoby, E. E., and Jacklin, C. N. *The psychology of sex differences.* Stanford, Ca.: Stanford University Press, 1974.

Maccoby, E. E., and Masters, J. Attachment and dependency. In P. Mussen (Ed.), *Carmichael's manual of child psychology*, Vol. 2. New York: Wiley, 1970.

Mack, D. E. Where the black matriarchy theorists went wrong. *Psychology Today*, January, 1971, 86–87.

Manpower Report to the President, 1975. *The changing economic role of women.* Washington, D.C.: U.S. Government Printing Office, 1975.

Marecek, J. Social change, positive mental health, and psychological androgyny. *Psychology of Women Quarterly*, 1979, *3*, 241–247.

Marieskind, H. The women's health movement. *International Journal of Health Services*, 1975, *5*, 217–223.

Martin, D. *Battered wives.* San Francisco: Glide Publications, 1976.

Martin, D., and Lyon, P. *Lesbian/woman.* New York: Bantam Books, 1972.

Maslin, A., and Davis, J. L. Sex-role stereotyping as a factor in mental health standards among counselors-in-training. *Journal of Counseling Psychology*, 1975, *22*, 87–91.

Maslow, A. H. *Motivation and personality.* New York: Harper & Row, 1954.

——. Self-esteem and sexuality in women. *Journal of Social Psychology*, 1942, *16*, 259–294.

——. *Toward a psychology of being*, second edition. New York: D. Van Nostrand, 1968.

Bibliography

MASTERS, W., and JOHNSON, V. *Human sexual inadequacy.* Boston: Little, Brown, 1970.

——. Human sexual response: The aging female and the aging male. In B. Neugarten (Ed.), *Middle age and aging.* Chicago: University of Chicago Press, 1968.

MATTHEWS, E., and TIEDEMAN, D. Attitudes towards marriage and career and the development of life style in young women. *Journal of Counseling Psychology,* 1964, *11,* 375–384.

MAXFIELD, M. Toward a feminist perspective in alcohol studies. Paper prepared for the Sessions on Women and Alcoholism, National Council on Alcohol Forum, Washington, D.C., Spring, 1979.

MEAD, M. *Coming of age in Samoa.* New York: William Morrow, 1932.

——. *Male and female.* New York: William Morrow, 1949.

——. On Freud's view of female psychology. In J. Strouse (Ed.), *Women and analysis.* New York: Grossman, 1974.

MEDNICK, M., and PURYEAR, G. Race and fear of success in college women: 1968 and 1971. *Journal of Consulting and Clinical Psychology,* 1976, *44,* 787–789.

MEDVENE, A. M., and COLLINS, A. M. Occupational prestige and appropriateness: The views of mental health specialists. *Journal of Vocational Behavior,* 1976, *9,* 63–71.

MILLER, J. B. *Toward a new psychology of women.* Boston, Mass.: Beacon Press, 1976.

MILLER, S., NUNNALLY, E. W., and WACKMAN, D. B. *Alive and aware: Improving communication in relationships.* Minneapolis, Minn.: Interpersonal Communications Programs, Inc., 1975.

MINUCHIN, S. *Families & family therapy.* Cambridge, Mass.: Harvard University Press, 1974.

MISCHEL, W. Sex-typing and socialization. In P. Mussen (Ed.), *Carmichael's manual of child psychology,* Vol. 2. New York: Wiley, 1970.

MONEY, J., and EHRHARDT, A. *Man and woman, boy and girl.* Baltimore: The Johns Hopkins University Press, 1972.

MORGAN, M. *The total woman.* Old Tappan, N.J.: Fleming H. Revell Company, 1973.

MOULTON, R. Some effects of the new feminism. *American Journal of Psychiatry,* 1977, *134,* 1–6.

MURRAY, S., and MEDNICK, M. Black women's achievement orientation. *Psychology of Women Quarterly,* 1977, *1,* 247–259.

McCANDLESS, B. R. Childhood socialization. In D. A. Goslin (Ed.), *Handbook of socialization theory and research.* Chicago: Rand McNally and Company, 1969.

McCONNELL, H. Study profiles: Substance abuse by women. *The Journal* (Addiction Research Foundation of Ontario), June, 1978, 9.

McEADDY, B. J. Women who head families: A socioeconomic analysis. *Monthly Labor Review,* 1976, *99,* 3–9.

National Commission on Working Women Fact Sheet. An overview of women in the workforce. Washington, D.C.: Center for Women and Work, 1979.

NEUGARTEN, B. L. (Ed.). *Middle age and aging.* Chicago, Ill.: University of Chicago Press, 1968.

——. The psychology of aging: An overview. *JSAS Catalog of Selected Documents in Psychology,* 1976, *6,* 97 (Ms. No. 1340).

———. Adaption and the life cycle. In N. K. Schlossberg and A. D. Entine (Eds.), *Counseling adults*. Monterey, Ca.: Brooks/Cole, 1977.

NEUGARTEN, B. L., and GUTTMAN, D. L. Age-sex roles and personality in middle age: A thematic apperception study. In B. L. Neugarten (Ed.), *Middle age and aging*. Chicago: University of Chicago Press, 1968.

———. (Eds.). *Personality in middle and late life*. New York: Atherton, 1964.

NEUGARTEN, B. L., MOORE, J. C., and LOWE, J. C. Age norms, age constraints, and adult-socialization. *American Journal of Sociology*, 1965, *70*, 710–717.

NIETO-GOMEZ, A. Heritage of La Hembra. In S. Cox (Ed.), *Female psychology: The emerging self*. Chicago: Science Research Associates, 1976.

NORRIS, G., and MILLER, J. A. *The working mother's complete handbook*. New York: E. P. Dutton, 1979.

OBERSTONE, A., and SUKONECK, H. Psychological adjustment and life style of single lesbians and single heterosexual women. *Psychology of Women Quarterly*, 1976, *1*, 172–188.

O'LEARY, V. E. *Toward understanding women*. Monterey, Ca.: Brooks/Cole, 1977.

O'LEARY, V., and HARRISON, A. Sex role stereotypes as a function of race and sex. Paper presented at Annual Meeting of American Psychological Association, Chicago, 1975.

OLIVER, L. Principles drafted for therapy and counseling with women. *APA Monitor*, 1978, December, 11.

O'NEIL, J. M., MEEKER, C. H., and BORGERS, S. B. A developmental, preventive, and consultative model to reduce sexism in the career planning of women. *Catalog of Selected Documents in Psychology*, 1978, *8*, 39.

O'NEILL, N., and O'NEILL, G. *Open marriage: A new life style for couples*. New York: M. Evans and Company, 1972.

OSIPOW, S. H. *Emerging woman: Career analysis and outlooks*. Columbus, Ohio: Merrill, 1975.

OTT, M. D. *Analysis of doctor's degrees awarded to men and to women, 1970–71 through 1974*. Washington, D.C.: U.S. Government Printing Office, 1977 (National Center for Education Statistics publication 77-333).

PADILLA, A. M., and RUIZ, R. A. *Latino mental health: A review of literature*. Washington, D.C.: U.S. Government Printing Office, 1976 (U.S. Department of Health, Education and Welfare No. ADM 76-113).

PAIGE, K. E. Women learn to sing the menstrual blues. *Psychology Today*, 1973, *7*, 41–46.

PAINTER, D. H. The black woman in American society. *Current History*, 1976, *70*, 221–234.

PANCOAST, R. E. The new feminist ego-ideal: Its function in feminist therapy. Scientific Proceedings in Summary Form: 128th Annual Meeting, American Psychiatric Association, 1975.

PARLEE, M. Psychological aspects of menstruation, childbirth, and menopause: An overview with suggestions for further research. Presented at the Conference on *New Directions for Research on Women*, Madison, Wisc., May 31–June 2, 1975.

PARSONS, J. E., FRIEZE, I. H., RUBLE, D. N., and CROKE, J. *Intrapsychic factors influencing career aspirations in college women*. Unpublished manuscript, 1975.

PATTERSON, L. E. Girl's careers: Expression of identity. *Vocational Guidance Quarterly*, 1973, *21*, 268–275.

Bibliography

PENDERGRASS, V. E. Sex discrimination counseling. *American Psychologist*, 1975, *31*, 36–46.

PEPLAU, L. A., COCHRAN, S., ROOK, K., and PADESKY, C. Loving women: Attachment and autonomy in lesbian relationships. *Journal of Social Issues*, 1978, *34*, 7–27.

PERLS, F. S. *Ego, hunger and aggression.* New York: Vintage Books, 1969.

PIETROFESA, J. J., and SCHLOSSBERG, N. K. Counselor bias and female occupational role, 1970 (ERIC Document Reproduction Service No. ED 044–749).

PIZZEY, E. *Scream quietly or the neighbors will hear.* Short Hills, N.J.: Erin Pizzey-Ridley Enslow Publishers, 1977.

PLECK, J. H. The male sex role: Definitions, problems and sources of change. *Journal of Social Issues*, 1976, *32*, 155–164.

———. Men's family work: Three perspectives and some new data. *The Family Coordinator*, October, 1979, 481–488.

———. The work–family role system. *Social Problems*, 1977, *24*, 417–427.

POLK, B. B. Male power and the women's movement. *Journal of Applied Behavioral Science*, 1974, *10*, 415–431.

POLOMA, M. M., and GARLAND, T. N. The myth of the egalitarian family: Familial roles and the professionally employed wife. In A. Theodore (Ed.), *The professional woman.* Cambridge, Mass.: Schenkman, 1971.

POLSTER, E., and POLSTER, M. *Gestalt therapy integrated: Contours of theory and practice.* New York: Brunner/Mazel, 1973.

POWELL, B. The empty nest, employment, and psychiatric symptoms in college-educated women. *Psychology of Women Quarterly*, 1977, *2*, 35–43.

PRATHER, J., and FIDELL, L. Sex differences in the content and style of medical advertisements. *Social Science and Medicine*, 1975, *9*, 23–26.

PREDIGER, D. J., and LAMB, R. R. The validity of sex-balanced and sex-restrictive vocational interest reports: A comparison. *Vocational Guidance Quarterly*, 1979, *28*, 16–24.

PRICE, R. R. The forgotten female offender. *Crime and Delinquency*, 1977, *23*, 101–108.

RADLOFF, L. S. Sex differences in depression: The effects of occupation and marital status. *Journal of Sex Roles*, 1975, *1*, 249–265.

RAMIREZ, M., III. Identification with Mexican family values and authoritarianism in Mexican-Americans. *Journal of Social Psychology*, 1967, *73*, 3–11.

RAPOPORT, R., and RAPOPORT, R. N. (Eds.). *Working couples.* New York: Harper Colophon Books, 1978.

RATHOD, H., and THOMSON, I. G. Women alcoholics. *Quarterly Journal of Studies on Alcohol*, 1971, *32*, 45–52.

RAVEN, B. H. Social influence and power. In I. D. Steiner and M. Fishbein (Eds.), *Current studies in social psychology.* New York: Holt, 1965.

RAWLINGS, E. I., and CARTER, D. K. (Eds.). *Psychotherapy for women: Treatment toward equality.* Springfield, Ill.: Charles C Thomas, 1977.

———. Divorced women. *The Counseling Psychologist*, 1979, *8*, 27–28.

REBECCA, M., HEFNER, R., and OLESHANSKY, B. A model of sex-role transcendence. *Journal of Social Issues*, 1976, *32*, 197–206.

RICE, D. G. *Dual-career marriage: Conflict and treatment.* New York: Free Press, 1979.

RICE, J. K., and RICE, D. G. Implications of the women's liberation movement for psychotherapy. *American Journal of Psychiatry*, 1973, *30*, 191–96.

RIDDLE, D., and MORIN, S. Removing the stigma: Data from individuals. *APA Monitor*, November 1977, 16 and 28.

RIDDLE, D. I., and SANG, B. Psychotherapy with lesbians. *Journal of Social Issues*, 1978, *34*, 84–100.

ROCHELLE, S. A. Psychological studies of rape. *Signs*, 1977, *3*, 423–435.

ROMER, N. Sex-related differences in the development of the motive to avoid success. *Psychology of Women Quarterly*, 1977, *1*, 260–272.

ROMNEY, S. L., and GRAY, M. J. *Gynecology and obstetrics: The health care of women*. New York: McGraw-Hill, 1975.

ROSEN, B. C., and ANESHEUSEL, C. S. The chameleon syndrome: A social psychological dimension of the female sex role. *Journal of Marriage and the Family*, 1976, *38*, 605–617.

ROSENSTEIN, M., and BASS, R. D. *Characteristics of persons served by the federally funded community mental health centers programs, 1974*. Washington, D.C.: U.S. Government Printing Office, 1979 (National Institute of Mental Health Series A, No. 20).

ROSSI, A. S. Barriers to career choice of engineering, medicine or science among American women. In J. Bardwick (Ed.), *Readings on the psychology of women*. New York: Harper & Row, 1972.

——. Equality between the sexes: An immodest proposal. *Daedalus*, 1964, *93*, 607–52.

——. The roots of ambivalence in American women. In J. M. Bardwick (Ed.), *Readings on the psychology of women*. New York: Harper & Row, 1972.

ROTTER, J. Generalized expectancies for internal versus external control of reinforcement. *Psychological Monographs*, 1966, *80* (No. 609).

RUIZ, R. A., and PADILLA, A. M. Counseling Latinos. *Personnel and Guidance Journal*, 1977, *55*, 401–408.

RYAN, W. *Blaming the victim*. New York: Random House, 1971.

SAARIO, T. N., JACKLIN, C. N., and TITTLE, C. K. Sex role stereotyping in the public schools. *Harvard Educational Review*, 1973, *43*, 386–416.

SANCHEZ-DIRKS, R. Reflections on family violence. *Alcohol Health and Research World*, 1979, *4*, 12–16.

SANDMAIER, M. *Alcohol abuse and women: A guide to getting help*. U.S. Department of Health, Education, and Welfare. Washington, D.C.: Government Printing Office, 1977 (DHEW Publication No. [ADM] 77–358).

——. *The invisible alcoholics: Women and alcohol abuse in America*. New York: McGraw-Hill, 1980.

SATIR, V. *Making contact*. Millbrae, Ca.: Celestial Arts, 1976.

——. *Peoplemaking*. Palo Alto, Ca.: Science and Behavior Books, Inc., 1972.

SAWHILL, I. Discrimination and poverty among women who head families. In M. Blaxall and B. Reagan (Eds.), *Women and the workplace*. Chicago: The University of Chicago Press, 1976.

SCANZONI, J. Sex roles, economic factors, and marital solidarity in black and white marriage. *Journal of Marriage and the Family*, 1975, *37*, 130–144.

——. *Sexual bargaining: Power politics in the American marriage*. Englewood Cliffs, N.J.: Prentice-Hall, Inc., 1972.

Bibliography

Scarato, A. M., and Sigall, B. A. Multiple role women. *Counseling Psychologist*, 1979, 8, 26–27.

Schiffer, L. J. Legal issues regarding sex bias in the selection and use of career interest inventories. In C. K. Tittle and D. G. Zytowski (Eds.), *Sex-fair interest measurement: Research and implications*. Washington, D.C.: National Institute of Education, 1978.

Schlossberg, N. K. The case for counseling adults. In N. K. Schlossberg and A. D. Entine (Eds.), *Counseling adults*. Monterey, Ca.: Brooks/Cole Publishing Company, 1977.

Schlossberg, N. K., and Goodman, S. A woman's place: Children's sex stereotyping of occupations. *Vocational Guidance Quarterly*, 1972, 20, 266–270.

Schlossberg, N. K., Troll, L. E., and Leibowitz, Z. *Perspectives on counseling adults: Issues and skills*. Monterey, Ca.: Brooks/Cole Publishing Company, 1978.

Schultz, A. P. Radical feminism: A treatment modality for addicted women. In E. Senay, V. Shorty, and H. Alkane (Eds.), *Developments in the field of drug abuse*. Cambridge, Mass.: Schenkman Publishing Company, Inc., 1975.

Seaman, B., and Seaman, G. *Women and the crisis in sex hormones*. New York: Rawson Associates Publishers, Inc., 1977.

Seiden, A. M. Overview: Research on the psychology of women. Gender differences and sexual and reproductive life. *American Journal of Psychiatry*, 1976, 133, 995–1007.

Seifer, N. *Absent from the majority: Working class women in America*. New York: National Project on Ethnic America, 1973.

———. *Nobody speaks for me: Self portraits of working class women*. New York: Simon & Schuster, 1976.

Seligman, L. Haitians: A neglected minority. *Personnel and Guidance Journal*, 1977, 55, 409–411.

Seligman, M. P. *Helplessness: On depression, development and death*. San Francisco: Freeman, 1975.

Sexton, L. *Between two worlds: Young women in crisis*. New York: Morrow, 1979.

Shafer, N. Helping women through the change of life. *Sexology*, 1970, 36, 54–56.

Sherman, J., Koufacos, C., and Kenworthy, J. A. Therapists: Their attitudes and information about women. *Psychology of Women Quarterly*, 1978, 2, 299–313.

Shertzer, B., and Stone, S. C. *Fundamentals of counseling*. Boston: Houghton Mifflin, 1968.

Shusterman, L. R. The psychosocial factors of the abortion experience: A critical review. *Psychology of Women Quarterly*, 1976, 1, 79–106.

Simon, E. J. The contemporary woman and crime. Washington, D.C.: U.S. Government Printing Office, 1975. (Department of Health, Education and Welfare, Publication No. [ADM] 76 2161).

Skalka, P. Farewell to the youth culture. *TWA Ambassador*, April, 1978, 43–48.

Skovholt, T. M. Feminism and men's lives. *Counseling Psychologist*, 1978, 7, 3–10.

Smith, E. J. Counseling black individuals: Some stereotypes. *Personnel and Guidance Journal*, 1977, 55, 390–396.

Smith, M. B. A map for the analysis of personality and politics. *Journal of Social Issues*, 1968, 24, 15–23.

Sommers, T. Aging is a woman's issue. *Response*, March 1976, 12–15.

——. The compounding impact of age on sex: Another dimension of the double standard. *Civil Rights Digest*, Fall 1974, 3–9.

SONTAG, S. The double standard of aging. *Saturday Review*, 1972, *55*, 29–38.

SPENCE, J. T., HELMREICH, R., and STAPP, J. The personal attributes questionnaire: A measure of sex-role stereotypes and masculinity–femininity. *JSAS Catalogue of Selected Documents in Psychology*, 1974, *4*, 43.

Spokeswoman. All in the family. March 1978, 8, 10.

——. Election analysis: Women make gains in state and local races. December 1978, 9, 8.

——. Women's campaign fund. March 1980, *10*, 9.

——. Cornell 11 fights sex discrimination. May 1980, *10*, 16.

ST. JOHN-PARSONS, D. Continuous dual-career families: A case study. *Psychology of Women Quarterly*, 1978, *3*, 30–42.

STANDLEY, K., and SOULE, B. Women in professions: Historic antecedents and current lifestyles. In R. E. Hardy and J. G. Cull (Eds.), *Career guidance for young women*. Springfield, Ill.: Charles C Thomas, 1974.

Statistics on Social Work Education in the United States. Council on Social Work Education, 111 8th Avenue, New York, New York, 1980.

STEIN, A. H., and BAILEY, M. M. The socialization of achievement motives in females. In M. T. S. Mednick, S. S. Tangri, and L. W. Hoffman (Eds.), *Women and achievement*. New York: Wiley, 1975.

STEINER, C. (Ed.). *Scripts people live*. New York: Grove Press, 1974.

STEINER, C., and WYCKOFF, H. Alienation. In C. Steiner (Ed.), *Readings in radical psychiatry*, 1974.

STERNE, B. Wife-beating. Session, National Conference on Women and Crime, National League of Cities and U.S. Conference of Mayors, Washington, D.C., 1976.

STRAUS, M. Sexual inequality, cultural norms and wife-beating. *Victimology: An International Journal*, 1976, *1*, 54–70.

SUE, D. W. Counseling the culturally different: A conceptual analysis. *Personnel and Guidance Journal*, 1977, *55*, 422–425.

SUE, D. W., and KIRK, B. A. Asian-Americans: Use of counseling and psychiatric services on a college campus. *Journal of Counseling Psychology*, 1975, *22*, 84–86.

TALBOT, D. B., and BIRK, J. M. Does the vocational exploration and insight kit equal the sum of its parts? A comparison study. *Journal of Counseling Psychology*, 1979, *26*, 359–362.

TANGRI, S. S. Determinants of occupational role innovation among college women. *Journal of Social Issues*, 1972, *28*, 177–199.

TAVRIS, C. Stereotypes, socialization, and sexism. In A. G. Sargent (Ed.), *Beyond sex roles*. St. Paul, Minn.: West Publishing, 1977.

TERRY, R. The white male club. *Civil Rights Digest*, 1974, Spring, 66–77.

THOMAS, A. H., and STEWART, N. R. Counselor response to female clients with deviant and conforming career goals. *Journal of Counseling Psychology*, 1971, *18*, 332–357.

THOMPSON, C. Cultural pressures in the psychology of women (1942). In M. R. Green (Ed.), *Interpersonal psychoanalysis: The selected papers of Clara Thompson*. New York: Basic Books, 1964.

Bibliography

THOMPSON, C., McCANDLESS, B. R., and STRICKLAND, B. R. Personal adjustment of male and female homosexuals and heterosexuals. *Journal of Abnormal Psychology*, 1974, 29, 86–90.

Time. It's your time in the sun. October 16, 1978, 48–61.

TITTLE, C. K., McCARTHY, K., and STECKLER, J. F. *Women and educational testing.* Princeton, N.J.: Educational Testing Service, 1974.

TITTLE, C. K., and ZYTOWSKI, D. G. (Eds.). *Sex-fair interest measurement: Research and implications.* Washington, D.C.: National Institute of Education, 1978.

TOFFLER, A. *Future shock.* New York: Random House, 1970.

———. *The third wave.* New York: William Morrow, 1980.

TRECKER, J. L. Women in U.S. history high school textbooks. *Social Education*, 1971, 35, 249–260.

TRESEMER, D. Fear of success: Popular, but unproven. *Psychology Today*, 1974, 7, 82–85.

TROLL, L. E. *Early and middle adulthood—The best is yet to be—Maybe.* Monterey, Ca.: Brooks/Cole, 1975.

———. The nature of the adult client: Developmental needs and behavior. In N. C. Seltz and H. V. Collier (Eds.), *Meeting the educational and occupational planning needs of adults.* Bloomington, In.: Indiana University, 1976 (ERIC Document Reproduction Service No. 143–885).

TROLL, L. E., and NOWAK, C. "How old are you?" The question of age bias in the counseling of adults. In N. K. Schlossberg and A. D. Entine (Eds.), *Counseling adults.* Monterey, Ca.: Brooks/Cole, 1977, 98–107.

TROLL, L. E., and SCHLOSSBERG, N. How "age-biased" are college counselors? *Industrial Gerontology*, Summer 1971, 14–20.

TURNER, B. F., and McCAFFERY, J. H. Socialization and career orientation among black and white college women. *Journal of Vocational Behavior*, 1974, 5, 307–319.

UNGER, R. K. Male is greater than female: The socialization of status and inequality. *Counseling Psychologist*, 1976, 6, 2–9.

UNGER, R. K., and DENMARK, F. L. *Woman—Dependent or independent variable?* New York: Psychological Dimensions, Inc., 1975.

U.S. Bureau of the Census. *Households and families by type.* (Current population reports. Series P–20, No. 282). Washington, D.C.: U.S. Government Printing Office, 1975 (a).

———. *Marriage, divorce, widowhood, and re-marriage by family characteristics.* (Current population reports. Population characteristics. Series P–20, No. 312). Washington, D.C.: U.S. Government Printing Office, 1975 (b).

———. *Money income in 1973 of families and persons in the U.S.* (Current population report. Series P–60, No. 97). Washington, D.C.: U.S. Government Printing Office, 1975 (c).

———. *Household and family characteristics.* (Current population reports. Population characteristics. Series P–20, No. 291). Washington, D.C.: U.S. Government Printing Office, 1976 (a).

———. *A statistical portrait of women in the United States.* (Current population reports. Special studies. Series P–23, No. 58). Washington, D.C.: U.S. Government Printing Office, 1976 (b).

———. *Household and family characteristics: March 1978.* (Current population reports.

Population characteristics. Series P-20, No. 340). Washington, D.C.: U.S. Government Printing Office, 1979 (a).

———. *Marital status and living arrangements: March 1978.* (Current population reports. Population characteristics. Series P-20, No. 338). Washington, D.C.: U.S. Government Printing Office, 1979 (b).

———. *Persons of Spanish origin in the United States: March 1978.* (Current population reports. Population characteristics. Series P-20, No. 339). Washington, D.C.: U.S. Government Printing Office, 1979 (c).

———. *The social and economic status of the black population in the United States: An historical overview, 1790-1978.* (Current population reports. Special studies. Series P-23, No. 80). Washington, D.C.: U.S. Government Printing Office, 1979 (d).

———. *Statistical abstract of the United States, 1979.* Washington, D.C.: U.S. Government Printing Office, 1979 (e).

———. *A statistical portrait of women in the United States: 1978.* (Current population reports. Special studies. Series P-23, No. 100). Washington, D.C.: U.S. Government Printing Office, 1980 (a).

———. *Money income in 1978 of households in the United States.* (Current population reports. Consumer income. Series P-60, No. 121). Washington, D.C.: U.S. Government Printing Office, 1980 (b).

U.S. Bureau of Labor Statistics. *U.S. working women: A data book.* Washington, D.C.: U.S. Government Printing Office, 1977.

———. *Women in the labor force: Some new data series* (Report 575). Washington, D.C.: U.S. Government Printing Office, 1979.

———. *Employment in perspective: Minority workers, First quarter 1980* (Report 602). Washington, D.C.: U.S. Government Printing Office, 1980 (a).

———. *Employment in perspective: Working women, 1979 summary* (Report 587). Washington, D.C.: U.S. Government Printing Office, 1980 (b).

———. *Perspectives on working women: A data book* (Bulletin 2080). Washington, D.C.: U.S. Government Printing Office, 1980 (c).

U.S. Citizen's Advisory Council on the Status of Women. *Women in 1975.* Washington, D.C.: U.S. Government Printing Office, 1976.

U.S. Commission on Civil Rights. *Women and poverty.* Washington, D.C.: U.S. Government Printing Office, 1974.

———. *Social indicators of equality for minorities and women.* Washington, D.C.: U.S. Government Printing Office, 1978.

U.S. Department of Health, Education, and Welfare. *Fact sheet on demographic trends affecting women.* Washington, D.C.: National Institute of Education, Women's Research Program, 1977 (a).

———. *Fact sheet on women doctorates.* Washington, D.C.: National Institute of Education, Women's Research Program, 1977 (b).

U.S. Law Enforcement Assistance Administration. Females commit more crimes as opportunities increase. *LEAA Newsletter,* 1978, 7 (7), 4.

———. The prosecution of sexual assaults. *LEAA News Release,* September 3, 1978.

———. Typical rape victim is poor, young, single. *LEAA Newsletter,* 1979, 8 (8), 4.

U.S. National Advisory Council on Women's Educational Programs. *Sex discrimination in guidance and counseling: Report review and action recommendations*. Washington, D.C.: U.S. Government Printing Office, 1977.

———. *Toward educational equity: A report of findings from outreach activities*. Washington, D.C.: U.S. Government Printing Office, 1976.

U.S. National Commission for UNESCO. *Report on women in America* (Department of State Publication 8923). Washington, D.C.: U.S. Government Printing Office, 1977.

U.S. National Commission on the Observance of International Women's Year. *To form a more perfect union: Justice for American women*. Washington, D.C.: U.S. Government Printing Office, 1976.

———. *Education: A workshop guide*. Washington, D.C.: U.S. Government Printing Office, 1977 (a).

———. *Female offenders*. Washington, D.C.: U.S. Government Printing Office, 1977 (b).

———. *Older women: A workshop guide*. Washington, D.C.: U.S. Government Printing Office, 1977 (c).

———. *Rape*. Washington, D.C.: U.S. Government Printing Office, 1977 (d).

———. *Sexual preference*. Washington, D.C.: U.S. Government Printing Office, 1977 (e).

———. *Wife abuse: A workshop guide*. Washington, D.C.: U.S. Government Printing Office, 1977 (f).

U.S. National Institute of Mental Health. *How women see their roles: A change in attitudes*. (New dimensions in mental health series). Washington, D.C.: U.S. Government Printing Office, 1976.

———. *Victims of rape*. (Department of Health, Education, and Welfare, Publication No. [ADM] 77–485). Washington, D.C.: U.S. Government Printing Office, 1977.

U.S. News and World Report. Surge in "no-fault" divorce and its spreading impact. July 25, 1977, 76.

———. America's changing profile: What official figures show. May 22, 1978, 56–57.

———. Labor trends. December 25, 1978/January 1, 1979, 102.

U.S. Social Security Administration. *Social security bulletin* (Vol. 43). Washington, D.C.: U.S. Government Printing Office, 1980.

U.S. Women's Bureau. *The myth and the reality* (Revised). Washington, D.C.: U.S. Government Printing Office, 1974.

———. *1975 handbook on women workers* (Bulletin 297). Washington, D.C.: U.S. Government Printing Office, 1975.

———. *Maternity standards: A reprint from the 1975 handbook on women workers*. Washington, D.C.: U.S. Government Printing Office, 1976 (a).

———. *Mature women workers: A profile*. Washington, D.C.: U.S. Government Printing Office, 1976 (b).

———. *Women of Spanish origin in the U.S.* Washington, D.C.: U.S. Government Printing Office, 1976 (c).

———. *Women workers today* (Revised edition). Washington, D.C.: U.S. Government Printing Office, 1976 (d).

———. *Employment needs of women offenders: A program design* (Pamphlet No. 13). Washington, D.C.: U.S. Government Printing Office, 1977 (a).

———. *Minority women workers: A statistical overview*. Washington, D.C.: U.S. Government Printing Office, 1977 (b).

Bibliography

——. *Women of Puerto Rican origin in the continental United States.* Washington, D.C.: U.S. Government Printing Office, 1977 (c).

——. *Working mothers and their children.* Washington, D.C.: U.S. Government Printing Office, 1977 (d).

——. *Brief highlights of major federal laws and order on sex discrimination in employment.* Washington, D.C.: U.S. Government Printing Office, 1978 (a).

——. *Why women work.* Washington, D.C.: U.S. Government Printing Office, 1978 (b).

——. *Economic responsibilities of working women.* Washington, D.C.: U.S. Government Printing Office, 1979 (a).

——. *20 facts on women workers.* Washington, D.C.: U.S. Government Printing Office, 1979 (b).

——. *The earnings gap between women and men.* Washington, D.C.: U.S. Government Printing Office, 1979 (c).

VETTER, L. *The majority minority: American women and careers.* In J. S. Picou and R. E. Campbell (Eds.), *Career behavior of special groups.* Columbus, Ohio: Charles E. Merrill Publishing Company, 1975.

VONTRESS, C. E. Racial differences: Impediments to rapport. *Journal of Counseling Psychology*, 1971, *18*, 7–13.

WALLACE, A. F. C. The heyday of the Iroquois. In A. Moogenboom and O. Moogenboom (Eds.), *Interdisciplinary approach to American history*, Vol. 1. Englewood Cliffs, N.J.: Prentice-Hall, Inc., 1973.

WALLACE, M. *Black macho and the myth of superwoman.* New York: The Dial Press, 1979.

WEINGARTEN, K. Interdependence. In R. Rapoport and R. N. Rapoport (Eds.), *Working couples.* New York: Harper Colophon Books, 1978 (a).

——. The employment pattern of professional couples and their distribution of involvement in the family. *Psychology of Women Quarterly*, 1978 (b), *3*, 43–52.

WEISSMAN, M. M., and KLERMAN, G. L. Sex differences and the epidemiology of depression. *Archives of General Psychiatry*, January 1977, *34*, 98–111.

WELCH, M. S. *Networking: The great new way for women to get ahead.* New York: Harcourt Brace Jovanovich, 1980.

WERTHEIMER, B. M. Labor unions in the 1980's: What role for women? *Spokeswoman*, May 1980, *10*, 6–7.

WESTERVELT, E. M. *Barriers to women's participation in post secondary education: A review of research and commentaries of 1973–1974.* Washington, D.C.: U.S. Government Printing Office, 1975 (National Center for Education Statistics No. 75–407).

WESTERVELT, E. M. A tide in the affairs of women: The psychological impact of feminism on educated women. *The Counseling Psychologist*, 1973, *4*, 3–26.

WESTON, P. J., and M. T. MEDNICK. Race, social class, and the motive to avoid success in women. In J. M. Bardwick (Ed.), *Readings in the psychology of women.* New York: Harper & Row, 1972.

WHISNANT, L., and ZEGANS, L. A study of attitudes toward menarche in white middle-class American adolescent girls. *American Journal of Psychiatry*, 1975, *132*, 809–814.

WHITE, M. S. Measuring androgyny in adulthood. *Psychology of Women Quarterly*, 1979, *3*, 293–307.

Bibliography

WILBORN, B. L. The myth of the perfect mother. *Counseling Psychologist*, 1976, 6, 42–45.

WILLIAMS, J. H. *Psychology of women: Behavior in a biosocial context*. New York: W. W. Norton and Company, 1977.

WILSNACK, S. C. Women are different: Overlooked differences among women drinkers. Keynote address, Symposium on Alcoholism and Women, Institute for the Study of Women in Transition, Portland, Maine, June 2–3, 1977.

WITT, S. H. Native women today: Sexism and the Indian woman. In S. Cox (Ed.), *Female psychology: The emerging self*. Chicago: Science Research Associates, 1976.

WOLCOTT, I. Meeting women's health needs. *Spokeswoman*, 1979, 9, 9.

WOLMAN, C., and FRANK, H. The solo woman in a professional peer group. *American Journal of Orthopsychiatry*, 1975, 45, 164–171.

Women in Crisis. Conference brochure, cosponsored by Project Return Foundation, Inc., and the School of Social Welfare, SUNY at Stony Brook, New York, June, 1980.

Women in Transition, Inc. *Women in transition: A feminist handbook on separation & divorce*. New York: Charles Scribner's Sons, 1975.

Women's Educational Equality Communications Network Newsletter. Did you read ——? San Francisco: Far West Laboratory, Spring, 1979, 5.

Women's Equity Action League. *Women & health*. Washington, D.C.: Women's Equity Action League, 1977.

WOOLLEY, S. F. *Battered women: A summary*. Washington, D.C.: Women's Equity Action League, 1978.

WYCKOFF, H. Banal scripts of women. In C. Steiner (Ed.), *Scripts people live*. New York: Grove Press, 1974.

——. Radical psychiatry for women. In E. I. Rawlings and D. K. Carter (Eds.), *Psychotherapy for women*. Springfield, Ill.: Charles C Thomas, 1977.

——. *Solving women's problems through awareness, action, and contact*. New York: Grove Press, Inc., 1977.

WYMAN, E., and McLAUGHLIN. Traditional wives and mothers. *Counseling Psychologist*, 1979, 8, 24–25.

YANICO, B. J. Sex bias in career information: Effects of language on attitudes. *Journal of Vocational Behavior*, 1978, 13, 26–34.

ZELLMAN, G. L. The role of structural factors in limiting women's institutional participation. *Journal of Social Issues*, 1976, 32, 33–46.

ZYTOWSKI, D. G. Implications for counselors of research on sex-fairness in interest measurement. In C. K. Tittle and D. G. Zytowski (Eds.), *Sex-fair interest measurement*. Washington, D.C.: National Institute of Education, 1978.

Index

Index

Index

Index

Index

Index

Unemployment, 132, 213
Unger, R. K., 8, 175
U. S. News and World Report, 88, 92
Unmarried women, 91–92

Valium, 208
Valle, V., 42
Vetter, L., 143
Vicarious achievement ethic, 140
Vocational education, 104
Vocational Education Bill of 1976, 147
Vocational Exploration and Insight Kit, 155
Vogel, S. R., 3, 8, 28, 32n, 49

Wackman, D. B., 66, 97
Wallace, A. F. C., 227
Wallace, M., 220
Wanberg, K. W., 205
War on Poverty, 230
Weinberg, M. S., 243, 246, 248
Weingarten, K., 69, 97, 98
Weissman, M. M., 41, 44, 54
Welch, M. S., 169
Welfare, 231, 257–258
Welling, M. A., 33
Wertheimer, B. M., 104
Westervelt, E. M., 103, 140, 145, 146, 216
Weston, P. J., 219
Whisnant, L., 175
White, M. S., 60
Whiteley, J. M., 4, 145, 155
Widowhood, 50, 89–91, 237
Wife abuse, 195–199
Wilborn, B. L., 96
Williams, J. H., 2, 3, 6, 31, 33, 41, 193, 194, 236
Wilsnack, S. C., 204, 205
Witt, S. H., 226, 227

Wolle, H. O., 165
Wolman, C., 45
Women in Crisis, 3
Women and Work Incentive Program, 145
Women's Bureau, 81, 89, 108, 129, 130, 131, 132, 133, 138, 144, 148, 159, 163, 164, 213, 214, 224, 226, 230, 252, 253
Women's Caucus of the American Society for Training and Development, 4
Women's Equity Action League (WEAL), 106n, 148, 178
Women's Health Movement, 175, 209
Women's movement, 12, 36, 96
Wong, D., 225, 226
Woolley, S. F., 196
Work conditions, 133
Working women, 99–102, 126–152: age of, 130; child care, 135–136, 144; double workload, 134–135; economic need, 131–132; education of, 102–105, 131, 145–146, 255–256; external barriers to achievement, 142–147; full-time versus part-time, 100; heads of families, 101, 130–131; homemaker, 99–100, 102; income of, 83–86, 126, 127, 131–132, 138–139, 147; intermittency, 100–101, 127, 137–138, 143; internal barriers to achievement, 139–142; job categories, 129, 143–144; marital status, 132–133; minority status, *see* Minority women; unemployment, 132, 213
Wyckoff, H., 38, 40, 274n

Yanico, B. J., 145

Zegans, L., 175
Zellman, G. L., 9, 140
Zytowski, D. G., 155, 156, 157
Zytowski's Theory of Career Development, 156–157